Taming the Disorderly City

ALSO BY MARTIN J. MURRAY

Cities in Contemporary Africa (co-edited with Garth Myers)

The Revolution Deferred: The Painful Birth of Post-Apartheid South Africa

Radical Sociologists and the Movement: Experiences, Lessons, and Legacies
  (co-edited with Martin Oppenheimer and Rhonda F. Levine)

*South Africa: Time of Agony, Time of Destiny. The Upsurge of Popular Protest
  in South Africa*

South African Capitalism and Black Political Opposition

The Development of Colonialism in Indochina, 1870–1940

Taming the Disorderly City

The Spatial Landscape of
Johannesburg after Apartheid

MARTIN J. MURRAY

Cornell University Press *Ithaca and London*

First published 2008 by Cornell University Press
First printing, Cornell Paperbacks, 2008

Printed in the United States of America

Library of Congress Cataloging-in-Publication Data

Murray, Martin J.
  Taming the disorderly city : the spatial landscape of Johannesburg
after apartheid / Martin J. Murray.
       p.   cm.
  Includes bibliographical references and index.
  ISBN 978-0-8014-4569-9 (cloth : alk. paper) — ISBN 978-0-
8014-7437-8 (pbk. : alk. paper)
  1. Sociology, Urban—South Africa—Johannesburg. 2. Urban
renewal—South Africa—Johannesburg. 3. City planning—South
Africa—Johannesburg. 4. Johannesburg (South Africa)—Social
conditions. 5. Johannesburg (South Africa)—Geography.
6. Johannesburg (South Africa)—Politics and government. I. Title.

  HN801.J64M87 2008
  307.3'4160968221—dc22

2008001452

Cornell University Press strives to use environmentally responsible
suppliers and materials to the fullest extent possible in the publishing
of its books. Such materials include vegetable-based, low-VOC inks
and acid-free papers that are recycled, totally chlorine-free, or partly
composed of nonwood fibers. For further information, visit our
website at www.cornellpress.cornell.edu.

Cloth printing   10 9 8 7 6 5 4 3 2 1
Paperback printing 10 9 8 7 6 5 4 3 2 1

Contents

Preface

The concept of progress must be grounded in the idea
of catastrophe.

Walter Benjamin (1999, 473)

In *Invisible Cities,* Italo Calvino recounts the story of a Venetian traveler,
Marco Polo, who entertains the aged Tartar emperor Kublai Khan with
apocryphal tales of the cities he has visited in his travels around the vast empire. In time, it gradually becomes evident that each of the fantastic places
that Marco Polo so artfully describes is really one and the same place: the city
of Venice. For Calvino, cities are constantly evolving places that resist objec-
tification, summary, and closure. As open-ended aggregates subjected simultaneously to both centripetal and centrifugal forces, cites never congeal into
cohesive universals or submit to totalizing perspectives. Among many other
things, Calvino was concerned with the connection between memory and the
experience of urbanity, or how place is the product of a relationship—part
internalization of existing external realities and part intersubjective projection onto space. For him, since all cities are different cities wrapped into one
(metaphorically at least), travelers never have to leave home to discover the
"strangeness" in the familiar (Calvino 1974; see Curtis 2001, 56–65).

It can be said that, speaking figuratively, Johannesburg resembles Calvino's
invisible Venice, for it is a prismatic, kaleidoscopic, and ever-changing metropolis that contains many cities in one (De Boeck 2002). It is at once a city of
monumental architecture and abysmal slums; a city of luxurious playgrounds
for the rich and empty wastelands for the poor; a city of utopian fantasy and
dystopian anxiety; and a city of collective memory and intentional forgetting.
Johannesburg is a place that cannot be truly grasped in its entirety as some
kind of fixed and stable whole, since its morphological form, its places, and its
people are in constant motion, continuously changing and evolving in ways
both planned and unplanned, anticipated and unanticipated. The physical

viii   *Preface*

remnants and cultural artifacts of past times are repeatedly subjected to destruction and ruination, whether the result of deliberate intervention or the consequence of benign neglect. The endless cycles of building and rebuilding have
endowed the urban landscape with a contingency and elusiveness that make it
difficult to classify, categorize, and define. This ontological instability attached
to the built environment has resulted in a gap between the city and its representations, that is, between its provisionality and the efforts to explain its erratic
patterns of growth and development in terms of conventional models, paradigms, or deductive theories of urban transformation (Abbas 1994, 442–445).

Well-established image categories—most apparent in political commentar-
ies, journalism, fiction writing, documentary film, popular media, and urban
scholarship—have portrayed Johannesburg after apartheid as a sprawling metropolis in constant flux, a disorderly and edgy place that is formless in structure, illegible in appearance, and difficult to decipher, manage, and negotiate.
Like all other cities, it consists of highly differentiated and heterogeneous
spaces that reflect a great diversity of experiences, activities, and lifestyles. Enthusiastic image makers have never tired of drawing attention to the city as the
"World's Greatest Gold Producer," the "New York of Africa," the "City of Record
Sunshine," and the "Heartbeat of South Africa" (Sihlongonyane 2005, 22). But
beneath the glittering veneer that endowed Egoli, the City of Gold, with its distinct qualities of place is a recurrent tale of boom and bust, of reinvention, recreation, and make-believe. It is a complicated story that did not end with the
demise of apartheid, but has continued to unfold as powerfully new schisms
along class and racial lines intersect in new and different ways to reshape the
city for future generations (Robinson 2002; Sawhey 2002; van Niekerk 1999).

As Johannesburg struggles to shed the visible (and not-so-visible) reminders of its odious past as the quintessential apartheid city, the city has become
something like a prism through which we can focus attention on a host of
questions concerned with the connections between the social forces reshaping the built environment, architecture, and urban design, on the one hand,
and enduring social and racial inequalities, national identity, and citizenship,
on the other. As with all cities in South Africa, the urban landscape of Johannesburg continues to bear the marks of racial separation and class division.
With the end of apartheid and the transition to parliamentary democracy, Johannesburg finds itself in a virtual frenzy of future projections, and, in line
with the roseate image of the "rainbow nation," in the midst of intense debates
about how to reshape the urban landscape in conformity with the genuine
commitment to racial harmony. The lack of regular work, affordable housing,
and social security for ordinary people has engendered increased demands
for the "right to the city," including spatial justice and legal enforcement of
the entitlements of full citizenship. In seeking ways to position Johannesburg

among elite cities with world-class aspirations, city builders have struggled to balance market-driven growth with the maintenance of social safety nets for the poorest of the poor. Yet these boosterist visions of a radiant future are both haunted by structural legacies and collective memories inherited from the past and undermined by city-building strategies that seem oblivious to addressing persistent inequalities of the present (see Huyssen 1997).

Put broadly, this book is an invitation to look at Johannesburg and other cities not only in formal and functional terms but in figural and symbolic ways as well. To make sense of the city-building processes that have spatially reconfigured the urban landscape of Johannesburg after apartheid requires the adoption of an interpretive approach that is capable of acknowledging the interplay between surface layers and the deep structural forms, that is, between scenographic visionscapes saturated with aestheticized images and their underlying material conditions of existence. The urban landscape consists not only of a built environment subject to radical alteration and modification but also of a constellation of outward signs that convey a host of overlapping, intersecting, and sometimes conflicting meanings. The visible appearance of buildings and other assembled material objects that make up the cityscape always gives rise to intuitive or evocative allusions. City-building processes oscillate between creative interventions, the fashioning of something new that never existed before, on the one side, and selective destruction, erasure, and elimination, on the other. The result is a hybrid layering of architectural sites, woven together and juxtaposed in sometimes strange and seemingly odd combinations (Boyer 1992; 1994a, 3, 5, 9, 19, 21, 25).

The methodological approach that informs this book seeks to bypass the crude reductionism, one-dimensionality, and abstract qualities of many deductive theories of urban transformation. Instead of trying to forcibly shoehorn the individual case of Johannesburg into a single explanatory logic derived from such available theories as "urban growth machines," "global cities," and postmodern urbanism, I seek instead to retain the detailed richness, complexity, and heterogeneity of the urban experience by focusing on different parts of the story and how these separate pieces fit together into a coherent whole. This synthetic approach, which manages to convey some sense of the panoramic totality of the city through the patchwork assemblage of fragments, finds a great deal of its inspiration in Walter Benjamin and his writings on Paris, particularly the unfinished *Arcades Project* (Benjamin 1999, 33–36, 65, 87). It involves the identification of persistent themes or common threads that, when brought into relation with one another, constitute something akin to a unified totality. This way of thinking, which resembles a montage of seemingly disconnected glimpses of city life, enables us to approximate a holistic vision of city building in Johannesburg after apartheid (Harvey 2003, 18–19).

Acknowledgments

Johannesburg is a habit that has proven impossible to break. From the first time I set eyes on this strange place in June 1977, I was immediately overwhelmed by the compact density of the downtown built environment, the sheer verticality of its monumental buildings, the boundless horizontal sprawl of its northern suburban utopias, and the bleak sterility of its artificial townships and squatter settlements. My fascination with Johannesburg stems in large measure from starkness of the contrasts: magnificent mansions and their luscious greenery contrasted with corrugated iron shacks forlornly sited on treeless, barren ground; spotlessly clean shopping malls in the northern suburbs contrasted with chicken feet grilled on open fires at taxi ranks in Soweto; expensive BMWs speeding past old black women trudging along the road after a hard day's work; and homeless street kids begging handouts from insouciant middle-class urbanites in a hurry to get to a restaurant appointment in some trendy new hot spot. Johannesburg has always been, and remains so today, a city of spectacle and a city of ruin, where the jarring mismatch between extreme wealth and abject poverty has contributed to an enduring sense of unease and discomfort. While Cape Town with its natural wonders and scenographic beauty has no difficulty in luring globe-trotting tourists, Johannesburg is an angular, jagged-edged place that has never completely shed its original identity as a coarse, unrefined mining town.

Scholarly interest in Johannesburg has steadily expanded since the demise of apartheid and the transition to parliamentary democracy. As an outsider writing on Johannesburg, I am acutely aware of the perils of carelessly trespassing into a stridently demarcated and vigorously defended intellectual territory in which theoretical and methodological differences are sometimes unduly exaggerated by interdisciplinary tensions, political affiliations, and firmly held beliefs. As with all scholarly work, we stand on the shoulders of giants who cleared the first, original paths. In this respect, I owe a debt of gratitude to three such figures who in their own ways inspired my thinking about Johannesburg: Charles Van Onselen, Clive Chipkin, and Keith Beavon.

The ideas expressed in this book remain marked by the circumstances under which they were produced. The questions that I explore here are a direct response to my experience of trying to negotiate the urban landscape of what is indeed a strange city, filled as it is with delights and dangers in perhaps equal measure. I have learned to deal with Johannesburg, especially its reckless drivers and dangerous roads, its crime and criminals, its great distances, its pretensions, and its cruelties. Yet I have also come to appreciate its funkiness, its music and art, and its Orlando Pirates, along with the warmth and generosity of its residents, who sometimes stand on opposite sides of the barricades.

Scholarly work is never produced in isolation; it is always rooted in intellectual, institutional, and social contexts. The completion of this book would not have been possible without the assistance and generosity of others, especially my family, friends, and colleagues, who provided encouragement, inspiration, and support through the long process of research and writing. As scholars, we create our communities out of the debates, conversations, and discussions we conduct as part of our everyday academic life. My thinking about urban spatiality has been enriched by numerous encounters with so many fellow academics and students at conferences and seminars that it is impossible to identify them all by name. Yet because of their unflagging encouragement and advice over many years, some friends and colleagues deserve special mention: Anne Pitcher (my greatest supporter and severest critic), Eric Mourier-Genoud, Garth Myers, Mary Moran, and Sean Jacobs. Jenny Robinson offered extremely useful suggestions at various stages about how to reshape the manuscript in ways that would highlight the main arguments. My friends in Cape Town (Ginny Volbrecht, Meshack Mochele, and Elaine Salo) provided invaluable logistical support. In Johannesburg Zwelahke Tshandu, Eddie Webster, Luli Callinicos, David Fig, and other colleagues at the University of the Witwatersrand helped me clarify my thinking. Yoon Park and Roland Pearson provided me with a wonderful place to stay and an instant family away from home. Their daughter Siana reminded me of the unadulterated innocence and joy of childhood. Besides arming me with a cell phone, Doug Tilton was a great traveling companion for our many excursions around the city. Patrick Bond has always been extremely generous and hospitable, particularly with inviting me to stay at his Kensington home. At the State University of New York at Binghamton, Jean-Pierre Mileur, dean of Harpur College, provided much-appreciated financial assistance; and Richardo Laremont, chair of the Department of Sociology, offered encouragement all along.

To a large extent, this book has been shaped by the institutional and professional settings within which its core ideas took form. I greatly benefited from the five-month research leave at the Shelby Cullom Davis Center, Princeton University, from September 2004 through January 2005, where significant portions of the writing of this book took place. The collegial atmosphere at the Davis Center created an ideal setting for all sorts of engaging conversations around public lectures, formal seminars, informal discussions, and social gatherings. Our group of fellows—Jordan Sand, Sarah Shrank, Pamela Long, Frank Mort, and Sheila Crane—worked well together. Office manager Jennifer Houle was a great help. Bob Tignor and Bill Jordan offered insightful comments on early drafts of chapters. But more than anyone else, the director of the Davis Center, Gyan Prakash, was responsible for establishing an incredibly stimulating and supportive environment. I am grateful for his invaluable insights, thoughtful comments, and helpful advice at numerous stages of this project.

Alan Mabin, head of the School of Architecture and Planning at the University of the Witwatersrand, offered me a temporary office at the Centre for Urban and Built Environment Studies (CUBES) during May and June 2006. Kate Mothapo was extremely gracious and helpful. Margot Rubin deserves a special acknowledgment for her friendship, logistical support, and generosity. I benefited enormously from conversations with numerous individuals at the University of the Witwatersrand, including Sarah Charlton, Phillip Harrison, Marie Huchzermeyer, and Tanja Winkler (all in the School of Architecture and Planning), Ivor Chipkin, André Czeglédy (Department of Anthropology), Sakhela Buhlungu (Department of Sociology), and Loren Landau (Forced Migration Studies Programme). I learned a great deal from conversations with community activist Dennis Brutus; Raymond Suttner, imprisoned for ten years under the apartheid regime and former South African ambassador to Sweden; and Bronwen Jones, director of Children of Fire. I enjoyed talking with people at MMA Architects (Johannesburg), especially its director, Mphethi Morojele, and Solam Mkhabela. They do great work.

Juanita Malan, the official photographer for the School of Architecture, University of the Witwatersrand, helped me to create a huge treasure trove of photographs from which to choose for the book. I also worked with Aubrey Graham, Colgate University, to produce several photographs for the book. Albert Fu provided invaluable technical assistance in the final stages of the project. Stephanie McClintick contributed her many professional talents in the construction of maps and in the arrangement of photographs. Peter Wissoker, my editor at Cornell University Press, supported the project from the beginning, and he moved the process forward swiftly, just as he promised. Joanne Hindman provided superb editorial suggestions that improved the manuscript enormously. I would like to acknowledge the extremely valuable comments of two anonymous readers for Cornell University Press who read the manuscript carefully. Their critical assessments provided me with a great deal of help in reshaping what was originally an unruly text.

The fieldwork that constitutes the empirical foundation for this book would not have been possible without the generosity of numerous individuals and institutions. While conducting research on this project, I have benefited greatly from the local knowledge of numerous city officials, urban planners, property developers, architects, city visionaries, and urban scholars who generously shared their time and ideas with me. My assessment of Johannesburg springs from an enduring interest in what they collectively do and from a profound respect for their commitment to making the city a better place.

A central component of my research strategy has involved on-site visits to particular locations, what Michel de Certeau has called "walking the city." I owe a special debt to a number of individuals who responded to my curiosities about Johannesburg by graciously accompanying me on various peripatetic excursions and exploratory field trips around the city. In this regard, I would like to acknowledge the gracious assistance of many people, especially Neil Fraser, Keith Beavon, Sarah Charlton, Graeme Gotz, Geoff Mendelowitz, Doug Tilton, Patrick Bond, Marie Huchzermeyer, Tanja Winkler, Mzwanele Mayekiso, and Trevor Ngwane.

While I have benefited greatly from formal interviews and from informal conversations with numerous individuals, the views expressed in this book are entirely my own. I suspect that I have interpreted events and processes in ways that differ from some of those whom I interviewed. I would like them to know that, although I have offered a critical assessment of city building in their city, I greatly admire their commitment to the betterment of Johannesburg. I hope that I have not offended them too greatly in this endeavor.

My four brothers offered much-needed distractions on our annual hiking expeditions out West. In their own ways, my two sons, Andrew and Jeremy, have provided real-world counterpoints to the almost surreal existence of research and writing. I am especially indebted to Anne Pitcher. As always, she is my best critic and my best friend. She offered thorough and thoughtful criticism of the entire manuscript and prodded me to bring closure to the project when the end seemed nowhere in sight. Her insistence that I make my arguments clear and concise has helped to make this a much better book. For that and much more, I am forever grateful. Our daughter Alida Pitcher-Murray is such a joy. She has endured the hardships of being the child of two hard-working academic parents who hauled her hither and yon across the African continent. She endured with a stoicism and patience worthy of something akin to sainthood. Every day she reminds me of the challenges and rewards of living in the world—rather than obsessing about making sense of Johannesburg. Finally, my mother, Margaret Louise Claeys Murray, passed away before this project could be completed. It is in her memory that I dedicate these assembled words.

MARTIN J. MURRAY

Binghamton, New York

Abbreviations and Nicknames

ABSA	Allied Banks of South Africa
AFHCO	Affordable Housing Company
AMPROS	Anglo American Property Services
ANC	African National Congress
APH	Aengus Property Holding
"Awake"	Mayivuke
BBP	Better Buildings Programme
CALS	Centre for Applied Legal Studies
CBD	Central Business District
CCTV	Closed Circuit Television
CID	City Improvement District
CJP	Central Johannesburg Partnership
COHRE	Centre on Housing Rights and Evictions
EMS	Emergency Management Services
GASC	Gauteng Alliance for Street Children
GJMC	Greater Johannesburg Metropolitan Council
GNP	Gross National Product
ICO	Inner City Office
iGoli	Johannesburg
JDA	Johannesburg Development Agency
JHB	Johannesburg
JHC	Johannesburg Housing Company

JICDF	Johannesburg Inner City Development Forum
Jo'burg	Johannesburg
Jozi	Johannesburg
JPC	Johannesburg Property Company
Madiba	Nelson Mandela
OPH	Olitzki Property Holdings
PAC	Pan Africanist Congress
POMA	Property Owners and Managers Association
SABC	South African Broadcasting Corporation
SAHRA	South African Heritage Resources Agency
SAPA	South African Press Association
SCA	Supreme Court of Appeals
Spaza Shop	Literally "Camouflage" Shop
TUHF	Trust for Urban Housing Finance

Taming the Disorderly City

Introduction:
The Untamed City of Fragments

Beautiful it was not. The Golden City was still too raw and drab
and dirty for that. But it was a real city, no one could deny it,
and a homely place in its fashion.

THOMAS PAKENHAM (1979, 47)

Johannesburg is both a material entity, identified and defined by its geographical boundaries, and an imagined place, or, to use a phrase coined
by the urban theorist Robert Park (1925, 1) a "state of mind." It is a restless,
unsettled city whose own self-identity has always revolved around its vitality,
its novelty, its crassness, and its seemingly boundless opportunities and insatiable appetite for material gain. The fluid, chaotic quality of the city life in Johannesburg after apartheid is reflected in the unresolved tension between the
overall plan of urban space and its specific details, between the durability of
the built environment and the transitory use of urban locations, and between
the deliberate regulation of spatial practices and the uncontrolled anarchy of
chance encounters in public places. Generally speaking, middle-class urban
residents have looked upon this lack of symmetry and order, this absence of
harmony and clarity, with a great deal of trepidation and anxiety. Yet there
is actually nothing surprising about this seemingly confusing, ambiguous
state of affairs: after all, like South Africa's other cities, Johannesburg is the
byproduct of colonialism in the postcolonial era of unrelenting globalization,
and it still bears the enduring imprint of the apartheid spatial order at a time
when its racially codified rules, regulations, and restrictions no longer apply
(Herwitz 1999, 404–421).

Unlike other cities that originated as ports, entrepôts, and gateways straddling major transport routes, Johannesburg owes its unlikely existence to
a fortuitous geological accident of nature. From the late nineteenth century, when the chance discovery of an ore-bearing reef along the Witwatersrand triggered the largest gold rush in world history and made instant

millionaires out of the great mine magnates known colloquially as the Rand-lords, the destiny of the city has been inextricably linked with the waxing and waning fortunes of this precious metal. Arising literally on top of the richest goldfields ever discovered, this restive, energetic metropolis acquired from the start a contingent, provisional identity that it has never really been able to shed.

The pragmatic accommodation to the insatiable worldwide appetite for gold strongly influenced the physical separation and spatial unevenness of the metropolitan landscape. Efforts aimed at imposing some kind of rational plan-ning or disciplinary order on the cityscape lagged far behind the frantic pace at which city builders alternated between the construction and the destruction of the built environment. Without a mountain, river, or the sea, Johannesburg has always struggled to invent an enduring image for itself that breaks with its historical origins as a gritty, frontier mining town located off the beaten track in the African interior. Unlike other aspirant world-class cities that point with pride to their originating myths, Johannesburg has always reacted with ambiva-lence and equivocation to its serial incarnations as a European outpost at the geographical margins of modernity, as a racially segregated colonial city, and as an unapologetic apartheid city during the heyday of white minority rule. In the headlong rush to distance themselves from a historical past that has been regarded as somehow too unbecoming, too crass, and too shameful to collectively remember and commemorate, city builders in Johannesburg have typically relied on a deft combination of concealment, erasure, and denial to reinvent what came before as a point of departure for an imagined optimistic future (Roberts 2002, 1–14).

Throughout its turbulent history, Johannesburg has always been torn be-tween the extremes of utopian dreamworld and dystopian nightmare. At its founding at the end of the nineteenth century, the city acquired a schizo-phrenic urban identity that has oscillated between the sacred and the pro-fane, or between a bountiful Garden of Eden and a frightening paradise lost, the contemporary prototype of ancient Babylon and Nineveh (van Onselen 1981a, 1981b). These extremes have a way of exaggerating differences, contrib-uting to fears and anxieties, and fostering distrust and resentment. The self-promoting city boosterism that can at one moment glorify and mythologize Johannesburg as the epitome of urban chic and cosmopolitan sophistication can just as easily metamorphose into its opposite. Dystopian images of the city as a miasmic cesspool of abject misery and human degradation, unpredictable crime, rampant disease, and interminable strife have often lent legitimacy for various kinds of municipal intervention into the existing social fabric of the urban landscape, where city officials have tried to erase or conceal what they wished to eliminate rather than deal with its root causes. The noir image of urban dystopia has frequently served as the administrative justification for the creative destruction and the rebuilding of the urban landscape. Grand urban renewal plans, from racial segregation and forced removals, from demolition of old buildings and the elimination of city streets, and from inner-city revitalization to stylized experiments with the New Urbanism, have derived their raison d'etre from the imagined disorder, misuse, and deterioration of urban space (Baeten 2002, 111–112).

Over the past several decades, spatial restructuring of the greater Johannesburg metropolitan region has produced a sprawling, polycentric landscape consisting of a galaxy of rival "edge cities" and rapidly urbanizing cluster points arrayed around a historic urban core and connected by a vast traffic grid of multilaned freeways, corridor highways, and arterial roadways. The downtown business district has come to resemble an archipelagic assemblage of fortified enclaves inhabited in the daylight hours by tens of thousands of white-collar employees, office workers, and blue-collar support staff, and abandoned at night to the legions of low-income residents and homeless squatters who have carved out tenuous shelter in the overcrowded and decaying apartment blocks scattered in pockets around the central city (Rutheiser 1999, 317–318).

The frenzied pace of high-modernist city building in Johannesburg that took off during the 1960s and 1970s produced a dense compression of new high-rise skyscrapers that coaxed the cityscape into a patchwork pattern of juxtaposed urban forms, a kind of geometric expression of exploding size and verticality. The voracious speed of real estate development left a colonized streetscape in its wake, consisting of concrete canyons lined with megastructures that deadened the pedestrian vitality of the central city. The synergistic effects of fast construction and quick profits often churned out what amounted to cookie-cutter buildings differentiated solely by superficial decorative stylistics. Some buildings have turned out to be extravagantly beautiful, others merely extravagant. Over time, the hurried construction of new high-rise office blocks resulted in the destruction of iconic buildings that symbolized earlier periods of the city's flamboyant history. Just as the 1982 science fiction film *Blade Runner* was set in the desolate aftermath of technology out of control, Johannesburg under the spell of 1960s and 1970s high-modernist city building managed its own self-destruction without much outside assistance. Rather than promoting the efficient and rational use of the urban center, the labyrinthine maze of freeways that encircled the downtown urban core fostered a spatial retreat to the suburban north. The high-modernist dreamscape of high-rise corporate office blocks, luxury shopping sites, and entertainment venues mutated into its opposite. What accompanied the techno-utopian fantasies of high-speed urban living all coming together in the downtown urban core was the dystopian nightmare of overcrowding, traffic gridlock, pollution, and metastasizing inner-city slums (Bremner 2005; Czeglédy 2004, 65–67).

Fractured Urbanism: Johannesburg Divided against Itself

The central argument of this book is that spatial dynamics of Johannesburg after apartheid have resulted in an unstable urban landscape where abandonment and neglect have left once-valued and -stable parts of the built environment in decline and in ruin, where unbridled growth and horizontal expansion have undermined herculean efforts at city planning and regulation, and where the steady expansion of sequestered sites of fantastic luxury has been matched by proliferation of places of degradation and despair. The contradictory impulses of centripetal and centrifugal urbanism have always operated in tandem, both tightening linkages between parts of the city where none existed before and fracturing the urban social fabric into a braided montage of kaleidoscopic and scattered, yet coexisting and mutually interdependent, fragments. Each of these discordant microworlds of the city contains distorted elements of the others, yet never in equal measure. Above all, this book seeks to capture the fragmentary and unsettled qualities of fractured urbanism in Johannesburg after apartheid, where the production of urban space is the outcome of an unstable mixture of opposing fields of force, and where the latent tensions between the anxious rich and the desperately poor are never completely out of sight and occasionally erupt into outright conflict in the most unexpected places.

The argument presented here rests on three distinct but overlapping premises. First, urban regeneration and urban ruin are not separate and disconnected features of the cityscape but integrally connected and mutually dependent processes that proceed in tandem. Like two sides of the same coin, one cannot be addressed without considering the other. Second, despite the fact that planning professionals look on urban landscapes as dynamic and flexible spaces subject to constant tinkering, city sites often prove difficult to unbundle and reconfigure, since they easily become fixed, obdurate, and securely anchored in their own histories as well as in the histories of the built environment around them (Hommels 2005, 10). This tension between the malleability of urban space and its obduracy establishes real constraints on the capacity of urban planners, municipal authorities, and city officials to fashion the kinds of cityscapes they imagine as befitting their world-class aspirations. Third, the reliance on market competition for access to strategic locations as the main underlying mechanism for guiding urban development unleashes the oscillating dynamics of inclusion and exclusion, whereby those with the greatest marketplace bargaining power are able to commandeer prime urban sites, and the rest are left to fend for themselves. The governing logic of entrepreneurial urbanism subsumes the right to the city under the rational calculus of market competition, with the result that affluent urban residents who have unencumbered access to all the city has to offer are able to enjoy the substantive benefits of full citizenship and those im-poverished urban dwellers with their restricted access to the advantages of city living are left with the hollow rights of empty citizenship.

In seeking to legitimate their efforts to foster urban rejuvenation through the creative destruction of the built environment, city builders have attached themselves to the animating fantasy belief that deliberate interventions aimed at reshaping the material form of the cityscape almost always produce a per-petually better future. Yet by ignoring how urban revitalization for some resi-dents invariably results in social catastrophe for others, municipal authorities, urban planners, and city boosters have inadvertently sustained the mythol-ogy of Johannesburg—and, by extension, all cities undergoing revitalization through rebuilding—as a dynamic place in constant pursuit of improvement, always aspiring to new heights of greatness. For city builders, this uplifting trope of progress has operated as a persistent metaphor to explain the cycle of destruction and rebuilding as self-evident and innocent, and as natural and inevitable. By constructing the alleged necessity for intervention through the simplifying (and hence distorting) lens of urban renewal and revitalization, real estate developers, city planners, and code enforcement officials are able to rationalize the need for the eradication of the places that provide the urban poor with shelter and their means of livelihood, and to justify the displace-ment of those city dwellers least able to fend for themselves. As a visual rep-resentation of progress, the serial arrangement of time-lapse photographs—the "then and now" comparisons that signify the "before and after" of city improvements—provide the classic portrayal of the transformation of cities. As Max Page has argued, the repeated use of these organic metaphors of natural growth to convey the image of cities as something akin to flowering plants has the effect of further obscuring a central dynamic of urban development, namely, city-building processes involve not only expansion and growth but also destruction and rebuilding. The resolution of this inherent tension de-termines the physical shape and composition of the urban landscape (Page 1999, 2–3). The endless search for new places with marketable potential even-tually renders buildings and building sites outdated and redundant, thereby producing vast quantities of premature waste. Both literally and figuratively, obliterating traces of these obsolescent artifacts of earlier city-building efforts effectively reinforces the modernist myth of endless and seamless urban prog-ress (Edensor 2005a, 2005b).

Behind every city plan, architectural project, and physical modification of the existing urban fabric lies a utopian belief that deliberate interventions inevitably result in collective improvements to the cityscape. By contrasting the present predicament with an imagined roseate future, city builders are able to justify their rebuilding efforts—even when these interventions displace ordinary urban residents or disrupt their livelihoods. The aesthetic discourses that animate urban regeneration campaigns construct the current state of affairs as deficient and wanting in order to legitimate and mobilize support for remedial action. But, like all historicist continuities, this idealized representation constructs city-building efforts as part of an unfolding, if periodically interrupted, flow of gradual-yet-steady progress toward a shared normative ideal. As such, it is founded on its own denials and exclusions, consigning to a separate, marginal domain the spatial frictions that disrupt its putatively seamless coherence. Yet sentimental appeals calling for urban regeneration conceal a calculated, instrumental rationality. No matter how objectifying and neutral-sounding the language within which they are framed, the aesthetic discourses that accompany urban redevelopment projects are, by virtue of their choice of subject matter, boundaries, and exclusions, also selective statements that define the problems and propose solutions for rebuilding city sites within a narrow range of options (Boyer 1994a; Deutsche 1996, 4–9, 49–50, 109–110).

The spatial transformation of Johannesburg after apartheid has not taken place along a linear path of progressive expansion (horizontal or vertical) and steady growth, but rather has unfolded in fits and starts, where regeneration and ruin have proceeded in tandem as distorted mirror images of each other. In seeking to unpack and make sense of this chaotic and contradictory process of destruction and rebuilding, this book explores the connections between city building and real estate capitalism, on the one side, and the tensions, negations, and resistances that have accompanied municipal efforts to regulate the orderly use of urban space, on the other. The point of departure for my excursion into the spatial politics of Johannesburg after apartheid is the contention—put forward most eloquently by Henri Lefebvre (1991, 14–18, 38–41) and since reinforced by numerous other scholars—that social space is not an empty container, inert void, or innocent background within which social action takes place but a powerful and creative social force in its own right. This spatial perspective enables us to view the urban landscape of Johannesburg as an evolving field of tensions and contradictions, in which the physical features of the cityscape are saturated with symbolism and meaning and where collective memories and imagined futures are inscribed in the built environment. To speak of the production of space in the ways that urban theorists such as Lefebvre intended is to acknowledge that the evolving urban form of cities always involves protracted struggles between contending forces, where the terrain for battle oscillates between mobile "wars of maneuver" and static "wars of position." This spatial perspective provides a platform from which to contest the uplifting discourses of urban renewal, revitalization, and regeneration and to disrupt the neutral-sounding, functionalist rhetoric of the property developers, land speculators, and urban planners. Despite the fact that city-building efforts frame cityscapes as dynamic and flexible spaces, never quite finished but always under construction, it remains very difficult to fundamentally reshape the existing built environment of cities. The structural configurations of cities become fixed, tightly anchored in their own histories and deeply rooted in the histories of their surroundings (Hommels 2005, 10–26).

As a general rule, urban planners, municipal authorities, and city officials have looked upon the cityscape as a malleable work in progress amenable to manipulation, tinkering, and improvement. They have visualized the urban landscape though the lens of the classical tropes of modernity, laying particular stress on efficiency, rationality, and functionality, especially with regard to land use and the compression of space and time as a means of fostering rapid circulation of people and goods. Drawing heavily on organic (and biological) metaphors as these relate to the unhealthy city, urban planners have focused on unsanitary and unsafe residential housing in the inner city, traffic congestion brought on by the unregulated taxi industry, overcrowded sidewalks choked with unlicensed hawkers, piles of rubbish accumulating in public parks, criminals and crime hot spots, disorganized street markets inundated with unwanted traders. Armed with their cognitive maps of what a "good city" should be and how it ought to function, they have operated with the premise that the physical elimination of blighted buildings, the forcible removal of unauthorized squatters, and the enforcement of city bylaws amount to self-evident, unquestionable, and inevitable prescriptions for bringing about the desired regeneration of the inner-city core. Having lost a great deal of moral authority because of their collaboration with white minority rule and its failed, racially segregated utopia, planning professionals in the postapartheid era have become more modest in their outlook, more judicious in their judgments, and more narrow in their concerns. In mimicking global trends in vogue in other aspirant world-class cities, urban planners in Johannesburg after apartheid have largely adopted the contemporary language of instrumentalism, negotiation, and performance assessment as a way of legitimating their active interventions. By relying on public-private partnerships and courting leading property-owning stakeholders, they have effectively shielded themselves from taking full responsibility for the plight of the urban poor (Dear 1989; Fainstein 2000; Loukaitou-Sideris 1993).

In contrast to this normative vision of the cityscape, this book seeks to understand the folly of the unending yet futile efforts to superimpose formal order, rational coherence, and spatial stability on the inherently unstable urban landscape. Instead of accepting the normative approach to urban planning at face value, I focus primarily on what comes between the conception and fulfillment of efforts to tame the unruly urban landscape. Taken together, rivalries and conflicts of interest, the endless cycle of negotiation and compromise, and the encroachments (at once steady, molecular, and impossible to regulate) of ordinary people on the use of urban space intersect and overlap in ways that ensure that city building is always unfinished business. It is my contention that cities operate—and hence evolve over time—according to multiple, overlapping, simultaneous, and often incommensurate logics that interact in sometimes surprising and unpredictable ways. In Johannesburg, as elsewhere, the intersection of these sometimes conflicting spatial practices ensures that city building always amounts to a provisional exercise, a permanently unsettled condition that the American social critic Jane Jacobs (1961) identified as "organized complexity."

In fashioning the central arguments for this book, I take my cue from Mike Davis (2002, 144), who contends that city-building efforts are "neither a purely natural metabolism (as neoliberals imagine the marketplace to be) nor an enlightened volition (as politicians and planners like to claim)." Rather, the spatial restructuring of urban landscapes—of which urban redevelopment, gentrification, the rule of law, and forcible evictions are a central part—amounts to an infinite game, a relentless competitive struggle among assorted social actors played not toward any definitive conclusion, closure, or fixed end-point, but toward its own endless protraction where the wealthy, privileged, and propertied battle the propertyless urban poor for control over the use of urban space (Davis 2002, 140–181).

The intellectual scaffolding that frames the analysis of this book combines ideas about architecture and urban design, the built environment, and real estate capitalism, on the one hand, with theories of urban modernity, social space, and city planning, on the other. I situate my investigation of the shifting terrain of city building in Johannesburg after apartheid within the multidisciplinary field of inquiry that Rosalyn Deutsche (1996, xi–xii) has called "urban-aesthetic" or "spatial-cultural" discourse. As she makes clear, this discourse itself is neither monolithic nor static, but, on the contrary, is continually changing and evolving in response to shifting conditions.

One cannot truly and fully grasp the growth and development of Johannesburg without understanding the symbiotic relationship between the metropolitan center and the peripheral edge (Cronon 1991; Brechin 1999). As a general rule, there is the tendency, in both the popular media and scholarly writing, to treat these spatially distinct localities as analytically separate places, more isolated from each other than connected. Yet the urban core and the peri-urban fringe not only share a common history, but they are also tightly bound together in a unified (albeit asymmetrical) field of interaction, exchange, and movement. Always and everywhere, city building is a contradictory and uneven process that differentiates the urban landscape along a spatial continuum ranging from sites of concentrated wealth and luxury at one pole to marginalized places of deprivation and impoverishment at the other. In Johannesburg the "urban glamour zone"—manifested in safely cocooned, high-rise office buildings, luxurious commercial and entertainment sites, and affluent suburban enclaves—represents the geographical antithesis to the sprawling townships, informal settlements, and squatter encampments that have proliferated around the exurban fringe of the city.

The story of Johannesburg is that of a constantly expanding megalopolis creating new and ever more elaborate and intimate linkages between the core areas of concentrated building and luxurious living and the environmentally degraded zones of impoverishment located on the metropolitan edge. As the city has grown and developed into the most important economic powerhouse on the African continent, so too has its geographical reach and its capacity to transform and disrupt the surrounding hinterland on which urban residents have come to depend. The metamorphosis of Johannesburg into the key command and control center in an expansive inland empire has meant that its tentacles have extended and stretched over vast distances. In a manner resembling an insatiable metropolitan growth machine, city building in Johannesburg has both attracted and consumed available resources, including accessible supplies of land, labor, and capital. But the growth and development of the city—in short, its material transformation—cannot take place without the disposal of useless waste (Kaika and Swyngedouw 2000; Gandy 2005b). Besides the physical detritus of the used-up resources, city-building efforts also involve the displacement of the urban poor as so much unwanted excess standing in the way of progress. Confined to the fetid wastelands on the margins of city life, the urban poor who inhabit the *terrain vague* of the cityscape are the expendable byproducts of luxury production in the urban core. The wasted lives of the expurgated poor provide ample testimony to the grim fact that city-building processes award winners and punish the losers (Bauman 2003; Bales 2004; Davis 2006).

Locating the Historical Specificity of Johannesburg

The analysis that I develop here relies on four separate but intersecting lines of argument. The first concerns the fickle imperatives of real estate capitalism that lie at the heart of city-building processes and modern urbanism more generally. Following the work of David Harvey (1982), Max Page (1999), David Scobey (2002, 7, 81–82, 93, 133–134, 153–154), and others, I argue that the metamorphosis of urban property, land uses, and locations into an assemblage of price-sensitive commodities, connected in a relatively unified field of market exchanges, puts in motion recurrent cycles of boom and bust, where capital investments in the built environment careen back and forth between volatility and inertia in the marketplace for urban space. City-building processes in Johannesburg—as in other cities—have conformed to these spatial dynamics. By subjecting property investment and land use to the unforgiving discipline of market rationality, real estate capitalism sorts the cityscape into a heterogeneous mosaic of widely discrepant zones that range from volatile arenas of hyperactive dynamism and growth, at one end of the spectrum, to lethargic immobility and capital-deprived sites of underdeveloped, underutilized, and neglected space, on the other.

While these polar extremes may appear disconnected and unrelated, I argue that they are merely the visible manifestations of the Janus-faced process of city building under the rule of real estate. Vitality and sluggishness are two sides of the same coin. The driving force behind the uneven spatial development of the urban landscape can be located in the underlying dynamics of real estate capitalism and their contradictory effects on city-building processes. Rather than treating underinvestment, senseless land use, congestion, overcrowding, decay, and ruin as the unfortunate byproducts of stunted growth or arrested or distorted development, or even the unfinished business of modernizing impulses not yet in full swing, I argue that these spatial disorders are part and parcel of city-building processes under the discipline of commodified land values. In short, these "frictions of capital," as David Scobey (2002) calls them, are not the unanticipated consequence of market inefficiency or of a temporary failure of the market to correct itself, or even unfortunate accidents of nature. On the contrary, such enduring features of the urban landscape as dysfunctional patterns of land use, physical stagnation, unstable property markets, capital flight, and disinvestment are the outcome of city-building processes subjected to the rule of real estate capitalism (Scobey 2002, 7, 81–82, 93, 133–134, 153–154).

In prescribing the kinds of entrepreneurial strategies for urban regeneration in vogue in aspirant world-class cities, city builders typically relate to the uneven development of the urban landscape in a one-sided way. In their way of thinking, market-propelled growth occurs at different locations at varying paces of cumulative development, ultimately spilling over to the advantage of all. In this blinkered field of vision, social inequalities appear as random disparities, unrelated and disconnected from one another. While they readily acknowledge that the benefits of prosperity are not evenly distributed, planning professionals typically focus on piecemeal, locally specific remedies to urban decay. On balance, ad hoc approaches to the manifest imbalances in urban growth tend to overlook, ignore, or even sometimes deny how uneven spatial development is a structural, rather than incidental or accidental, feature of real estate capitalism. This failure to fully comprehend the inherent structural imbalances in market-led strategies of urban growth results in a largely Sisyphean approach to city building, one in which well-meaning proclamations of success often prove to be a transitory optical illusion, neither permanent nor enduring (Deutsche 1996, 49–51).

The second line of argument finds its inspiration in the claim, put forward by Michel de Certeau (1988, 3–5), that every new time finds its source of legitimation in what it displaces and excludes. The boosterist self-image of Johannesburg after apartheid locates its historical specificity in its rejection and repudiation of formalized racial segregation that took place under white minority rule. City builders after apartheid have self-consciously sought to separate the present moment from a disreputable past, to break with virtually everything that has occurred up the point of transition. The new discourses of postapartheid city building rest on the presumption that the modes of thought that governed the division of the cityscape into racially demarcated zones with their own rules, protocols, and regulations have become unthinkable and must be expunged or suppressed in the new urban imaginary. In order for the new cosmopolitan city of Johannesburg (along with its world-class aspirations) to be born, the old representational forms have to be repudiated and treated as outmoded and moribund.[1]

Yet the city-building processes inaugurated in the aftermath of apartheid did not begin de novo. Such topographical features as the original streetscape and the spatial unevenness of the built environment are not easily modified or eliminated. So it is not surprising that the spatial separations, racial divisions, and structural imbalances that characterized the apartheid city have insinuated themselves into the postapartheid cityscape and its representational forms. The uplifting discourses of egalitarianism and constitutional rights that accompanied the transition to parliamentary democracy typically attributed the source of ongoing urban inequities, socioeconomic hardships, and racial imbalances to the lingering legacies of the odious past, thereby drawing attention away from a sanguine and critical appraisal of the extent to which contemporary planning policies and practices are inadequate as sufficiently powerful mechanisms for challenging and eradicating the spatial imprint of the apartheid past. I argue that city-building efforts—including the profit-driven approaches of property developers and the interventions of city officials and planning professionals—have not only contributed to the maintenance of the spatial divisions inherited from the apartheid past but also introduced new kinds of cleavages that have reinforced the yawning gap between affluence and impoverishment.

1. For a stimulating critique of the Eurocentric roots of urban planning efforts, see Sihlongo-nyane (2005, 22–30).

The third line of argument relates to the shift in urban management away from conventional models of modernist-inspired urban planning to new, postliberal modes of urban governance that stress public-private partnerships, outsourcing of service delivery, and the adoption of cost-recovery market principles as the lynchpin of service provision. The emergence of what has been called "privatized urbanism" has gone hand-in-hand with the spatial partitioning of the urban landscape into fortified luxury enclaves at one pole and vast, informal settlements, overcrowded shantytowns, and inner-city slums on the other. The steady accretion of citadel office complexes, gated residential communities, and enclosed shopping malls for the affluent propertied classes has proceeded apace with the shrinkage of well-maintained public spaces dedicated to civic engagement, social congregation, and chance encounter. In the entrepreneurial city the reigning ethos of market competitiveness, cost recovery, and "pay-as-you-go" has dwarfed the conventional welfarist notions of distributive justice, public goods, and social safety nets, where the marketplace bargaining power of key property-holding stakeholders has triumphed over low-cost provision of physical infrastructure and basic services.

As a general rule, debates over postliberal (or neoliberal) modes of urban governance pay insufficient attention to how discourses of entrepreneurialism, possessive individualism, and consumerism work to reconfigure the everyday practices and politics of citizenship. While conventional juridical-legal definitions of what it means to be a citizen revolve around political rights and obligations with respect to a sovereign nation-state, these formal conceptualizations inhibit our ability to understand how citizenship is constructed through discourse, practice, and the imagination. In contrast to these abstract idealizations, a growing number of scholars stress how the privatizing logic of the competitive marketplace has restructured the meaning of public citizenship in ways that bring it into line with notions of personal consumption. The private consumer lays claim to the city by seeking to fashion a civic urbanity—grounded in notions of orderliness and convenience and in opposition to a public urbanity, which is deemed to be disruptive and unpredictable—in ways that reconfigure the normative ideal of citizenship. The construction of this civic urbanity involves a distinction between citizens who assert their rights to the well-mannered and orderly use of urban space through their capacity to consume, and "anti-citizens" who are unable to move freely about the city because of their restricted marketplace bargaining power. The freedom of consumption is linked with the freedom to move in an uninhibited way through the urban landscape. In this way, the public citizen articulates with the figure of the private consumer. In the social logic of the entrepreneurial city, the discourse of citizenship undergoes a shift from an understanding that centers on the enjoyment and protection of formal rights to one that stresses entitlements, exclusionary rights, and the freedom to make consumer choices (Lukose 2005; Holston and Appadurai 1999).

The fourth line of argument focuses on the discourses and practices of urban planning and their relationship with the contradictory dynamics of inclusion and exclusion. As a general rule, the primary mechanisms for social inclusion into the mainstream of urban life are regular work and stable income, the availability of authorized residential accommodation, and access to physical infrastructure and basic social services. These institutional props are the main instruments that promote social integration and incorporation into the urban fabric and hence anchor urban residents to a rightful place in the city. Where these are absent, the centripetal forces of social exclusion, displacement, and marginalization are set into motion.

In conventional academic and policy usage, social exclusion has remained a largely opaque, loose, and open concept, typically deployed alongside a constellation of related terms and local idioms such as isolation, marginality, and insularity. It is often deployed as a descriptive marker, referring to a lack of integration into mainstream activities of urban life (Leontidou, Donnan, and Afouxenidis 2005). Social exclusion originates in the determined efforts of urban planners, city officials, and real estate developers to homogenize urban space by minimizing differences and limiting diversity under the guise of restoring social harmony and maintaining spatial cohesiveness. In seeking to fashion the well-managed city, municipal authorities adopt various strategic initiatives designed to impose order, establish boundaries, and define proper use of space. As a general rule, they justify exclusions by appeals to aesthetics (cleaning up and beautifying derelict places), utility (adopting "the highest and best use" of urban space), and functionality (making the city work efficiently and smoothly). By mobilizing a technocratic, protectionist discourse of permanence and continuity, municipal authorities, real estate developers, and urban planners are able to celebrate the preservation of historic landmarks, architectural diversity, and neighborhood revitalization while laying the bulk of the blame for urban decay, degradation, and blight on the irresponsible poor (Deutsche 1996, xiii, 50, 52–54, 58).

There is little dispute that the urban poor are deprived of a rightful place in the city through the deliberate actions of municipal authorities, city planners, and property owners. The enforcement of city codes, the use of restrictive covenants, and land-use regulations create a juridical-legal patina through which the urban poor are displaced or denied entry to places where they are unwanted. Yet the brute, coercive force of market-driven, competitive economics ensures that social exclusion, displacement, and marginalization are insinuated into the normal routines and rhythms of everyday life. In short, the inability of the urban poor to get ahead through market competition puts them at a distinct disadvantage in securing a rightful place in the city through regular work, authorized residential accommodation, and access to infrastructure and social services. The banality of such exclusionary practices makes it seem that the plight of the urban poor is somehow natural, inevitable, or unavoidable. Those city dwellers who are without work, without officially sanctioned shelter, and without the requisite social capital to buy a place in the city, find themselves continuously off balance, out of place, and on the move. In the headlong pursuit of the ephemeral status of world-class city, the urban poor have become expendable, sacrificed on the altar of urban progress and revitalization.

Yet the urban landscape is always a contested terrain, where the propertied, privileged, and powerful seek to establish one set of rules governing the use of urban space that is compatible with their city vision, and, conversely, the propertyless, underprivileged, and powerless make use of whatever means are at their disposal to challenge the status quo. In other words, official efforts aimed at imposing a coherent spatial order on the cityscape are never frictionless undertakings with uncontested outcomes. Building the planned (or figured) city is always mirrored in the simultaneous growth and development of the unplanned (or disfigured) city. Municipal authorities, urban planners, and city officials invariably encounter opposition, ranging from noncompliance to outright resistance. In this sense all cities lead what amounts to an unsettling double life: the unintended use of urban space always operates in tandem—as a kind of parallel dimension of everyday life in the city—with the official version of the orderly cityscape. By utilizing urban space in ways that facilitate their immediate survival needs, the urban poor have transformed the cityscape—not through a significant alteration of the physical environment but through a redefinition of it. The urban poor make use of the cityscape in ways never intended by its original builders, planners, and designers. This steady encroachment of ordinary people on the officially sanctioned prerogatives of the propertied, privileged, and powerful constitutes a formidable social force in its own right (Bayat 1997a, 57; 1997b; Baviskar 2003; Staub 2005).

1

Social Justice and the Rights to the City

The right to the city is like a cry and a demand,…a transformed and renewed *right to urban life*.
HENRI LEFEBVRE (1996, 158)

In linking geographical mobility with contemporary globalization, Zygmunt Bauman (1998, 77) has declared, "Nowadays we are all on the move." In distinguishing between different groups of mobile travelers, Bauman divides people on the move into affluent tourists and impoverished vagabonds, that is, between those who travel from place to place as "vicarious or actual privileged consumers of the world as a globalized spectacle" and those uprooted, desperate people who are forced to move by straightened circumstances beyond their control (quotation from Faulkner 2004, 93). For affluent tourists, faster forms of travel, streamlined border controls, and a ballooning service industry catering to their every need and desire have transformed what were once inaccessible places into exotic adventure lands for the leisure class. In contrast, the movement of vagabonds takes place out of necessity, not as a consequence of the calculated choice of consumer preference. As Bauman (1998, 94) puts it, "the vagabond is the alter ego of the tourist." While tourists and vagabonds are separated by their dissimilar experiences of travel, their movements within the global economy are structured and shaped by overlapping and intersecting forces that allow a privileged few to enjoy the freedom of movement and at the same time deny these options to others. Indeed, the expansion of global spheres of privilege not only enables the temporary translocation of the tourist but also acts to limit the freedom (and choice) of movement of the world's poor. Whereas affluent travelers can subject their choice of destination to the rational calculation of consumer preference, the rootless poor are often forced to move against their will (Faulkner 2004, 93–94).

Pulled by the illusive dream of steady income or pushed by despair and hopelessness, tens of thousands of recent arrivals have come to the greater

Johannesburg metropolitan region in search of a better life. Yet opportunities for socioeconomic advancement are largely restricted to those urban residents with inherited wealth, talents, and educational attainment. Johannesburg after apartheid has metamorphosed into a city where sociospatial stratification, racial inequality, and marginalization have become entrenched features of the urban landscape. An intricate mosaic consisting of an overlapping grid of legally sanctioned property regimes, statutory regulations, zoning ordinances, and institutionally enforced bylaws has helped to generate and reinforce these pervasive urban processes that have reconfigured the spatial landscape. Johannesburg is a city almost entirely constructed around a forbidding architecture of enclosure. The gradual expansion of such fortified urban enclaves as citadel office complexes, city improvement districts, gated residential communities, and sequestered shopping malls have produced a spatially uneven and hierarchically arranged landscape where large-scale property owners—protected by legally sanctioned barriers to entry, restrictive covenants, and exclusionary codes—clash with the claims of the propertyless urban dwellers who assert their right to the city by demanding a more egalitarian and collective understanding of land use (Blomley 2004, xiii–xxi).

Exclusionary Urbanism and Spatial Injustice

In Johannesburg as elsewhere, the technocratic urge toward eliminating ambiguity, indeterminacy, and uncertainty in urban space is an ingrained habit of city building. Seen through the moralizing lens of those planning discourses that stress the need to maintain the orderly city, displacement mutates into spatial purification. The paranoid vision of workless legions of rootless vagabonds wandering aimlessly around the city has played a pivotal role in the construction of the postapartheid identity of the propertied residents of middle-class suburban neighborhoods. Middle-class anxiety about the dangerous city has spilled over into a visceral distrust, resentment, and indifference to the plight of the poor. As propertied and privileged urban residents retreat behind walls, the jobless poor are forced to survive in the atrophying public spaces of the city, with their deteriorating infrastructure, inadequate services, and limited opportunities for income generation.

Displaced persons have little choice but to continue carrying out what amounts to a nomadic existence shuffling between the cracks and crevices of social space. In contrast to the mapped and monitored spaces of sovereignty and municipal authority, the lived spaces of the displaced—the temporary shelters, the squatter camps, the unauthorized shantytowns, abandoned buildings, parks, cemeteries, prisons—exemplify the marginalization of those for whom there is no rightful place in the city. These dispersed, pulverized, indeterminate spaces constitute the "Invisible City," and they exist outside the boundaries of official scrutiny and institutional governance. Those who occupy these marginal sites are "both invisible and too visible." Even if their voices are not silenced, their protests and complaints are largely unheard—and hence unrecognized (Delaney 2004, 847–848; see also Kihato and Landau 2005; Landau 2005, 2006; Groth and Corijn 2005).

In the past several decades, displacement has emerged as one of the most persistent themes in human rights law, as well as a central focus in the scholarly fields of migration, diasporic, and refugee studies. Such scholarship has been instrumental in prompting a greater interest in questions of the forced mobility of unwilling subjects, along with the linkage of these concerns to discourses of social justice and universal human rights, citizenship, and national belonging (Bales 2004; Bauman 2003; Landau 2006; Ong 1999; Simone and Gotz 2003). As a conceptual framing device, displacement is linked to various modalities of coercive movement, the spatialization of power, and the infrapolitics of inclusion and exclusion. In a global age that typically celebrates hypermobility as the emblematic embodiment of personal and collective freedom, displacement focuses instead on mobility as a distinctive kind of coerced movement, "as against the will or wishes of subjects" (Delaney 2004, 848) who, because they are deemed to be out of place, are compelled to relocate. As a concrete manifestation of enforced deterritorialization, displacement draws attention to the microtechnologies of power, or how people are denied entry or removed against their will. The spatial practices of expulsion and exclusion blend together in ways that bring to light the capillaries of the workings of power hidden in everyday life (Delaney 2004, 848).

Viewing displacement through the prism of an inaugural or threshold episode, such as the moment of eviction, forced removal, deportation, expulsion, or arrest, has the effect of reducing what is less a singular event than an ongoing state of being, or what sometimes becomes a permanent condition of existence (Kawash 1998). Displaced people—those who are uprooted and evicted—are literally put into motion, compelled to be constantly on the move in search of work, adequate shelter, and access to basic resources. Often it is brute force that operates as the active agency behind displacement: people flee or retreat when "confronted with men with guns"(Delaney 2004, 849). Yet undue stress on the threat or use of physical violence as the *driving force* behind coerced movement overlooks the ordinariness and banality of displacement as an integral element of everyday life. Coerced movement is also brought about by the persuasive force of reason, or the application of legal authority: the enforcement of such routine regulations as municipal bylaws, statutes, immigration laws, and health and safety codes, can result, no less than the use of physical violence, in the dispersal and coercive scattering of people (Delaney 2004, 849; Mbembe 1992).

Assorted figures of displacement—the unemployed, those who occupy abandoned buildings, asylum seekers, undocumented immigrants, refugees, runaway youth, prostitutes, and the itinerant traders—inhabit a material world that is saturated with the legal signifiers of property and ownership, sovereignty and territorial governance, nationhood and citizenship. This inextricable conjunction of spatial emplacement and legal rights makes the lifeworlds of city dwellers meaningful in terms of the exercise, circulation, and justification of power. The ever-shifting interplay between material locations and legal signifiers renders ostensibly equal city dwellers legible as either legitimate city users (citizens, property owners, consumers, tenants, and guests) or illegitimate occupiers of urban space (undocumented immigrants, trespassers, squatters, or itinerant traders). Those who do not belong or are out of place are subject to removal and expulsion, exclusion and banishment (Blomley 2003; Flusty 2001; Landau 2005, 2006).

For newcomers to the city and for young people entering adulthood, social integration into the mainstream of urban life generally occurs through a combination of overlapping mechanisms: absorption into the everyday world of regular work, incorporation into the market for decent and affordable housing, and access to reliable physical and social infrastructure (piped water and sewerage, electrical power, social services such as health, education, welfare, and police and fire protection). These three mechanisms of social inclusion—steady income, decent housing, and access to basic urban services—intersect and complement one another. In combination, they anchor urban residents into a relatively stable place in the sociocultural fabric of the city. The rootedness in place—linked as it is to the materiality of locality and a sense of belonging—enables urban residents to mobilize and tap into the kinds of social networks necessary for their material survival (Keyder 2005, 124–125, 127).

Conversely, social exclusion refers to a failure of the mechanisms of social integration to incorporate the urban poor into the mainstream of urban life. The shrinkage of wage-paid employment under juridical-legal supervision, the lack of affordable residential accommodation, and highly restricted access to the physical and social infrastructure of the city has rendered the daily lives of the urban poor vulnerable in the extreme. Without regular work, authorized shelter, and basic social services, the urban poor are cast adrift from the ties that bind them to the urban fabric (Kihato and Landau 2005; Landau 2005, 2006).

The variegated multitudes of impoverished urban residents have crystallized into a permanent underclass, constantly moving back and forth between casual and informal work, self-employment, and unemployment, largely dependent on the outside assistance of others for their survival (Rogerson 1996b; Keyder 2005, 132). Displacement, exclusion, and marginalization of this propertyless underclass are the result of both deliberate policy choices of property owners and municipal authorities and the everyday operations of property regimes, land markets, and the legal enforcement of codes, regulations, and bylaws. The visible expressions of revanchist urbanism—such as forced removals of homeless squatters from unauthorized settlements and arresting vagrants and beggars—constitute a war on the poor (Smith 1996, 1998). Municipal authorities have effectively criminalized the urban poor by treating the structural problems that arise from unemployment and poverty as matters of law enforcement. In the official mind popular illegalities such as drug dealing, prostitution, sleeping in public parks, erecting curbside stalls on the pavements, and panhandling, contribute to the disorderly city and therefore must be eradicated in order to fashion a cityscape that conforms to middle-class sensibilities (Merrifield 2000; Mitchell 1997).

But to focus exclusively on the draconian measures designed to drive the urban poor out of the city ignores the everyday routines that make it virtually impossible for the truly disadvantaged to survive in the city. The triumphant rise of market liberalism has tied the provision of such basic urban services as water, electricity, education, health care, and welfare to the commercial ethos of supply and demand. The commodification of urban services—with its "pay-as-you-go" logic of cost recovery—has driven a wedge between the haves and the have-nots. The inosculated overlay of property regimes, restrictive covenants, city bylaws, and land-use regulations has ensured that unwanted and undesirable people are denied entry to the fashionable zones of the urban landscape.

At a time characterized by diasporic peoples, hybrid subjects, and porous borders, it is not possible to understand or make sense of displacement and exclusion simply or exclusively in terms of citizenship and national belonging (Merry 2001; Sanchez 1997, 2001). Rather, new modes of urban governance have come to depend on strategies of spatial governmentality, that is, the adoption of regulatory techniques that aim "to manage populations in place" by grafting technologies of sociospatial control with discourses of community, risk minimalization, and security (Sanchez 2004, 871). These new modes of spatial governance operate along the lines of *legitimacy*, that is, on what side of the *criminal* law one stands. As a central organizing principle governing the use of urban space, exclusion revolves around the question of legality. The identification, categorization, and differentiation of urban space in terms of which city dwellers are legally entitled to use particular places has the effect of criminalizing some individuals and their behaviors while incorporating others "into the domain of the city" (Sanchez 2004, 866).

As part of a wider deployment of a range of technologies of control, spatial governmentality depends on a delicate balance between differential inclusion and differential exclusion. The theory and practice of differential inclusion rest on a hierarchical classification of social collectivities in terms of the relative value and usefulness of their labor power at any given historical moment. In contrast, the theory and practice of differential exclusion direct their attention toward supernumerary urban dwellers, that is, those "surplus people" whose numbers are deemed excessive and whose working capacity is superfluous from the vantage point of their failed absorption into existing labor markets. The urban poor who inhabit unauthorized squatter encampments, who invade abandoned buildings, and who sleep on the sidewalks typically survive outside the law and the legitimacy and entitlements it provides. Enforcement of the plethora of municipal statutes, city laws, and health and safety regulations that outlaw such practices as constructing self-built shelters in unauthorized places, occupying abandoned buildings or vacant lots, sleeping on city sidewalks or in public parks, curbside trading, begging and panhandling, selling drugs, and prostitution constitutes a form of spatial governance that seeks to draw a protective boundary between the everyday spaces of privileged, propertied urban residents and the bare life of those whose toil is not counted as legitimate work. As an expression of municipal authority, power operates both as a totalizing force of urban order and discipline and as an individualizing mechanism that divides and differentiates the urban poor into different legal categories and classifications by criminalizing their survivalist strategies. In other words, power is efficacious because it defines who belongs and who does not, and because it differentiates between what rights to the city are legitimate and which are not. Because of their precarious existence at the margins of urban life, the urban poor are forced into a constant struggle to be *less excluded*. Exclusionary practices are effective precisely because they operate partially and differentially for different categories of the urban poor, thereby turning the struggles of displaced persons into a competition to be less excluded than someone else. Put in another way, exclusion thus becomes a matter of degree and distance. For the urban poor, it is the degree of exclusion and distance from the rights and privileges of citizenship that help to explain its efficacy. For the practice of exclusion is far more effective a strategy for keeping the urban poor off balance if "it is not an all-or-nothing proposition," as Lisa Sanchez contends, "if it instills and perpetuates a hierarchy of the excluded who stand divided against power and who have a partial stake, a glimmer or hope, relative to those more excluded, of achieving inclusion and legitimacy" (Sanchez 2004, 881).

The Politics of Location: Struggling to Survive in the Depleted Landscapes of Despair

Like sprawling urban agglomerations elsewhere, Johannesburg after apartheid has been subjected to the twin pressures of order and disorder. Ordinary people—those whose marginal existence has been overlooked in the official planning scenarios—have encroached upon the interstitial spaces of the city, infringed upon official regulations governing the proper use of urban space, and intruded into orderly places where they are not wanted. The unsatisfied demand for proper residential accommodation has led to the proliferation of illegal building occupations, unauthorized shantytowns, and unofficial, informal settlements. The lack of wage-paying employment has forced discouraged work seekers into the bloated informal sector where they compete for space in already overcrowded niche markets. The legal geographies of various regulatory regimes have effectively criminalized all sorts of activities closely associated with the survival strategies of the urban poor, adding another layer of vulnerability to their daily existence (Landau 2005; Baviskar 2003).

Despite some notable achievements in assistance programs designed to bring relief to the "poorest of the poor," Johannesburg after apartheid has remained a city where those residents who occupy the bottom rungs of the socioeconomic ladder have to scramble to find even a precarious foothold in the furious race for space and work. The inability of the municipality to keep up with the demand for low-cost housing has ensured that unauthorized, informal settlements are the only possible option for shelter. While the official gaze of urban planners looks on these encroachments as disfiguring the urban landscape, the urban poor have little choice but to take advantage of whatever opportunities for enterprise present themselves. The spatial unevenness accompanying the implementation of different strategies for disciplining the urban poor has left room for negotiation and accommodation in some places, while making violence and repression inevitable in others (Bremner 1999, 2002).

The conjoined practices of social exclusion, marginalization, and isolation do not exist in a vacuum. Instead they are embedded in a network of social practices that, taken together, constitute a contested field of sociocultural action whereby the propertied, privileged, and powerful seek to maintain (and even extend) the prevailing hierarchies and structural imbalances in the social order and, conversely, the propertyless, underprivileged, and powerless employ whatever means are at their disposal to challenge the status quo. Social collectivities such as trade unions, mass political parties, and social movements make use of conventional avenues of mobilization and popular protest, including strikes and work stoppages, political rallies, street demonstrations, and mass marches, in order to press for the redress of grievances. In contrast, such structurally atomized individuals as the unemployed and the unemployable, homeless squatters, curbside hawkers, itinerant work seekers, casual toilers, informal workers, migrants, refugees, immigrants, and other socially marginalized and excluded people constitute free-floating social clusters that operate outside the formal institutional frameworks of organized workplaces, schools, and associations. This fluid condition of peripatetic nomadism means that these groups therefore lack the institutional capacities necessary for sustained, coordinated, and collective demand-making protests, since they do not possess the organizational power of disruption—that is, the means to withhold critical resources on which others depend. Instead they rely on various kinds of individualized direct action that Asef Bayat (1997a, 57; see also 1997b) has characterized as the "silent encroachment of the ordinary"—the intractable, molecular, protracted, patient, and persistent infringement of ordinary people on the prerogatives of the propertied, privileged, and powerful in order to survive socioeconomic hardships and to improve their lives. For the most part, these modes of everyday struggle are sufficiently fluid, open ended, and fleeting that they escape notice. In this sense they constitute what James Scott (1990, 118–119) has termed an "infrapolitics of the powerless." These kinds of everyday encroachments typically take place without clearly defined leadership, coherent ideology, or structured organization (Bayat 1997a, 1997b).

Instead of constituting a central part of self-conscious political campaigns directed at the entrenched sources of urban power, these individualized actions are aimed primarily at extracting incremental concessions from property owners and city officials, where these marginalized, disenfranchised, and subaltern groups are driven primarily by the force of necessity—the need to survive and to live a dignified life (Bremner 2002). The institutionalized powerlessness of the urban poor is compensated for in their versatility and inventiveness in taking direct action, whether it is individual or collective, piecemeal or dramatic. These free-forming and largely spontaneous activities are directed primarily at the redistribution of social goods, including the unlawful and direct appropriation of means to life (squatting in unused buildings, tapping into electricity lines), the acquisition of objects of collective consumption (land, shelter, piped water, sanitation facilities, building materials), access to social services (schooling, health clinics, family assistance), encroachment on public space (sidewalks, street pavements, intersections, parks, parking lots), and the seizure of opportunities for petty entrepreneurialism (Bayat 1997a, 59).

All in all, these quotidian acts of insubordination, noncompliance, and transgression are linked to demands for official recognition of individual as well as collective rights to the city, that is, the capacity of ordinary people to participate in and enjoy the social benefits of inhabiting urban space (Emdon 2003; Kihato and Landau 2005; Pile 1997). What compels these disparate groups to adopt these largely spontaneous modes of small-scale direct action is not only the desire for an alternative mode of life but also the lack of institutional supports and conventional mechanisms through which they can collectively express their grievances and legitimately resolve their problems. In the official mind, these "silent encroachments of the ordinary" disrupt and destabilize the urban social fabric. Municipal authorities, urban planners, and law enforcement officials are virtually unanimous in their distain for these unauthorized and often lawless actions, condemning them for disturbing their idealized vision of what the urban landscape should be and how it should function (Bayat 1997a, 58).

In order to survive, ordinary people who are excluded from the world of regular work, who are denied access to social services, and who are unable to afford decent housing must move through and transform urban space. Through their disruptions of the stylized aesthetics of what a good city should look like, these expressions of "insurgent urbanism" offer a resistant alternative to the institutionalized domain and dominant principles of planned urban development (Sandercock 1998b, 120–121; Holston 1999, 157–158, 165). In their struggles to carve out alternate ways of living, the urban poor engage in a politics of location, that is, a politics of lived spaces. These mobile tactics (at once blurred, awkward, and ambivalent) frustrate the efforts of urban planners to fix boundaries, regulate the authorized use of space, and facilitate movement and circulation. In the official mind, these spatial transgressions of the urban poor disrupt and destabilize the urban social fabric. As a consequence, conventional urban planning discourses construct unflattering images of the urban poor as outsiders who have transgressed spatial boundaries where they are not wanted and hence do not belong to the city. These demeaning stereotypes serve to legitimate municipal intervention into the life-worlds of the urban poor, where the criminalization of their survival tactics creates outcast groups of alleged lawbreakers (Bayat 1997a, 58).

Managing the Fragmented City: Locating Citizenship in the Postliberal City

Everyday space is not only not self-evidently innocent but
also bound into various and diverse social and psychic dynamics
of subjectivity and power.
GILLIAN ROSE (1993, 37)

Captivated by the desire to propel Johannesburg into the lofty status of a world-class city, municipal authorities, urban planners, and city boosters have inscribed the story of the postapartheid metropolis in the conjoined narrative of developmentalism, cosmopolitanism, and modernity. But this trope of world-class city, as a specific modality of linear temporality, is not simply about making requisite improvements to the physical infrastructure, creating sites of luxurious spectacle, and introducing signature architecture. It is also about subjecting urban residents to a life-aesthetic that effectively transforms them into law-abiding, model citizens who spontaneously and obediently comply with the normative ideals about how a good city should function. In other words, it is about regulating, managing, and controlling the ways that urban residents meet their daily needs in proper and moral ways. Yet for the urban poor, everyday survival largely consists of associating and moving in ways that are not conducive to such notions of citizenship (Simone 2002, 30–31; 2003; 2004c).

With its permeable boundaries and porous borders, Johannesburg has evolved over the past several decades in ways that urban planners could not have foreseen, let alone managed or controlled. Hence it is not surprising that recurrent, proleptic visions of a stable and orderly city have been tempered by an uneasy sense of imminent crisis and potential breakdown. Despite the elegance of their future projections, urban planning practices always come face-to-face with the countervailing impulses of antiplanning: the corrosive effects of unexpected friction, disruption, and resistance brought about by the stubborn refusal or reluctance of ordinary people to conform to the established rules governing the use of urban space. Urban planning regimes typically fail to grasp how the exercise of administrative power is necessarily open to inconsistencies, fissures, and ambivalences that allow for the emergence and persistence of an unanticipated, spontaneous urbanism (Pile 1997). City dwellers who lack places of their own have little choice but to opportunistically take advantage of overlooked gaps in existing power grids to reappropriate and reanimate indeterminate spaces, remaking them to serve their immediate needs (Groth and Corijn 2005, 503–505; Pile 1997). These improvised, extemporaneous expressions of the lived city constitute a perplexing paradox for urban planning practices. On the one hand, municipal authorities in Johannesburg have remained committed to eradicating the structural imbalances put in place under white minority rule and to addressing the plight of the poorest of the poor. These bottom-up reappropriations of indeterminate spaces reflect the inability of municipal planning practices to accommodate the needs of the urban poor, and their failure undermines the political legitimacy of the city administration. On the other hand, the capacity of informal actors and the urban poor to evade the municipality's disciplinary apparatus exposes the inherent weakness of urban regulation: the inability of the urban planning regime to obtain the normative ideal of governable subjects. These improvised expressions of the lived city project onto space and time an alternative mode of living in the city that challenges institutionalized authority and the dominant principles of planned urban development (Groth and Corijn 2005, 503–505; Simone 2001a, 2001b, 2002).

In Johannesburg after apartheid city builders have focused on reshaping the negative image and rejuvenating the neglected built form of the central city

(Bremner 2000, 185–193). These "imagineering efforts" encompass the disparate activities of all those cultural producers who create the discursive fields in which the practices of urban revitalization are conceptualized, debated, and transformed into facts on the ground (Rutheiser 1986). The key figures involved in imagineering efforts include city officials, urban planners, large-scale property owners, real estate developers, and corporate builders, along with their hired cadres of architects, landscape designers, engineers, advertising experts, real estate agents, and public relations specialists. This assortment of individuals in no way constitutes a unified group with a common ideology and common interests. Nonetheless, differences of professional identity and conflicts of interest are frequently transcended by a shared belief in the same strategic vision of Johannesburg after apartheid as a socially progressive, racially harmonious, aspirant world-class city with a postindustrial, high-tech future of cosmopolitan urbanity (see Rutheiser 1999, 322–323).

The new ethos of privatized urbanism has gone hand in hand with a shift to postmanagerial modes of urban governance, an emphasis on downtown renaissance, and the privatization (or commercialization) of municipal services. Instead of cultivating the enlargement and upgrading of urban public space, the entrepreneurial agenda has fostered new kinds of fortified urbanism: siege architecture and its disciplinary technologies (electronic surveillance and monitoring of movement) combined with the use of legal remedies to construct purified spaces cleansed of the unwanted urban poor. This "annihilation of space by law" entails the criminalization of the survivalist strategies of the urban poor, including the adoption of legal sanctions that restrict the use of post-public spaces (Mitchell 1997, 303).[1] In seeking to eliminate indeterminacy from the cityscape, urban planners typically call for a hardening of the urban landscape, looking for a reinforcement of boundaries and distinctions (Mitchell 2003, 381). The presence of homeless people, beggars, and idle youth across the urban landscape is the visible expression of joblessness and persistent poverty. Typically employing rhetoric that is couched in such phrases as "reclaiming the streets for law-abiding citizens" or "promoting the quality of urban life," property owners and city officials have exploited "compassion fatigue," or the growing intolerance that alleges a widespread erosion of public sympathy for the homeless and the unemployed. This new realism has bred a kind of callous indifference to the plight of the poor and the downtrodden, who come to be regarded as a nuisance. With the selective appropriation of a punitive or revanchist political repertoire, propertied urban residents

---

1. Ideas derived from interview with John Penberthy, Business Against Crime, June 19, 2003, and interview with Nazira Cachalia, program manager, City Safety Programme, City of Johannesburg, May 30, 2006. The interpretation is entirely mine.

have turned away from concerns with the protection and expansion of the rights of the most disadvantaged and instead have endorsed spatial strategies designed to keep the poor, the unemployed, and the unwanted out of their privatized places of work, residence, and entertainment (Mitchell 2001, 71). In this wholesale embrace of the enterprise culture, the imperative to appease entrenched business interests, along with the clamor to adopt fiscal austerity measures, has trumped the well-meaning political efforts to extend the rights of social citizenship, including the provision of basic social services, to the neediest urban residents (MacLeod 2002, 609–610).

The steady expansion of enclosed spaces—such social gathering places as upscale shopping malls and leisure and entertainment sites for affluent urbanites—represents the materialization of class privilege. Restricted entry to these places serves to communicate a sense of hierarchical space. Yet the ingenuity of these prohibitions, by their combination of strict enforcement and capriciousness, has managed to demonstrate in a concrete way the absolutist nature of regimes of private property. Rules, regulations, and restrictions function as constant reminders to the poor and unwanted that there are some barriers, no matter how trivial, that they overstep at their own peril (Bremner 2002; Landau 2006; Kaviraj 1997, 87). While they have jettisoned racial segregation as the principal regulative principle governing the use of urban space, municipal authorities after apartheid have nevertheless introduced new codes and sanctions that have reinforced the powers of exclusion. This hierarchical differentiation of the urban landscape has crystallized into a new post-public cityscape where the suffocation of public space has gone hand in hand with the steady accretion of privatized places with restricted access (Lipman and Harris 1999).

Under white minority rule the so-called nonwhite majority of the South African people experienced citizenship negatively, that is, as a package of formal rights and entitlements of which they were deprived. A central element of the antiapartheid struggle was the demand for universal citizenship rights in an undivided South Africa. In postapartheid South Africa, as elsewhere, there is an unresolved tension between the unconditional values and universal human rights that citizenship embodies and "the sociohistorical conditions of its appearance" (Bouillon 2002, 81). This opposition between citizenship as an ontological status grounded in a "statutory body of inalienable rights" (Bouillon 2002, 81) and citizenship as a contingent praxis, or the practical enunciation of what it means to belong to a place, lies at the heart of ongoing struggles over what Henri Lefebvre (1996, 173–174, 195) has called "the right to the city." Competitive battles over which urban residents have legitimate access to and rights over specific places and available resources constitute the central dynamic of what it means to belong to the city. For Lefebvre, the right to the city is linked to claims of city dwellers to a legitimate presence in the city through the appropriation of urban spaces. Conversely, the right to the city legitimates the refusal of city dwellers to be excluded or removed from "the networks or circuits of communication, information, and exchange" that endow urban places with their meaning (Lefebvre 1996, 173–174, 195). In the postliberal city, everyday practices of exclusion and marginalization effectively qualify citizenship rights by making formal entitlements conditional on securing legitimate access to places and resources. Excluded from or chased out of places in the city, the urban poor have little choice but to try to reshape the locations where they find refuge in order to meet their immediate needs for shelter and for other basic resources. Taken together, these efforts of the urban poor to appropriate spaces of the city, to transform them and use them in ways designed to ensure their everyday survival constitutes what James Holston (1999, 157–158, 165) has called "spaces of insurgent citizenship."

The demise of classical liberal modes of thought has gone hand in hand with the shifting meanings of citizenship (Ong 1999). New strategies of postliberal urban governance "conceive of citizens, individually and collectively, as ideally and potentially 'active' in their own [self-management]" (Rose 2000, 97). By ceasing to be a possession defined by simple rights of persons, citizenship becomes a capacity to act in relation to the particular circumstances in which individuals find themselves. By extending the logic of competitive marketplace into arenas previously monopolized by the municipality, new modes of urban governance have fostered a kind of entrepreneurial citizenship in which calculating actors strive to realize and actualize themselves through the range of choices available to them. This radical transformation from citizenship as possession to citizenship as capacity, as Nikolas Rose (2000, 99) puts it, "is embodied in the image of the active and entrepreneurial citizen who seeks to maximize his or her lifestyle through acts of choice, linked not so much into a homogeneous social field as into overlapping but incommensurate communities of allegiance and moral obligation." In the postliberal city the practice of citizenship involves enrolling alert citizens in an active engagement with minimization of risk and maximization of choice, whether through Safer Cities initiatives or Neighborhood Watch groups or through private schooling or participation in contractual associations (such as gated residential communities). By attaching itself to the popular rhetoric embodied in such slogans as "zero tolerance" and "no broken windows," this entrepreneurial image of citizenship seeks to awaken a sense of individual moral obligation and responsibility directed at the policing of personal conduct. The postliberal vision of a purified, hygienic, moral space inhabited by a well-regulated citizenry serves to justify and legitimate the spatial exclusion of anti-citizens—those who threaten the project of citizenship itself—from the alleged virtuous places of the city (Rose 2000, 97, 99, 103, 106; Merrifield 2000; Smith 1998).

The new ethos of municipal governance represents a sea change in official thinking whereby the strict assignment and enforcement of individual responsibility has replaced the emphasis on communal and collective values (Brodie 2000, 124). But unlike the minimalist night-watchman state imagined by conventional advocates of neoliberal policies, these new modes of post-liberal urban governance have defined a new role for municipal agencies and bureaucracies as active partners in managing the affairs of the city, seeking to facilitate, enable, shape, and stimulate the self-governing activities of a multitude of dispersed entities—associations, business enterprises, communities, and collectivities of all kinds—who assume for themselves many of the powers, responsibilities, and duties previously controlled by municipal authorities. The characteristic features of these new strategies of urban governance are familiar: downsizing and streamlining the bureaucratic administration of the municipality, decentralizing decision making, devolving power to intermediate bodies (such as public-private partnerships, trusts, and associations), privatizing many functions of the municipal machinery and exposing them to marketplace pressures and entrepreneurial styles of management, introducing managerialism and competitive pressures to guide policy decisions, and displacing the monopoly of knowledge controlled by state functionaries with the knowledge of review generated by financial experts and paid consultants. These new modes of urban governance not only pluralize the agencies and bureaucratic bodies involved in municipal administration, but also introduce novel kinds of monitoring, regulation, and control through the techniques of the new public management. All in all, this shift from old-style managerialism to competitive entrepreneurialism requires a "reduction in the scope of direct management of [urban] affairs by state-organized programmes and technologies, and an increase in the extent to which the government of diverse domains is enacted by the decisions and choices of relatively autonomous entities" (Rose 2000, 96–97; see also Harvey 1989b, 3–7).

Citizens without a City: The Ontological Insecurity of Irregular Work and Impermanent Shelter

> The breeding places of disease, the infamous holes and cellars in which the capitalist mode of production confines our workers night after night, are not abolished; they are merely *shifted elsewhere!*
>
> FRIEDRICH ENGELS (1970, 74)

Johannesburg has come to resemble what urban theorists have called the "dual city": the urban expression of multiform processes of spatial restructuring whereby two equally dynamic sectors—the high-flying, information-based formal economy and the downgraded, labor-based informal economy—co-exist, intersect, and interact, albeit in highly uneven ways. The aesthetics of consumption reflect this process of class differentiation. At one extreme, up-scale malls offer low-volume, high-quality commodities to the discriminating middle classes. At the other, the informal marketplaces catering to the laboring poor provide high-volume, low-quality commodities and rudimentary services. By their stylized architectural design, upscale shopping malls enforce the spatial boundaries between formal and informal economies. Formal commercial transactions are sequestered behind protective barriers, leaving informal barter, or the spontaneous trade of everyday life, to the small-time vendors, hawkers, and service providers who occupy the outside streets and sidewalks. These remnants of public space are reconfigured as the last refuge of the desperately poor, the marginalized, and the unwanted. In the postliberal city, the atrophied streetscape no longer operates as the congregating space for middle-class strollers celebrated in the modernist imagination. Instead, stripped-down public spaces are forced with an increasingly dispassionate narrow-mindedness into the exclusive role of conduits for the uninterrupted flow of vehicles and the dumping grounds for the urban poor (Landau 2006, 125–145; Simone 2001a, 2001b; Flusty 1994, 14–16).

The steady influx of newcomers who have flocked to the greater Johannesburg metropolitan region, including displaced rural migrants, immigrants from other African countries, and itinerant work seekers from surrounding areas, has placed enormous pressure on the municipality to provide basic infrastructure, to extend the delivery of social services, and to introduce proper governance procedures. The proliferation of vast informal squatter settlements on the ex-urban fringe, the severe overcrowding in the existing townships, and unauthorized occupation of decaying buildings in the inner city reflect the acute housing shortage where the supply of stable, decent, and affordable residential accommodation has failed to match the rising demand. This lack of properly approved housing has given rise to all sorts of unregulated housing arrangements, including illegal land seizures, unauthorized occupation of abandoned buildings, and homeless encampments in public parks, on the streets, and in alleyways. In those inner-city neighborhoods, informal squatter settlements, and shantytowns where the municipality has achieved only limited administrative control, the urban poor have been forced to organize the provision of virtually every aspect of their basic needs, from clean water to building materials, from food to sources of heat, from fire suppression to informal policing. City dwellers who inhabit unauthorized housing accommodation face constant danger, ranging from uncontrolled fires and flooding to the predations of criminals and racketeers who seek to exploit their weaknesses. Those who have illegally commandeered makeshift shelter also face the constant threat of eviction at the hands of municipal authorities who use the strict enforcement of city bylaws, building codes, and health and safety regulations to close down "bad buildings."[2]

In the sprawling informal settlements that have proliferated on the ex-urban fringe, in the decaying inner-city neighborhoods of Hillbrow, Berea, and Joubert Park, and in the backyard shacks of the townships, the experience of daily life has produced a general sense of acute insecurity, displacement, and loss of place (Landau 2006, 125–145; de Boeck and Plissart 2004, 13–61). The movement of newcomers and old-timers in and out of these unstable locations has cultivated a kind of spatial fluidity that undermines the need for permanence, belonging, and stability. City dwellers who occupy these indeterminate spaces and marginal sites where the institutional supports of municipal governance barely exist, if at all, inhabit a sociocultural world where survival takes precedence over the kinds of enjoyment, fulfillment, and realization of potential that an alert citizenry have come to expect as their entitlement as rightful residents of the city. This state of exception is a zone not simply of exclusion but of abandonment as well, where, as part of the rational calculus of everyday living, emergencies become a normal state of affairs and tragedy becomes routine. The exception—expressed as constant menace and the threat of social death—becomes the general rule. This liminal state of being is characterized by the absence of the rule of law and its protections, where there is limited recourse to appeal to higher, official authority for redress of grievances, to ensure safety, and to gain access to municipal services (Agamben 2005, 23–24, 86–88; Landau 2005, 2006).

Estimates of the numbers of homeless squatters squeezed into overcrowded, unhygienic informal settlements on the metropolitan fringe are largely guesses, extrapolations from known data derived from small-scale surveys, official statistics, and journalistic impressions. These numbers refer to quantities that, at best, yield patterns and trends over time. Leaving aside the question of their accuracy or reliability, these figures indicate nothing about the movements in and out of homelessness, tactics that households employ to survive on a daily basis, and collective efforts required to make these places work. Equally important, these numbers fail to reveal anything about shack dwellers as human beings: their social relationships, their identities, their daily movements, or their survival techniques.

2. Municipal authorities coined the term "bad buildings" to refer to run-down, unsafe apartment complexes and hotels in the inner-city residential neighborhoods. For comparative purposes, see Gandy (2005a, 49–50). Ideas derived from interview with Graeme Gotz, specialist in policy and strategy, Corporate Planning Unit, Office of City Manager, City of Johannesburg, May 26, 2006; and interview with Geoff Mendelowitz, program manager, Better Buildings, City of Johannesburg Property Company, June 2, 2006.

All sorts of urban poor inhabit the city: paupers, beggars, the infirm, aged or sick people with little or no means of support; orphaned and runaway children, unprotected mothers with young children, widows, and other castaways without visible means of subsistence; jobless and idle youth, the casually employed, the chronically unemployed, along with the casualties of labor markets that favor the literate, the skilled, and the able-bodied. In their daily lives the urban poor suffer from the chronic insecurity of irregular and low-paying work, impermanent and unhygienic housing, poor or nonexistent health care facilities, and limited access to the panoply of social services that the middle classes take for granted. The forms of distress and social misery that the urban poor suffer include not only poverty in the strict sense of lack of reliable income but also the breakdown in the fabric of relationships that tie them organically to places, networks, and groups. In other words, the disaffiliation of the urban poor involves the intersection of two separate trajectories. On the one hand, positions along the axis of relationship to work range from attachment to a secure occupation, through participation in insecure, casual, and seasonal jobs, to the virtual absence of income-generating activities. On the other hand, positions on the axis of integration into social relationships vary from involvement and participation in solid social networks and intricate webs of interdependencies to social isolation and dissociation. The zone of disaffiliation thus entails both the breakdown in the reproduction of daily existence through income generation and a rupture in social bonds that link individuals to places, networks, and relationships. At the extreme, socioeconomic "insecurity becomes destitution and fragility of relationships becomes isolation" (Castel 2000, 520). Homeless vagrancy represents the near-total rupture in the social bonds of belonging, expressed most profoundly by a literal and figural detachment to place, whether a community, a neighborhood, a work site, or a social group. The pathetic figure of the homeless stranger, stigmatized as a dangerous idler, excluded everywhere, and condemned to roam in a sort of floating, liminal state of ceaseless movement, epitomizes this condition of disconnection and disaffiliation. Deprivation is not simply an extreme state of social misery and insecurity; it is the effect of a cumulative logic of exclusion that involves both expulsion from the income-generating world of work and a disintegration of social networks of support (Castel 2000, 520, 523–524; Delaney 2004; May 2000; Kihato and Landau 2005). Without structured responsibilities and unable to rely on the certitudes that govern the daily existence of the urban middle class, the urban poor inhabit places only temporarily and undertake movements that are often erratic, unpredictable, and circuitous. Efforts to eke out everyday survival are almost always provisional, impromptu, and uncertain (Kihato and Landau 2005; Simone 2002, 29–30).

For those without steady work and without access to permanent shelter, the spatial dimensions of social vulnerability dovetail with a breakdown in the cohesive networks of social belonging, where physical insecurity and social isolation are transformed into exclusion. In their daily lives the urban poor are subjected to a wide range of interdictions that impinge on their unimpeded movement in the city and that operate to keep them constantly on the move. These spatial interventions take the form of physical barriers (such as walls, gates, and checkpoints), surreptitious monitoring by omnipresent surveillance cameras, denial of entry to privatized enclosures, constant harassment, forcible evictions from illegal occupation of abandoned buildings, and arbitrary arrest. These accumulated technologies of dislocation produce disaffiliated persons who lack the kinds of social bonds, connections, and relationships that provide privileged access to the sites of cosmopolitan urbanity enjoyed by those with money and status. The urban poor are pushed to the interstitial spaces on the margins and fringes of the metropolis. Taken together, the concatenation of these social exclusions amounts to a denial of formal entitlements to the city, or a kind of truncated or empty citizenship of hollow rights that offer little protection in the conduct of everyday life (Lukose 2005; Caldeira and Holston 1999).

In a city where steady income, decent housing, and stable family life provide a secure platform for laying claim to the full benefits of citizenship, those who lack these accoutrements find themselves at a distinct disadvantage in claiming their right to a place in the city. The inability of the poor to assert their right to the legitimate entitlements of urban citizenship—like police protection, educational opportunities, health facilities, and access to the judicial system in seeking redress of grievances—has rendered them socially, legally, and spatially marginal. As virtually invisible occupiers of urban space, they are unstable inhabitants—rather than stable residents—of the city (Robinson 1999, 170–171; Simone 2001a, 2001b, 2004).

Newcomers to the city, and particularly recently arrived immigrant communities, have charged ahead, not waiting for city officials to accommodate them, carving out their own niches in the indeterminate spaces in the city (Simone 2000). The diversity and unpredictability of disparate informal economies and the variety of networks that constitute urban spaces ensure that new opportunities for place-making are always potentially available. As white shop owners and small-scale manufacturers abandoned the central city, new arriviste black entrepreneurs, artisans, and traders filled in the available spaces with small- and medium-scale enterprises encompassing both retail and manufacturing. Countless numbers of small-scale enterprises that originated in the shadow lands between formality and informality have redefined and reconfigured the meaning of urban entrepreneurialism. Fledgling entrepreneurs have occupied the porous zone between legality and illegality, taking advantage of the loose application of legal statutes, of zoning regulations, and of code enforcement (Robinson 1999, 170–171; Simone 1999, 173–187).

In the whirlwind world of fierce competition, small-scale enterprises typically pool resources, mobilize the assistance of extended family networks, and draw on the support provided by community ties, religious affiliation, and ethnic identification both within and beyond the city. Many of these small-scale ventures survive on the margins of legality, operating from largely invisible sites tucked away in the neglected spaces of the city. Informal, non-monetary exchange arrangements enable those facing financial hardship to trade vital services and, at the same time, learn valuable skills, work experience, and organizational capabilities for future use. The ceaseless competition of the impersonal marketplace has no regard for social justice, no patience for fairness, and no place for responding to genuine social needs. Cities are at once delightful sites of splendor, spectacle, and vitality, as well as frightful places of utter destitution, degradation, and immiseration. They bring together stark inequalities of wealth, lifestyle, and living conditions. But this does not make them any less fearful, insecure, or predatory places (Simone 1999, 2001a, 2001b).

More than anything else, it has been the rapid expansion of both the numbers and size of informal squatter settlements after the end of apartheid that has illustrated the failures of urban planning to accommodate the needs of the vast multitudes of shelterless work seekers who have poured into the greater Johannesburg metropolitan region. These informal settlements—with their broken-down or nonexistent infrastructure, patchwork of residential patterns of self-built, poor-quality housing squeezed onto tiny plots, and virtual absence of requisite social services (most notably health, education, and welfare facilities)—have become the new dumping grounds for the urban poor who lack a proper place in the formal city. These forlorn, featureless encampments are fluid sites of nervous movement, evolving, metastasizing, expanding, and contracting. The restless sojourners who have found refuge in these places of temporary residence seem to be constantly on the move, in transit from one place to another. These informal settlements, with their deprived spaces defined by their need for just about everything and their improvised income-generating activities, have become incubators for inventive survival strategies where inhabitants have begun to reclaim available space for multiple uses, develop their own specific forms of collaboration and cooperation, and reterritorialize their connections both inside and outside the city. The growth and development of informal trading networks have infused the city with their own temporal dynamics, practices, and values. The logic of survivalist economics—with its peculiar dynamics of collaboration and competition, casual work, and informal trading and exchange—has infused the urban world, as Filip de Boeck and Marie-Françoise Plissart (2004, 43) describe in another context, "both metaphorically and practically, with its own moralities, its own ethics of accumulation, expenditure, and redistribution, and its own specific pathways of self realization."

The provisionality of daily life in the city not only opens up opportunities for the accumulation of resources but also poses the danger of downward mobility, exclusion, and marginalization. The rhizomatic circuits of power and domination that insinuate themselves into everyday urban practices have triggered a variety of responses, ranging from surrender and subservience to subversion and resistance. Ironically, those highly localized struggles for empowerment and inclusion that work against the forces of oppression and domination tend to reinforce the conservative imagery of cities as places of unpredictable chaos, disorder, and moral decay, rather than as contested spaces where there is at least some hope for negotiation, compromise, and accommodation (Swyngedouw 2005, 128–129).

Zones of Indistinction: Social Vulnerability and Disaffiliation in the Postliberal Metropolis

In the [squatter] camp, the state of exception, which was
essentially a temporary suspension of the rule of law on the basis
of a factual sense of danger, is now given a permanent spatial
arrangement.

GIORGIO AGAMBEN (1998, 169)

Seen abstractly, the hallmark of modernist city building is the radical separation between private space and public space—a demarcation that corresponds, metaphorically at least, to the demarcation between inside and outside, where the former refers to the interior space of private domesticity and the latter to the exterior space of public sociability. On the one hand, private space functions as the exclusive domain or sequestered preserve of intimately connected individuals. On the other hand, public space operates as the shared realm of exposure and exchange, the neutral and accessible terrain of social interaction, and the interpersonal arena of chance encounter among strangers (Madanipur 2003, 200, 202, 232–233, 240). In Johannesburg after apartheid the erection of walls and barriers that encircle virtually every house and building, shielding them from unwanted encroachment or violation of private space, marks the visual achievement of the duality of inside and outside (Mbembe 2004, 385).

In the contemporary postliberal metropolis, however, this analytical distinction between public and private space is too blunt and crude an instrument to fully capture the intricacies and nuances of how power geometries structure everyday life of the cityscape. The blurring of the boundaries between public and private space has brought into existence new subdivisions of the urban landscape, along with new functions and new meanings attached to particular places. In the postliberal city power to regulate, control, and authorize inclusion and exclusion to post-public spaces is typically diffuse and fragmented, polyvalent and invisible (de Cauter 2002).

In Johannesburg after apartheid a host of new mechanisms (both legal and extralegal) have come into existence through which the urban poor and the marginalized are expelled from where they are not wanted. These powers of exclusion are both concentrated in the formal agencies of the state administration and widely dispersed in the quotidian practices of everyday life. On the one hand, exclusionary practices operate through the deliberate actions of municipal officials who use their administrative authorities to regulate the use of urban space. For the most part, law enforcement and the court system function as the most visible expressions of formal state power. On the other hand, exclusionary practices come into play in the tangled skein of everyday life where, in cities fragmented into an agglomeration of privatized enclosures, urban residents lacking requisite skills, proper qualifications, sufficient money, and cultural capital are denied entry to secured sites of luxury. These powers of exclusion operate spatially through the intersection of ordering principles that categorize and stigmatize certain individuals or groups in accordance with their qualifications to belong and the identification of the localities or places where they belong. Without access to formal housing or to recognized sources of income, the jobless poor have literally no place to belong (Castel 2000; Simone and Gotz 2003).

To fully grasp how the powers of exclusion operate in the everyday life of the city requires us to visualize how the urban landscape is arranged as a bewildering, rhizomatic maze of disconnected spaces. The elaborate layers, barriers, and boundaries that overlay the cityscape facilitate the safe passage of middle-class residents, at the same time preventing the easy movement of the urban poor. As Steven Flusty (2001, 658) has put it, the emergent "urban panopticon" quite readily "translates into a city that has, in many parts, become a veritable labyrinth of interdictory spaces: barricaded streets, privately administered plazas, police helicopter over-flights, and traffic lights festooned with panning, tilting, and zooming video cameras." The steady buildup of such "paranoid building typologies" as gated residential communities and similar "luxury laagers," citadel office complexes, enclosed shopping malls for the affluent, and closed-off suburban neighborhoods has partitioned the urban landscape into a mosaic of fortified enclaves surrounded by the dead space of blighted zones with decaying infrastructure, inadequate service delivery, and deteriorating built environments. The intersection of architectural design and regulatory mechanisms has produced a new spatial order and an urban environment characterized by intensified forms of spatial differentiation (Flusty 2001, 658–659; Christopherson 1994).

The urban landscape of Johannesburg is polarized along the axis of luxurious wealth at one extreme and abject impoverishment at the other. These multiple modernisms—on the one side, dynamic, cosmopolitan, and future-oriented, and, on the other, stagnant, survivalist, and immediate—coexist as polar extremes within the same evolving urban topography. Such spaces of chic cosmopolitan urbanity as the Johannesburg International Airport, the Sandton City Shopping Mall, Melrose Arch, and Montecasino entertainment resort stand in stark contrast to such "sites of indistinction" (Agamben 1998, 122, 170) as the rundown tenements, seedy brothels, and drug hotels of inner-city neighborhoods (Hillbrow, Berea, Joubert Park, Yeoville), and the proliferating informal squatter settlements on the metropolitan fringe. New modes of postliberal urban governance seek to unleash the profit-making powers of entrepreneurialism to restructure and refashion the cityscape in the image of vibrant, cosmopolitan urbanity befitting an aspirant world-class city, on the one hand, and to eradicate the miasmal parts of the cityscape while at the same time dislodging and removing those urban residents who inhabit them, on the other (Robins 2002).

These dual dynamics of space and power are grounded in a continuous differentiation between privileged insiders and excluded outsiders: while insiders enjoy the right to participate fully and directly in the collective life of the cosmopolitan city, outsiders are relegated to the margins of urban life, divested of legal protections and entitlements, and reduced to the limbo status of subjects, guests, or unwanted trespassers (Kihato and Landau 2005; Landau 2005, 2006). It is this force field of spatial liminality—at once material and symbolic—beyond the threshold of the law that constitutes what Giorgio Agamben (2005) has called the "state of exception." The combination of intermittent work and precarious shelter with insecurity of tenure gives rise to an ontological state of being where the urban poor are terrorized by not knowing when and to what circumstances the next tragedy will intrude on their lives. For them, everyday life is a persistent state of emergency. The confluence of socioeconomic marginalization, resource deprivation, and physical subjugation reproduces this state of exception, where the urban poor are deprived of their legal and civil rights and reduced to an existential condition of biological necessity at the mercy of a sovereign power (Agamben 1998, 143, 159, 176–177; Landau 2005). Those who inhabit these sites of indistinction find themselves cast adrift from the institutional supports and juridical-legal frameworks that underpin and sustain the contemporary city. These sites emerge outside the conventional boundaries of municipal governance and beyond the scope of administrative regimes of municipal authority. The resulting juridical-legal abandonment leaves those who occupy these marginal spaces suspended in a lawless, extra-legal limbo (Agamben 2005, 21–26, 45–46). In functional terms these places are vast dumping grounds for warehousing and containing the poor, disposal sites for depositing the wasted lives of marginalized urban inhabitants who, with no actual prospects for formal employment, have no real value within the circuits of capital that constitute the new global economy (Bauman 2003).

Conventional enclosures ranging from prisons, barracks, and asylums to households, schools, and factories are well-known sites of discipline and confinement. As monitored spaces folded in upon themselves, these enclosures are common sites where those in authority seek to instill habits of work and discipline, to produce a homogeneous orderliness, and to regulate and individualize the conduct of people in accordance with certain normative prescriptions. This juridical-institutional model of disciplinary enclosure enables us to grasp how the microphysics of power operates in confined spaces with fixed boundaries and immobile populations. Yet this Foucauldian-inspired approach is not particularly helpful in helping us to make sense of such marginalized sites of exclusion as refugee camps, informal squatter settlements, and homeless encampments. Unlike conventional disciplinary enclosures defined by order, predictability, and regulation, these places are characterized by mobility, fluidity, and liminality.[3]

As unordered areas of spontaneity, unpredictability, and indeterminacy, these marginal sites obey a different set of conventions, protocols, and rules outside and beyond the boundaries of municipal regulation. The countless multitudes of homeless squatters who inhabit zones of indistinction at the metropolitan edge find themselves cut adrift from the institutional and juridical-legal frameworks that underpin the operations of the modern city. Without running water or electricity, squatters are compelled to forage on their own in order to ensure their daily survival (Kihato and Landau 2005; Landau 2006).

These sites of exclusion are not just spaces defined by movement, but they become what they are through movement. They are characterized by mobile habits: fleeting relationships, casual encounters, temporary work, and passing connections that homeless squatters assemble in their everyday struggle to survive (Simone 2001a, 2001b). Unlike enclosed disciplinary spaces, the marginal sites occupied by squatters are not cellular or contained, since they have permeable boundaries. They do not instill the kinds of codes of conduct amenable to what city officials would consider the civic virtue of law-abiding

3. Agamben's (2005, 10–11, 34–35) contention that the refugee camp is a place of legal exception becomes all the more compelling when he also suggests that this condition can be naturalized or stabilized as a prototype that reappears at such places as border crossings, airports, and informal squatter settlements on the outskirts of cities.

citizens. Homeless squatters experience a kind of nomadic displacement forged out of a "culture of the marginalized" (Shields 1991, 3–6). Those who occupy these spaces of squatter marginality engage in a variety of different behaviors, since in the struggle for survival, codes of conduct are situational, where no single set of rules applies, bargaining is always provisional, and there are no standard ways to act (Shields 1991, 3–6; Simone 2001b, 2003, 2004a, 2004c).

2

Ruin and Regeneration
Intertwined

[W]e should study not only how cities evolve but also *how they decline.*
ALDO ROSSI (1992, 152)

A s a general rule, cities are always experienced in space but studied in time. In other words, cities historicize space. As sites where the duration and depredation of objects, persons, and memories take place in time, cities are haunted by their own histories. In this way, they not only stretch across time but also extend through space. Whatever traces of the past that remain provide a partial glimpse of what once was. Cities accumulate metonymic objects, artifacts, and discarded residues of the past as a kind of involuntary memory. To elicit this city memory is to arrive at a moment of recognition of how the present is both a fading reflection of what came before and a prescient foretaste of what is to come. City futures are immanent in the past. In this sense they are never complete but always already in a state of ruin. As emblematic artifices in the allegory of modernity, cities stand for the failure of intentionally planned futures to realize utopia. Susceptible to the countervailing forces of design and chance, cities are sites for the perpetual negotiation and compromise between the providential and the unpredictable, between the anticipated and the fortuitous (Patke 2000, 5–6; Cuff 2000, 18, 19, 37–39).

Expressed in theoretical terms, scholarly efforts to explain the itineraries of urban transformation in terms of available models like modernization, dependency, and developmentalism fail to acknowledge that the evolution of cities does not necessarily follow a predictable linear progression, each succeeding step unfolding logically from what came before. Urban biographies are shaped by such unexpected, extraordinary, and catastrophic events as war, popular rebellion, famine, disease, and natural disaster that leave a residue of physical wounds and psychic scars in their wake. It is in this sense, then, that cities do not constitute unified wholes or coherent entities that are defined by what are considered their essential characteristics. Rather, they exist as agglomerations of fragments, held together tenuously, sometimes by originating myths that speak of a unified past and sometimes by the uplifting promise of a radiant future (Abbas 1994).

As both an object of nature and a subject of culture rooted in history and memory, every city mutates, evolves, and unfolds into a kaleidoscopic plurality of different cities that coexist at the same time and place (see Calvino 1974). These "analogous cities" (Rossi 1992, 166, 176) take shape from seemingly endless repertoires of associations that include not only contrasting architectural styles, design motifs, and planning interventions but also collective memories, personal reminiscences, and subjective experiences of urban residents. Although they occupy the same temporal and spatial coordinates, analogous cities presuppose a juxtaposition of sometimes intersecting and sometimes opposing temporalities, where urban artifacts left over from past city-building efforts struggle for survival against the relentless forces of decay and oblivion; at the same time the imaginary City of Tomorrow strives to be born amid the chaotic clutter of the ever-advancing present (Rossi 1992). It is in this sense, then, that city building is always provisional, tentative, and incomplete, a kind of ceaseless, Sisyphean task without finality or closure (Jaguaribe 1999, 295–296, 299–300; Cuff 2000, 18, 19, 37–39).

As material objects buildings suffer the same fate as all other commodities.[1] Property speculation means that every built structure in Johannesburg and elsewhere, however monumental, spectacular, and up-to-date at the moment of its creation, is potentially a decaying ruin, transformed with the passage of time into an anomalous inconvenience, blocking the path to progress in the impatient rush to the future. Under the impulse of modernist city building, the originality and novelty of every new addition to the built environment is counteracted by rapid turnover and accelerating obsolescence. As material objects constructed in accordance with historically specific guidelines, buildings struggle from the start against their inevitable degeneration, ruin, and potential disappearance. The urban landscape mutates and changes over time, making the cityscape of the past sometimes virtually unrecognizable in the present. Without constant vigilance and attention, the built environment

---

1. In Marxist terms the metamorphosis of commodities takes place through a tripartite cycle: the sphere of production, where value is embedded or imprinted in material objects; the sphere of circulation, where value enters into the circuits of capital via the exchange of equivalents; and the sphere of consumption, where value is depleted through use over time. Commodities begin their journey through the life cycle as something new, exciting, and pristine and terminate it as something old, discarded, and useless.

of the city suffers from the effects of neglect, misuse, and decline. As the animating spirit behind municipal planning, urban regeneration takes its meaning from breathing new life into lifeless, moribund places in the city. As the platonic ideal of an uplifting process without end, these planning tropes are paradigmatic exemplars of the master narrative of progress, improvement, and growth. In the discourse of urban planning they acquire their cachet precisely because they are the antithesis of stasis, stagnation, and disorder (Abbas 1994; Huyssen 1997).

Disappearing Acts: The City Vanishes

> The old city dies and the new city rises on its ruins—not gradually, but in a burst, suddenly—as the butterfly emerges from the cocoon of the caterpillar.
>
> Le Corbusier (Charles-Edouard Jeanneret)

Over the course of its history Johannesburg has accumulated a varied symbolic repertoire of iconic buildings that have embodied the dreams and aspirations of the city builders who initiated their construction. Built to convey a sense of the new and the up-to-date, these structures came into being under the sign of the future, that is, as material embodiments and symbolic place markers that projected an imagined Future City. Yet like all constructed objects, the built environment mutates over time into a motley assortment of urban artifacts—decaying buildings, deteriorating districts, dead zones, congested streetscapes, in-between spaces—that testify by their modified uses and by their decomposition to the provisionality and transience of a past modernity and its accompanying utopian projections that were never fully realized. By surveying the wreckage of decayed modernist and hypermodernist architecture, it is possible to detect the failed utopias of successive waves of city building that have taken root in Johannesburg over time (Jaguaribe 1999, 298–299).

Meanings attached to place cannot be understood apart from their spatial location in the urban landscape and from their historically specific temporality (or specific moment in time). Fashioned to be both functionally useful and to convey symbolic meaning, buildings lose their newness not only because of physical erosion and accelerated obsolescence, but also due to the fragmentation and disappearance of the ethos that influenced their construction. In their decline buildings translate into ruin the ephemerality of the utopian impulses that accompanied their initial creation. As emblematic expressions of originality and novelty, new buildings project a future that over time becomes outdated and outmoded (Edensor 2005a, 2005b; Jaguaribe 1999, 298–299; Page 1999).

Conventional approaches to urban revitalization—and especially those associated with urban ecology—look upon the revalorization of landed property as the welcome outcome of an adjustment process guided by the self-regulating, invisible land of the capitalist marketplace. By employing biologistic analogies that rest on assumptions about the organic nature of urban growth and development, these mainstream perspectives conceive of modifications to the built environment solely in terms of laws of competition, dominance, succession, and invasion. When viewed through the lens of the functional and efficient use of urban space, spatial restructuring appears to be governed by natural, mechanical, or organic processes. Severed from its social production, urban space is thus fetishized as an objective entity, thereby enabling city boosters to look upon urban regeneration as the outcome of the heroic conquest of hostile environments by risk-taking pioneers (Boyer 1994a, 104–108, 234–237; Deutsche 1996, 50–52, 70–72, 75–76).

Far from a uniform process, however, urban revitalization takes place in different locations at varying speeds. The uneven development of urban space is a structural, rather than incidental, feature of revitalization efforts. The visible symptoms of material prosperity—gentrified neighborhoods, upscale shopping and entertainment, luxury housing, and clean and safe physical environments—are not distinct from, but are integrally connected with, the overt manifestations of urban blight: neglect, deterioration, and ruin. The devalorization of real estate—brought about by abandonment, disinvestment, and redlining—results in a situation where investment in alternative land uses can create opportunities for profitable return. Revitalization is thus the consequence of the uneven development of urban space. While revitalization is the remedy for the deterioration of the built environment, it is also the case that decay and ruin are the preconditions for urban revival (Deutsche 1996, 50–52, 54, 70–72, 75; Scobey 2002, 153–154).

The logic of real estate capitalism ensures that all forms of landed property, including residential housing, office blocks, and retail shops, are commodities to be exploited for profit. The expansion of profit-maximizing real estate development involves the creative destruction of the built environment, where the revalorization of landed property results in some groups profiting at the expense of others. The occupants and users of revamped spaces are faced with the conversion of their residential neighborhoods into refurbished areas they can no longer afford. Real estate developers, municipal authorities, and city boosters legitimate displacement, evictions, and exclusions as the necessary byproduct of progress and change (Deutsche 1996, 75–76; Page 1999).

Starting in the 1980s, the massive exodus of large-scale corporate enterprises from the Johannesburg inner city reinforced the disorders of the city-building process, rewarding the "sweating" of the built environment (by squeezing profits out of unimproved properties), dysfunctional land use (overcrowding, building conversions that defied the best and highest use), and the transformation of public space into a residual dumping ground for the poor. As a result, city streets grew more congested, chaotic, and unmanageable, locked in a seemingly inexorable downward spiral of decline and ruin. Public parks, vacant lots, and other open spaces became congregating places for the homeless, providing surrogate homes for those who had nowhere else to go. Decaying residential buildings devolved into overcrowded, dilapidated barracks for warehousing the urban poor. Rather than generating ever-widening circles of social wealth through the spark of economic competition, market mechanisms actually triggered the opposite effect. Starved of capital and deprived of infrastructural improvements, the built environment of the inner city experienced disinvestment and neglect, decay and abandonment. Real estate capitalism undermined itself: on the one hand, property markets in land and buildings became too rigid (because of capital fixed in place); on the other hand, they became too makeshift (as property was no longer put to its highest and best use). As a consequence, real estate capitalism by itself was unable to regulate land values, capital flows, commerce, and social stability in strict accordance to the laws of supply and demand (Blomley 2004, 32–34, 86–87, 142–144; Scobey 2002, 153–154).

For those new postapartheid urban elites who looked upon the urban landscape as a prophetic text, these frictions of capital have come to represent a serious obstacle to Johannesburg taking its rightful place in the global hierarchy of leading cities (Bremner 2000, 2005; see Scobey 2002, 153–154). As urban planners, city officials, and large-scale property owners viscerally understood, spatial disorder threatened to undermine the future prospects of postapartheid Johannesburg as a cosmopolitan world-class city. Respectable, middle-class observers were troubled by all sorts of vexing problems: crime-ridden slums in the inner city, congested and dangerous streets, overcrowded tenements, filth in public places, abandoned buildings, and historic sites in woeful states of ruin. The spatial unevenness of the built environment, in short, challenged the most cherished material and moral ambitions of the new generation of city builders who had ascended to political power after the end of apartheid. They responded by imagining how Johannesburg should look and how they should rebuild and govern it. Beginning with the introduction of various regeneration strategies unveiled in serial displays of confident optimism about the city yet to come, a diverse collection of city-building elites—large-scale property owners (including the historic mining houses with deep roots in the central city, commercial and investment banks, insurance companies, and real estate holding companies), politicians and city administrators, intellectuals and social reformers, journalists and design professionals—cobbled together new plans to reconfigure the decayed cityscape, to coordinate its growth and development, and regulate its debilitating disorders (Tomlinson 1999a, 1999b, 2002).[2]

The Figured City of the Topographical Imagination: The Illusionary Fantasy of Coherence

> [T]he essence of metropolitan culture is change—a state of
> perpetual animation.
> REM KOOLHAAS (1994, 296)

As a normative ideal, the figured spaces of the planned city consist of well-designed, artfully arranged, and carefully maintained places of strong visual identity and aesthetic appeal, where such regulative mechanisms as contextual zoning ordinances, standardized design guidelines, and code enforcement operate as a protective shield to preserve the integrity of the urban form. They are not always physically connected, yet the spatial enclaves that comprise the figured city are linked imaginatively to each other, to other aspirant world-class cities, and to a shared history of cultural meanings that reinforce attachment to place. The semiotic effect of such seamless ordering of material objects is the construction of a mental map of stable, coherent, and legible space: the regulated city of the elite imagination. The demarcation of the figured spaces of the planned city is tantamount to the production of boundaries, spatial hierarchies, and spatial separations (Boyer 1995, 81–109).

In contrast, the disfigured spaces of the unplanned city consist of those abandoned, neglected, or overlooked places where the operations of spatial discipline are largely ignored, bypassed, and subverted. As the site of decay and ruin, the disfigured city is characterized by an excess of discarded waste—unwanted matter out-of-place (Edensor 2005a, 2005b). Because they are cast adrift and detached from the well-designed ornamental nodes of the planned city, the disfigured spaces of the unplanned city appear mundane and inconsequential, constituting a kind of formless void without identifiable functions and discernible uses. As superfluous appendages not needed or wanted in the figured city, the nomadic poor who inhabit these "placeless" places occupy a kind of ontological state of nonbeing (De Cauter 2004, 11; Augé 1995, 85, 94–95, 102; Bauman 2003; Davis 2006).

---

2. Information derived from interview with Richard Tomlinson, consultant in urban economic development and project management, Johannesburg, June 4, 2001. Interpretation is entirely mine.

The figured city and the disfigured city constitute spatially distinct geographies that inhabit the same urban landscape. Yet the scenographic power of the former renders the latter largely invisible. The interstitial spaces of urban banality that constitute the disfigured city are easily forgotten and dismissed, allowing instead a rational and imaginary ordering of things glorifying the figured city to dominate the remembered and lingering afterimage of the city. The points where they intersect and overlap often metastasize into zones of antagonism and conflict. The production of material excess in the figured city is expunged as so much useless waste and ruin to the disfigured city (Boyer 1995, 82–83).

In Johannesburg after apartheid the steady expansion in the figured spaces of the planned city has evolved alongside the proliferation of the disfigured spaces of the unplanned city. Spatial restructuring of the urban landscape has not only resulted in the extensive growth and development of new sites of cosmopolitan urbanity but also reinforced tendencies toward fragmentation, polarization, and separation. The steady accretion of citadel official complexes, gated residential communities, enclosed shopping malls, and other fortified enclaves of luxury for affluent city dwellers has gone hand in hand with severe overcrowding in the impoverished sections of existing townships, the proliferation of informal squatter settlements along the peri-urban edge of the metropolis, and unauthorized squatting in such in-between spaces of the city as abandoned buildings, unattended lots, public parks, unused alleyways, under bridges, and along the banks of streams (Czeglédy 2004). Like other aspiring world-class cities that have sought to move upward in the ranked hierarchy of urban sites, Johannesburg has experienced the shock of rapid integration into transnational networks and global markets that define what Manuel Castells (1996) has called the "informational city."

This abrupt insertion of Johannesburg into global "space of flows" (Castells 1996, 407–459) of capital, information, and power has led to increased differentiation between those urban residents who are able to become part of these transnational networks and those who are left out. On the one side, the privileged urban residents have retreated into gated residential communities, gentrified neighborhoods, and townhouse cluster developments safely cocooned behind walls. They spend their leisure time and discretionary incomes in the new luxury spaces that replicate analogous ones in other aspirant world-class cities. On the other side, the propertyless urban poor are forced to eke out a meager existence on the margins of urban luxury (Bremner 2004a). The spatial transformation of the urban landscape has reinforced the already deeply engrained structural inequalities between these two poles of the social spectrum. The great disparities in income, accumulated wealth, and power that separate the comfortably rich from the desperately poor are visibly apparent in the obvious juxtaposition between places of residence, cultures of consumption, and practices of everyday life. Surely the mechanisms of differential inclusion have created gradations in the experience of luxury, where only those at the apex of the socioeconomic pyramid have virtually unencumbered access to whatever they need or want and whenever they desire (Castel 2000; Deutsche 1996; Keyder 2005).

The locus of power in the contemporary city of Johannesburg has shifted from concentrated and visible manifestations of state-sanctioned municipal authority (such as city bureaucracies, law enforcement agencies, and regulatory agencies) to a diffuse and diversified set of networks dominated by the large-scale owners of capital, such as real estate interests, corporate builders, large-scale property owners, finance and banking, and well-entrenched lobbying surrogates. No longer the focus of high-modernist schemes to impose a strict kind of functional order and rational efficiency on the cityscape as a coherent whole, the postliberal city has experienced a profound restructuring whereby powerful private interest groups have carved up the urban landscape into separate zones that amount to their own privatized fiefdoms (Bremner 2005).

Johannesburg after apartheid has experienced at one and the same time growth, expansion, and transformation along with contraction, polarization, and decay. The greater Johannesburg metropolitan region has developed and mutated in ways that are beyond the reach of city planners to fully control. This process, which Matthew Gandy (2005a, 51–52) has called "amorphous urbanism," has resulted in a sprawling, distended metropolitan form where the countervailing forces of connection, integration, and coherence, on the one hand, and separation, polarization, and differentiation, on the other, are locked in fierce competition with each other. The constantly evolving urban morphology and the sheer scale of the greater Johannesburg metropolitan region, infused with the polarizing extremes of wealth and poverty, have presented real obstacles to the imposition of order onto the physical environment or discipline onto the social fabric. The fragmented, disjointed physical layout of the urban landscape has largely deprived the city of a comprehensive institutional logic or planning discourse capable of "tying its heterogeneous residents together in some inclusive conviction of common belonging," with shared beliefs and mutual points of reference (Simone 2004c, 4). As such, it is not difficult or unusual for affluent urban residents to go their own way, carrying on their daily lives, not knowing and oblivious to the grim realities of deprivation that encircles the city (Bremner 2002; Simone 2001a, 2001b, 2002).

Shades of Noir: The City as Spectacle and Ruin

The ruin creates the present form of a past life, not according
to the contents or remnants of that life, but according to its
past as such.

GEORG SIMMEL (1911, 265)

In Johannesburg after apartheid the anxious rich and the resentful poor live
in distinct physical environments and locations: one static, monumental, and
safely cocooned behind barricades, walls, and barriers; the other metastasizing on the outer edges and fringes of the city, sprawling haphazardly along
major transportation routes or crammed into any available crevices of abandoned buildings, alleyways, or invisible sites of the inner core. Seeking to escape what they perceive as the miasmal city, affluent residents have partitioned
the urban landscape into a patchwork assemblage of bunkered enclaves that
provide the fanciful illusion of sanitized, first-world cosmopolitanism in the
midst of third-world impoverishment. At the same time, numerous and poor
newcomers have shaped the spatiality of the cityscape in ways that have frustrated the efforts of city planners to impose the kind of order and stability on
the urban landscape that they believe is befitting an aspirant world-class city
(Bremner 1999).

At the risk of oversimplification, it is possible to imagine the urban landscape of the greater Johannesburg metropolitan region in terms of a layered
hierarchy of three distinct zones of activity that give substance and meaning to radically different modes of urban living. While these three spheres
cannot be conceived of as separate and autonomous "spatial envelopes" (Jameson
and Speaks 1990, 32–37) disconnected from one another, they each conform to
their own distinctive spatial dynamics, institutional logics, and temporal rhythms.
In addition, they also invoke their own circuits of power, rely on their own rules
of conduct, and fashion their own norms of civility, reciprocity, and exchange
(Simone 2004c, 2).

At the apex of the hierarchy, city-building efforts represent a mode of spatial
engineering designed to serially reproduce and incorporate showcase sites as
key nodal points in the global space of flows. In Johannesburg after apartheid
municipal authorities, urban planners, and city boosters alike have set their
sights on securing the place of Johannesburg as a genuine world-class city.
City officials have provided the kinds of basic physical infrastructure and support services required to generate greater flexibilities for large-scale business
enterprises with headquarters or major office complexes in the city to both
extend their geographical reach and to consolidate their capacities to compete
in the global marketplace. The integration of Johannesburg after apartheid
into the ephemeral world of the globalized space of flows has brought about

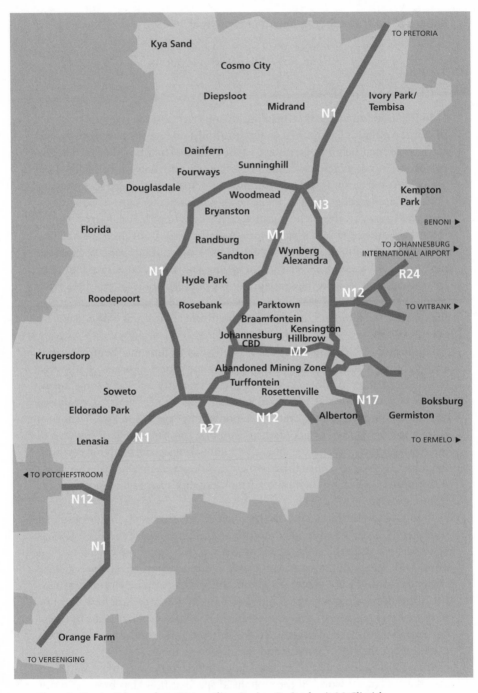

Figure 1. Greater Johannesburg Metropolitan Region. By Stephanie McClintick

the spatial concentration of advanced telecommunications, information technologies, and financial services required for fast-track commercial transactions and business decision making at cocooned enclaves that are separated from the everyday activities of ordinary people in the city. These policy initiatives have taken place in arenas outside the histories, experiences, and livelihoods of the majority of urban residents (Sassen 2000).

In this cosmopolitan City of Spectacle, elite city builders retreat behind the utopian projection of the "emancipatory city," an imaginary urban landscape consisting of an assemblage of sequestered sites saturated with fanciful dreams of plenitude, pleasure, and relaxation (Lees 2004, 3–20). Such spatial enclaves as city improvement districts, citadel office complexes, gated residential communities, and other secured urban fortresses have become exemplary expressions of the kind of privatized urbanism that characterizes the city-building efforts of aspirant world-class cities. Separated from the institutional grid of municipal service provision, these cocooned, fortified enclosures provide their own private policing and surveillance-monitoring systems, establish their own protocols enabling entry and exit from their privately owned premises, and supplement municipal services with their own refuse disposal, beautification campaigns, and auxiliary sources of electrical power. Such "globalized villages" as Sandton, Rosebank, Fourways, Sunninghill, Ilovo, Bryanston, and Hyde Park have become key nodal points in a chain of strategic sites where a multiplicity of globalization processes assume concrete, localized forms. These localities cater to an affluent minority who identify with a global vision of cosmopolitan urbanity. As such, these places bear little relation to the daily experiences of the majority of urban inhabitants. As glitzy shrines to consumption, such luxury sites as enclosed shopping arcades, gated residential communities, and other verdant playgrounds for the rich have so detached themselves from the urban landscape that they are capable of relocation anywhere. By eliminating chaos and disorder, by expunging environmental degradation and pollution, and by expelling human squalor to places outside its boundaries, the City of Spectacle keeps alive the enduring myth of progress. The serial reproduction of fantasy-islands for affluent urbanites, safely quarantined behind walls and barriers, enables the real city—with its disorganized spaces and accumulated waste—to gradually disappear from view. In other words, by maintaining the fictional illusion of the perfectly managed city, the City of Spectacle nurtures the unrealized dream of earthly urban paradise (Boyer 1994a, 46–59, 474–476, 1994b; Buck-Morss 1995, 25; Kaika and Swyngedouw 2000, 135–136).

The second tier (or middle level) of city building involves the assembly, or the piecing together, of the physical and social infrastructure, the institutional and administrative networks, and the appropriate technologies of rule that enable the municipality to function on a daily basis. Cities are built not just around the fantasy distractions of architects but on the technological prowess of engineers. In order to function efficiently cities require the massive and calculated mobilization of vast material resources to maintain the physical environment, to secure the continuous flow of social services, and to regulate the use of urban space (Gandy 2005b).[3]

City building is never finished or complete. The cityscape is always a provisional work in progress, where the debilitating effects of broken-down and outmoded infrastructure, overtaxed social services, decaying buildings, and squalid housing conditions exemplify the fallacy behind the mythical construction of "the perfectly managed city" (Kaika and Swyngedouw 2000, 136). Because it regulates the habitats within which city dwellers conduct their daily lives, physical infrastructure, particularly its quality and spatial distribution, functions as a key element in the material technology of urban governance. The maintenance, repair, and improvement of roadways, streetscapes, illumination, sewerage, gas mains, water systems, and electricity require constant attention and vigilance (Kaika 2005; Otter 2002, 1, 5, 6).

The shift toward neoliberal strategies of urban governance has meant local municipalities have largely relinquished their commanding place in overseeing the urban environment and regulating its residents and have adopted instead new functional roles that stress coordination and facilitation. New entities cobbled together under the rubric of public-private partnerships have increasingly assumed control over the provision of social services, the maintenance of basic infrastructure, and the regulation of urban space. Municipal funds are increasingly directed at enhancing the capacities of local entrepreneurship, attracting large-scale investor capital, and promoting various kinds of growth alliances and development coalitions among powerful urban stakeholders. This movement away from holistic urban management and toward a new role as facilitator has deprived local municipalities of the centralized powers and administrative authority they once enjoyed, thereby decentering, diluting, and diminishing their room for maneuver. The new broadened networks of urban governance have meant that policy making and implementation have come to depend on a wide array of participants, including property owners and alliances of entrepreneurs, chambers of commerce, social welfare agencies, churches, consultants, and local community organizations (Mayer 1995).

The fragmentation of the urban landscape into a confusing mélange of separate property regimes, administrative jurisdictions, and regulatory entities has thwarted the efforts of municipal authorities to impose a single, all-encompassing package of procedures, rules, and norms on the cityscape. In

3. See Nicolai Ouroussoff, "How the City Sank," *New York Times,* October 9, 2005, for an insightful treatment of city catastrophe in New Orleans after the onset of Hurricane Katrina.

negotiating their way through the labyrinth of overlapping and sometimes rival interest groups, city officials have introduced a number of initiatives aimed at the provision of essential urban services through outsourcing, public-private partnerships, and outright privatization of delivery systems. The results of this Faustian bargain with neoliberal modes of urban governance are evident, particularly the transformation of privileged zones of the urban landscape into self-sufficient luxury enclaves while other parts of the city, dependent on faltering city services and neglected infrastructure, are allowed to fall into ruin. With overcrowded hospitals and health clinics, under-resourced schools and social service facilities, and overburdened infrastructure always in need of repair, municipal authorities are compelled to engage in a kind of urban triage, deciding which projects will live and which will die. Under circumstances in which public financing is nonexistent, municipal authorities have worked with private social service agencies, such as the Salvation Army, church groups, and nongovernmental organizations, to provide basic assistance to those most in need. The development of these municipal initiatives largely takes place with very circumscribed territorial parameters that tend to support particular communities at precisely the historical moment when the unrelenting pressures of joblessness, precarious shelter, and vulnerability to disease operate against the sustainability of permanence, stability, and rootedness necessary for the sustainability of local identities (Simone 2004c, 2; Winkler 2006).

In the main, the bottom tier of the urban hierarchy consists of those unauthorized spatial zones that functionally operate outside of the control of any formal or legitimate arm of public authority, with the exception of periodic incursions to clean up what is deemed to be unacceptable behavior. As normal access to the formal life of the city becomes increasingly inaccessible for the urban poor, so too those domains, localities, and circuits where impoverished residents of the city operate become increasingly impenetrable to official scrutiny, classification, and control. The absence of the ordinary surveillant technologies of urban governance, combined with the collapse of basic infrastructure and the absence of social service provision, has left large parts of the city in a liminal state of virtual ungovernability (Landau 2005, 2006; Simone 2004b, 10–11, 12–14, 92–93, 140–142, 206–208).

The haphazard growth and expansion of the greater Johannesburg regions has gone hand in hand with the proliferation of vast informal settlements on the ex-urban fringe, with overcrowding in the existing townships (particularly backyard shacks) and with new shantytowns that have metastasized around their edges, with squatter occupations of abandoned buildings in the inner city, and with extra-legal land invasions of such interstitial places as public parks, unused alleyways, under bridges, and along the banks of streams. On balance, these "zones of indistinction"—to borrow a phrase from Giorgio

Agamben (1998, 122, 170, 174)—have developed independently of the efforts of city officials to regulate, contain, and control them. The inability (and sometimes unwillingness) of municipal authorities to properly maintain urban infrastructure, to provide requisite social services for those who cannot provide for themselves, and to establish workable frameworks of law and order, health and safety, has left whole areas of the urban landscape outside the institutional framework of urban governance. This failure of the assembled apparatus of municipal administration to extend the reach of urban governance to the metropolis as a whole has resulted in the emergence of zones that fall outside official rule and regulation (Simone 2001a).

City dwellers who occupy the environmentally degraded and resource-depleted spaces of the urban landscape are compelled to conduct their daily lives amid the fracturing and fragmentation of the cityscape, the declining usefulness of atrophied physical infrastructure, and the breakdown of service delivery systems (including health, welfare, and police and fire protection). These straitened circumstances have generated a confusing mélange of informal, unregulated activities that revolve around cobbling together livelihoods that typically involve the unconventional or illicit use of the built environment, the redirection of existing institutional arrangements, and the commandeering of whatever resources are available. Where opportunities for regular employment are few and far between, the urban poor engage in a wide range of activities designed to establish some sort of stability in a sociocultural world defined by instability, impermanence, and uncertainty. These arts of survival assume many guises, some heroic, uplifting, and exemplary, and others dangerous, degrading, and harmful to body and soul (Rogerson 1996b; Simone 2001a, 2001b, 2002, 2004a).

While the numbers represent little more than educated guesses, city officials estimated that by 2005 around 190 informal settlements accommodating many hundreds of thousands of homeless squatters had metastasized around the outer edge of the greater Johannesburg metropolitan region, where large vacant tracts of publicly owned land are located. Most informal settlements have sprouted on the fringes of the former black townships, further exacerbating the latent tensions between somewhat privileged insiders and impoverished outsiders seeking residential accommodation on almost any terms. This trend is especially evident in the southwestern areas of greater Johannesburg, particularly around the outer edge of Soweto and nearby Lenasia (Huchzermeyer 2004).[4]

4. See Michael Wines, "Shantytown Dwellers in South Africa Protest the Sluggish Pace of Change," *New York Times,* October 24, 2005. Information also derived from interview with Graeme Gotz, specialist in policy and strategy, Corporate Planning Unit, Office of the City Manger, City of Johannesburg, May 26, 2006, and from various on-site visits to the area.

Whether officially authorized or not, the proliferation of these unplanned and unregulated informal settlements that are geographically dispersed over a wide area represents the spatial incarnation of a kind of spontaneous urbanism, where municipal authorities can do little more than react to what has already taken place on the ground. These places take shape as a checkered mosaic of mixed spatial practices, with the result that makeshift shelters, workplaces, shops, and sites of worship are intertwined in an untidy profusion of apparent chaos. The urban poor who live in these environmentally degraded places have negligible access to essential shelter-related services, such as piped water, sewage and sanitation facilities, electricity, and refuse collection. Schools, playgrounds, and health clinics are virtually nonexistent. The substandard conditions that prevail in these sprawling encampments of self-built shelters ensure that residents are subjected to high rates of debilitating disease, crime, and other kinds of personal hardships. Within these liminal zones of marginality the normal operations of legal rights and protections, or more generally, the duties and responsibilities of citizenship, no longer apply in any real sense, and the accepted conventions of the social contract are suspended. The conjoined impact of social isolation, juridical-administrative abandonment, and legal limbo has produced a culture of distress, hopelessness, and despair, where inhabitants see no appreciable advantage in making any long-term investment in permanence (Landau 2005; Agamben 2005).

Taken as a whole, the specific spatial dynamics, temporal rhythms, and institutional logics associated with these three spheres of city building have reconfigured the relationship between Johannesburg and cities elsewhere. They have also revamped the relationships between residents and the built environment of the cityscape and introduced new patterns in the flow and movement of goods, information, and people across the urban landscape (Czeglédy 2004). The slightest shifts in production systems, market capacities, commodity circuits, money trails, and consumption patterns can have far-reaching effects on the value of urban financial investments, the sustainability of infrastructure, the use of urban space, and the worth of human resources. Business success of transnational corporations has become increasingly dependent on complex communication systems, sophisticated information technologies, and infrastructure inputs tailored to economic transactions in the global marketplace that are conducted in real time but across virtual space. Yet, ironically, this growing dependency on connecting to world markets has the effect of exacerbating the deleterious effects of the low technologies on which most urban residents rely in the conduct of their daily lives. In an urban environment where city-building efforts have concentrated their investments in fortified urban enclaves that showcase the first-world qualities of the glittering Johannesburg cityscape, the infrastructural grid and the public spaces in neglected parts of the city have fallen into disrepair. In those forsaken places where municipal authorities have found it difficult to offer and enforce the kind of overarching administrative governance that enables the city to operate with a modicum of efficiency and predictability, urban residents are left to fend largely for themselves. City dwellers who lack access to basic resources compensate for the lack of reliable infrastructure, the breakdown of service delivery, and the absence of opportunities for regular work by developing livelihoods that re-volve around repair and recycling, piracy and seizure (or the reuse of found objects), and the provision of personal services. To a large extent, these in-formal activities involve the subversive, unanticipated, and sometimes hereti-cal uses of urban space, including the unauthorized conversion of structures, squatting in abandoned buildings, and sidewalk trading. The constantly evolv-ing and widely discrepant uses of the urban environment have far exceeded the capacity of municipal authorities to identify, measure, and map what is going on, let alone prevent these disruptions of the orderly city from taking place (Harrison 2006; Kihato and Landau 2005; Simone 2003, 2004a, 2004c; Simone and Gotz 2003).

Spatial (Un)discipline: The Contested Terrain of Urban Space

> The modern [capitalist] concept of property is pretty well
> confined to the right of an individual or corporation—a
> natural or artificial person—to exclude others from some use
> or enjoyment of some thing.
> C. B. MACPHERSON (1987, 78, 80)

In the typical case, urban planning experts, architects, and design profes-sionals are emboldened by the twin ideals of rational order and uncontested omnipotence.[5] They often believe themselves to function in the role of fair-minded democratic negotiators, sensitive community advocates, neutral so-cial scientists, proponents of the aesthetically beautiful, or masterful builders of useful space. Yet they act only as a small part of much broader, much more deeply entrenched systems of economic power, political authority, and cultural signification. All too often urban planners, architects, and design experts look upon the built environment through the lens of aesthetics, thereby ignoring

5. Macpherson (1987, 78, 80) continues, "Property as an exclusive right of a natural or arti-ficial person to use and dispose of material things…leads necessarily, as in any kind of market society,…to an inequality of wealth and power that denies a lot of people the possibility of a reasonably human life….The right not to be excluded from some use or enjoyment of some thing cannot, by its very nature, be marketed."

and masking the structures of power that underlie the uses and functions of urban space (Borden, Kerr, and Rendell 2001, 4–5). Urban planning practices, with their strongly utopian roots, "have often presumed a fixed spatial order underpinning an idealized social stability." Broadly speaking, urban planners have presumed an ideal correspondence between the spatial form of the cityscape and regular, mechanical social processes. By imposing static and utopian schemes on the spatial form of the city, they have fixed futures in "an often banal or repressive caricature" of the intended outcome (Read 2005, 5). While discourses of urban planning have more often than not portrayed deliberate interventions into the urban fabric as a technical, scientific, and rational process free from partisanship and politics, official efforts designed to reshape the cityscape are actually never far removed from the exercise of power. The built form of the city frames everyday life by authorizing certain uses of urban space while simultaneously delegitimizing others. Architecture and urban design mediate power by inscribing a complex mixture of seduction, authority, and coercion into the built form of the city. The exercise of power moves almost seamlessly from one form to another, thereby naturalizing and masking itself behind the aura of legitimacy. As Foucault (1980, 86) has argued, "power is tolerable only on condition it masks a substantial part of itself. Its success is proportional to its ability to hide its own mechanisms." The built form of the city is literally saturated with latent, simmering conflicts that regularly mutate into open power struggles over the use and meaning of places (Dovey 1999, 9–16).

As a general rule, planning professionals conjure up imaginary forms of spatial unity and historical continuity in their abstract models of the city, and these serve to suppress, ignore, or deny the contested nature of urban space. By looking on the urban landscape as a physical form amenable to technical mastery, expert manipulation, and regulatory control, city builders tend to overlook and ignore the conflicts that arise because of the alternative uses and rival meanings attached to place (Blomley 2004, 53–54; Gandy 2000, 368–369). Viewed from the perspective of everyday life and social practice, the cityscape is a contested terrain of both social discipline and resistance, where ordinary urban residents who live and work in the city are not just passive recipients of grandiose municipal planning schemes but active agents in carving out places for themselves in the interstices of urban space. Cities function not only as administrative hubs from which order, control, and hierarchy emanate, but also as places where those kinds of stabilizing forces are challenged and disrupted (Solnit and Schwartzenberg 2000, 18–19). This subversion originates within the marginal, hidden spaces of the cityscape where urban residents who have been excluded from mainstream participation in urban life (that is, casual laborers, homeless squatters, street hawkers, informal traders, unlicensed taxi operators, prostitutes, and petty thieves) have been forced to flee. In short, the urban landscape is forged by conflict and cooperation, by negotiation and compromise, between those who seek to impose order and discipline on the use of urban space and those who seek to mold it to their own purposes. While city builders have tried to fix the shape of the urban landscape from above, the social collectivities that inhabit the city have left their mark from below (Ballard, Habib, Valodia, and Zuern 2005; Simone 2001b, 2003).

Conventional urban planning schemes seek to impose rational order and a modicum of stability and predictability on the cityscape by establishing formal rules and regulations governing "the proper [and expected] use of certain kinds of spaces" (Robinson 1999, 170–171). The effect of "representing social space as a substantial unity that must be protected from conflict, heterogeneity, and particularity" is to conceal the inherent messiness of urban life, and hence to naturalize and justify exclusions of undesirable city dwellers from where they are not wanted (Deutsche 1996, xiii). Yet ordinary people are always inventively experimenting with new ways of reusing and remaking urban space. With the disappearance of the apartheid regulations that governed the use of urban space, the formal city of the past quickly metamorphosed into an entirely new landscape in which the informal economy has come to play an increasingly significant role in the provision of goods and services. Faced with stagnant local markets in impoverished townships and squatter settlements, many informal traders relocated to the Johannesburg central city. The streets of downtown Johannesburg, once the exclusive playground and shopping area for white middle-class residents of the city, have evolved into vast, open-air marketplaces that operate primarily to service the retail needs of residents of Soweto and other outlying townships. By the mid-1990s the sidewalks of the city center were blanketed with makeshift stalls "set out in the shadows of the skyscrapers, selling everything from fruit to handbags, cosmetics, and clothes, providing haircuts, shoe repairs, photographic services, [and] telephone calls" (Robinson 1999, 170; see also Simone 1999, 2004a). Although informal markets have put retail businesses under enormous competitive pressure, it must be remembered that for many South Africans these activities constitute their only available source of income. By 2000 transactions in the informal economy accounted for the production of an estimated 40 percent of South Africa's gross national product (GNP). Faced with the unavoidability of informal trade, municipal authorities in Johannesburg have experimented with innovative programs designed to carve out a niche in urban space for these activities. Instead of the one-dimensional approach of spatial segregation under apartheid, city officials and urban planners have established alternative sites for informal trading through the creation of designated enclaves with uniform stalls organized at regular intervals. Yet these official efforts to formalize and institutionalize informality have not produced the desired results. Only the heartiest traders are able to survive the stiff competition, and an estimated 10 percent fall by the wayside. For the most part, informal traders have resisted the payment of rent and have resented what they regard as unwarranted interference (Beerends 2000, 58–59; Rogerson 1996b; Simone and Gotz 2003).[6]

Whereas the known city is saturated with the visible signs of scenographic spectacle and public theatricality, the unknown city remains hidden from view, concealed by layers of deception and subterfuge, devoid of collective memory, misrepresented in myth and rumor, and waiting to be discovered (Pile 2001). Framed in this way, invisible Johannesburg consists of those hidden places of the city that exist outside the grasp of casual observation. The hidden spaces of the city—the voids that contrast with the solids—belong to those residents of the city who engage in what Michel de Certeau (1984, 30–31) called "tactics," that is, everyday spatial practices adopted by people who are aware that they have no territory recognized by municipal authorities as their own.

Workless and shelterless urban dwellers negotiate the hidden spaces of the city, getting by and making do in whatever ways they can. Homeless squatters have seized opportunities whenever and wherever they find them, constructing semipermanent shelters in the interstitial spaces of the cityscape such as abandoned buildings, alleyways, and under bridges. Ephemeral squatter communities have materialized in vacant lots where buildings once stood, in derelict warehouses, and in cemeteries. Harassed by the police and by private security enforcers, the silent legions of the homeless circulate around the city, in constant search for temporary shelter and food. Inexperienced newcomers and more vulnerable homeless families are more likely to seek shelter on the more abundant, but more remote, vacant lands on the edges of the city. Not waiting for the world-class city to materialize, or for the alleged benefits of neoliberal economic policies to trickle down to ground level, ordinary people have redrawn and reimagined the boundary lines of the city. These boundary transgressions have taken place outside the abstract models, operational frameworks, and conceptual grids of mainstream planning visions. Operating beyond the scope of municipal authority and legal sanction, these ordinary people become effectively invisible nonpersons without access to the legal

6. Information and ideas derived from interview with Yael Horowitz, project manager, Johannesburg Development Agency, June 20, 2003; interview with Neil Fraser, executive director, Central Johannesburg Partnership, June 12 and July 3, 2003; interview with Lael Bethlehem, chief executive officer, Johannesburg Development Agency, City of Johannesburg, May 30, 2006; interview with Li Pernegger, program manager, Economic Area Regeneration, Department of Finance and Economic Development, City of Johannesburg, May 30, 2006; and interview with Nathi Radebe, former street trader and inner-city building manager, Johannesburg, May 25, 2006. The interpretation is entirely mine.

means to protect their citizenship rights (Kihato and Landau 2005; Lipman 2006, 133–136; Robinson 1999, 170; Simone 2004a, 409–427).[7]

Spaces of indeterminacy exist in all cities. In the typical case these unplanned locations are pluralistic, fuzzy, and chaotic, which urban residents—particularly the marginalized and the poor—can identify with, take advantage of, and use without the need of legal ownership. The scale of such places varies considerably, from substantially large areas to run-down sites in out-of-the-way locations, or what urban planners have often dismissively described as dead zones or voids, as well as the countless in-between spaces located in the cracks, crevices, and gaps of the cityscape. The fluidity and provisionality of these spaces of indeterminacy constitute a threat to the imaginary conception of disciplinary order that urban planners seek to impose on the cityscape (Lim 2002; Doron 2000).

7. See *Sunday Independent,* "Jo'burg Targets City Buildings for Renewal," April 27, 2002; and *South African Press Association (SAPA)*, "Four Derelict Jhb Buildings to Be Demolished," April 24, 2002.

3

The Fixed
and Flexible City

[Johannesburg is] a city of the present with so little of the past,
a city of the future moving forward at full tilt with no time
to look back into its history.

ELLEN PALESTRANT (1986, 7)

As an enduring testimonial to its original city planners, the spatial morphology of the greater Johannesburg metropolitan region has been more
or less a dismal failure. From its earliest frontier days as a rapidly expanding boomtown at the epicenter of the thriving gold-mining industry through
successive waves of downtown building booms and urban renewal projects,
Johannesburg has resisted efforts to tame its unruly landscape. Driven by the
imperatives to forge order out of the seeming chaos and confusion, a long line
of urban planners, municipal officials, civil engineers, sanitarians, business associations, and civic leaders have tried in vain to impose a modicum of stability and coherence on the ungainly urban form, but often with only temporary
and marginal success (Beavon 2004; Bremner 1999, 49; Beall, Crankshaw, and
Parnell 2002; Mabin 1999, 268–277).

The two-dimensional maps of city planners give a synoptic view of the spatial
configuration of the cityscape from the panoramic vantage point of above
and beyond. By implying connections between zones of the urban landscape where none actually exist, this bird's-eye view imposes an artificial, and
hence false and misleading, unity on the topographical surface of the city.
A grounded view of the cityscape from the street level, however, enables urban
residents to become acutely aware of the true artifice of spatial construction
or how city planners arbitrarily create spatial districts and presumptively
assume the legibility of the urban form (Boyer 2001, 45; de Certeau 1984,
91–110).

Whatever coherence observers can discover, or seek to impose upon, an
urban landscape as vast and complex as the Johannesburg municipality is
necessarily selective and arbitrary, and it is also usually figurative. Over the

course of its relatively short history, Johannesburg has been most often read and seen metaphorically, as a manifestation of something else—a rollicking frontier town, a European outpost at the southern edge of Africa, a glittering city of gold, the quintessential embodiment of apartheid, an industrial megalopolis, the African Manhattan, or an emerging world-class metropolis (Melvin 2000, 36–37).[1] Critical analysis and commentary have often reflected the implicit values found in these one-sided idealizations. The different ways of imagining Johannesburg can be most readily seen in the two contrasting approaches: on the one side, there are those who treat the city as a text to be deciphered; on the other side, there are those who look upon it as a body to be fashioned and put to specific uses. For journalists, essayists, fiction writers, and filmmakers, Johannesburg has more often than not been regarded as an assemblage of messages to be decoded, symbols to be interpreted, or scripts to be deconstructed. In contrast, city builders, urban planners, architects, and landscape designers, typically conceive of the city as undifferentiated matter to be shaped, fashioned, and molded into useful and hence meaningful forms (Roberts 2002, 1–14; McClung 2000, 2–3).

The urban planners who designed the original cityscape of Johannesburg laid out the spatial grid of the city to facilitate mining, banking, industry, commerce, leisure, and work, as well as to efficiently administer the racially ordered use of urban space. From the start the built environment conformed to an idealized model that exemplified "essentialized distinctions between colonizer and colonized" (Herwitz 1999, 419). Moreover, in its architectural stylistics and formulas it reflected a European aesthetic taste strangely out of place at the southern edge of Africa. The early city builders anointed the long, dusty, straight streets with sober, aristocratic British names like Anderson Street, Commissioner Street, and Pritchard Street—or else marked them with designations—Banket Street, Nugget Street, and Claim Street—associated with the great windfall riches that lay beneath the city's surface. The city center became "solid and respectable," a predictable place of implacable, "stone-faced commercial buildings in the classical style and broad pavements lit by gaslights" (Pakenham 1979, 47). Yet from the grounded perspective of those who have inhabited the city, Johannesburg has always exhibited the rich hybridities of other immigrant cities, where diverse people arrive, amalgamate, and sometimes even assimilate,

---

1. As Jonathan Crush (1994, 257) has put it, "Travelers to South Africa visit Johannesburg, and many write about it. As they do, they bring narrative order, significance, and meaning to the city's landscape. Johannesburg is a city of signs, of moral coherence, of essence. Its landscape encodes stories about its origins, its inhabitants, and the broader society in which it is set."

where old identities are discarded and new ones adopted seemingly over-night, where streets, neighborhoods, and suburbs collide in the formation of an ever-changing urban agglomeration that contains its own chaotic im-brications of meanings and lifestyles, sometimes clashing and sometimes blending in novel ways (Herwitz 1999, 419–420).

Whatever its other attributes, Johannesburg is a city largely defined by its main traffic arteries, by the idea of rapid movement, and by the heterogeneity of its spatial form and design (Czeglédy 2004). With the collapse of the rules governing the use of urban space under apartheid and the absence of widely accepted new ones, a withering array of differing ways of life have come to the surface, each with their own formal and informal cultural standards regu-lating interpersonal contact in the public realm. The result is a fluid urban matrix in which the likely outcomes of chance encounters are unpredictable and contingent, where boundary making and boundary breaking are part and parcel of daily life, and where uninitiated newcomers often ignore or misread territorial signs at their own peril. As social groups and individuals go about their daily business, they typically cross paths and inevitably encroach on one another's space, frequently causing social distrust, friction, and resentment. In response to the myriad uncertainties and tensions that characterize this frag-mented yet dynamic urban milieu, those social groups with privileged access to financial resources have carved out defensible spaces as a way of segregating themselves from the perceived threats to their lifestyles, properties, and sense of well-being (Flusty 1994, 44–45; Simone 2001a, 2001b; Swyngedouw 2005, 134–135).

As the era of white minority rule came to an abrupt end, middle-class urban residents began to move indoors, safely ensconced behind a prohibitive laby-rinth of interdictory spaces. The proliferation of enclosed suburban shopping malls, gated residential communities, and fortified office complexes on the ex-urban fringe, together with the steady expansion of underground parking ga-rages with restricted entry and above-ground walkways that bypass the streets, interior gardens, landscaped atriums, and sequestered gathering places, has usurped the conventional role of town squares, public parks, and downtown sidewalks as sites for everyday social interaction. This expanding network of cocooned urban environments—publicly inhabited but privately owned places—has fundamentally reshaped the uses and meanings of urban space in the new South Africa. Barriers, walls, and security perimeters are the visible signs of paranoid urbanism and the growing fortress mentality in urban South Africa after apartheid (Lipman and Harris 1999, 731–733; Jurgens and Gnad 2002). The rapid proliferation of enclosed places signifies the expansion of post-public space in the postliberal city (Dawson 2005).

The Spatial Fix: The Enduring Legacy of the Past

> Cities tend to remain on their axes of development, maintaining
> the position of their original layout and growing according to
> the direction and meaning of their older artifacts, which often
> appear remote from present-day ones.
>
> ALDO ROSSI (1992, 59)

Since its founding in the late nineteenth century, Johannesburg has experienced distinct periods of extreme stress and turmoil caused by war, economic depression, or internal conflict. During each of these periods the need to quickly restore order and stability and to repair damage to the physical environment led municipal authorities to think in modernist terms of comprehensive urban planning as the primary instrument for reconstructing the unsettled cityscape. Before the collapse of apartheid, there were five key junctures where holistic planning schemes took center stage in reshaping the urban landscape: after the South African War (1899–1902); after the First World War and into the 1920s; after the Great Depression of the 1930s; during and after the Second World War; and during the high tide of apartheid rule in the 1960s and 1970s. These successive waves of modernist and high-modernist city building required the systematic subtraction of the cityscape to ensure a tabula rasa on which to inscribe the new. At each stage of urban reconstruction city builders found inspiration in modernist planning ideas appropriated from abroad as they carried out the task of initiating large-scale rejuvenation projects designed to replace decaying sites and to rid the urban landscape of unwanted structures standing in the path of progress. On balance, municipal authorities looked on the disorder of the city through the lens of developmentalism: curing the ills of the city could best be achieved through the top-down implementation of holistic, citywide planning objectives carried out by value-free professionals and trained experts committed to the public interest (Robinson 2005). Over the course of the twentieth century, the modernist impulse that has suffused the mind-set of city planners has imposed a functional homogeneity and, with the demolition of historic Victorian, Edwardian, Beaux-Arts, and art deco buildings, an aesthetic monotony on the downtown urban landscape. While narrow streets, short blocks, and far too many corner lights slowed vehicular traffic to a crawl, the steady accretion of sprawling megastructures absorbed and cannibalized available open space, thus helping to shrink the public realm of the city and to diminish—such as it was under apartheid rule—the vitality of difference and heterogeneity intrinsic to a vibrant and healthy urbanity (Chipkin 1993, 1999; see Sandercock 1998a).

In Johannesburg and in other South African cities the rationality of capitalist homogenization and fragmentation of the urban landscape was overlaid by a purposefully political ordering of space, a deliberate intervention into the shaping of the cityscape which took its cue from modernist planning practices while simultaneously drawing on colonial notions of racial superiority (Dewar 1999, 368–375; Mabin 1999, 269–277). Land-use zoning, which Henri Lefebvre (1991, 317) has described as responsible for "fragmentation, breakup, and separation under the umbrella of bureaucratically decreed unity," laid the foundation for the idealized segregated city on the basis of a calculation of racial difference. From the start municipal planners worked tirelessly to eliminate unwanted diversity from the urban spaces, to create monofunctional and racially homogeneous places of work, residence, and leisure, "to keep apart rather than bring together, to separate out the colourful mix" that genuinely cosmopolitan urban traditions celebrate, advocate, and emulate (Robinson 1999, 169).

The referential role of modernist planning principles featured prominently in the construction of the apartheid city in the decades following the Second World War. State bureaucrats, urban planners, architects, and design specialists borrowed extensively from the modernist rhetoric of urban planning as they sought to fashion a purified European cityscape by institutionalizing racially segregated zones of work, residence, and leisure (Mabin 1999; Parnell 1997). In the design of the urban landscape, form and function were smoothly incorporated into the logic of institutionalized racial separation that had as its program the partition of the cityscape into spaces of fulsome civility for white citizens and spaces of confinement for nonwhite subjects. The construction of a white utopia in urban space was the dream of those National Party ideologues who imagined apartheid spatiality as a stable and orderly system of institutionalized racial separation. It was the driving force behind the modernizing visions of functionally separate zones of the cityscape radiating outward from a central downtown core, of efficient modes of transportation, and of proficient city management. The dream was itself an immense natural power that transformed the urban landscape, erasing what stood in the way and investing the built environment with a spatial fix resistant to change. This legacy of spatial planning under white minority rule has acted as an obstacle to dreams of beginning anew (Beavon 2004; Robinson 1992, 1995, 1998, 1999).

The evolving material form of a city provides a visual signature of its sociocultural identity. The collage of diverse elements that constitutes the built environment of the cityscape offers an immediate reading of its modernity, its originality, and its ambition. The vertical skyline of cities offers a material medium through which a wide variety of different economic, social, and aesthetic meanings are signified. Despite the imaginary projection of rationality and unity, cities in actuality consist of a patchwork of spatially dispersed sites, unbalanced infrastructures, and diversified activities, tethered to the illusion of wholeness and coherence. The presence of decay, obsolescence, and ruin connotes the failure of what was once a confident vision of progress through holistic planning (Parker and Long 2004, 40–41).

As a general rule, city-building efforts are animated and energized by optimistic images of what a good city should look like and how it should function. Yet like all material entities, cities are constantly subjected to the countervailing forces of growth and decline, of renewal and decay. "In the convulsions of the commodity economy," Walter Benjamin (1978, 162) suggested more than a half century ago, "we begin to recognize the monuments of the bourgeoisie as ruins even before they have crumbled." This image of the city as a site of disappearance provides a grim reminder that corporate builders, property speculators, and real estate developers look upon the built environment as a collection of exchange values that suffer the same fate of all other commodities when they outlive their usefulness (Abbas 1994). On the one hand, the uplifting powers of urban renaissance have produced rejuvenated environments of refurbished buildings and reconfigured sites that carry the aesthetic appeal of novelty and originality. On the other hand, the corrosive powers of degeneration have resulted in deteriorating environments where neglected buildings fall into disrepair and deteriorating physical infrastructures become so disjointed and disarticulated that they lose their capacity to generate the kinds of services they were designed to provide. These contradictory dynamics have produced a heterogeneous cityscape, where urban revitalization heralds the replacement of the old with the new and whatever is neglected falls into ruin. With the passage of time, what city builders once hailed as new, original, and fashionable eventually becomes outmoded and obsolete, telltale signs that the urban landscape never stands still but is always changing, evolving, and mutating. What once offered the fresh promise of a radiant future eventually becomes an iconic emblem of a redundant past. The cityscape is saturated with the decaying ruins of unrealized promises and past dreams (Edensor 2005a, 2005b; Hillis and Tyler 2002; Kolson 2001).

Efforts at city building always involve both a material and a symbolic dimension: the dynamic impulses that result in the creative destruction of the built environment cannot be separated from the iconographic meanings and mythological significance attached to erased places. In Johannesburg after apartheid city builders have fashioned their ideas about urban revitalization around twin narratives that combine an idealized projection for a radiant future with a condemnation of the past (King 1996, 1997). Specifically, this kind of boosterist storytelling relies on a double movement, namely, bringing a "politics of vision" into alignment with a "politics of erasure" (Parker and Long

2004, 38–40). First, narratives of urban regeneration require the creation of a forward-looking politics of vision, that is, a "horizon of expectation" (Parker and Long 2004, 55) toward which confident city builders project their hopes for establishing and showcasing the credentials of Johannesburg as a future world-class city—a transnational location for global investment and trade, a cosmopolitan tourist destination, and a prosperous metropolis with market-based and entrepreneurial opportunities for upward mobility. The creation of this "aspirational city imaginary" for the radiant Johannesburg yet-to-come involves not only the physical restructuring of the built environment but also the construction of a new image, or a new "symbolic economy" (Zukin 1995, 3, 7–10, 46). At their core these narratives of urban regeneration privilege the enterprise culture that functions as the driving force behind entrepreneurial urbanism (Parker and Long 2004, 39, 40, 51–52, 55). Second, narratives of urban decline require the construction of a politics of erasure that, in turn, depends on dramatizing existing places suffering from neglect, ruin, and decay. By evoking a spectacle of shame that highlights such features as failing infrastructure, a deteriorating built environment, dangerous inner-city slums, and vast shantytowns metastasizing on the ex-urban fringe, city builders are able to legitimate the destruction of these unappealing locations and to justify the displacement of the urban poor—all in the name of urban regeneration, progress, and future betterment. As a key element in imagining Johannesburg as a vibrant, cosmopolitan metropolis with world-class aspirations, the politics of erasure views the blighted, insalubrious, and mephitic spaces of the cityscape as sources of urban ills that, once they are eradicated, will clear the way for the anticipated rebirth of the city. In the rational calculation of urban regeneration, the displacement of the urban poor who inhabit these run-down spaces is a necessary but unavoidable means to a better end (Parker and Long 2004, 39, 40, 46, 51–52, 55).

Yet both of these urban images—the ruinous city standing in the path of progress and the aspirational city of pure potential—tend to ignore how the cityscape is a disputed terrain, where urban residents struggle over alternative uses for urban spaces and the different meanings attached to them. The spatial restructuring of the urban landscape in the name of revitalization typically eradicates the visible manifestations of neighborhood blight, infrastructural decay, and cluttered streetscapes but without addressing their root causes (Deutsche 1996, 32–33). Behind the bland facade of urban revitalization—couched in the roseate language of gentrification, beautification, and regeneration—lurks the "haunting memory," as Michel Foucault (1977, 198) put it, of desperate people, removed and displaced, "who appear and disappear, who live and die in disorder."

"A Site for Sore Eyes": The Decaying Central City and the Prospects for Urban Revitalization

Too many white South Africans have never really lived in Africa
in their own minds...that they were able to live such pleasant
lives only at a terrible cost to their fellow black citizens did not
appear to dilute their level of comfort.

JUSTICE RICHARD GOLDSTONE (Quoted in Lipman 1998, 21)

Like other rapidly expanding urban agglomerations where the centripetal forces of deindustrialization, decentralization, and suburban sprawl have substantially reconfigured the urban landscape, the greater Johannesburg metropolitan region has become a vast, disjointed megalopolis without clearly recognizable boundaries, a spatially fragmented and increasingly polycentric conurbation on the boundless scale of Los Angeles, Las Vegas, and Phoenix.[2] The historic downtown urban core has lost its luster as the preferred location for corporate office facilities, upscale entertainment venues, and high-end retail commerce catering to affluent consumers. This secular decline of the Johannesburg inner city did not take place overnight. The early warning signs of approaching decay appeared in the late 1970s when the first large-scale corporate enterprises decided to relocate their headquarter offices away from the central city. This process of spatial relocation accelerated during the 1980s and reached a crisis point by the early 1990s. The stagnation of the central city has gone hand in hand with the unprecedented horizontal growth of the greater Johannesburg metropolitan region. This "urbanization of suburbia" has reversed the conventional relationship between historic urban core and dependent periphery. As white-owned businesses, large and small, joined the headlong rush to exchange their premises in downtown Johannesburg for new facilities close to the new urbanizing growth points to the north, rival edge cities (Sandton, Randburg, Rosebank, Kempton Park, and Fourways) have blossomed on the peri-urban fringe, absorbing the lion's share of fresh capital investments (Beavon 1997; Bremner 1999; Goga 2003; Lipman and Harris 1999, 731–733; Tomlinson 1999a).

Like other elemental components of the city-building process, capital flight—a shrill, moralistic term for the regular cyclical movements of investment capital seeking highest profitability—deprived the Johannesburg inner city of the upscale vibrancy that stamped it as the premier business center of the nation, let alone the African subcontinent. This wholesale disinvestment from the central city left a great deal of under-utilized space, declining property values, abandoned buildings, collapsing infrastructure, and neglected

---

2. This section's title, "A Site for Sore Eyes," is taken from Caroline Kihato (1999, 6).

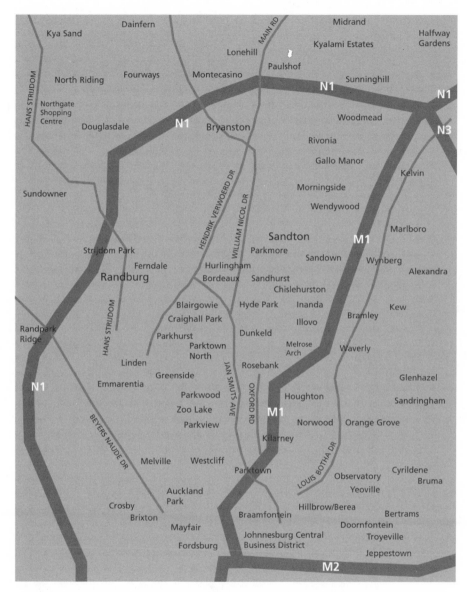

Figure 2. Northern Suburbs. By Stephanie McClintick

facilities in its wake. The telltale signs of urban blight were visible every-where: littered streetscapes, broken windows, boarded-up storefronts, vacant buildings, homeless encampments, and the rising menace of predatory street crime. As once-elegant high-rises fell into disrepair and rental rates for office space in the central city plummeted, enterprising newcomers were quick to fill the void: convenience stores and fast-food outlets replaced upscale restaurants, long-stay boarding houses with no-frills, spartan service supplanted glitzy five-star hotels, and inexpensive clothing and apparel shops sprang up where upscale boutiques once catered to an affluent white clientele. The changing topography of the Johannesburg central city gave rise to a disorderly urban landscape, a volatile spatial configuration consisting of unstable boundaries, sharp and sometimes violent edges, colliding interests, and widely dissimilar spaces. The poor, the desperate, and the audacious were quick to take advantage of the changing circumstances, filling the desolate, in-between, unoccupied spaces. Homeless squatters sought out desolate and deserted spaces to carve out rudimentary accommodation for themselves, seizing abandoned buildings and unused warehouses and establishing modest living quarters in the most unlikely places. Hawkers commandeered sidewalks and busy street corners, selling whatever they could to passersby. Taxi owners staked a claim to particular routes and ranks, turning to violence when competitors sought to encroach on their turf (Simone 2000; Tomlinson and Larsen 2003).[3]

All sorts of commentators, writing both in the popular press and in professional publications, have focused considerable attention on providing comprehensive listings of the characteristic features that accompanied this ongoing process of urban deterioration. But a simple enumeration of the various factors contributing to inner-city decay overlooks how these elements overlapped, interacted, and combined to yield unexpected outcomes (Kihato 1999, 1–6).[4] While historians, economists, and other social scientists have sought to uncover the underlying causes for the secular decline of the Johannesburg inner city, urban planners, city officials, real estate developers, and property owners have directed their efforts not to understanding the past but to shaping the future (Beavon 2004).[5]

Starting with the accumulated monotony and misery of the apartheid city, those experts in charge of city building in Johannesburg have faced a highly resistant urban landscape that bears the historical imprint of an inglorious past. It should come as no surprise, then, that the precarious future of the postapartheid Johannesburg inner city has been the source of continuous, and often acrimonious, debate and accusatory finger-pointing. Alarmist newspaper

---

3. See C. Paton, "The Rainbow Alienation," *Sunday Times*, April 18, 1999; and Ferial Haffajee, "City Streets: Where South Africa's Economy Is Changing," *Mail & Guardian*, July 7–13, 1998.

4. See *The Star*, "Alarm over Crime-and-Grime Exodus," September 10, 1996.

5. See, for example, Rowan Philp and Sabelo Ndlangisa, "Welcome to the Promised Land," *Sunday Times*, February 4, 2001; and Richard Tomlinson, "Jo'burg's Dynamo Will Hum in 2010," *Mail & Guardian*, June 26–July 2, 1998.

headlines, such as "City in Ruins: Entering a City in Filth," "Jo'burg on the Road to Calcutta," "Spectre of Overcrowding Hangs over Africa's Cities," "Big Business Loses Out in the CBD," "Great Trek Out of CBD Continues," "How to Put the Glitter into City of Gold," and "Jo'burg Is in a State of Decline" effectively convey—through the selective use of alarmist metaphor and anxious hyperbole—the uncertainty surrounding the country's largest and most well-known city.[6]

Under current conditions of intense global competition, urban planners, policy makers, and municipal authorities have sought to endow Johannesburg with visible marks of distinction that enable the city to be recognized for its unusual qualities and its unique features. Prescriptions for city revitalization vary greatly. The most aggressive city boosters have looked forward to a future time when Johannesburg can assume its rightful place as a world-class city, and they have proposed that the key to the rebirth of the city center pivots around a kind of entrepreneurial urbanism, where urban planners derive new ideas from international best practices, municipal authorities practice good governance, and public-private partnerships take direct charge of city-building projects.[7] Other, less-ambitious commentators have suggested that future prospects for inner-city revitalization depend on building a genuine African city, with a particular stress on retail and residential housing schemes and sponsorship of small-scale manufacturing and cross-border trade. These contrasting visions of the future city relied on different values regarding stakeholder participation in decision-making processes, different managerial styles, and different kinds of urban revitalization projects (Kihato 1999, 2).[8]

The mass exodus over the past several decades of large-scale corporate enterprises—among them DeBeers, Gold Fields, and the Johannesburg Stock Exchange—and the closure of major upscale, service-oriented businesses such as the Carlton Centre, has gone hand in hand with the declining fortunes of

6. See, for example, *City Press*, "City in Ruins: Entering a City in Filth," March 2, 1997; *The Star*, "Jo'burg on the Road to Calcutta," November 2, 1997; *The Financial Gazette*, "Spectre of Overcrowding Hangs over Africa's Cities," November 20, 1997; Lee-Ann Alfreds, "Big Business Loses Out in the CBD," *The Star*, April 23, 1998; Maggie Rowley, "Great Trek Out of CBD Continues," *Star Business Report*, December 10, 1996; *Saturday Star*, "How to Put Glitter into the City of Gold," March 28, 1998; and Melanie-Ann Feris, "Jo'burg Is in a State of Decline," *The Star*, October 26, 1999.

7. Personal observation; interview with Neil Fraser, Central Johannesburg Partnership, 12 June 2003; and interview with Yael Horowitz.

8. For information here and in following paragraphs, see interview with Lindsay Bremner, head of Department of Architecture, School of Architecture and Planning, University of the Witwatersrand, June 12, 2003. For a wider discussion of these ideas, see Lindsay Bremner, "Johannesburg: Rescue 011," *Sunday Times*, March 3, 2002; and Tomlinson, "Jo'burg's Dynamo."

middle-class retail shopping and leisure venues, the changing nature of socio-economic activities in the inner city, the shifting social composition of urban residents, and a dramatic transformation in the functional uses to which city buildings, open places, and streets are put. To a certain extent, the physical decay of the inner city has been brought about by the inability of the built environment to accommodate the changing functions and uses of city space. On the one hand, office space is available and abundant for those with the financial means to pay the asking rental prices. On the other hand, places of residence are severely overcrowded, and hawkers have claimed some of the sidewalks, squeezing out pedestrian traffic. The demand for space in the inner city has shifted away from plush office complexes for corporate tenants and toward small retail outlets catering to low-income consumers, housing for low-income families, and secure places where informal traders can sell their wares (Tomlinson 1999a).[9]

The out-migration of large-scale corporate and commercial business from the inner city has proceeded in tandem with the physical deterioration of buildings, environmental degradation of the built environment, and the expansion of the visible symbols of impoverishment such as garbage and littered streets, petty crime, and homeless people seeking shelter wherever they can find it. The lack of investor confidence in inner-city recovery has meant that property owners have been reluctant to renovate their buildings and to maintain proper standards. This inattention to upkeep has resulted in the general decline of property values (Goga 2003; Kihato 1999, 2–3). By a kind of perverted logic, capital disinvestment from the inner city has created new spaces of opportunity for those excluded from formal economic activities, creating room for small-scale (largely black-owned) business enterprises and enabling thousands of small-scale traders, itinerant hawkers, and petty entrepreneurs to gain a precarious foothold in the urban landscape. Microenterprise, survivalist trade, illicit commerce, cross-border trade, and immigrant entrepreneurship have become significant structural features of the inner-city economy (Bremner 2000; Kesper 2003).[10]

Spatial engineering under apartheid entailed the dispersal of once tight-knit communities to far-flung townships on the urban fringe, resulting in serious material deprivation and long-distance commutes for work and for shopping (Beavon 1997; Robinson 1995, 1998). Influx controls artificially kept a large portion of the population out of the city in order to promote the state policies of

---

9. See Lee-Ann Alfreds, "Big Business Loses Out"; *The Star,* "Jo'burg Has a Future"; Audrey d'Angelo, "Reports Show Business Is Moving Back to CBD," *Star Business Report,* July 1, 1996; and Karin Schimke, "Inner City on the Rise despite Dire Predictions," *The Star,* April 16, 1997.

10. Interview with Neil Fraser, chief executive officer, Central Johannesburg Partnership, and Ian Fife, "Jo'burg CBD Shows Signs of Life," *Financial Mail,* January 2, 2001.

racial segregation and to lessen social and welfare expenditures on a large non-white labor force. Legislative enactments denied black people the right to live in the city and barred them from owning businesses or property. Further legislation prohibited rural migrants from settling in the teeming townships and squatter settlements on the peri-urban fringe. When white minority rule and the apartheid system disintegrated, municipal authorities in Johannesburg and other South African cities were unprepared administratively to handle the large numbers of impoverished work seekers streaming into the cities. In particular, Johannesburg experienced a large influx of people from surrounding townships, from the rural areas, and from neighboring countries, migrating to the inner city in search of economic opportunities and residential accommodation close to sites of work (Lester, Nel, and Binns 2000; Robinson 1992).

The declining fortunes of the central city have not only posed a direct challenge to large-scale property owners with huge financial stakes in downtown real estate but also undermined the roseate, boosterist image of postapartheid Johannesburg as an emergent world-class city. In seeking to halt the hemorrhage of businesses leaving the central city, to stabilize the built environment, and to safeguard existing real estate investments, a coalition of large-scale property owners joined forces with leading municipal authorities, civic-minded boosters, and urban planners to stitch together a corporate-driven strategy of urban revitalization that has linked an emphasis on personal safety and business security with site-specific clustered development and social homogeneity in the use of urban space. In embracing this ambitious program of environmental regulation and spatial reconfiguration, these key figures representing powerful vested interests have viscerally understood that the rejuvenation of the central city was first of all a work of imagination. In constructing the cosmopolitan ideal around which they measured their efforts, they drew on a complex set of assumptions about what a globally competitive metropolis should look like and how this new generation of postapartheid city builders should respond to the challenges of revitalization. Their programmatic thinking was saturated with ideas borrowed from North American and European city planning models (Bremner 2000). The new habits of mind that have shaped the discourse of city building in Johannesburg after apartheid were derived from a fixation on what were known as "international best practices" (Tomlinson 1999b, 2002).

Planning the Postapartheid Future: Revitalizing the Dormant Center

There is a strong similarity, as Françoise Choay observed some time ago, between the way that modernist town planners and architects approach the urban landscape, on the one hand, and utopian literature, on the other. Both operate with almost totalizing visions, seeking to bring every aspect of urban life under whatever particular organizing scheme of perfection they favor at the moment (Choay 1980; Holston 1989). Put abstractly, mainstream modernist urban planners typically begin with a particularly Cartesian conception of space as their central organizing principle: space as transparent, homogeneous, divisible, empty, ready to be filled with social content and to be demarcated and subdivided. Conceived of as more or less an unimpeded blank slate, space is not only able to be ordered (clinically, rationally, and purposefully) but also functions as a source of order. Specifically, space becomes a source of order because it offers "practical and strategic possibilities for control and division by means of lines on maps and clinical separations of unsuitable activities." Seen through this optic, modernist urban planning is about envisioning the city as a perfectly disciplined, rationally and efficiently managed, and smoothly functioning spatial order (Robinson 1996, 335–337).

In seeking to accomplish the utopian promise of material progress and social advancement, modernist urban planning has always been consumed by the desire to impose visual regimentation, symmetrical uniformity, and legible coherence on the unruly cityscape. This urge to aesthetic abstraction (embodied in straight lines, right angles, and serial repetitions) reveals an inability of mainstream urban planners to establish an actual rapport with the material realities of city life and the lived daily experience or urban residents. What is created is a wide gap between those experts concerned with a stylized conception of rational order and those dependent on the actual social conditions and ambiguities of city living. To the extent that it rests solely on abstracted notions of grids, zones, and districts, conventional planning theory is not capable of grasping the actual substance and nuanced intricacies of social life. The planning imagination requires making sense of urban form and texture through lenses that occlude the ability to engage with the actual conditions of daily life (see Boyer 1983; Scott 1998, 55–57, 80–83).

Modernist urban planning is a normative exercise that involves an idealized image of a better future, and one that equates its solution-driven practices with material progress (Sandercock 1998a, 1–6). Yet the urban landscape is cluttered with the accumulated deadweight of the past: material objects fixed in space that once offered the promise of a radiant future metastasize into disused, obsolete ruins haunting the present. The physical tracks of prior city building are still visible in such locational characteristics as the spatial grid of city blocks, the patterns of the streetscape, the shape and size of buildings, and the placement of civic monuments and other public sites (Mabin 1990; Body-Gendrot and Beauregard 1999, 7–8; Edensor 2005b). Whatever their personal politics and their animating ideologies, design professionals, architects, political activists, advocates for the poor and displaced, municipal authorities, and city planners must operate within the circumscribed limits of what came before. Their scope for maneuver is restricted by the preexisting fixity of the built environment, the crystallized powers of capital, and the material force of entrenched wealth in landed property. The competing demands that are placed on the use of urban space insure that whatever urban planning schemes that are proposed cannot easily follow a unified aesthetic or social vision. However well-meaning and intentionally progressive, efforts to restructure the urban landscape are compromised from the start. There is little by way of an obvious, coherent alternative to the entrenched patterns of capitalist investment based on profit-seeking, on real estate speculation instead of rehabilitation, on the spread of legally sanctioned private enclaves instead of meaningful public spaces, on frenzied consumption and self-absorbed individualism instead of shared political vision, and on all forms of waste: deterioration and decay of inner city neighborhoods, the idleness of those willing and able to work, minds and bodies atrophied by drug and alcohol abuse, and the creative energies of the poor who have been systematically denied the opportunities to reach their fullest potential (Bremner 1999; Simone 1999).

Since 1990 municipal authorities, government officials, and corporate interest groups in Johannesburg have come together to spearhead a number of different local economic development initiatives to restructure, reinvent, and reimagine its inner-city landscape. These efforts at urban rejuvenation have been underpinned by two intertwined objectives: first, to reverse the socio-economic decline of the central city urban core and, second, to position Johannesburg in the world economy as a globally competitive world-class city. In order to accomplish these goals urban planners have worked closely with civic boosters to self-consciously construct roseate images of the city's future, around which they have sought, with varying degrees of success, to mobilize investment (both overseas and domestic), public opinion, and social agreement (Bremner 2000, 185; Tomlinson et al. 2003, 10–14). At the heart of these endeavors have been deliberate interventions into urban place making and city marketing, or what Charles Rutheiser (1986) in another context has called "imagineering."

The first revitalization effort originated during the dying days of white minority rule, at a time when corporate interest groups were seeking to establish their bona fide credentials as proactive, progressive agents for positive change, to cement their proprietary rights in the urban core, and to ingratiate themselves to the political leadership of the African National Congress (ANC), the new ruling party. The twenty-year erosion of the industrial and manufacturing base of the Johannesburg central city, the flight of corporate capital and the resulting free fall of property values, the changing racial demographics of its inner-city residential suburbs, and the burgeoning informal economy transformed downtown Johannesburg from the premier financial, corporate, and commercial hub of sub-Saharan Africa into an almost lifeless wasteland of vacant office buildings, shuttered storefronts, and abandoned warehouses: an increasingly hollowed-out dead zone of unused, empty space (Beavon 2004; Crankshaw and White 1995; Rogerson 1996a). In seeking to rekindle the former dynamism of the central city, city builders unveiled a series of ambitious yet ill-conceived master plans encompassing a range of programs that focused primarily on the physical rehabilitation of the built environment through fresh investment in derelict buildings and improvements to aging infrastructure. The aim of these urban renewal projects, in combination with a host of initiatives designed to tackle crime, homelessness, litter, informal trade, overburdened infrastructure, and taxi management, was to quickly restore the competitiveness and enhance the vitality of the historic downtown core (Tomlinson 1992, 1999b).[11]

This early revitalization effort was inspired by conventional models of urban regeneration and entrepreneurialism primarily drawn from the experiences of North American and Western European cities (Bremner 2000, 2005). As such, this corporate-centered strategy largely conformed to what Robert Beauregard (1993, 267) has called the "mainstream approach" to urban economic revival. It virtually ignored the bitter (and divisive) historical legacy of the apartheid past, that is, a divided city characterized by white middle-class indifference, entrenched racial segregation, and gross disparities in wealth, income, and opportunities for socioeconomic advancement. The strategy sought instead to capitalize on the imminent reentry of postapartheid South Africa into the world economy, using the negotiated settlement ending white minority rule and the 1994 popular elections as a propitious opportunity for reinventing Johannesburg as the vibrant gateway to Africa (Bremner 2000, 185, 187; Rogerson 1996a, 141). For the most part, this boosterist approach involved an elite-dominated planning process that focused on the massive infusion of public resources into basic urban infrastructure and the cobbling together of public-private partnership schemes targeting flagship projects in retailing, leisure, and commercial development (Rogerson 1996a, 139; Fitzsimmons 1995, 7–8). It sought to resuscitate the dormant central

11. See *The Star,* "Jo'burg Has a Future."

business district by transforming key zones into the modern corporate image: a financial, administrative, and professional services center with an emphasis on recommercialization rather than reindustrialization and an orientation toward luxury consumption with entertainment and commercial facilities that appealed to young corporate managers, educated professionals, conventioneers, out-of-town visitors, and overseas tourists. The various business-friendly strategies devised to revitalize the city center revolved around property-led development programs (particularly intensive investment of private capital in signature undertakings) that included an aggressive city marketing campaign that shamelessly glossed over the apartheid past and presumptuously flouted (without any substantiation) Johannesburg as South Africa's "most integrated city" (Rogerson 1996a, 146–147). In order to highlight the unique qualities of place, these promotional schemes (sometimes called place-marketing, place-promotion, or branding) also laid particular stress on sports, arts, and culture (exemplified by exhibition halls and convention centers, museums, galleries for the performing arts, and large spectator facilities for sporting events) as vehicles for urban regeneration (Rogerson 1996a, 146–147; Tomlinson et al. 2003, 10–14; Boyer 1992, 1995; Fainstein and Judd 1999, 1–17; Holcomb 1999).[12]

Municipal authorities recognized that Johannesburg, like other aspirant world-class cities, required a distinct urban identity in order to attract overseas investment and international tourists. In seeking to enhance its desired image as an internationally recognized modern metropolis, they began to portray Johannesburg as the Tokyo or New York of Africa. In order to promote the city to overseas investors, pro-business boosters sought to situate the city in the new economic geography of global capitalism. By stressing its locational advantages, its developed and up-to-date communications infrastructure, and its modern financial and banking facilities, they touted Johannesburg as a convenient, stable launching pad for corporate investors seeking to tap into the vast under-exploited hinterland of Africa (Bremner 2000, 187; Rogerson 1996a, 135; 1996b, 167–179).[13]

One underlying aim of this image-making offensive was to counter the unremittingly pessimistic noir vision of Johannesburg as a "nightmare city" on the brink of catastrophe. Despite its modernist pretensions, Johannesburg under apartheid had acquired a much-deserved reputation as a cold, brutal city of racial exclusivity where white minority rule found its deepest expression (see Crush 1993, 1994). To repair this tarnished image as an urban center

12. Information derived from interview with Li Pernegger, program manager, Economic Area Regeneration, Department of Finance and Economic Development, City of Johannesburg, May 30, 2006; and interview with Lael Bethlehem, chief executive officer, Johannesburg Development Agency, City of Johannesburg, May 30, 2006.

13. See Bremner, "Johannesburg: Rescue 011."

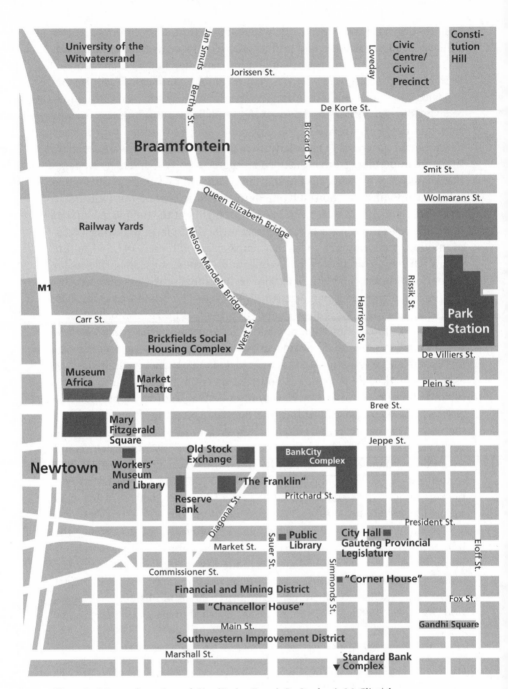

Figure 3. Johannesburg Central City (Facing Pages). By Stephanie McClintick

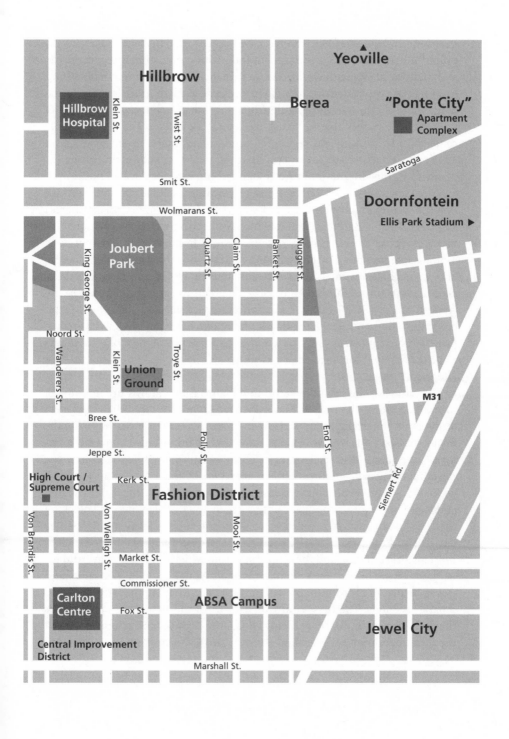

irretrievably stigmatized by its oppressive past required the wholesale reinvention of Johannesburg as a vibrant cultural melting pot, an inviting, inclusive, and multiracial city with world-class pretensions. In marketing Johannesburg to potential corporate investors, civic boosters went to great lengths in the dying days of white minority rule to picture Johannesburg as "a world city showroom" that was able to "assert itself unequivocally as the key economic center of a subcontinental region."[14] Amid great fanfare, urban planners in 1991 unveiled ten strategic projects designed to attract and retain private investment in the CBD, and to vault Johannesburg into the coveted position of an elite world-class city. These initiatives included a R200 million light-rail link between the high-rise inner-city suburbs (Hillbrow, Joubert Park, Berea) and the CBD; the Baralink project, which connected Soweto to downtown Johannesburg via a sixteen-mile growth corridor linking a development zone around Baragwanath Hospital with the central city; infrastructural upgrading and physical improvements to inner-city housing in order to attract middle-class tenants; the establishment of closed markets to accommodate inner-city street trading; a R200–300 million convention center added to the Carlton complex in the central city; the development of a R100 million jewelry manufacturing site, known as Jewel City, in the eastern sector of the CBD, which was to be fashionably constructed as a commercial theme park to attract tourists (Rogerson 1996a, 152).[15]

A keystone of the urban revitalization plan was downtown urban renewal. Municipal authorities invited Meyer Pienaar Architects and Urban Designers to initiate a comprehensive restructuring plan as a way of bringing to life the bland, soulless CBD by giving focus and symbolic importance to the city's historic Civic Spine—the axial sequence of under-utilized public spaces between the library, city hall, and the old Rissik Street Post Office. Whatever the overall goals, this scheme was subject to intense controversy from the start. The first and less contentious component of this urban renewal plan involved blocking off Civic Square, which forms the city's "sacred heart" and which is defined by city hall and the post office. The design focused on the post office, the city's most historic building and the central site from which distances away from Johannesburg are measured. A circular fountain symbolizing the Witwatersrand was to be placed in front of this building, thereby dividing the street into two separate sections. The most controversial part of this new design project was the enclosure of the library gardens. The spatial layout of this scheme involved the introduction of underground parking, small shops, and a restaurant and

---

14. Rogerson (1996a, 148–149) quotes from an unpublished Johannesburg City Council 1993 memorandum.
15. Interview with Keith Beavon. See also Beavon, "The City That Slipped."

ni니

pub. This commercial use of public space triggered an outcry from those who regarded this project as a further example of the ongoing suffocation of what little publicly accessible places remained in central Johannesburg (Muwanga 1998, 151–152; Rogerson 1996a).

In plotting a strategy aimed at recapturing the city center in the rapidly suburbanizing region, boosterist image-makers enthusiastically billed Johannesburg as the premier sports, cultural, and entertainment venue in Africa. To give substance to this emergent city myth, municipal authorities initiated several projects. One involved rehabilitating the Ellis Park Sports Precinct on the eastern edge of the central city. By completing a thirty-five-thousand-seat athletics stadium in 1995 and streamlining roadways for convenient entry and exit, city officials transformed what had become an under-utilized site into a premier sports entertainment complex (which will host the 2010 World Cup football matches). City officials also turned their attention to a long-neglected, council-owned tract of land on the western edge of the city center, committing substantial public-sector investment in upgrading derelict buildings and rechristening the site as the Newtown Cultural Precinct. Through the inauguration and sponsorship of such lavish events as the annual Arts Alive Festival and the Johannesburg Biennial, city authorities sought to establish the area as a recreational and cultural theme park. Ceding all power to the imagination, enthusiastic culture brokers visualized a revitalized Newtown Cultural Precinct as a beachhead for urban renewal on the western edge of the city center and as a welcome counterweight to the northward drift of cultural life. By proposing the construction of a primary school, a library, a gymnasium, a police station, and eight thousand middle-income apartments around an artificial lake, urban planners envisioned a kind of imitation Greenwich Village in downtown Johannesburg, a gentrified enclave emulating waterfront developments in Baltimore, Boston, San Francisco, and Cape Town.[16]

Without massive influx of capital and a concomitant reversal in business confidence in the central city, these efforts to reassert the downtown geography of power were doomed for failure from the outset. In a real sense these overly ambitious exercises in urban alchemy and city mythmaking represented the dying gasp of an old propertied elite trying to salvage downtown Johannesburg as the exclusive preserve of a privileged few. After the historic 1994 national elections, urban governance in the greater Johannesburg metropolitan region underwent a wholesale restructuring: municipal boundaries were redrawn, administrations redeployed, and powers and functions redistributed.

16. E. Horak, "Jo'burg Gets Ready to Shape Up," *Engineering News*, 21 January 1994; and Beavon, "The City That Slipped." Interestingly enough, those who endorsed constructing an artificial lake seemed to blithely ignore the problems with illegal dumping and persistent pollution at Bruma Lake on the eastern edge of downtown.

With investor confidence at a low ebb, corporate interest groups were generally reluctant to commit themselves to what they regarded as risky undertakings in the central city. The 1995 popular elections fundamentally altered the social composition of the new metropolitan and local councils. Almost immediately the new city officials demoted or fired the key architects who had put together the late apartheid revitalization plan for Johannesburg, cut the budgets for the ten strategic projects, and began to cobble together a more inclusive rejuvenation program for the Johannesburg inner city.[17]

Although the late apartheid vision for urban regeneration largely depended for its success on a speculative gamble for world-city status, the second reimaging effort redirected attention toward local initiatives. The first revitalization plan was bold, expansionist, and buoyant. In contrast, the second was considerably less ambitious in its grandiose design and more cautious in its projected outcome. City planners adopted an environmentally led program directed at stabilizing inner-city decline and promoting neighborhood organization as a precursor to growth (Bremner 2000, 191; Tomlinson 1999b).[18] These plans were developed through an inclusive partnership involving government, civil society, labor organizations, and private business in an umbrella organization known as the Johannesburg Inner City Development Forum (JICDF). Adopted in 1996, its vision rested on the corporeal metaphor of Johannesburg as the Golden Heartbeat of Africa. Packaged under the name *Mayivuke* (Awake, Johannesburg), this imagineering effort portrayed Johannesburg as the city with a heart of gold, staking its identity on its founding and its most popularly recognizable feature. In contrast to the late apartheid plan that envisioned Johannesburg as Africa's inviting gateway, this second regeneration effort situated the city as its center, and, figuratively speaking, its life force and its heartbeat. For the first time, municipal authorities acknowledged the location of Johannesburg as a vital part of Africa, rather than placing it ambivalently on its margins, and they sought to incorporate its Africanness into its image of itself. This focus of development was not primarily directed at the attraction of overseas investment, but rather at local improvement, including better service delivery, fighting crime, and upgrading existing infrastructural facilities. The driving force of economic development was trade and

---

17. With little personal experience and few progressive role models to emulate, new city officials and planning professionals came face-to-face with the daunting task of managing and servicing the city, particularly the huge problems associated with maintaining and developing a crumbling infrastructure, with confronting unchecked peripheral urbanization, and with combating the threat—real or imaginary—of crime (see Tomlinson 1999a, 1670–1673). Information also derived from interview with Richard Tomlinson, consultant in urban economic development and project management, Johannesburg, June 4, 2001.

18. See *The Star*, "Rebirth of the CBD."

commerce rather than sport and culture (Bremner 2000, 189–190; Tomlinson 1999a, 1670–1673; 1999b).[19]

This second revitalization effort marked a shift in emphasis from showcasing spectacle to rebuilding the physical environment as the cornerstone of urban regeneration. This optimistic vision of Johannesburg's reinvigorated inner city received a great deal of positive reinforcement in the popular media and in city-sponsored promotional material. Repeated often enough, uplifting slogans like "a dynamic city that works," "a 24-hour city," "livable, safe, well-managed, and welcoming," and "a city for residents, workers, tourists, entrepreneurs, and learners" became the unofficial manifesto of the reimagined Johannesburg at the onset of the twenty-first century (Bremner 2000, 189–190).[20] New legislation facilitated the creation of semiautonomous legal entities known as city improvement districts, thereby enabling private business associations to work together with municipal authorities to strengthen service provision (garbage collection, security, street cleaning) in specially demarcated zones of the inner city.[21]

Despite the great fanfare that accompanied the 1997 launch of the *Mayivuke* inner-city renewal plan, municipal authorities faced an uphill battle to make visible improvements to the urban environment and to counter the skeptics and prophets of doom who envisioned a once-great, first-world city "on the verge of an abyss," slipping inexorably into ruin and decline. Stories in the popular press hammered away at the betrayal of Johannesburg: a mismanaged, under-resourced city "in the throes of an irreversible rigor mortis," where majestic skyscrapers were "cob-webbed and boarded up," where once-fashionable downtown shopping areas had evolved into a dangerous "ruffian's paradise," where the streets were littered with refuge and garbage, and where pavements were unnavigable because aggressive hawkers plying their trade had commandeered every inch of space. For the propertied elite who had abandoned the city center, downtown Johannesburg was a filthy, chaotic, and uninviting place that was on the road to decline such as Calcutta, Nairobi, Mombasa, or Harlem experienced, and there was little, if anything, that could be done to stop it.[22]

19. *The Star,* "A New Johannesburg." Ideas and information for this and the following paragraphs derived from interview with Neil Fraser, Central Johannesburg Partnership, 12 June 2003.

20. Bremner (2000, 189–190) provides this list of slogans. *The Star,* "A New Johannesburg"; and interview with Yael Horowitz.

21. *Sunday Times* (Metro), "Working Together to Make the CBD Safe," March 3, 1996.

22. The quotations and information taken from *The Star,* "Jo'burg on the Road to Calcutta"; Anso Thom, "CBD Still Alive but Needing a Shot in the Arm," *The Star,* October 19, 1997; *Saturday Star,* "Jo'burg Can Be Great Again"; Adele Shevel, "Awakening an Inner City," *Star Business Report,* November 25, 1997; and *Saturday Star,* "How to Put Glitter."

The Johannesburg municipal council focused its efforts on stabilizing downtown decline and resisting the northward flight of capital. The Turbine Square Project in Newtown, the introduction of social housing projects catering to moderate income households, and the refurnished downtown taxi ranks around Joubert Park formed integral parts of a greater urban renewal plan designed to reconquer the central city (Swilling 1999).[23] In the minds of urban planners, the redevelopment of the Newtown Cultural Precinct, located at the western rim of the downtown business district, has provided a potential catalyst not only to rejuvenate the ramshackle central city but also to define the role the new South Africa could potentially play in southern Africa in the twenty-first century. Before its upgrading, the Newtown precinct consisted of a collection of under-utilized and dilapidated buildings that had long been locked in a struggle between urban entropy and bootstrap self-improvement. In trying to redraw the frontiers of urban decay, municipal authorities endorsed a number of projects (including the construction of the Johannesburg branch for the South African Reserve Bank at a site adjoining the proposed Turbine Square Project), sponsored the conversion of derelict buildings into a medley of different uses in what they hoped would become a cultural precinct accommodating a range of arts and entertainment venues (like MuseumAfrica and the Market Theatre), and worked with Johannesburg Housing Company to complete the massive Brickfields social housing scheme at the northeast corner. In order to provide convenient highway access, city officials completed the construction of the soaring Nelson Mandela Bridge connecting Newtown with Braamfontein across the railroad lines to the north. With the exception of the self-governing city improvement districts that have carved the cityscape into an assemblage of cocooned enclaves primarily serving the interests of the property-holding elite, the Newtown Cultural Precinct has remained an isolated middle-class beachhead in the overall plan to eventually reconquer the city center (Muwanga 1998, 11–12).[24]

While they continued to allocate resources to maintain investments previously committed to sport and cultural facilities, municipal authorities identified key priorities for stabilizing the physical environment of the inner city, including the management and development of informal street trading, the regulation of the lawless caprice of the taxi industry, and creation of public-private investment projects in inner-city residential housing accommodation. Infrastructural projects included a R160 million upgrade of the Johannesburg

23. Ideas and information for this and the following paragraphs gathered from interviews with Neil Fraser and interview with Yael Horowitz.

24. See Anonymous, "The South African Reserve Bank," *Architecture SA* (1993): 16–18.

central railroad station, three taxi management facilities catering to six thousand taxis, the refurbishment of squares and parks in the inner city, and the provision of six housing facilities for homeless people. In addition, municipal authorities sponsored the formation of a quasi-government development agency, called the Informal Trade Management Company, to take responsibility for restructuring informal trade within the inner city. This initiative called for the construction of six marketplaces combining market stalls, housing units, and storage facilities, all designed to give an estimated twenty-four hundred informal traders a more permanent stake in the inner-city economy (Bremner 2000, 189–190; Tomlinson 1999a).[25] Within several years urban planners hailed these strategic initiatives as modest successes in bringing about a steady reduction in inner-city crime, improved cleanliness, and increased demand for downtown office space.[26]

The inner city of Johannesburg has always presented urban planners with a rapidly changing, highly fractured, and deeply contested urban milieu. In trying to grapple with the diverse uses and histories of urban space that made any kind of coherent urban planning difficult, Johannesburg municipal authorities turned their attention to small, manageable projects. Created in 1998 as a special branch of the Johannesburg Metropolitan Council, the Inner City Office (ICO) quickly acquired a reputation as the most innovative agency within the municipal bureaucracy. From the start, the ICO functioned as a project design and facilitation unit, structuring a range of urban environmental upgrade and social and economic development projects. From 1998 to late 2002 the ICO initiated an estimated forty large-scale regeneration and development projects. One initiative was to demarcate distinctive precincts within the urban landscape, encouraging various kinds of activities to develop across different locales and places of the city. This approach acknowledged the multiplicity of spatial uses in the city and tried to find ways to manage their coexistence. It also involved channeling different kinds of flows into and beyond the inner city, where the opportunities for synergies in services and the built environment might be able to be realized (Simone and Gotz 2003; Robinson 2003).[27]

---

25. Themba Sepotokele, "Small Firms Trickling Back to Jo'burg CBD," *The Star*, July 26, 1998; and *The Star*, "Businessmen Roll Up Their Sleeves."

26. *Saturday Star*, "How to Put Glitter"; Themba Sepotokele, "Small Firms Trickling Back"; and Adele Shevel, "Awakening the Inner City."

27. Information and ideas for this and later paragraphs derived from interview with Neil Fraser, chief executive officer, Central Johannesburg Partnership, 12 June 2003; interview with Yael Horowitz; and interview with Graeme Gotz, specialist for policy and strategy, Corporate Planning Unit, Office of City Manager, City of Johannesburg, May 26, 2006.

Ordering the Cityscape: Urban Governance
in Johannesburg after Apartheid

> It's an open secret that taking a decent walk through Johannes-
> burg is almost impossible. Our parks have been destroyed.
> Many of our pavements are dotted with zillions of hawkers who,
> despite the appreciable fact that they're trying to earn an honest
> living, make life in the city rather unbearable.
>
> JR at Large

In Johannesburg after apartheid municipal authorities have sought to strike
a balance between addressing the basic needs and service backlogs of all urban
residents and promoting sustained economic growth and global competitiveness.[28] They have tried to reconcile these conflicting policy agendas in
ways that both mark a radical break with past urban planning practices and
conform to recent global trends in urban governance. Yet regardless of their
personal politics, urban policy makers are trapped in a dilemma. On the one
hand, in seeking to bring about the radical redistribution of scarce resources
in favor of the urban poor, they have to tackle the structural legacies of separate development, particularly the deplorable living conditions, huge (and
growing) backlog of poor quality housing, and inadequate basic services that
persist in the older, settled townships and newer, informal settlements on
the metropolitan periphery. In addition, policy makers are faced with the
vexing problem of deteriorating housing, high levels of unemployment, and
socioeconomic inequalities that characterize the life-worlds of the inner-city
poor concentrated in residential neighborhoods close to the central city (Beall,
Crankshaw, and Parnell 2000, 118–119; Mangcu 2003). On the other hand,
the pursuit of economic growth depends on, as Christine Boyer (1983, 59–60)
has put it in another context, the imposition of a specific "disciplinary order
within and under the surface of the urban form," that is, a set of entitlements
and obligations that are in harmony with the laws of private property and
the needs of capital accumulation and that internalize "the rules for efficient
capitalist expansion and circulation." Luring new investment into the inner
city in order to stimulate economic revitalization requires a strict regulatory
regime that can effectively implement procedures governing land-use planning, infrastructural improvements, building standards, code enforcement,
zoning regulations, tax abatements, and the policing of public places. Because its principal purpose is to create a favorable business climate, this regulatory regime is one that caters to the profit-making interests of powerful

---

28. Quote is from JR at Large, "City of Gold Needs to Clean Up," *The Star,* June 8, 2001.

property-holding stakeholders (Beall, Crankshaw, and Parnell 2000, 107; 2002, 7–24).[29]

Confronted with these policy choices, municipal authorities in Johannesburg have endorsed new modes of urban governance that reflect emerging trends in managing cities all over the world. Because they have endorsed technocratic principles that favor a business-friendly environment and because they are compelled to operate within the constraints of fiscal responsibility, urban policy makers have limited maneuverability in implementing a basic-needs approach that can address quality of life concerns for all citizens. Budgetary constraints, an overtaxed civic administration, and a bureaucratic maze of overlapping jurisdictions and competing mandates have greatly restricted the scale, quality, and timing of service delivery. In postapartheid Johannesburg as well as throughout urban South Africa, municipal authorities, urban planners, and neighborhood activists have faced an uphill battle against fickle property owners whose investment decisions are governed by profitability above all else (Beavon 1992).[30]

Captured in such slogans as "One City, One Future," urban planners have focused their attention on the difficult goal of drawing together the once disparate parts of the greater Johannesburg conurbation into a cohesive, non-segregated metropolitan whole where equality for all citizens under law and shared resources govern decision-making processes. From the outset, the first postapartheid city administration faced two immediate tasks: first, to establish effective fiscal, administrative, and service-delivery systems out of the chaos inherited from the past; and second, to reconceptualize the process of local governance, focusing attention on reorienting municipal resources and regulatory powers toward meeting the needs of the urban poor. Prior to the enactment of the Local Government Transition Act of 1993, the governing structures of Johannesburg consisted of thirteen independent (and racially defined) local council administrations (each with their separate operating budgets) and two black local authorities that were, in turn, funded by the Regional Services Council. This checkerboard configuration of rival jurisdictions resulted in an inequitable distribution of financial resources and basic services, creating a geographic polarity along a north-south axis. In a concerted effort to bridge this yawning gap that was even further exacerbated by rapid peripheral urbanization along the northern boundary of the sprawling metropolis, the 1993 Act amalgamated the fifteen governing bodies into seven administrations. A revision of the legislation in 1996 further consolidated these seven administrations

29. Information also derived from interviews with Neil Fraser; and interview with Yael Horowitz.

30. Information and ideas also gathered from interview with Keith Beavon.

into a single entity named the Greater Johannesburg Metropolitan Council (GJMC), with four substructures, or metropolitan local councils (MLCs). Despite these far-reaching steps to eliminate the apartheid-era administrative confusion, the resulting agglomeration of five administrative bodies—whose functions were duplicated, uncoordinated, and unwieldy—made the decision-making process overly bureaucratic and time-consuming, where available financial resources were not sufficient to meet demands for municipal development (Govender and Aiello 1999; 650–651, 654, 656; Tomlinson 1999b).[31]

Faced with persistent shortfalls of municipal revenues and bottlenecks in provision of municipal services, the GJMC unveiled a visionary plan in 1999 called iGoli 2002, an ambitious framework of institutional and fiscal transformation that spelled out a three-year plan to establish a more secure fiscal platform for the city and to radically reduce the direct role of local government in service delivery (Tomlinson et al. 2003, 10–14). The animating slogan that underscored this administrative restructuring effort was "Making the city work: it cannot be business as usual."[32] The immediate, short-term aim of the iGoli strategy was to put the city's finances in order, a first step regarded as a prerequisite for addressing the organizational, institutional, and service-delivery challenges facing the GJMC. The cornerstone of this new approach to urban governance rested on a comprehensive program for restructuring and rationalizing municipal services by streamlining, outsourcing, and privatization.[33]

At its core, the iGoli 2002 scheme called for managing the city like a private business, and it was premised on market-driven, cost-recovery, and entrepreneurial principles derived from neoliberal policy perspectives. Its proponents envisioned transforming Johannesburg from a debt-ridden, inefficiently operated, disjointed agglomeration of dispersed local governments into a financially healthy, vibrant "unicity" that would also serve as a role model for other South African municipalities (Govender and Aiello 1999, 7).[34] City planners looked upon the restructuring of municipal governance principles in Johannesburg as a litmus test for urban local government across South Africa. With the end of apartheid the pressing issues of urban planning that promoted spatial integration across racial lines, infrastructural development that targeted the impoverished zones of the municipality, and efficient administration of the city

---

31. Lindsay Bremner, "Johannesburg"; and interviews with Neil Fraser; and interview with Yael Horowitz.

32. Rapule Tabane, "Expertise, Cash Boost for iGoli 2002," *The Star*, October 13, 1999.

33. Peta Krost, "End of the Line for Jo'burg Metro Gravy Train," *The Star*, July 14, 2000; and Prince Hamnca, "Jo'burg Boss Moloi Aims for World-Class City," *The Star*, April 3, 2001.

34. Interviews with Neil Fraser; interview with Yael Horowitz; and interview with Lael Bethlehem, chief executive officer.

assumed national significance. The GJMC operated with a budget twice the size of any other South African local authority. By proclaiming that fiscal discipline tied to a coherent administrative chain of command was a first and necessary step toward the trickling down of socioeconomic benefits to the poorest of the poor, the planning discourse that framed the iGoli program offered an ideological justification for reconciling the conflicting agendas of economic growth and satisfying basic needs (Beall, Crankshaw, and Parnell 2000: 110–111, 118–119).

The iGoli 2002 blueprint called for the privatization of city-owned properties in order to ease the short-term cash shortfall and to improve service delivery. By selling such prime assets as the Johannesburg International Airport, the Ellis Park Stadium, and valuable parcels of public land, the municipal council hoped to inject much-needed capital into its depleted coffers. Financial experts estimated that the city could save an estimated $300 million in two years by outsourcing such utilities as water supplies, sanitation, electricity, housing, roads, and the metro bus service.[35] As part of the iGoli 2002 program, the city council established a stable of municipally owned but privately managed businesses as a means of improving the delivery of services. The municipal council established such entities as Johannesburg Water, City Power, and Pikitup (garbage collection) as independent, private utility companies, wholly owned by the City of Johannesburg but under private management, to serve the greater Johannesburg metropolis. The council also formalized ownership over two other types of entities: corporate units such as MetroBus and semiautonomous agencies such as the Johannesburg Roads Agency. The transformation of the city administration from a service provider to a service coordinator marked a kind of privatization by stealth.[36]

As pressure mounted on municipal authorities to deliver on the promised revitalization of Johannesburg, they responded with one ambitious scheme after another. Whereas the iGoli 2002 program amounted to little more than an introverted rescue plan to address the budgetary constraints brought about by revenue shortfalls, the longstanding financial crisis, and institutional malaise, the iGoli 2010 strategy sought to position Johannesburg as a globally competitive African world-class city. Unveiled at the end of 2000 before popular elections for the new post of executive mayor, the iGoli 2010 program gradually fell out of favor because it tried to be all things to all people.

---

35. Gilbert Lewthwaite, "South Africa Repolishes Tarnished 'City of Gold': Johannesburg Hopes That Zero Tolerance Privatization Will Help," *Baltimore Sun*, December 28, 1999.

36. Eamonn Ryan, "iGoli 2002 Starting to Deliver the Goods," *Sunday Times*, June 30, 2002. Ideas and information for this and the following paragraphs also derived from interviews with Neil Fraser; interview with Yael Horowitz. Interpretation is mine alone.

In contrast, the next economic revitalization plan, an ambitious, far-sighted blueprint called iGoli 2030, envisioned the integration of Johannesburg into the world economy as a world-class city by the third decade of the twenty-first century. The goal of this renaissance scheme was to wean the city from its historic dependence on mining, manufacturing, and other heavy industries, and to reconfigure its economic profile by transforming Johannesburg into a vibrant, export-oriented metropolis with increased global integration.[37] The iGoli 2030 plan called for promoting Johannesburg as an information technology and service-oriented regional hub with transport, trade, financial, and business services; utilities; tourism; food and beverage; and chemical and professional equipment as the top priorities for private investment. The main impetus of the iGoli 2030 strategy was to encourage new private investment with the goal of raising economic growth by between 7 and 9 percent, thereby bringing about an increase—expected to be sustainable—in both the standard of living of residents and their quality of life. As a way of emphasizing its global pretensions, the iGoli 2030 vision dropped any reference to a globally competitive African world-class city, and instead endorsed the mantra of transforming Johannesburg into a "world-class business location."[38]

These postapartheid urban revitalization efforts revolved around three strategic initiatives: a commitment to enhancing the livability of the city, tackling the so-called crime-and-grime syndrome, and a marketing plan designed to bolster the city's international credentials. The high-octane, booster script for Johannesburg after apartheid thus rested on three assumptions: first, globalization has created an unavoidable climate of worldwide competition where the only way forward entails carving out both a market niche and a compelling brand image; second, the City of Tomorrow depends on a postindustrial developmental trajectory imbricated with the global marketplace; and third, to compete successfully requires the subordination of divisive class-based loyalties and partisan politics in the broader interests of the generic, pro-business team effort (Hall and Hubbard 1996).

In order to move away from the city's historical dependence on gold mining and heavy industry, city officials sought a postindustrial development trajectory that emphasized three interrelated goals: first, to promote the metropolitan region as an inviting site for environmentally clean information technology industries, as well as leisure and cultural activities, scientific research, and the media arts; second, to establish Johannesburg as a transportation hub for ecotourism in the southern African region; and, third, to situate the city as

---

37. Anna Cox, "Jo'burg—No Longer Just a Mining Town," *The Star*, February 18, 2002.
38. Quote from Lindsay Bremner, "Johannesburg"; and Anna Cox, "Jo'burg—No Longer Just a Mining Town."

the preferred location for financial services, banking, insurance, professional, and producer services. To this end, the iGoli 2030 revitalization scheme overlapped with the highly touted Blue IQ growth strategy endorsed by the Gauteng Provincial Government. This scheme called for a R1.7 billion initiative to invest in ten projects related to tourism, transport (including a high-speed rail link connecting Johannesburg and Pretoria), and high value-added manufacturing. In seeking to attract R100 billion in foreign direct investment, the Blue IQ plan envisioned the creation of a "smart province" revolving around information technology industries and skilled employment clustered in a mini Silicon Valley close to Midrand (Bénit and Gervais-Lambony 2005).[39]

39. Tom Nevin, "Gauteng: The Smart Province," *African Business,* May 2000, pp. 17–18; and Tom Nevin, "Africa's Silicon Valley?" *African Business,* May 2000, pp. 20–22.

4

Disposable People
at the Peri-Urban Fringe

At the end of a road that meanders through dismal mealie fields,
fire-blackened veld, and winter smog lies South Africa's newest
settlement [at Bredell], our own little piece of Zimbabwe.

PATRICK BULGER

In late June 2001 thousands of landless squatters seized a barren piece of
vacant land at Elandsfontein farm close to a suburb called Bredell, outside of
Kempton Park on the eastern outskirts of Johannesburg.[1] The homeless squatters who came to this forlorn place near the Johannesburg International Airport
were indeed the poorest of the poor and surely the most vulnerable citizens
of the new South Africa: single mothers with young dependent children; the
old, the infirm, and the sick; newcomers to the city; the casually employed;
and the chronically jobless. Within days these expectant homesteaders, who
numbered around 10,000 persons, had carefully marked out individual plots
and erected close to 1,200 shacks on this expansive swath of open land, tow-
ered over by rusty pylons and squeezed between a chicken farm, some ragged
mealie patches, and a petrol pipeline. Lured by the hope for a better life, they
tried to make the dry, dusty place seem a little like home, hanging curtains and
rolling out worn rugs to cover the rocky red soil.[2]

Without proper sanitation, clean water supply, or any other of the social
amenities required for a decent life, this inauspicious stretch of land seemed an
unlikely setting for such a bitter standoff, pitting the desperately poor against

1. Patrick Bulger, "Battlelines Are Drawn in the Bredell Dust," *Sunday Independent,* July 7,
2001.
2. For this and the following paragraphs, see Rachel Swarns, "South Africa Confronts Landless Poor and Court Sends Them Packing," *New York Times,* July 12, 2001; Evidence wa ka Ngobeni, Bongani Mjola, and Khadija Magardie, "'Save Us from Hell on Earth,'" *Mail & Guardian,*
July 13–19, 2001; Phomello Molwedi and Rapule Tabane, "Desperate People Flock to Buy Land
for R25," *The Star,* July 3, 2001; and Patrick Bulger, "Battlelines Are Drawn."

state housing authorities, who were determined to prevent an informal settlement from taking root on the site. For the homeless squatters, the occupation of Elandsfontein farm represented a better option than the overcrowded squalor of the dismal backyard shacks in nearby Tembisa from whence they had escaped. For municipal authorities, in contrast, the unauthorized land seizure symbolized a lawless disregard for proper administrative procedures in the fledgling new democracy. After weeks of legal wrangling, the municipal officials won a court order, allowing them to dismantle the shantytown and forcibly remove the squatters. As nearly a thousand heavily armed riot police stood by, more than two hundred employees of Wozani Security Company, whose notorious reputation had earned them the nickname *Rooi Gevaar* (Red Danger) or the Red Ants, embarked on the task of demolishing the squatter encampment. As distraught middle-aged women stripped naked as a way of demonstrating their anger at the evictions, the Red Ants, clad in their distinctive red overalls, used crowbars and axes to indiscriminately smash and bash the flimsy shacks, "bringing roofs down on the possessions inside," and destroying the "pitiful belongings of the desperately poor squatters."[3]

Seen in the broad context of pent-up frustration with the slow pace of housing delivery in postapartheid South Africa, the land invasion at Bredell and the subsequent, forcible removal of the homeless squatters who sought to make a life for themselves there were not particularly unusual events. After all, since the birth of the new South Africa in April 1994, tens of thousands of newcomers have poured into the greater Johannesburg metropolitan region, crowding into existing informal settlements or creating entirely new ones, swallowing up available tracts of empty land, and putting an almost unbearable strain on already over-burdened municipal resources. According to reliable estimates, by the late 1990s the numbers of new arrivals to the greater Johannesburg metropolitan region exceeded twenty thousand per month, and these numbers have not abated. Between 1996 and 2004 the eight largest cities in South Africa experienced a population growth rate of 4.4 percent per year—more than twice the national average. During the same time period, the population of the greater Johannesburg metropolitan region jumped 25 percent, while the number of individual households expanded by one third.[4] By 2005 the number of new households was growing at an average annual rate of 6.7 percent. If these trends continue (and there is no reason to expect that they will not), the number of households in greater Johannesburg will double in the next twelve years.[5]

3. Anele ka Nene and Mariette le Roux, "Squatters 'Willing to Die' for R25 Plots," *South African Press Agency (SAPA)*, July 6, 2001; and *BBC News*, "Police Evict SA Squatters," July 12, 2001.

4. Editorial, "Housing Dilemma," *Business Day*, July 12, 2004.

5. Interview with Graeme Gotz, specialist in policy and strategy, Corporate Planning Unit, Office of City Manager, City of Johannesburg, May 26, 2006.

As in other cities around the country, municipal authorities in Johannesburg have been unable to keep pace with the accelerated demand for decent and affordable housing. According to World Bank figures for the period 1996 to 2001, the number of informal shacks in the Johannesburg municipality expanded an astonishing 42 percent to almost a quarter million, despite the fact that the number of formal dwellings increased by over 220,000 units.[6] According to the 2004 State of the Cities Report, an estimated 22.5 percent of households—close to one quarter of the population of Johannesburg—were without formal shelter.[7] In a report issued in late 2006 housing experts estimated that the municipal backlog (as indicated by the waiting list for subsidized units in greater Johannesburg) had crept steadily upward to somewhere between 250,000 to 300,000 units. While the elapsed time between filing an application for subsidized housing and actual occupation was estimated at seven years in 2000, available evidence for 2006 suggested that the wait on the subsidized housing list for the greater Johannesburg metropolitan region had inched closer to ten years.[8]

Unlike the earlier waves of work seekers who were lured to the burgeoning Johannesburg conurbation in response to rapid industrialization, recent arrivals have limited prospects for finding regular work in the formal sector. The influx of newcomers to the greater Johannesburg metropolitan region has continued despite accelerating deindustrialization, high rates of urban unemployment (estimated at close to 40 percent of the economically active population), and falling real wages for unskilled workers (Beall, Crankshaw, and Parnell 2002, 29–44). As elsewhere in the world, this kind of perverse urbanism—where urban population growth has accelerated without a corresponding expansion of wage-paid employment—has contributed to all sorts of problems related to environmental degradation, unchecked horizontal spread of informal settlement patterns, and unhealthy living conditions of unprecedented severity in slums and shantytowns (Davis 2006).

With the country's housing backlog estimated at close to three million dwellings in 2005, newcomers to the cities—as well as those squeezed out of existing places of residence—have little choice but to rent backyard shacks in the established townships, to squeeze into already overcrowded informal

6. "Housing Dilemma," *Business Day*; and Peter Honey, "Spread of Squatter Shacks Reflects Policy Failure," *Financial Mail*, March 5, 2004.

7. Kecia Rust, Andreas Bertoli, and David Gardner, "Review of Johannesburg's City Strategy, Opinion Piece 1: Housing Pressures, Residential Opportunities, and Asset Investment Choices," report prepared for City of Johannesburg Corporate Planning Unit, June 23, 2005, pp. 33, 39 (henceforth, referred to as "Review of Johannesburg's City Strategy").

8. Interview with Kecia Rust, consultant in housing finance and development policy, June 1, 2006; "Review of Johannesburg's City Strategy," pp. 11–12; and Trafalgar Properties, *The Trafalgar Inner City Report 2006* (unpublished pamphlet, pp. 5–12, 20–26).

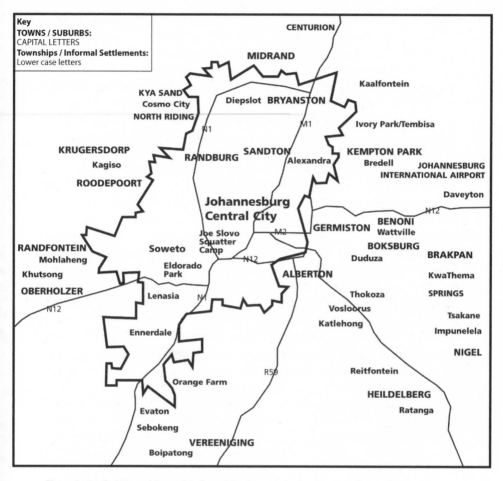

Figure 4. Settled Townships and Informal Settlements in the Greater Johannesburg Metropolitan Region. By Stephanie McClintick

settlements, or to unlawfully occupy vacant land and erect makeshift shelters with whatever materials are available.[9] While state housing officials have pledged to provide land and suitable shelter for the urbanizing poor, they have also drawn a clear line: they vowed to meet unauthorized and illegal occupations of land with prosecutions and evictions.[10]

9. See Mungo Sottot and Tangeni Amupadhi, "A Human Flood Is Drowning Gauteng," *Mail & Guardian,* May 10–16, 1997; and South African Cities Network, "Govt Shift on Shack Dwellers," *Mail & Guardian,* July 13–19, 2004.

10. Rachel Swarns, "South Africa Confronts Landless Poor."

The social origins of bitter contestation over access housing on the peri-urban fringe of the greater Johannesburg metropolitan region can be traced to the convergence of rising expectations of impoverished, landless squatters who literally have nowhere else to go, on the one hand, and the failure of market-led policies, based on the principle of willing buyer, willing seller, to provide sufficient land for the landless and adequate homes for the homeless, on the other. State housing and land policies, particularly after the late 1990s, have not catered to the truly destitute (Bond 2000, 122–155; Huchzermeyer 2003b). With the end of apartheid, the new ANC-dominated government pledged to redistribute 30 percent of white-owned land to landless black people in a time frame of five years. But more than a decade later, the government has managed to transfer only about 2 or 3 percent of the land into black hands. Market-led policies have failed to deliver sufficient land for housing into the hands of the millions of truly desperate people from whose ranks the Bredell squatters were drawn. Because they were unable to meet the qualifications that would make them eligible for access to formal housing, the poorest of the poor have been left to fend for themselves in seeking rudimentary shelter wherever they could find it.[11] Yet despite notable achievements in the field of housing delivery, the availability of affordable residential accommodation for the poor has failed to keep up with the accelerating demand for affordable accommodation. Postapartheid housing authorities have pointed with pride to their accomplishments: the construction of around 1.6 million formal dwellings in authorized residential sites over the decade beginning in 1995—a 10 percent increase in the country's formal housing stock. Nevertheless, the official backlog has continued to expand.[12] Between 1996 and 2004 the numbers of informal settlements in South Africa's largest cities grew by about 30 percent. Whereas there were an estimated forty-seven informal settlements in Gauteng Province in 1990, the number skyrocketed to around two hundred by 2006. In 2004 somewhere between seven and eight million impoverished people—mostly but not exclusively South African citizens—lived in "unsatisfactory dwellings"—many with the legal status of squatters, that is, as unauthorized occupants of the land on which they had constructed rudimentary shelter.[13] The lack of affordable

11. Editorial, "Nobody Wins," *Mail & Guardian*, July 8–13, 2001; *Pretoria News*, "Fears of a Mugabe-Style Land Grab Stalk SA's Farmlands," January 14, 2004; Zakes Hlatshwayo, "Land Invasions Are Inevitable if the State's Hands Are Tied," *Mail & Guardian*, June 15–21, 2002; and Richard Tomlinson, "Subsidies Benefit Only a Few," *Mail & Guardian*, September 22–28, 2001.

12. "Housing Dilemma," *Business Day*.

13. According to the South African Human Rights Commission, close to eleven hundred informal settlements blossomed around the country in 2001 alone. For quotation, see *SAPA*, "Failure to Spend 'Contributes to Housing Backlog,'" April 22, 2003; Jan Hennop, "South African Township Riot Highlights Housing Problem," *Agence France-Presse*, July 7, 2004; and South African Cities Network, "Govt Shift on Shack Dwellers"; interview with Graeme Gotz.

and decent housing has come to symbolize in a highly visible way not only the enduring legacy of apartheid rule but also the failure of the democratically elected government to respond to the material needs of its poorest citizens (Guillaume and Houssay-Holzschuch 2002). Newcomers have flocked to the greater Johannesburg metropolitan region not only from the impoverished rural hinterlands but also from across the African continent. Along with malnourished and unhealthy bodies, irregular housing (overcrowded backyard shacks in existing townships, illegal occupation of unused buildings, and makeshift shelter of any kind) is perhaps the most visible expression of urban poverty. Municipal authorities have tried to upgrade authorized settlements and to contain the spread of unlawful occupation of land. Despite these efforts, unlawful squatter encampments have mushroomed in the peri-urban fringe (Huchzermeyer 2004, 1–4, 83–104).

City officials have acknowledged a catalog of problems that have plagued the supply of affordable residential dwellings. Housing delivery programs have lacked the social and economic development components required to address historical disparities in access to decent residential accommodation. Land prices in more desirable locations near the main transport nodes and employment cores are invariably higher than large tracts of land situated on the metropolitan periphery. Private investment in residential dwellings has remained stagnant in the historically marginalized townships and new low-income settlements. Even where housing delivery has occurred, the provision of social services and physical infrastructure has lagged behind community requirements.[14]

The combination of resource constraints, lack of capacity, and unwillingness to interfere in the free play of market forces has limited the capability of state housing authorities to deliver affordable shelter for the poor. Almost from the start, the entire system of housing delivery became entangled in numerous problems, including cumbersome bureaucratic approval processes, the creation of such stringent criteria for household eligibility that countless numbers of the poorest of the poor failed to qualify for subsidies, and agonizingly long waiting lists (Dewar 1999, 368–375).[15] At the same time, allegations of unauthorized expenditure and outright fraud, financial irregularities involving builders and contractors, shoddy construction, and unwarranted queue jumping have undermined public confidence in the fairness, propriety, and equity in housing delivery.[16] No longer willing to wait patiently for

14. "Review of Johannesburg's City Strategy," pp. 28–29.

15. Rapule Tabane and Fikile-Ntsikelelo Moya, "R43m Spent on Ghost Houses," *The Star,* December 11, 2002; and Yolanda Mufweba, "Gauteng Housing Department Explains Expenses," *Saturday Star,* January 16, 2004.

16. "Gauteng Declares War against Corruption in Housing," "R400 Gauteng Housing Scam," and "Shambles in Jo'burg Housing: JHD Demoted," *Housing in Southern Africa* (June 2003): 1, 2, 4.

state housing officials to fulfill their promise of delivering adequate shelter to those in need, homeless squatters in Johannesburg and elsewhere have seized whatever opportunities arise to occupy land without official authorization (Huchzermeyer 2003b).[17]

Privileged Insiders and Excluded Outsiders: The Social Roots of the Housing Crisis

> The invaders came to the wasteland [Bredell] by the hundreds two weeks ago, dragging splintering planks, rusting metal sheets, and wilting squares of cardboard.... Here, in the ragged stretch of land owned by government agencies and a private farmer, the poor believed they were finally tasting the fruits of black liberation.
>
> RACHEL SWARNS

> Steve: have you got a nice big bedroom? All we want is a piece of ground the size of your kitchen. How many can sleep in your garage? We don't want land that belongs to others, there is enough land in this country for everyone. Please tell us, Steve, how long must we wait?
>
> PLACARDS HELD BY BREDELL SQUATTERS AND ADDRESSED TO MINISTER OF SAFETY AND SECURITY STEVE TSHWETE

At first glance the July 2001 land invasion at Bredell seemed an unlikely catalyst for such a bitter standoff that pitted homeless squatters—who vowed to die rather than leave—against municipal authorities equally adamant about driving the unwanted intruders off Elandsfontein farm and restoring the place to its rightful owners. After all, homeless squatters in small numbers had continuously occupied state-owned land at Bredell since 1995.[18] Over the years, the Ekurhuleni metropolitan council on the East Rand engaged in an ongoing battle with the squatters, paying a private company named ACME Training to evict them and tear down their makeshift dwellings, at a cost of somewhere between R360 and R485 for each shack demolished.[19]

What distinguished the Bredell case from similar actions at other times and other places was that this particular land occupation coincided with heightened

---

17. Nawaal Deane, "Removals Spark Legal Battle," *Mail and Guardian*, July 7–13, 2001; Evidence wa ka Ngobeni and Nawaal Deane, "Bredell Squatters Challenge Evictions," *Mail & Guardian*, July 21–27, 2001; and Ngwako Modjadji and Nawaal Deane, "In Search of the 'Promised Land,'" *Mail & Guardian*, July 1–6, 2001.

18. Rachel Swarns, "South Africa Confronts Landless Poor"; the placards are cited in Evidence wa ka Ngobeni, Bongani Mjola, and Khadija Magardie, "'Save Us from Hell on Earth.'"

19. Evidence wa ka Ngobeni, "E. Rand Council Moves Illegal?" *Mail & Guardian*, July 14–20, 2001.

anxiety over the unsettled state of affairs in neighboring Zimbabwe, where President Robert Mugabe had cavalierly sponsored widespread seizures of white-owned farms despite worldwide condemnation. Regardless of the political motivations that lay behind those expropriations, the sheer scale and scope of the seizures of white-owned farms in Zimbabwe raised the profile of the land question in South Africa and the region. Municipal authorities in urban South Africa reacted to these unfolding events with grave concern, fearing that unauthorized land occupations could trigger a chain reaction of lawlessness that would disrupt political stability and undermine international investor confidence (Greenberg 2004a, 6–7).

The Pan Africanist Congress (PAC)—a South African opposition political party that openly expressed admiration for the orchestrated land invasions in Zimbabwe—aided and abetted the squatters at Bredell, setting up registration booths at Elandsfontein farm and luring homeless squatters with the promise of plots on which to erect their own shacks in exchange for a R25 "donation." African National Congress (ANC) officials responded viscerally to the involvement of the PAC, accusing that group's leaders of seeking to capitalize on growing land hunger in urban South Africa by encouraging the landless to seize white-owned farms as part of the "unfinished business of liberation."[20] There was some truth to the claim, put forward by the journalist Patrick Bulger, that the PAC had successfully "stolen the march on the ANC government, whose progress in 'settling' the land issue has been conspicuous by its failure." In its eagerness to offer the impression that it would not allow land invasions of the sort that brought ruin to Zimbabwe, the ANC leadership "turned quickly to derision and slander [of its political opponents] and to the courts and the police bully boys of yesteryear to impose its will."[21] In seeking legal justification to authorize the forcible removal of the unwanted squatters, the owners of Elandsfontein farm argued before the Pretoria High Court that the land occupation posed serious and immediate safety risks to the squatters since the property was crisscrossed by electricity pylons, railway tracks, and an underground oil pipe. They also contended that the squatters faced the risk of contracting diseases like cholera and dysentery, and the cold weather posed a fire hazard due to the possibility of runaway shack fires.[22]

20. Mariette le Roux, "Invaders Taking What Belongs to Them—PAC," *SAPA*, July 5, 2001; *SAPA*, "Land Is the Unfinished Revolution, Says PAC," August 14, 2001 (quotation comes from this source); Anele ka Nene and Mariette le Roux, "'Land Owners' Threaten Violence if Evicted," *SAPA*, July 14, 2001; and Andrew Donaldson, "Still No Sign of Missing Bredell Land Money," *Sunday Times*, August 5, 2001.

21. Patrick Bulger, "Battlelines Are Drawn." See also Rapule Tabane, "PAC Members 'Selling' Land to Homeless," *The Star*, July 2, 2001.

22. The owners of the land were the Ekurhuleni municipality, Transnet, and a private company called Groengras Eiendomme—along with servitude holder Escom. There were unsubstantiated

The bitter and tragic standoff at Bredell highlighted the scope and depth of land hunger that had simmered largely unnoticed since the end of apartheid. As an ominous gesture of possible futures, the squatter occupation of Elandsfontein farm inspired a spate of similar illegal land invasions by homeless squatters, in places as far apart as Rietvlei and Olifantsfontein outside Pretoria and at numerous sites around Cape Town.[23] In the weeks following the upsurge of land invasions, state officials worried aloud about the negative impact of these illegal actions, fearing that international investors would tar them with the same brush as the worldwide condemnation of the land invasions in Zimbabwe. South African Reserve Bank governor Tito Mboweni went so far as to cite the Bredell land invasion as one of several factors that contributed to the depreciation of the rand (as it plunged to record lows against the U.S. dollar). Municipal authorities insisted that they would not tolerate illegal land occupations, vowing to use the courts to prosecute squatter leaders and pledging a willingness to resort to physical force if necessary to dislodge unauthorized land invaders.[24]

While the property owners inundated the courts and the popular media with pious platitudes about lawless land invaders, the unmitigated catastrophe that resulted from forcible evictions of homeless squatters faded from view. Most shack-dwellers ejected from their impermanent home at Bredell were scattered to the four winds, and their fate is unknown. Yet it is possible from journalist accounts to trace the harrowing journey of fifty-four homeless families evicted from Bredell. This seemingly aimless odyssey of these poor people represents in microcosm the hapless plight of countless numbers of unwanted squatters who have become invisible vagabonds in the land of their birth. Following their expulsion from Bredell, these itinerant families (who had been informed by Bavumile Vilakazi, the mayor of the Ekurhuleni metropolitan council, to "go back where they came from") found refuge for six months at several churches in Tembisa on the East Rand. But after their continued presence exhausted the patience of parishioners, they were once again forced to move on. Following

rumors that the Ekurhuleni metropolitan council had agreed three months before the crisis erupted to sell the property to a Dutch company with plans to establish a game lodge on the disputed land. Baldwin Ndaba, "Tshwete Is a Drunkard, PAC Tells Squatters," *The Star,* July 11, 2001; Allan Seccombe, "State Urges Court to Evict Squatters," *Reuters,* July 9, 2001; and SAPA, "Judge Halts State Bid to Evict R25 Squatters," *The Star,* July 6, 2001.

23. *The Star,* "Police Muscle In to Stop Second Land Grab," July 9, 2001; Nashira Davids, "Builders Chased Away as Homeless Despair," *Sunday Times,* October 14, 2001; Tom Hood, "Land Invaders Win Court Battle," *Sunday Times,* September 30, 2001; and Murray Williams, "Bredell Struggle Inspires Cape Squatters," *Cape Argus,* July 14, 2001.

24. Ed Stoddard, "Tempers Flare as Police Arrest Land Invaders," *Sunday Independent,* July 5, 2001; Estelle Randall, "Mboweni Says Bredell a Factor in Falling Rand," *Sunday Independent,* September 28, 2001; and *Cape Argus,* "PAC Man Blamed for the Rand's Latest Woes," August 22, 2001.

an agreement reached between the South African Council of Churches and the provincial housing authorities, the squatters were transported to land set aside in Palm Ridge near Alberton. Yet local residents objected to the unwanted influx of so many newcomers, so police moved them first to the Elden Park police station before finding them shelter at the Elden Park fire station, where they stayed for several days. Eventually they were transported to another site in Palm Ridge called Phase 4, where they were unceremoniously dumped without water, sanitation facilities, or proper building materials.[25]

Although the tragic saga of the Bredell squatters received worldwide media attention, the predicament of dozens of other squatter encampments scattered across the urban landscape remained in the shadows, outside the purview of public discussion or debate. Land invasions have dramatized the failures of the state administration to deliver on its pledge to provide decent shelter for the poor. They signal that the challenge of homelessness on the metropolitan edge cannot be solved simply by building brick houses for those who can afford to pay for rates and services, but by concentrating on providing land and services for the most marginalized citizens—the new immigrants to the cities and those spilling out of overcrowded townships. In the face of increasing land hunger among the urban poor, municipal authorities have appealed for patience while at the same time pursuing what amount to "strong-arm tactics against those who illegally invade land" (Ramutsindela 2002).[26]

This new wave of unchecked urbanization that began in the early 1990s has posed new challenges for the Johannesburg municipality. City officials have grappled with constructing a coherent urbanization strategy within existing budgetary and administrative constraints. But most new residents who have flocked to Johannesburg live in wretched conditions. They rarely have access to clean water, sewage facilities, or refuse removal (Greenberg 2004b, 31–33). Squatters exist in a permanent state of legal and social insecurity because, as a general rule, they usually build shacks on the land they inhabit without official authorization and are hence under the constant threat of eviction. This insecurity of tenure has greatly diminished any incentive for shack dwellers to invest in improvements, and it has only exacerbated social stress associated with fear of eviction (Guillaume and Houssay-Holzschuch 2002).[27]

25. Baldwin Ndaba and Gudrun Heckl, "Ray of Hope after Day of Tears at Bredell," *The Star*, July 12, 2001; SAPA, "Churches to Accommodate Evicted Squatters," July 12, 2001; Chimaimba Banda, "Land for Bredell Squatters Remains Elusive," *The Star*, December 2, 2001; and Rapule Tabane, "Bredell Invaders Still Waiting for Their Land," *The Star*, December 19, 2001.

26. Marianne Merten and Evidence wa ka Ngobeni, "Poor People Are Not Stupid," *Mail & Guardian*, July 1–6, 2001.

27. Mungo Sottot and Tangeni Amupadhi, "A Human Flood"; Bongani Majola, "Wits Offers Postgraduate Program in Housing," *Mail & Guardian*, July 27–August 3, 2001; and South African Cities Network, "Govt Shift on Shack Dwellers."

In each of the three components of urban growth (namely, job creation, housing policy, and provision of basic services), the short-term costs have been disproportionately borne by the poorest of the poor. The groundwork of post-apartheid housing policy was negotiated during the period of political transition from 1990 to 1994. After a lengthy process of consultation, municipal authorities settled on a housing delivery policy that in the end has amounted to little more than a market-driven, developer-led approach to the provision of shelter. In formulating their housing delivery policies after the end of apartheid, city officials borrowed heavily from what were regarded as international best practices. Amid great fanfare the housing department under ANC and Communist Party stalwart Joe Slovo promoted a program of mass housing delivery that initially promised the construction of one million houses a year. The driving force behind this mass housing initiative was the active engagement of private banks and construction companies, where municipal authorities used the developmentalist rhetoric of building public-private partnerships and mobilizing mortgage bonding financing from private lenders (Bond 2000, 35–67; Desai and van Heusden 2002). For those low-income nuclear families who qualified, municipal authorities offered a once-only R16,000 subsidy, a sum that covered the costs of installing the basic infrastructure required to deliver water, sanitation, and electricity to households. The amount of financial assistance was calculated on the basis of the number of household members served. Yet in the terms of stringent eligibility requirements, persons living in backyard shacks in the townships were not able to obtain a housing subsidy to improve their dwellings. HIV- and AIDS-infected adults and children who were separated from their families were similarly ineligible for a housing subsidy (Huchzermeyer 2003).[28] Financing for new houses or improvements to existing structures was largely skewed toward those with higher incomes because they had the capacity to gain access to bank credit (Bond 2000, 136, 145, 146; Porteous and Naicker 2003).

Municipal housing policies and programs have proven incapable of dealing with the vast backlog of promised shelter or responding to new demands for affordable accommodation. In circumstances where municipalities have provided housing stock, building practices have typically taken the form of the construction of mass, monofunctional, site-and-service schemes that are "undertaken on disconnected parcels of land and characterized by a low-density, undifferentiated blanket of freestanding housing shells" (Khan and Ambert 2003, xxv; McDonald 1998).[29] Despite the official promise of integrated cities

---

28. Richard Tomlinson, "Subsidies Benefit Only a Few"; and interview with Kecia Rust.

29. "Site-and-service" schemes refer to subsidized housing programs where the municipality assembles the land and provides basic infrastructure (roads, sewerage, electricity, water) but relies

and compact cities, municipalities have largely built these subsidized housing projects at the metropolitan edge, thereby reinforcing existing spatial patterns inherited from apartheid town-planning initiatives and creating new locational imbalances. The resulting socioeconomic hardships—for instance, long-distance commutes to places of work—for those who are forced to live there has added to the burden of living in informal settlements (Royston 2003, 234).

For the most part, housing authorities have looked on mushrooming, self-built squatter encampments as illegal, disorderly, and unwanted "blots on the landscape." Housing intervention has been directed at removing this "scourge of informal settlements" and at preventing the outbreak of unauthorized land invasions. Critics have charged these policies are actually counterproductive, simply replacing one set of harmful dynamics with another.[30] Despite official condemnation and the persistent threat of forced removal, squatter collectives have little choice but to seek makeshift shelter wherever they can find it (Khan 2003; Huchzermeyer 2003b, 2004). Housing experts have increasingly voiced concerns that this kind of technocratic intervention paradigm—with its narrow fixation on externally defined, market-driven, and product-oriented solutions to the eradication of informal dwellings—has failed to take into account local needs. The mandate to deliver quantities of standardized housing units has pushed aside concerns with existing community organization, local initiative, collective ideas for improvements, and fragile livelihoods that depend on informally established land-use patterns and interhousehold ties (Huchzermeyer 2004, 3, 5–7, 234–236).

While most informal settlements and low-income housing projects are concentrated south of the central city, almost all new jobs have been created in the urbanizing north, especially along the M1 highway between Johannesburg and Pretoria (Tomlinson et al. 2003, 14). The predicament in Johannesburg is complicated by a shortage of suitable land for human habitation, stubborn resistance by mostly middle-class homeowners to poor black settlements encroaching on their suburban neighborhoods, and a municipal development strategy that for all intents and purposes would like to "wish away informal settlements."[31] State housing officials have targeted informal settlements for

on self-help for dwelling construction. Housing consists of detached, single-family units laid out in long rows on individual plots. Building materials include brick exteriors and some wooden framing (Huchzermeyer 2004, 27, 30, 50, 55).

30. Quotations from "Review of Johannesburg's City Strategy," pp. 11–12, 27–28, 45–46; and interview with Kecia Rust.

31. Peter Honey, "Spread of Squatter Shacks." It should be noted that there are disputes regarding definitions of housing backlogs and numbers of unsatisfactory dwellings. See "Review of Johannesburg's City Strategy," pp. 11–12, 28–29.

eradication, earmarking some for upgrading while condemning others to demolition alongside the relocation of their squatter residents to other sites. Critics have questioned the practical wisdom of this approach, arguing that formalization or upgrading of existing informal settlements invariably means reducing the overall number of shack dwellings to make room for roadways, sewerage pipes, and power lines (Huchzermeyer 2003b, 2004, 3, 5–7, 145–178). It also requires the relocation of residents to planned site-and-service schemes such as Vlakfontein, southwest of the city, or the sprawling informal settlement at Diepsloot to the north. These sites have become so overcrowded with new-comers that their flimsy infrastructure has been stretched to the limit, and they are located far from jobs and employment opportunities, schools, and other amenities that drew the squatters to the city in the first place. Aside from dis-rupting the lives of desperate people, the interventionist practice of shuffling homeless squatters from one temporary transit camp to another has failed to diminish their number, but has merely raised the prospect of continued land invasions and reinforced the shadowy practice of shack farming, whereby un-scrupulous land owners take advantage of the plight of the homeless poor by inviting them onto their land in exchange for a fee.[32]

Unauthorized Land Seizures: Low-Intensity War on the Peri-Urban Edge

> Tumbledown shacks fashioned from corrugated iron and
> cardboard jostle for space with stagnant pools of sewage
> [at Modderklip]. Dogs forage on heaps of rubbish and the
> singsong lilt of Portuguese travels along the shantytown's dusty
> alleys. At first glance, this sprawling slum could be in any city
> in Portuguese-speaking Africa. Yet this corner of South Africa
> and the shantytown, filled with migrants from neighbouring
> Mozambique, has sprung up on what were once the lush maize
> fields of a white-owned farm.
>
> DAVID BLAIR

During the early to late 1990s the number of land invasions escalated dra-matically both in anticipation of the end of apartheid and in the immediate aftermath of the transition to parliamentary democracy.[33] In June 1994, two months after the historical April 1994 liberation elections, municipal authori-ties, civic organizations, and representatives of squatter communities agreed

32. Peter Honey, "Spread of Squatter Shacks"; personal observation, shack farming near Kya Sand industrial area, north of Randburg, 4 June 2006.
33. David Blair, "Shanty Town Battle Sparks Land Grab Fears for S African Farmers," *Daily Telegraph* (London), December 15, 2004.

to a moratorium on land invasions and evictions. According to the agreement, squatters settled before June 1994 would not face eviction proceedings. But all land invasions after this period would be considered illegal and hence subject to forcible removal. Municipal authorities used this agreement to carry out a number of evictions of unwanted squatter encampments from such places as Moffat Park (south of Johannesburg), the Far East Bank of Alexandra, Parktown in the older northern suburbs, Eldorado Park (near Soweto), Langlaagte (on the western fringe of the city center), Thokoza Unit F (East Rand), Tembisa (near Kempton Park), Kaserne and Liefde en Vrede (both southeast of the central business district), and Nietgedacht (near the Lion Park in the far north). These forcible removals—sometimes conducted with the kind of indifferent brutality that characterized the darkest days of apartheid—highlighted the growing housing crisis for the swelling ranks of homeless squatters who were ceaselessly on the move in search of suitable places to find shelter.[34]

In numerous locations earmarked for upgrading and economic revitalization, the technocratic application of land-use planning has meant that informal settlements and makeshift squatter encampments have been cleared to allow for the more rational, efficient, and productive use of the vacated space (Greenberg 2004a, 11). While examples could be multiplied many times over, a few cases should suffice to illustrate the persistent use of forcible removals of unauthorized squatter settlements to meet municipal policy objectives.[35]

At Kliptown (Soweto) the construction of the mammoth heritage project and tourist attraction—named Walter Sisulu Square to mark the historic signing of the Freedom Charter in 1955—required the eviction of hundreds of squatter households in ramshackle shanties close to the site.[36] At Eikenhof informal settlement (otherwise known as the Jacksonville squatter camp), south

---

34. *SAPA*, "Police Monitor Land Invasion at Nietgedacht," October 26, 1996; Thuli Nhlapo, "Squatters Freeze While Mayor Eats Salmon," *Mail & Guardian*, March 1–8, 2001; and Glenda Daniels, "Government Officials Pass the Buck on Forced Removals," *Mail & Guardian*, February 16–22, 2001.

35. There are numerous cases of forcible removal of squatters from unauthorized shack settlements on the peri-urban fringe. I mention several here. For the poignant example of the destruction of the Harry Gwala informal settlement near Wattville on the East Rand, see Lee Rondganger, "Commotion as Red Ants Evict Squatters," *The Star*, May 31, 2006. Angry squatters barricaded Beyers Naude Drive after law enforcement agencies demolished shacks at Zandspruit near Honeydew, west of Johannesburg; see Poloko Tau, "Many Homeless as Cops Destroy Illegal Shacks," *The Star*, September 26, 2006. In a graphic display of brute force, the Red Ants forcibly removed forty thousand squatters and razed their shacks at the Angelo and Dunuza informal settlements in Germiston. As the Red Ants moved in to demolish the shack settlement built on a mine dump on the Main Reef Road, they were greeted with a barrage of rocks and stones. See Lee Rondganger, "Homes Torn Down in Blitz on Mine Dump," *The Star*, June 2, 2005; and *SAPA*, "Squatters Move Out Overnight," June 2, 2005.

36. A. Milazi, "Makeover in Kliptown," *Financial Mail*, November 28, 2003, p. 35.

of Johannesburg, municipal authorities called on the Red Ants to carry out the forcible removal of three hundred families in order to make way for a cemetery. The families were then relocated to Vlakfontein, where the promised access to water and sanitation failed to meet their expectations. The municipal decision to demolish the site triggered internal strife, as residents were divided about the relocation, one group voluntarily moving to Vlakfontein and the other vowing to remain.[37] The squatter invasion of Modderklip farm next to Daveyton township outside Benoni eventually blossomed into the largest land grab in South Africa's postapartheid history. The six-year battle to remove the estimated forty thousand squatters highlighted the legal complexity of land and housing rights in the new South Africa, pitting private landowners, municipal authorities, and the landless in a triangular conflict over property rights and land for housing.[38]

The eviction of close to two thousand families from Mandelaville informal settlement in Diepkloof (Soweto) in January 2002 exemplifies the official practice of displacing settled squatter communities to make way for anticipated commercial development. Following five years of failed negotiations the City of Johannesburg obtained a court order authorizing local authorities to demolish the Mandelaville shack settlement and transport the squatters to overcrowded, violence-prone Durban Deep hostel near Roodeport. The first squatters at Mandelaville erected illegal shacks on the site in 1976, and many of the original inhabitants had remained in the intervening 26 years. Over time Mandelaville expanded into a sprawling squatter encampment of fifteen thousand residents crammed into a dense warren of ramshackle, one-room huts where movement was restricted to narrow dirt pathways. City officials complained that the squalid conditions, chronic joblessness, and lack of social amenities made the place a breeding ground for disease and lawlessness. In lengthy discussions with housing authorities, squatters refused offers to relocate to Silverton at a place called Snake Park, to Orange Farm, to Devland, and, finally, to Durban Deep. With the breakdown of negotiations, city officials turned to Wozani Security Company to carry out the demolition of the shack settlement and to forcibly remove residents and their meager possessions.[39]

After police arrested and handcuffed squatter leader Daniel Rabbie, the resistance to the forced removal dissipated. The efforts of angry residents to protect their homes were no match for the infamous Red Ants, who seemed

37. *Sunday Times,* "Up, Up, and Away," January 26, 2003; *SAPA,* "Eikenhof Squatter Camp Relocation Voluntary," January 26, 2003; and *SAPA,* "Two Comrades Arrested," January 26, 2003.
38. *Sowetan,* "40,000 Squatters Take Over Farm," July 20, 2001; and David Blair, "Shanty Town Battle Sparks Land Grab Fears."
39. For this and the following paragraphs, see Baldwin Ndaba, "Tension in Mandelaville as Eviction Starts," *The Star,* January 7, 2002; and *The Star,* "A Community Uprooted," January 7, 2002.

to take a sort of perverse delight in destroying tin shelters, scattering possessions, and harassing impoverished shack dwellers. As local Diepkloof residents cheered their departure, disconsolate squatters boarded trucks bound for Durban Deep hostel, a deserted mine compound that had once housed mine workers in overcrowded barracks. Although city officials assured them that the move was in their best interests, what the relocated squatters discovered at Durban Deep was far worse than what they had been promised. Upon arrival, the newcomers were met with hostility from residents from the nearby Sol Plaatje informal settlement, who had appealed without success to local authorities for permission to occupy the buildings allocated to the Mandelaville squatters. Months later, life for the former Mandelaville residents had changed very little. In a scathing report that focused on the callous disregard of the municipal authorities in handling the matter, the South African Human Rights Commission declared that the new arrivals were living under appalling and subhuman conditions at Durban Deep, in violation of their fundamental human rights. The mine compound was in a derelict state, with filthy walls and caved-in ceilings and without electricity, doors, bathrooms, or proper toilets. Four or five families shared a single-compound dwelling, partitioned into a kitchen, dining room, and bedrooms. Men, women, and children took turns using outdoor toilet facilities. Mandelaville had lacked running water and sanitation, was overcrowded, and had no street lights, but at least residents could get transport to work, children could go to school, and residents were close to shops and health clinics.[40] With the site finally cleared of unwanted squatters and fenced to prevent their return, the Johannesburg Property Company (JPC) formally announced that the "prime property" in Diepkloof Zone 3 was available for commercial development. Proclaiming its intention to upgrade the area through commercial enterprise, the JPC promised to bring "retail and business facilities closer to the community."[41]

Sites of Impossibility: Land Hunger and Squatting on the Metropolitan Fringe

The right to decent shelter is inextricably tied to access to land. For the shelterless poor, the unauthorized occupation of vacant or under-utilized

40. Baldwin Ndaba, "Residents Cheer Squatters' Eviction," *The Star,* January 8, 2002; Thabang Mokopanele, "Squatter Families Going to Durban Deep Hotel," *Business Day,* January 8, 2002; "Khumalo Street Gets Down to Business," *Mail & Guardian,* January 19–25, 2002; and Thabo Mohlala, "Down in the Dumps," *Mail & Guardian,* March 30–April 5, 2002.

41. Nick Wilson, "Opportunity for Developers in Soweto," *Business Day,* November 19, 2003; and on-site visit with Trevor Ngwane, community activist and resident of Pimville, Soweto, June 8, 2006.

land—what municipal authorities have referred to as illegal land invasions—
has come to symbolize a clever tactical maneuver in an ongoing and wider
struggle over the right to decent and affordable accommodation. Homeless
squatters who have occupied land on the peri-urban fringe without official
permission have revealed through their collective actions an awareness of the
necessity of cooperation and collaboration. For Michel de Certeau (1984,
xiv–xv), urban dwellers who are compelled by necessity to occupy indeterminate, unauthorized, or illegitimate space must rely on various clandestine
tactics, that is, spatial practices that involve taking advantage of gaps, fissures,
or voids in the structure of authority in order to seize propitious moments
in time. Along with such inventive actions as the occupation of abandoned
buildings in the inner city, unauthorized squatting on the metropolitan fringe
epitomizes these makeshift tactics that de Certeau has celebrated, or that James
Scott (1985, xvii–xviii, 331–333) has called "weapons of the weak" and Asef
Bayat (1997a, 53–72; 1997b) has termed the "quiet encroachment of the ordinary." Unauthorized seizures of under-utilized or vacant land have become
the dominant method of redistributing property through the self-activity of
landless squatters. Although these collective actions indicate active agency and
deliberate choice, one must avoid the temptation to overly romanticize land
seizures, since they frequently involve competition, contention, and intimidation in combination with cooperation, reciprocity, and coordination (Simone
2004a, 2004b, 12–13, 95–96, 205–206).

The proliferation of informal squatter settlements on the urban fringe has
brought about the horizontal extension of the metropolitan boundaries of Johannesburg. A quick glimpse at the scale and scope of land invasions that have
mushroomed along both sides of the Golden Highway (R553) that runs south
from Soweto to the Vaal triangle represents perhaps an exaggerated version
of the general trend. Beginning in the early 1990s, at least a dozen or more
separate squatter settlements sprang up along this so-called highway of zinc
in anticipation of the postapartheid dispensation. At an average of every five
kilometers from Eldorado Park (abutting Soweto) to Sebokeng approximately
50 kilometers south, shantytowns sprawled haphazardly along both sides of
the R553 freeway. Nearly three-quarters of a million impoverished people
have taken up temporary residence in makeshift shacks that are constructed
of corrugated iron, sheet metal, scrap wood, and plastic sheeting. Two squatter encampments—Freedom Park and St. Martin's Trust—ramble down a hill-
side, opposite Eldorado Park. Mjazana was erected just across the main road.
Thembelihle and Protea South cropped up to the west, near Lenasia. Residents
draw their water from taps in the yards of homes located in nearby townships.
About eight kilometers farther south, squatters had poured into Vlakfontein
and Grasmere, abutting the Ennerdale railway station. Weiler's Farm spread out

across the highway. A small shantytown called Eikenhof came next. The sprawling shack settlement of Orange Farm, housing perhaps 10 percent of the total population of Johannesburg, and its smaller northern appendage called Sweetwaters (along with the Kwamajazana squatter settlement) were located across the Golden Highway. Drieziek 4, Evaton North, and Ithobvallen Ntshanyane (next to the Sebokeng hostel and Zone 16) followed next along the highway, around five kilometers south. Inkatha refugees who fled from KwaMadala hostel settled at John Duoy, a grim place set back off the highway on the right. Immediately after the historic April 1994 elections that brought the ANC to power, four new squatter settlements sprang into existence. Long-hidden homelessness in the older, established townships—rather than rural-to-urban drift—underlay the explosion of shantytowns. Recent arrivals reported that they were no longer willing to live with parents or older relatives, or to pay high rents for backyard shacks. What had begun as a trickle in the late 1980s turned into a flood, as accelerating numbers of newcomers pushed out of the overcrowded townships of the Vaal (Evaton, Sebokeng, Boipatong, Sharpeville) and from Soweto to the north, expunged from the plots and recession-mired white-owned farms in the surrounding countryside, driven from violence-plagued townships and informal settlements on the East and West Rand, and, arriving from Mozambique and Zimbabwe, poured into the mushrooming shantytowns.[42]

The chronic shortage of affordable housing for the poor is the root cause for the proliferation of self-built, informal squatter settlements that encircle the peri-urban fringe of the greater Johannesburg metropolitan region. The social origins of two informal settlements located southwest of the Johannesburg central city—Orange Farm and Thembelihle—are fairly typical of the general patterns of precarious living on the urban margins. Looking at these in some detail, then, can assist us in understanding the historically specific dynamics that distinguish these kinds of self-built housing from officially sanctioned site-and-service schemes, backyard shacks, and shantytowns located inside existing townships (Beall, Crankshaw, and Parnell 2002, 131–132).[43]

From its modest origins in 1990 Orange Farm has exploded into a sprawling informal settlement of almost Brazilian proportions. Confronted with the massive and growing demand for shelter, the Transvaal Provincial Administration began to construct various site-and-service schemes in the early 1990s in order to regulate the mounting influx of homeless squatters. With central Johannesburg forty-five kilometers to the north and Vereeiging twenty-nine kilometers to the south, this virtually treeless, barren expanse of land was from

42. Drew Forrest, "The Highway of Zinc," *Mail & Guardian*, September 22–30, 1995; and Peter Honey, "Spread of Squatter Shacks."

43. On-site visits to Orange Farm (June 14, 2003), Thembelihle (June 8, 2003), and Weiler's Farm (June 14, 2003).

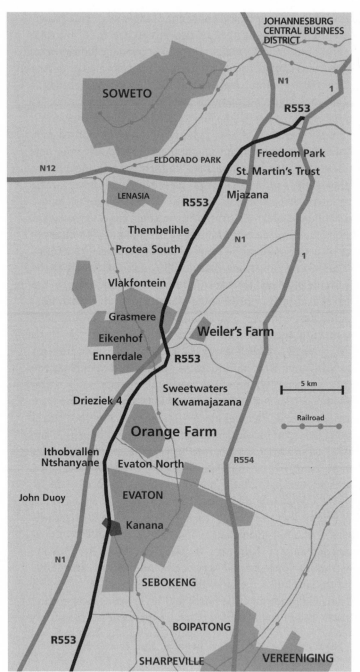

**Informal Settlements
North to South**

Freedom Park
St. Martin's Trust
Mjazana
Thembelihle
Protea South
Vlakfontein
Grasmere
Weiler's Farm
Eikenhof
Ennerdale
Sweetwaters
Kwamajazana
Drieziek 4
Orange Farm
Evaton North
Ithobvallen Ntshanyane
John Duoy
Kanana

Source:
Drew Forrest, "The Highway
of Zinc," *Mail & Guardian*, 30
September 1995; and Peter
Honey, "Spread of Squatter
Shacks Reflects Policy Failure,"
Financial Mail, 5 March 2004; On
site visit with Trevor Ngwane,
community activist and resident
of Pimville, Soweto, 8 June 2006.

Figure 5. Informal Settlements in 2006 along the Highway of Zinc (R553).
By Stephanie McClintick

the outset a dismal place with few social amenities. By 1995 the population of Orange Farm had skyrocketed to around 250,000 residents, where the number of individually serviced sites had expanded to thirty thousand units that were spread over seven separate extensions. The intensified pressure of so many new residents pouring into the area caused the established system of site allocation to collapse. To get a place on the waiting list for serviced sites, would-be home-steaders were required to pay a fee of R64. But because of *tjotjo* (bribery), people were allowed to jump ahead in the line. Just as ominously, self-appointed street committees had begun charging fees for access to laid-out sites in their zones of control. The fierce competition for land triggered ethnic animosities, as homeless squatters from Mozambique (called *Mashangaan*) were targeted for abuse. At nearby Drieziek 4, chaos reigned supreme. Widespread abuse of the waiting lists led the municipal authorities to suspend the allocation of serviced sites, thereby triggering unauthorized encroachment of land for shelter. Despite the great distances to places of work and the virtual absence of basic infrastructure and social services, Orange Farm—along with nearby Evaton to the south—has become one of the fastest-growing residential areas in South Africa, with an annual growth rate of 4 percent and a population in 2004 of around 400,000 people crammed into 102,000 housing units.[44]

Thembelihle (or "good hope" in Zulu) is an informal settlement that sprang up on vacant land next to Lenasia, an older, settled township set aside for urban residents of Indian origin and located about thirty kilometers southwest of the Johannesburg city center. The origins of Thembelihle can be traced to 1983, when a few entrepreneurs started to use the site (left vacant because it rested on unstable dolomite rock that is prone to sinkholes) as an open-air market-place to sell home-brewed beer to domestic servants, gardeners, and casual laborers who worked in Lenasia. The first permanent residents arrived in 1986, and they quickly organized themselves into a civic organization with the pro-claimed objective of regulating the use of the available space. The civic associa-tion laid out a grid-like street plan with relatively large, green plots, and several wide avenues. Newcomers poured into the area, squatting on whatever vacant land they could find. The squatter camp grew from an estimated six thousand residents in 1990 to nearly thirty thousand in 2004. The majority of squatters came from nearby Soweto where they had been living in overcrowded (and rack-rented) backyard shacks and single rooms. The fifty-eight hundred shacks in the sprawling settlement did not have access to water or to electricity, even though the Lenasia power lines pass directly above (Guillaume and Houssay-Holzschuch 2002, 90–91; and du Plessis and Wilson 2005, 86–91).

44. Drew Forrest, "Highway of Zinc"; and SoundRock Property, "Orange Farm Gets Upmar-ket Shopping Complex," *EPROP, Commercial Property Marketplace,* April 18, 2005.

Since 1995, local officials have sought to upgrade portions of the informal settlement at Thembelihle, introducing public toilets, garbage containers, and regular caravans for police and health services that have been located at the entrance. Residents have consolidated close to 20 percent of the shacks into permanent dwellings. Yet while some residents moved toward establishing permanent residence at the site, other squatter households—with a tenuous grip on security of tenure—were confronted with the real threat of forcible removal. From the start, apartheid-era municipal officials had regarded the land as unfit for human habitation and had vowed to evict the unauthorized squatters. With the transition to parliamentary democracy, the new local authorities resuscitated these earlier plans to relocate the unwanted land invaders by using the carrot of financial subsidies and land title in the relocated site and the stick of the threat of forced removal. As in the case of other municipal efforts to relocate illegal squatters, some households were lured away from Thembelihle with promises that they would acquire alternative housing sites, with title deeds, and be provided with bulk services and rudimentary infrastructures. Ironically, just as Thembelihle squatters abandoned their plots, impoverished residents from the nearby informal settlement of Vlakfontein invaded the vacated land. Yet a group of long-term residents of Thembelihle adamantly refused to move, claiming that the municipal plan to relocate them was politically motivated and linked to racial discrimination because middle-class Indian residents from Lenasia did not want to associate with impoverished black people, and arguing that the proposed subsidies were insufficient to build a proper house in another location (Guillaume and Houssay-Holzschuch 2002, 90–91).[45]

In June 2002 protesters from Thembelihle disrupted the Kliptown ceremonies marking the forth-seventh anniversary of the signing of the Freedom Charter. The lofty ideals of this historic document adopted in 1955 at the height of popular protests against the apartheid regime remained a mirage for the Thembelihle squatters. The irony was evident: while the five thousand dignitaries who attended the formal proceedings were celebrating the freedoms enshrined in the charter, including the right to decent housing, the protesters were demanding a reprieve from their forced relocation from Thembelilhe to new plots laid out at Vlakfontein.[46] The simmering tension reached a crisis point early the next month when residents of Thembelihle barricaded the squatter settlement to protest their forced removal to Vlakfontein, an area they claimed was without proper water and sanitation. A small splinter group went on a rampage in nearby Lenasia, petrol-bombing a school building, setting

---

45. Personal observation from on-site visit, June 8, 2006.
46. Rapule Tabane, "And There Shall Be Housing for All," *The Star,* July 26, 2002.

fire to several shops, looting businesses, ransacking a butcher shop, smashing cars, and attacking bystanders. The Thembelihle protesters acted on the belief that local Indian business owners were behind their relocation, but municipal authorities countered with the rationale that the sedimentary rock on which the squatter encampment had been erected made the area unfit for human habitation.[47]

Self-Built Dwellings and Vernacular Architecture: Symbolic Expressions of the Longing for Home

Whatever else shack settlements lack—and that's a great deal—
they are not without creative planning and design talent.
ALAN LIPMAN (2006, 136)

In cities everywhere land-use policies typically emphasize the protection and regulation of the central business district and the urban core of upscale residential zones, affluent leisure sites, and commercial districts. The administrative support that property law provides for city users tends to progressively diminish as urban residents move toward the ex-urban periphery. The panoply of codes, bylaws, and regulations governing land use constitute the juridical-legal framework within which disputes are adjudicated. Operating outside the protective framework of the law, residents of unauthorized squatter settlements are vulnerable in the extreme. With no legal claim to remain where they are, squatters are subject to unilateral municipal actions designed to uproot them from their temporary abodes. To adjust to this precariousness, residents of unauthorized settlements tend to forego making long-term investments in improving their living arrangements beyond the most rudimentary shelter, or in developing social ties in their immediate surroundings. Instead, they seek out opportunities that enable them to spread their affiliations and connections across the city. This spatial strategy lays particular stress on movement rather than permanence, since it involves breadth of connections rather than depth of social relationships (Simone 2001a; 2001b; 2004a; 2004b, 206).

For the most part, land invaders have been astute trespassers. In the typical case, squatter leaders have been well-informed, careful planners who have been aware of their legal rights (however tenuous these may be) and of the reluctance of some municipal officials and local councils to confront them or to evict them (especially in the cold winter months) without the availability of alternative shelter. Those who have masterminded squatter invasions typically

---

47. Baldwin Ndaba, "Rioters Petrol Bomb School," *The Star,* July 18, 2002; Baldwin Ndaba and Thuli Nhlapo, "Children Flee Bombs and Riots in Terror," *The Star,* July 18, 2002; and Caiphus Kgosana, "Bail Keeps 'Human Dumping Zone' Seven in Jail," *The Star,* July 22, 2002.

follow a well-rehearsed scenario: often striking in the early morning hours, groups of men armed with bags of chalk and a flag assemble on an empty field. They quickly mark out plots with chalk, leaving open space for streets and pathways. In a matter of hours, they can lay out the grid of an enormous informal settlement. They then raise the flag (often the national colors), name the squatter camp after a prominent leader, and quickly bring in as many women and children as possible. Taken together, the steady accretion of land invasions that began slowly in the late 1980s and gathered momentum by the mid-1990s fundamentally transformed the spatial landscape of the greater Johannesburg metropolitan region. Whereas the old apartheid laws allowed state officials to erase squatter settlements with bulldozers, postapartheid legislation has empowered local magistrates to preside over applications for evictions and to investigate whether suitable land exists to which squatters can be transferred.[48]

The vast informal settlements that have proliferated since the end of apartheid share a number of characteristics that distinguish their built form from the older settled townships like Soweto, Lenasia, Eldorado Park, and Westbury (on the southwest); Katlehong, Voslorous, and Thokoza (southeast); Wattville (Benoni); KwaThema (Brakpan/Springs); Duduza (Boksburg); Daveyton (Far East Rand), Alexandra and Tembisa (northeast). In the typical case, informal settlements consist of jumbled rows of self-built shacks cobbled together from discarded wood, salvaged cardboard, corrugated iron, and whatever other detritus of urban living can be commandeered from the surrounding landscape. The makeshift shelters are small enclosures of no more than two or three rooms with barely enough space to accommodate those who crowd into them. The flimsy materials provide only a modicum of protection from the elements. Shacks are generally poorly equipped and sparsely furnished with conventional household amenities. Basic infrastructure such as electricity, running water, indoor plumbing, and paved roads is virtually nonexistent, or available only to a privileged few households. Because all available land is quickly occupied, there is no room for open spaces, parks, or sports facilities of any kind (Huchzermeyer 2004, 206–214).[49]

Although informal settlements may appear to be formless assemblages of makeshift shacks distributed haphazardly over featureless landscapes, the layouts of these rudimentary encampments typically conform to deliberate patterns that reflect a collective desire for convenience, security, and orderliness. Rows of shacks are positioned in relation to pathways linking residents to *spaza* shops (i.e., informal businesses operated from a home or shack), communal

48. Mungo Sottot and Tangeni Amupadhi, "A Human Flood."
49. Information based on numerous on-site visits to various squatter settlements from 2001 to 2005.

water outlets, exits and entrances to the settlements, and community assembly points of one sort or another. The physical and social arrangements of the squatter settlements are typically not fortuitous: they are negotiated communally, endorsed by informal peer pressure, and often backed by agreed-upon codes of conduct. While individual shelters are often crowded together in clusters, their placement generally avoids intrusion on neighbors. Residents design the internal organization of their shack dwellings along rationalized lines to optimize the efficient use of limited space. Typically, the interior spaces of shacks are at once private and public: a location for social relations, for reception, and for representation. Residents use this social space to enhance their sociocultural standing, to offer outsiders an ideal representation of household members, and to outwardly display the cultural values of those who live there. This interior serves both a useful function as living space and a sociocultural function as exhibitionary space: "the home ideal of many informal dwellers is the common representation of a modern, Western, middle-class interior." The interior serves as a platform for the display of material possessions: a television and other electrical appliances, crockery in a glassed case, second-hand furniture, and walls decorated with photographs of children and relatives. Shack dwellers place a premium on maintaining an immaculate appearance in the interior spaces and immediate exterior. Along with all the other visible signs of attentive housekeeping, residents regularly sweep the earthen forecourts, maintain "serried rows of neat washing lines," and cultivate flower gardens (Guillaume and Houssay-Holzschuch 2002, 89; Lipman 2006, 133–136).

The spatial organization of shack interiors mirrors the public space of informal settlements. For instance, shack dwellers frequently use their residences as launching pads for conducting informal businesses, for storing goods for sale, or for neighborhood meeting places. In the typical case, informal settlements lack the provision of basic infrastructure: water services (with the exception of standpipe), electricity, sewers, paved roads, and sidewalks. Municipal services such as schools, clinics, police, and emergency facilities are virtually nonexistent. Residents seek to meet their immediate survival needs either by providing informal services, such as crèches, *spaza* shops, and haircare. To a limited extent, municipal authorities have legally recognized the existence of some informal settlements and have sought to regularize their existence by providing upgraded services like communal taps and toilets, paved main roads, electricity, and fire and emergency services. Ironically, the uneven pattern of upgrading and improvements has put into motion the early signs of social differentiation, thereby engendering resentment, rivalry, and conflict (Guillaume and Houssay-Holzschuch 2002, 88–91).

As a general rule, municipal authorities and housing officials have looked upon informal settlements as aberrant and anarchic living arrangements that deviate from the stated goal of formal housing with its standardized rules, bureaucratic procedures, and legible measurements. Yet there is mounting empirical evidence that suggests that these places are actually rational arrangements that are largely responsive to the immediate needs of their residents, often in the face of unresponsive policies (Huchzermeyer 2004, 179–226).[50] Since the material qualities of housing—its cost in time and money, its structural durability, its legality, and its physical design—are of fundamental concern to the inhabitants of informal squatter settlements, it should come as no surprise that this arena is one place where shack dwellers have advanced creative solutions to what appear to be intractable problems (Appadurai 2002, 36–37). Informal settlements often evolve in ways that are self-rationalizing, that is, the people who live there construct the socioeconomic networks that make their lives functional and create the kinds of social organizations that enable them to adapt to the demands of city living (Simone 2001a, 2004c).[51] Residents have used all sorts of inventive approaches to compensate for the woeful lack of amenities and basic infrastructure. For example, some shack dwellers have tapped into existing power lines and underground pipes to divert electricity and water to their places of residence. Others have erected solar panels on the roofs of their shacks and use storage batteries in order to provide sufficient electricity to power such modern conveniences as CD players, TVs, and VCRs.[52]

Languishing in the Limbo of the Outcasts: Squatter Vulnerability and the Shape of Disadvantage

South Africa's housing policy, however well-intentioned and whatever the success in unit delivery, has been a qualitative and economic disaster. The decision to build freestanding dwellings in peri-urban areas has not only perpetuated apartheid geography; it has resulted in massive wastage because billions of rands have been pumped into housing that has no [marketable] value.

Itumeleng Mahabane, Communications and Investor Relations Consultant

The overwhelming majority of squatter households that have settled on the metropolitan fringe have occupied land without official permission to do so.[53]

---

50. Interview with Kecia Rust; and "Review of Johannesburg's City Strategy," pp. 45–46.

51. "Review of Johannesburg's City Strategy," pp. 45–46.

52. Drew Forrest, "Highway of Zinc"; and personal observation at Orange Farm, May 28, 2003.

53. Itumeleng Mahabane, "Housing Policy Increases Barriers in War on Poverty," *Sunday Times*, October 19, 2006.

The availability of unused land, the indeterminacy of land titles, and the often ambiguous and contradictory response of municipal authorities to land occupations have provided the wedge through which squatters have pried open space for themselves on the urban fringe. The modes of slum settlement have varied across a wide spectrum, ranging from carefully orchestrated land invasions of vacant land to diversified kinds of rental arrangements that take place under conditions of insecurity of tenure.[54] As a general rule, land invasions have come about as a result of the collective, coordinated actions of homeless squatters acting more or less on their own initiative, sometimes without much forethought or long-range planning. Unlike organized political movements that rely on a great deal of ideological solidarity, these squatter collaborations are typically fluid, provisional, and tenuous, where the immediate aim of gaining access to shelter provides the ties that bind the collective enterprise together. Without formal land titles or security of tenure, squatters are vulnerable in the extreme, oftentimes pressured into dependent relationships with self-styled leaders whose interests are far from communitarian (Huchzermeyer 2003b; Greenberg 2004b, 30–33).

The ugly flip side of squatter ingenuity, collaboration, and cooperation is the emergence of opportunists, con men, and tricksters who have taken advantage of the desperate plight of homeless people in order to fleece them. In the absence of an effective housing program that provides accommodation for those in need, an embryonic land mafia—such as that which rules squatter settlements in Brazilian cities—has come into existence in the greater Johannesburg metropolitan region. These shadowy groups have access to networks that can coordinate the placement of up to five thousand people—along with requisite building materials—onto a piece of land in a fortnight. Usually the self-styled organizers of these unauthorized land occupations charge an average of R80 a month per site: R50 rental, R20 protection fees, and R10 for a legal defense fund in the event the municipal authorities try to forcibly remove people. These land mafia groups typically acquire legitimacy through the resources they control and by forming themselves into some sort of residents' association. In many areas local councilors have begun to ally themselves with these land mafia in order to win the political allegiance and support of the residents.[55]

Squatter ecology revolves around the supply of land for shelter (Davis 2006, 121–137). It is not unusual for homeless squatters to be duped into paying money to people claiming to be housing agents with official permission to

54. Interview with Sarah Charlton, School of Architecture and Urban Planning, University of the Witwatersrand, June 1, 2006; and "Review of Johannesburg's City Strategy," pp. 45–46.
55. Victor Khupiso, "Homeless Being Duped," *Sunday Times*, April 21, 2002.

settle squatters on particular plots of vacant land. Despite warnings from municipal authorities, countless numbers of gullible people in such spatially dispersed sites as Ivory Park (Midrand), the Barcelona settlement outside of Daveyton, and Bredell near Kempton Park have been conned into paying money to phony land brokers who claimed to have official permission to settle squatters on the land but in the end absconded with huge sums.[56] In addition to these land scams, vulnerable squatters have also suffered at the hands of rank-renting landlords. Just like the draconian rental agreements that sometimes characterize the backyard shacks that have proliferated in the established townships of Alexandra, Soweto, and Katlehong, self-styled landlords in places like the Joe Slovo squatter camp (located outside Crosby on the West Rand on private land owned by Transnet) have rented out shacks to newcomers for up to R200 to R300 per month.[57] One local power broker—known as Majapere ("he who eats dead horses")—has ruled over the informal settlement as if it were his personal fiefdom. Majapere has managed to acquire somewhere between fifteen and twenty shacks whose occupants provide him with a steady income. He also owns a *spaza* shop (where household necessities are for sale at inflated prices) and the main shebeen that has monopolized the sale of alcohol. Rack-renting landlords such as Majapere have no interest in improving living conditions, since upgrading would threaten to undermine their power and take away their multiple sources of income.[58]

Homeless squatters have also fallen victim to the shadowy practice known as shack farming. This particular kind of land occupation, in which white landowners rent out subdivisions on their properties to thousands of shack dwellers, has surreptitiously taken root at various locations around the metropolitan fringe. Saddled with rising debt or declining prices for farm products, hard-pressed white farmers have sometimes turned to shack farming as a last-ditch way of squeezing income out of unprofitable or under-utilized land. While municipal authorities have condemned this practice, they have been unable to eradicate it altogether. Shack farming has taken hold at various sites northwest of North Riding and in the vicinity of Kya Sand. In Region 5, near Roodepoort, city officials confirmed that at least seven landowners had subdivided their plots into small sections, renting out the estimated ten thousand makeshift hovels to shack dwellers for about R250 a month, but without the provision of any services. It was estimated that some landowners were able to

56. Victor Khupiso, "Homeless Being Duped."

57. Interview with Bronwen Jones, executive director, Children of Fire Trust, May 27, 2006. Transnet is a freight transport company.

58. This information is derived from personal observation from on-site visits and interviews with residents of the informal settlement who wished to remain anonymous, conducted in the summer of 2006.

Figure 6. Joe Slovo Camp. Photograph by Martin J. Murray

make around R100,000 a month with this rack-renting practice. Municipal authorities worried that without running water, refuse collection, electricity, proper sanitation, or toilet facilities these shack farms were environmental disasters waiting to happen. Municipal authorities were powerless to evict the squatters, since this "booming business" that was "spreading like wildfire" flourished on privately owned farmland. They also worried that if the offending landowners were legally forced to evict the squatters on their properties, they would in all likelihood be unable to pay the costs of removal and would consequently simply abandon their farms to foreclosure. Once this kind of land use took hold, it became difficult to prevent its spread. Neighboring land-owners, unable to sell their properties because of illegal squatter camps on their doorsteps, have followed a similar route, also turning to shack farming as a way of recovering their losses due to dwindling income and declining value of their properties.[59]

In many ways the bitter struggles over access to suitable housing in Alexandra have come to epitomize the plight of homeless people elsewhere. Since the end of apartheid, an estimated twenty thousand squatters have established makeshift accommodation in unused factories, abandoned warehouses, and derelict buildings on the outer fringes of Alexandra. Disgruntled property owners have angrily described these squatter occupations as carefully planned invasions of a once-thriving industrial strip on the northeastern edge of sub-urban Johannesburg. By the mid-1990s squatters had occupied vacant proper-ties in Wynberg (west of Alexandra), Kew and Linbro Park (to the south and west), and Marlboro (to the north). By 2000, squatters occupied at least fifty-five abandoned and derelict buildings in these declining industrial areas. In Marlboro alone, the epicenter of the self-housing movement, squatters seized more than sixty buildings—almost half of all properties in the area. During the apartheid years, factory owners in Marlboro had taken advantage of strict enforcement of urban residential segregation to tap into the vast catchment area of nearby Alexandra for their steady supply of cheap labor. The squalid, rat-infested shelters that the squatters have constructed inside buildings are often no more than cardboard and Masonite boxes, with poor or nonexistent ventilation, inadequate sanitation, and no electricity.[60]

These ongoing disputes between disgruntled factory owners and home-less squatters in Alexandra has revealed deep fissures in the postapartheid era where the lack of decent and affordable housing for the legions of jobless poor is a visible marker of pariah status in the new South Africa. Simmer-ing tensions over access to adequate accommodation in Alexandra came to a head in mid-2000 after angry residents accused local housing officials with rampant corruption in the allocation of new housing units, including an es-timated eighty houses and sixty flats at a development called Tsutsumani Vil-lage and two hundred houses in the Far East Bank. Those families who had waited patiently for new housing discovered to their dismay that corrupt of-ficials had allocated houses to numerous people who did not qualify, including

59. Quotations from Anna Cox, "Smallholders Raking It In as 'Shack Farmers,'" *The Star,* Au-gust 12, 2001; interview with Graeme Gotz; interview with Sarah Charlton; and personal observa-tion from on-site visit, June 4, 2006.

60. Phomello Molwedi and Themba wa Sepotokele, "Victory for Joburg's Homeless," *The Star,* May 30, 2001. This information is also derived from personal observation from numerous on-site visits in 1999, 2001, and 2003.

local councilors and nonresidents, while many other units remained vacant. As the scandal unfolded, victims of housing bribery scams came forward to allege that they secretly paid bribes to expedite their applications for access to housing. One such victim was Nelson Silawu, a fifty-eight-year-old man living with his mother and father, his four children, and his wife in one room in Alexandra. Alleging that he paid a bribe of R6000 to jump the waiting-list queue, he acquired documents with keys and moved into his new house—only to be evicted six weeks later when the details of the scam came to light.[61]

In November 2000, a number of community organizations, including the Alexandra Civic Association, the East Bank Civic Association, the Concerned Alexandra Residents Association, and the Alexandra Homeless Youth and Families, joined forces to stage a protest march to the Union Buildings in Pretoria. Frustrated with what they regarded as official foot-dragging, angry residents seized about four hundred houses that had remained empty for almost a year at Tsutsumani Village and the Far East Bank over the next several weeks.[62] The failure of Johannesburg municipal authorities to reach a negotiated settlement with the homeless squatters culminated in police raids in early January 2001, resulting in the arrests of over a hundred squatters and evictions of those alleged to have illegally occupied houses.[63] Housing officials hired Wozani Security to guard empty houses in the Far East Bank as homeless squatters were forced to fend for themselves on the open veldt.[64]

Moving in the Shadows: The Ordinariness of Everyday Exclusion

> You either plan with the poor or the poor will plan for you.
>
> GAUTENG DEVELOPMENT EXPERT

The geographical limits of the city are defined by its cartographic invisibility.[65] However detailed and accurate they pretend to be, maps of the city fail to reproduce the integral wholeness of the sprawling metropolis. Countless numbers of city dwellers inhabit those blank spaces on maps that are devoid of place-names or site identifications of any kind. Just as with other cities, the

---

61. Anna Cox, "Alex Plans March over Housing Issue," *The Star*, November 22, 2000.

62. This land invasion followed in the wake of a previous seizure that had occurred three months earlier. See Anna Cox, "No House, No Vote, Say Alex Invaders," *The Star*, November 29, 2000.

63. *SAPA*, "Rampaging Mob Damages 50 Houses in Alex," December 14, 2000; *SAPA*, "Cops Swoop on 'Illegals' in Alexandra Houses," January 11, 2001; and Sheena Adams, "Children Detained with 39 Alex Squatters," *The Star*, January 11, 2001.

64. Anna Cox, "Alex Activists behind Bars," *The Star*, February 22, 2001.

65. Development expert quoted in Peter Honey, "Spread of Squatter Shacks."

urban landscape of Johannesburg is liberally littered with its unacknowledged nobodies and nowheres. The failure of the cartographic representation of the cityscape to register the presence of marginalized people who inhabit unacknowledged places effectively renders them unknown and hence unknowable, expunging them from history and memory (Pinder 1996, 405–427).

Postapartheid housing policies of the Greater Johannesburg Metropolitan Council have revolved around the dual strategy of replacing existing informal settlements with regulated site-and-service schemes, on the one hand, and preventing unlawful infringement or illegal occupation of land, on the other. Fearing that the gathering momentum of land invasions might begin to resemble what happened in Zimbabwe, municipal authorities moved quickly and decisively to halt unlawful seizures. Following the "No Land, No Vote" campaign launched by the Landless People's Movement that accompanied the April 2004 national elections, municipal authorities in Johannesburg reiterated their uncompromising stance to counter unauthorized squatter occupations with force if necessary. The postapartheid legal regime that governs secure access to land in urban and peri-urban areas has laid particular stress on procedural guidelines for evictions rather than adopting strategies that seek negotiation or provide alternative options (Huchzermeyer 2004, 227–236). The Prevention of Illegal Evictions and Unlawful Occupation of Land Act (1998) served as the principal legal framework for regulating the eviction process. For the most part, homeless squatters who are forcibly removed from illegal encampments have not acquired improved circumstances. Municipal authorities have narrowly interpreted the constitutional right to "legally secure tenure or comparable redress" for all citizens to mean that squatters forcibly removed from a particular site can be relocated to an alternative location with similar insecure circumstances (quotation from Greenberg 2004a, 11–16).

In an effort to slow the increase in informal settlements that mushroomed on the outskirts of the greater Johannesburg metropolitan region, municipal authorities took decisive steps in 2004 to strengthen the legal framework governing unlawful occupation of land. Provincial authorities sought to implement a strict land invasion policy that would grant law enforcement agencies the power to evict squatters within 48 hours of their illegal occupation. Under this proposed land-use regime, state authorities expected municipalities to strictly enforce the removal of illegal squatters. This proposed modification to existing legislation represented a serious setback for land activists who relied on protracted court proceedings to delay the eviction of illegal squatters until all legal remedies had been exhausted. In addition, provincial authorities sought to tighten the grip over unlawful infringement of property rights by making it a criminal offense to organize land invasions and by considering it a criminal act to collect funds to cover the legal costs of combating evictions.

Previous laws contained no reference to individuals or groups who organized illegal land invasions or who collected fees for legal purposes to fight court evictions. Provincial authorities also vowed to crack down on the practice of shack farming.[66]

Under apartheid, the demand for land and for housing was subsumed under the broader national struggle for equal political rights and for popular democracy. Popular movements did not target the housing question per se, but looked upon insecurity of tenure and propertylessness as a visible expression of the racism of the white minority regime and symbolic of the denial of equal citizenship rights in an undivided South Africa. The persistence of insecurity of tenure in the postapartheid era, coupled with the slow pace of redistribution of legal ownership, has exposed the limits of the formal achievements of political democracy and formal deracialization. The landless movement has rearticulated longstanding grievances—access to basic services, freedom of movement and freedom to remain in one place, security of tenure, and popular participation in local governance—that relate directly to the land question. The landless movement has exposed one dimension of the failure of municipal authorities in Johannesburg and elsewhere to address persistent poverty, joblessness, and inequality in the new South Africa.[67]

The intense demand for adequate housing has gone hand in hand with ongoing contestation over access to land, ranging from marginal, almost invisible encroachments on miniscule slices of land to large-scale land seizures involving thousands of squatter homesteaders. Many, if not most, of the informal settlements that have come into existence around the main conurbations can trace their origins to unlawful land invasions that in time acquired authorization and legal status. By making visible the demands of impoverished constituencies that have been ignored and marginalized within the postapartheid discourse of world-class cities, the Landless People's Movement has challenged the dominant construct of citizenship rights and has thereby opened up new terrain for political contestation. The repressive response of municipal authorities to unauthorized land seizures has effectively redefined the political landscape after the end of apartheid and the transition to parliamentary democracy. As a liberation movement, the ANC welcomed mass mobilizations from below as part of the strategy of making the townships ungovernable. Yet as the ruling party in government, the ANC has vowed to strictly enforce the distinction between legitimate forms of protest and illegitimate acts of defiance outside the law.

66. Sphiwe Mboyane, "Gauteng to Get Tough on Land Invasion," *Business Day,* June 10, 2004; and Hopewell Radebe, "Law Set to Stop Land Invaders in their Tracks," *Business Day,* September 3, 2003.

67. See Kwanele Sosibo, "One Toilet for Five Families," *Mail & Guardian,* March 17–23, 2006.

By employing apartheid-era legislation along with the threat of physical force, municipal authorities have effectively criminalized resistance to land and housing policies, thereby converting the hard-fought liberal-democratic rights that guarantee public protest, gathering, and association into illegal acts. The blunt response of municipal authorities to illegal occupation of land seems to suggest that they consider these acts of defiance as a threat to political stability and social order (Greenberg 2004a, 11–16).

With the end of white minority rule, the elimination of the legal barriers to the geographical mobility of work seekers has resulted in new kinds of movements that are considerably more complex than the once-dominant prototype of rural-to-urban migration (Kihato and Landau 2005). One highly significant but often overlooked consequence of the collapse of the migrant labor system that prevailed under apartheid has been the loosening of the ties that once bound urban (and peri-urban) households with rural homesteads. Under apartheid the constant flow of cash remittances from urban wage earners to rural homesteads not only enabled large-scale employers to maintain downward pressure on wages but also allowed municipal authorities to keep a tight reign on the provision of formal housing, thereby denying nonwhites the possibility of home ownership in the urban areas. For all intents and purposes, the breakdown of the structural link between urban wage earners and rural families has exposed those without regular employment to new pressures of movement (Greenberg 2004b, 30–33).

Freedom of movement—a significant victory in the popular struggle against apartheid—has assumed quite different substantive meanings for citizens of the new South Africa who are distributed unequally across the class spectrum. For the propertyless and jobless, the freedom to choose where to go has been reduced to perpetual movement, or the necessity of moving from here to there. This situation has arisen because the structural imbalance between job seekers and job creation after apartheid does not provide the necessary stability to allow freedom of movement to be a choice among varying options. Intraurban (both between but principally within cities) migration has assumed greater urgency in the lives of those excluded from regular employment in the formal economy. Available empirical research has suggested that a typical migratory pattern consists of movement from a rural area or small town to an established township like Alexandra, Soweto, Thokoza, Tembisa, Daveyton, or Katlehong, where newcomers share accommodation with relatives, occupying either rooms or backyard shacks. But overcrowded conditions, high rentals, interpersonal conflicts with landlords, or changing circumstances have often driven people to seek alternative accommodation. Faced with limited options, newcomers feel the considerable gravitational pull of informal squatter settlements on the outskirts of cities, in large measure because rental costs are either very low or nonexistent (Greenberg 2004b, 30–33; Bond 2000, 122–151).

The stories of jobless work seekers scattered around the urban landscape reveal most starkly the constant pressure to constantly change residential locations because of the economic necessity to respond to whatever new opportunities arise for making ends meet. The structural impediments that deny access to steady employment in the formal sector have created a mobile class of rootless work seekers who oscillate between the necessity to move from place to place and the longing to settle in one place in order to create a stable life. Under these straitened circumstances, the instrumental role of social networks, associational ties, and multiple households has assumed considerable importance. One significant element in the art of getting by depends on success in the fashioning and maintenance of such relationships as family (i.e., blood) and kinship ties, "home-boy" connections, religious affiliations, ethnic bonds, and business linkages. Households are often multinodal, with members moving between three and four different residences: the mother with children in one part of the city; the father renting a room close to work; and other children located with relatives in the rural areas (Greenberg 2004b, 31–33).[68] Therefore, individuals may maintain attachments to several households located in different sites around the greater Johannesburg metropolitan region. Immediate and extended family, and even friends and acquaintances, often provide temporary shelter for mobile people who are constantly in search of a stable foothold near key points in the urban landscape (Simone 2001a, 2004a). Under these circumstances, the relocation policies of municipal authorities have only served to further destabilize and disrupt the fragile survival strategies of the poor, both by eliminating places that people have created to settle temporarily and by keeping them constantly on the move. In the absence of alternative residence with long-term stability and security of tenure, or of long-term employment and work opportunities, municipal policies that uproot those who have illegally occupied places of shelter merely reproduce the underlying structural imbalances (Greenberg 2004b, 31–33).

These circling, floating masses of jobless people, constantly seeking ways to survive amid the wealth of the richest city on the African continent, have become the new outsiders, the new pariahs, the new urban outcasts in Johannesburg and other South African cities. Because of their permanent condition as nomadic beings, inhabitants of unauthorized squatter settlements are always already bodies out of place. Squatters are figures of perpetual motion, elusive and ghostlike, both illegal and excluded. Faced with intensified global competition, large- and medium-scale employers in the formal economy have

68. Ian Fife, "Riches to Be Had," *Financial Mail,* July 2, 2004.

increasingly turned to subcontracting, outsourcing, and other temporary labor arrangements to lower their costs of doing business. The vast surplus army of labor provides a readily available pool of casual workers that can be hired or fired at will. Labor laws may offer some protection to permanent workers, but for temporary, part-time, nonunionized workers, legal protection provided by labor legislation is as ephemeral as ownership of fixed property. Countless sites that ring the outskirts of Johannesburg have become the gathering places for the mobile, rootless poor who are invariably "squeezed between the rural and urban economies that are equally incapable of meeting their [immediate] needs" for decent shelter, income-generating work, and realistic opportunities for a stable life. The urban-rural interface around Johannesburg proper—commonly referred to as peri-urban—has been transformed from that fuzzy in-between place where city meets the countryside and instead has become a compact, densely settled combat zone that pits impoverished households seeking stable shelter against municipal authorities who have vowed to prevent illegal squatting. Neoliberal strategies for economic growth cannot possibly absorb this reserve army of labor, and new modes of urban governance cannot regulate or control it. Continually shifting and moving people from one place to another within this in-between zone, in the vain hope that they might fade away or somehow disappear in the process, has proven to be a pipe dream (Greenberg 2004b, 31–33).

5

The Spatial Dynamics
of Real Estate Capitalism

Doctors, we are told, bury their mistakes; planners, by the same
token, embalm theirs.
ROBERT MOSES (1970, 793)

Like other aspiring world-class cities, Johannesburg after apartheid has been
subjected to a steady stream of regeneration efforts designed to breathe new
life into dead spaces of the urban landscape. Borrowing from planning motifs
in vogue in North America and Europe, city builders in Johannesburg have
unveiled a series of ambitious projects that aim to revive decaying, blighted,
and abandoned parts of the cityscape, thereby reinvigorating or reinventing
the civic and public life of the city. These regeneration efforts are integrally
tied to what Sharon Zukin (1995, 23–24) has called the "symbolic economy"
of cities. In her view, the symbolic economy features two parallel production
systems that are crucial to the material life of the city: first, the production
of the built environment, "with its synergy of capital investment and cultural
meanings"; and, second, the production of symbols, which provides "both a
currency of commercial exchange and a language of social identity." These
much-publicized efforts to reshape the urban landscape are designed to enhance the city's competitive edge on a "global catwalk" (Degan 2003, 867–868),
by parading constructed (and aesthetically pleasing) images of different parts
of the cityscape that advertise these refurbished places as attractive to capital
investments, business locations, and leisure and entertainment activities. By
providing facelifts to the physical environment, boosterist city builders engage
in a kind of "imagineering" sleight of hand, trading on romance and nostalgia
to construct historicist simulacra of what once was (Degan 2003; King 1996;
Rutheiser 1986, 1999).

Looking to cities like Glasgow, Turin, Amsterdam, Belfast, and Barcelona
that have successfully engineered the transition from industrial city to postindustrial metropolis, the champions of downtown renewal in Johannesburg

have found inspiration in the regeneration strategies that stress the role of public-private partnerships in place-making, where the connections between quality of life, work, accessibility, and sustainability are made through design alterations and an acute awareness of what makes a city competitive. They have hammered out a market-driven approach to urban revitalization, one that stresses the enabling and facilitating role of municipal authorities in fostering private investment in targeted projects (see Hannigan 1998).

As a general rule, the spatial dynamics of real estate capitalism insinuate their own irrationalities, dysfunctionalities, and incongruities into the urban landscape. The expansive cycle of entrepreneurial investment in the built environment tends to break down over time, generating disorders that market imperatives by themselves are unable to sort out, manage, or resolve. New institutional arrangements that involve deliberate municipal interventions are required to restabilize the built environment by creating new opportunities for profit-making capital investment. By reasserting the spatial power of market forces, city building can once again take off (Harvey 1982; Page 1999; Scobey 2002).

Yet, seen in theoretical terms, large-scale, mixed-use urban redevelopment projects designed to enliven once-derelict downtown areas rely on the functional interdependence of property sectors for their success. The achievement of this functional interdependence, however, does not automatically take place through the operations of a frictionless market logic of supply and demand. Because investments in residential, commercial, retail, and entertainment sectors conform to different micrologics (with dissimilar temporal rhythms and time-horizons) that are often in conflict with each other, property development in downtown housing initiatives is freighted with uncertainty. The social, institutional, and place-specific qualities of real estate investment—or what Robert Beauregard (2005) calls the "thickness" of property markets— often create practical difficulties for revitalization efforts. Put specifically, such real-life frictions as sectoral differentiation, specialization, and competition for prime locations impede the fluidity of abstract property markets as they actually operate on the ground. As a consequence, the functional interdependence required for successful urban redevelopment largely depends on coordination and timing among local property sectors. Without this cooperation, even the best-laid plans can easily fall apart (Parker 2004, 104–105).

Imagining the Postindustrial Metropolis: The Sisyphean Task of Urban Regeneration

Always and everywhere, city building is a contradictory and uneven process, where competing logics intersect, overlap, and clash to produce an incongruous patchwork of urban artifacts layered—both literally and figuratively—on top of each other. Over the past several decades, Johannesburg has experienced a massive horizontal building boom of unprecedented proportions that has not only pushed the geographical boundaries of the metropolis away from its historic downtown core, but also triggered the metamorphosis of what were once out-of-the-way suburban places like Sandton, Midrand, and Fourways into genuine urbanized edge cities. This urbanization of suburbia marked the collapse of the conventional center-periphery model of urban growth and development. The massive expansion of high-rise corporate, financial, and commercial office buildings clustered in various nodal points in the northern suburbs has brought about a monumental shift in the socioeconomic center of gravity away from the Johannesburg central city (Bremner 2000, 187). During the 1970s, commercial life in the central city began to suffocate as the overuse of automobiles and the lack of off-street parking gridlocked the traffic flow on the narrow streetscape. What began as a trickle in the late 1970s gradually turned into a flood by the mid-1980s as large-scale business enterprises, giant mining houses, banks and other financial institutions, and real estate holding companies took flight from the downtown urban core, relocating their corporate office facilities to clean, safe, and secure enclaves in the rapidly urbanizing nodal points of the northern suburbs. The causes for this massive exodus of large-scale capitalist enterprises were complex and have been explored admirably elsewhere (Beavon 2004, 212–269; Goga 2003). As the Johannesburg central city relinquished its once-prominent place as the prime location for corporate business and finance, the built environment underwent a long and protracted process of decline, neglect, and abandonment that left decay and ruin in its wake. In short, it was this powerful combination of capital flight and disinvestment that tipped the scale from unstable dynamism to paralysis and locational stagnation (Tomlinson 1999a).

The spatial unevenness of the urban landscape is also registered in the divergent temporal rhythms of real estate capitalism. The speeding-up and slowing-down of real estate investments function as a kind of regulatory mechanism for city-building processes more generally. Caught between the vision of a vibrant city in constant flux and the fear of a motionless city in paralyzing stasis, real estate capitalism careens back and forth between accelerated investments in dynamic locations and decelerated disinvestments in stagnant ones. Uneven spatial development of the urban landscape has made slowness, or, rather "behindness," a penalty in the feverish global race for world-class status (Highmore 2002, 172, 173, 175).

As a contradictory process, city building goes hand in hand with the uneven development of the urban landscape that always and everywhere brings dynamism together with inertia, grand spectacle with decay and ruin, and boundary making with boundary breaking. The built environment of Johannesburg after apartheid consists of a jumbled mélange of monumental sites reflecting commercial vibrancy, civic refinement, and technological progress juxtaposed with abandoned spaces of perverse use, indifferent disregard, and wasteful neglect. The environmental and social disorders of the inner city— dilapidated buildings, failing infrastructure, criminality, lack of social services— were not the unfortunate result of the failure to keep pace with the march of progress. Rather, they were the result of city-building processes where the capitalist marketplace largely shaped the pace and character of investment decisions (see Scobey 2002, 153–154).

The driving force behind real estate capitalism, or profit-seeking investments in the built environment, is the relative advantage of location. The sheer exuberance attached to such new, hypermodern (or eclectic postmodern) extravagances as the five-star, Renaissance-style Michelangelo Hotel at Sandton Square, the Tuscan-style Montecasino leisure and entertainment site at Fourways, and the trendy, cosmopolitan experiments with new urbanism at Melrose Arch offers the mesmerizing spectacle of globalized consumerism under the full sway of market dominance (Dirsuweit and Schattauer 2004; Jaguaribe 1999, 298–299; Mbembe 2004, 373–405). These enclosed luxury enclaves set aside for affluent urban residents stand in stark contrast to the decaying built environment of the inner city. This spatial unevenness is the paradoxical outcome of the *interdependence* of the location market. Speculative investments in new locations operate in tandem with disinvestment in others. Unlike most commodities, the exchange value of urban locations is "almost completely relational, its price set by the larger geography of activities and contiguities in which it is embedded" (Scobey 2002, 145). The dynamism of real estate capitalism thus depends on the capacity of private investments in the built environment to generate sufficient commodity exchanges and commercial transactions to sustain its profitability. This paradoxical mixture of exclusiveness (where land is put to its "highest and best use") and locational interdependence enable land values to operate as a powerful arbiter of spatial transformation (Scobey 2002, 145). But these qualities also promote self-serving, blinkered, and economically perverse choices within the narrow confines of the real estate market. In seeking higher rates of return, real estate capitalism encourages speculative investments and improvements. Yet, in seeking to avoid financial losses, it promotes cost-cutting neglect, disinvestment, and eventual withdrawal (Scobey 2002, 144–164).

Blight (ghettoization) and renewal (gentrification) are thus the two faces of real estate capitalism. On the one hand, private investments in the built environment create locational advantages that establish favorable conditions for profitable returns. On the other hand, real estate is subject to disabilities that hinder it from responding quickly and fluently to market cues. The spatial inertia associated with fixed investments with long turnover time places constraints on continued profitability.[1] Put in theoretical terms, real estate capitalism relies on fixed capital investments embedded in specific places to create necessary conditions for its profitability, only to find that its fixity (or the specific geographical distribution of investments) restricts its mobility and thereby becomes an obstacle to ongoing capital accumulation. The ongoing tension between the volatility of frenzied competition for locational advantage and the paralyzing stagnation associated with past investments in place produces the chronic instability where the real estate market is under constant threat of devaluation (Harvey 1982, 393–395; Smith 1996, 58–62).

In the main, the theoretical analysis of urban regeneration has tended to focus narrowly on rehabilitation of the built environment as simply a welcome solution to urban blight. This one-sided, static view tends to ignore how neglect, disinvestment, and decline of urban space are actually necessary preconditions for renewal, gentrification, and displacement (Lees 2000; Smith 1996, 58–62). The contradictory dynamics of abandonment (or devaluation of fixed capital in the built environment) and gentrification (the restoration of value) are inextricably linked together as the conjoined outcomes of real estate capitalism (Deutsche 1996, 75).

As an essential part of their professional ethos, urban planners typically frame the disorderly city as a problem that can be solved through the application of the proper solution. Yet the "frictions of space" (Scobey 2002, 134–135) cannot be simply reduced to merely a matter of unfinished progress calling for efficient intervention. Put in strictly theoretical terms, urban blight is caused less by the incompleteness of city-building efforts than by its contradictory effects. Urban blight, decay, and decline are the results of city-building processes, the byproducts of urban transformation. City-building processes under the rule of real estate capitalism by themselves reinforce the uneven development of the urban landscape (Scobey 2002, 142, 144, 145–146).

As a discourse grounded in a vision of the better future, urban regeneration locates the creative destruction of urban space within the grand narratives of material progress, uninterrupted growth, and civic improvement. Whether large or small, urban renewal campaigns represent not only actual modifications in the physical form of the cityscape but also symbolic interventions that

---

1. Private ownership of land confers near-monopoly control over the use of property and the nature of improvements, thereby putting into motion a kind of path dependency that fixes land use. The fixity of investments in place prevents redevelopment from occurring until invested capital has expended its economic life. The long turnover time required to realize profitability discourages further development. Taken together, these characteristics create barriers to capital accumulation in the built environment. For the source of these ideas, see Smith (1996, 58–62).

naturalize and justify disruptions of the prevailing status quo (Blomley 2004, 86–87). As a complicated process without end, the repetitive cycle of building and rebuilding of the urban landscape plays itself out on the shifting terrain of power and ideology. The choice and implementation of different visions of urban renewal highlights the tension between market forces at the heart of real estate capitalism and city planning efforts that have sought to direct capitalist investment to particular ends. While physical demolition has often been seen as the inevitable, natural solution to the vexing problem of metastasizing slums, the story of the creative destruction of dilapidated buildings is in fact quite complex. Low-income tenants in desperate need of inexpensive accommodation, property owners seeking to squeeze profits from past investments in decaying buildings, and city officials wishing to revitalize dead space are locked in bitter struggles over rival visions of whose right to the city trumps the others. These battles over how to deal with decaying buildings unfit for human habitation reveal not only the fault lines in the attitudes of affluent city dwellers toward the urban poor, but also the failure of the private real estate market to regulate itself (Page 1999, 12, 72; Scobey 2002).

During the course of the meteoric rise of Johannesburg from impermanent mining camp to aspirant world-class city, successive waves of city building have recast the urban landscape in ways that the early town planners who laid out the original orthogonal street grid could never have imagined. Figuratively speaking, downtown revitalization represents only the tip of the iceberg: it is the topographical surface appearance of a deeper structural transformation that has involved not only the spatial restructuring of the urban landscape but also a marked shift in the center of economic gravity away from mining and manufacturing and toward services and consumption. Until the 1980s, when capital flight stripped the central city of a substantial proportion of corporate headquarters office buildings, banking and financial establishments, and high-end commercial and retail outlets, downtown Johannesburg resembled the quintessential industrial city of large-scale capitalist enterprise geared toward mining, manufacturing, banking, and finance. In contrast, city builders after apartheid have envisioned the birth of a new kind of postindustrial city, where the ethos of consumption, recreation, and leisure supersedes the diligent habits of work and industry (Beall, Crankshaw, and Parnell 2002, 29–44; Tomlinson et al. 2003, 3–20).

Urban regeneration is always a complex story that involves money and location. In the untamed imagination of some postapartheid urban planners, the Johannesburg future city resembles San Francisco, London, or Tokyo, where the expansion of the gentrification frontier produces a heterodox mixture of middle-class residential areas; concentrated zones of professional, administrative, and managerial employment; small-scale manufacturing and artisanal production; and up-market recreational and entertainment facilities that cater to affluent consumers. Borrowing from the "shrinking cities" paradigm advocated by such new urbanist theorists as Witold Rybczynski, city builders have envisioned an incremental restructuring of downtown Johannesburg that involves abandoning the pipe dream of ever revitalizing the central business district as the principal location for corporate headquarters office buildings. The "shrinking cities" model entails managing the contraction of the historic central business district to an area concentrated at the southwestern corner around Marshall and Main streets. It also means the promotion of new uses for old spaces, particularly the conversion of modernist office blocks into residential buildings, the encouragement of small-scale manufacturing (such as specialized jewelry and fashion districts), and the substitution of pedestrian-friendly streets for modernist-inspired thoroughfares catering almost exclusively to automobile traffic.[2]

Borrowing from design motifs and successful urban regeneration strategies emanating from cities in North America and Europe, pioneering property developers in Johannesburg have begun to retrofit historic, grand, and majestic office buildings in the central city with luxury apartments, condominiums, and spacious lofts for affluent newcomers. Urban planners have unveiled ambitious schemes for boutiques, restaurants, and outdoor cafes to lure middle-class consumers back to the central city. Despite countervailing pressures, city officials have largely embraced an ethos of urban regeneration with only fleeting regard for the urban poor whose presence as residents of deteriorating buildings stands in the way of progress.[3]

The Perverse Logic of the Slumlord Economy: The Temporal and Spatial Rhythms of the Building Cycle

> [Building hijacking] is the quickest and easiest way of
> making millions of rands. [Building hijackers] are making
> the city ungovernable.
>
> PROPERTY CONSULTANT WHO ASKED TO REMAIN ANONYMOUS

Conventional theories of urban transformation typically portray the metamorphosis of cities through the juxtaposition of a series of time-lapse photographs, the then-and-now comparisons or before-and-after contrasts, depicting

---

2. Interview with Neil Fraser, Urban Inc., Urban Consultants, May 29, 2006. See also Colin Hossack, "Next Generation Jo'burg—Africa's San Francisco?" JOBURG, City of Johannesburg Official Website, http://www.joburg.org.za/feb_2002/2030.stm, February 21, 2002.

3. Danielle de Jager, "Finesse in the District," *Business Day*, August 20, 2004; and Janice Healing, "Inner-City Blues Starting to Lift," *Business Times*, April 4, 2005.

the urban landscape as something akin to a living organism moving forward over time in accordance with a natural cycle of growth and development.[4] Despite the elegance and parsimony of this formulation, this simple, linear narrative of organic growth and development tends to ignore, overlook, or obscure the convulsive (two steps forward, one step back) cycles of creative destruction and intentional rebuilding of the cityscape. Urban transformation is a contradictory and uneven process in which the alternating dynamics of growth and stagnation, development and decline, and expansion and contraction operate in tandem. Rather than looking on the disorder and chaos that accompany the growth and development of cities as the accidental effects or dysfunctional byproducts of urban transformation, it is much more fruitful to understand these debilitating traits, or "frictions of space" (Scobey 2002, 134–135), as integral components of city-building processes. Put in another way, contraction, stagnation, and decay are as central to the dynamics of real estate capitalism as growth, development, and expansion. Each reinforces the other. This mutual dependence of apparent opposite impulses lies at the heart of the city-building process (Scobey 2002, 143–146; Page 1999, 23–35). The city can be, at one and the same time, orderly and disorderly, stable and unstable, vibrant and moribund, or, as Rem Koolhaas (1994, 20) has put it in describing Manhattan, "a metropolis of rigid chaos."

The Johannesburg inner city includes the central business district; the dense concentration of office blocks in Braamfontein at the northern edge; the high-density residential neighborhoods of Berea, Joubert Park, and Hillbrow; the lower-density eastern residential neighborhoods of Yeoville, Bertrams, Lorentzville, Troyeville, Judith's Paarl, Doornfontein, and New Doornfontein; City Deep to the south; and the western areas of Newtown, Fordsburg, Pageview, Mayfair, Mayfair West, and Vrededorp. Residential properties vary from freestanding, owner-occupied homes to medium-density blocks of flats and high-rise apartment complexes. Ownership of residential property in the Johannesburg inner city is divided along a broad continuum, ranging from large-scale real estate holding companies with extensive holdings in apartment blocks with multiple rental units—like Trafalgar Properties and the thirty (or so) other large-scale property-owning groups organizationally linked under the auspices of the South African Property Owners Association (SAPOA)—to small-scale individual entrepreneurs, like retirees or pensioners, who rent a house or a building to a few tenants in order to supplement their incomes.[5]

---

4. Epigraph is from a property consultant quoted in Anna Cox, "Property Hijackers Coining Millions in Joburg," *The Star*, April 5, 2005.

5. Trafalgar Properties, *The Trafalgar Inner City Report 2004* (unpublished pamphlet, pp. 1–13); and interview with Andrew Schaefer, managing director, Trafalgar Property Management, June 5, 2006.

The residential heartland consists of the eight neighborhoods that are collectively referred to as Zone 4: Hillbrow, Berea, Yeoville, Lorentzville, Troyeville, Judith's Paarl, Bertrams, and Doornfontein. Over the past two decades, Zone 4 has experienced a downward spiral of neglect, abandonment, and decline. As white middle-class residents have abandoned inner-city residential neighborhoods for what they considered safe and secure suburbs elsewhere, increasing numbers of low-income newcomers, overwhelmingly young, black jobholders or work seekers, particularly immigrants from across the African continent, have taken their place. The mounting pressure of new arrivals in desperate need of low-cost shelter has taken place alongside the physical deterioration of existing housing stock. The physical decline of the built environment originated in the once-fashionable residential neighborhoods of Hillbrow, Berea, and Joubert Park, quickly metastasized, and spread outward, engulfing Jeppestown and Malvern at the southeastern corner and moving inexorably eastward through Bertrams, Troyeville, Judith's Paarl, and into Bezuidenhout Valley. At the western edge of the central city, the early warning signs of inner-city blight have appeared in deteriorating neighborhoods around Mayfair, Brixton, and Fordsburg. Slumlords have invaded declining places like Vrededorp, Pageview, Vredepark, and Jan Hofmeyr, subdividing vacant houses that not too long ago were owned by Afrikaans-speaking white families and renting them to several families at around R300 per room.[6] South of the vast unpeopled mining belt, the lower middle-class neighborhoods of Turffontein and West Turffontein (which served at one time as the main point of entry for Portuguese-speaking whites into the greater Johannesburg metropolitan region) have fallen on hard times. The once-stable residential neighborhood of Rosettenville has degenerated into such a "cesspit of crack houses, druglords, and prostitutes" that some cynical observers have rechristened it "Rottenville."[7]

From 1999 to late 2004 the number of identifiable "bad buildings" in the inner city almost doubled, increasing from 120 to 235.[8] According to the Trafalgar Inner City Report for 2004, an estimated 25 percent of residential buildings in Zone 4 were in an "extremely poor," "very poor," or "poor" state of repair.[9] Municipal housing officials attributed a great deal of this deterioration

6. Lizeka Mda, "Making a Standing in Vrededorp," *Mail & Guardian,* March 1–6, 1998; and Noor-Jehan Yoro Badat, "'Brixton Will Not Become Another Hillbrow,'" *The Star,* May 25, 2003.

7. Shaun Smillie, "'Rottenville' Moves to Reclaim Its Streets," *The Star,* March 28, 2005; on-site visit with Graeme Gotz, Corporate Planning Unit, Office of City Manager, City of Johannesburg, June 3, 2006; and on-site visit with Kuben Govender, Trust for Urban Housing Finance (TUHF), June 6, 2006.

8. A "bad building" is one that has deteriorated to such an extent that its market value is below the outstanding debt owed. The term is commonly used by Johannesburg municipal authorities.

9. In a survey of seventy-two inner city properties conducted in September 2003, city officials identified nineteen as "bad buildings." Extrapolating from these figures, city bylaw enforcement

of residential housing stock to several causes, including flat hijacking, where unauthorized individuals seize control of derelict buildings abandoned by their owners and demand payments from residents; building invasions, where homeless squatters have opportunistically occupied vacant properties; and subletting, where tenants invite expanding numbers of newcomers to sublet rooms, thus severely overcrowding the premises and overloading the building infrastructure.[10]

In the real estate market, location and timing mean everything. Steady deterioration of the built environment has paradoxically encouraged property owners to withhold land from its "highest and best use," either by extracting immediate gain from it without enhancing its physical or locational value, or abandoning it altogether. Seen in this way, slum making cannot be rationalized as the unwanted byproduct of market failure or inefficiency, or even lagged development (requiring time to catch up). Instead, slum-making is a process that must be understood as part and parcel of the contradictory dynamics of real estate capitalism itself. Faced with sagging market demand and shrinking profits, residential property owners within the capitalist marketplace have no choice but to shift their buildings to alternative uses, as once-elegant hotels have given way to no-frills, short-stay boardinghouses catering to low-income transient work seekers, as upscale apartment blocs are converted into over-crowded tenements, and as trendy nightclubs metamorphose into gritty bars and pool halls, seedy brothels, and drug dens (Leggett 2001, 122–152).[11]

The failure of the real estate market to create and sustain decent and affordable residential accommodation for low-income residents of the inner city has spawned a largely underground "slumlord economy" of absentee ownership, overcrowding, rack-renting, and building hijacking—where property owners have frequently stopped making repairs and paying taxes or bonds and where tenants have stopped paying rent and making payments for municipal services like water and electricity. In the whirlwind world of intense competition directed at satisfying the persistent demand for cheap residential accommodation, this destructive dynamic of slumlordism has reproduced itself and thrived on the margins of urban respectability. Put in strictly economic terms, the slumlord economy has opened up all sorts of opportunities that

personnel estimated that close to 30 percent of inner-city buildings needed to be cleared of tenants and either refurbished or demolished. See Peter Honey, "The Man Who Is Trying to Bring Down an Elephant," *Financial Mail*, October 10, 2003; and *The Trafalgar Inner City Report 2004*.

10. Christina Gallagher, "Slumlords Invade Johannesburg," *The Star*, February 5, 2005; Trafalgar Properties, *The Trafalgar Inner City Report 2005* (unpublished pamphlet, pp. 4–5); and interview with Geoff Mendelowitz, program manager, Better Buildings Programme, City of Johannesburg Property Company, June 2, 2006.

11. Information derived from interview with Kuben Govender, Trust for Urban Housing Finance (TUHF), June 6, 2006, but the ideas expressed here are mine alone.

have enabled crafty entrepreneurs, located both inside and outside formal legal authority, to extract huge profits from the captive poor who are desperate enough to pay to live in overcrowded, unhealthy, and unsafe conditions. Unregulated markets provide advantages to skillful, unscrupulous entrepreneurs to tap into these sources of perverse profitability. Slumlords have encouraged the overcrowding of residential buildings, since they charge rent per occupant instead of per flat. By reducing maintenance and repairs to a bare minimum or eliminating them altogether, absentee landlords have also been able to squeeze the last drops of profits out of decaying, dying buildings before abandoning them altogether. Abandonment has opened up opportunities for enterprising individuals—who typically call themselves management agents and claim to be operating at the behest of unknown property owners—to hijack buildings from their lawful owners, diverting rental payments into their own pockets.[12] These con artists—"agents provocateurs," as one frustrated property lawyer referred to them—typically use the promise of reduced rent to lure frightened and unsuspecting residents into making rental payments to them without ever intending to pay municipal service fees for water and electricity.[13]

City officials have complained bitterly that crafty entrepreneurs have wrested control out of the hands of lawful owners of properties by approaching tenants and, "by paying a fraction of the rent they would to the legitimate landlord," persuading them that "they can get their water and electricity for free."[14] With their rental income diverted into the hands of these building hijackers, lawful owners have often stopped paying municipal service charges and making bond payments. Faced with the absence of income from their property investments and with the prospect of an expensive and time-consuming process of eviction of tenants, frustrated owners have sometimes simply abandoned their properties to the vagaries of circumstance.[15] Wily

12. Anna Cox, "My Building Has Been Hijacked," *The Star*, September 29, 2004.

13. Property lawyer is quoted in David Pincus, "Law Is Not on Landlords' Side," *The Star*, February 5, 2005; and on-site visit to inner-city buildings with George Chauke, Better Buildings Programme, City of Johannesburg Property Company, June 7, 2006.

14. Quotations from Christina Gallagher, "Slumlords Invade Johannesburg."

15. While forcible evictions of impoverished residents have become a frequent occurrence, the actual process in individual cases is expensive and time consuming. Evictions require that a court order be served on tenants. It takes time for municipal authorities to subcontract the services of private security firms to assist in the actual process of removing occupants before the work of removal can begin. All in all, the process can take as long as six months. Evictions can cost much more than the property is worth. For an average-sized family home, the removal of unlawful tenants can cost the city as much as R30,000 to enlist the services of a subcontracting private security company appointed by the sheriff of the court. The municipality can incur added financial burden of R30,000 for the cost of legal services. In addition to legal fees, it can cost as much as R1 million to evict residents from larger properties, such as a block of flats. See Christina Gallagher, "Slumlords Invade Johannesburg"; and David Pincus, "Law Is Not on Landlords' Side."

entrepreneurs who have hijacked residential properties typically transform the buildings into what amount to rent farms, subdividing rooms into tiny cubicles and squeezing as many occupants into these cramped spaces as possible and charging exorbitant rates.[16] More ominously, criminal gangs have also seized abandoned buildings, transforming them into warehouses for stolen goods, houses of prostitution, key centers for drug trafficking, and havens for illegal immigrants. In addition, drug lords have gained access to what are called "sleazy hotels," using them as launching pads for all sorts of criminal enterprises (Leggett 2001, 122–152).

Building hijacking has blossomed into perhaps the greatest single obstacle standing in the way of municipal efforts to rejuvenate the inner city. By 2006 the sinister practice had become so widespread that it threatened, in the words of a property consultant who borrowed a popular phrase coined during the height of the antiapartheid struggle, "to make the city ungovernable." Hindered by limited cash resources and available personnel, municipal law enforcement agencies were unable to respond quickly enough to prevent its spread. The shadowy syndicates that were behind the upsurge of building hijackings turned the practice into a "multimillion rand business."[17]

As a collective practice outside the law, building hijacking was ingenious and cunning in its simplicity. Hijacking syndicates, which have highly organized, coherent chains of command, monitor all the empty buildings scattered around the inner city. They also employ "touts," individuals who monitor the main bus and train gateways into the inner city, luring new arrivals with the promise that, if they "pitch up" (i.e., show up) at a particular place at a specific time, they can obtain a rental unit in an unoccupied residential building. When the time is right, they send in busloads of armed gangs into vacant

---

See also Zukile Mancunga and Anneliese Burgess, directors of television news program, "Slums," *SABC Special Assignment,* June 20, 2000. Information for this and the following paragraphs derived from interview with Kuben Govender.

16. One property agent acting on behalf of an absentee owner who lived in Australia charged that slumlords had unlawfully seized the property, renting out tiny rooms with no toilet facilities at an exorbitant rate of R400 per month "for a space that could take only a mattress and a chair." See Anna Cox, "My Building Has Been Hijacked"; and interview with Geoff Mendelowitz. See also David Pincus, "Law Is Not on Landlords' Side"; and Anna Cox, "Property Hijackers Coining Millions in Joburg."

17. A knowledgeable property consultant claimed that syndicates were able to reap profits of up to R10 million a month, but there is no way to assess the accuracy of these figures. It was also believed that the head of the main syndicate is the brother of a well-known politician, who works with his attorney wife. Quotations and information derived from Anna Cox, "Property Hijackers Coining Millions." See also Phomello Molwedi, "Building-Hijack Probe Runs Deep, Says State," *The Star,* November 1, 2006.

buildings, threaten private security guards with firearms (if necessary), and then begin renting rooms to unsuspecting tenants at R500 to R600 per month. Local agents living in the commandeered buildings collect rent for six to eight months, knowing that the legal system is painstakingly slow and that, by the time the lawful owners obtain eviction orders, they will have reaped enormous profits. When law enforcement agencies finally get around to carrying out the eviction orders, they "simply walk away," leaving the evicted tenants to fend for themselves on the streets.[18]

Frustrated property owners have complained that the odious practice of building hijacking has gained momentum in the inner city.[19] With the number of hijacked buildings in the inner city steadily increasing to well over fifty by 2006, desperate landlords have complained that even well-managed and fully occupied buildings were at risk. As the vicious cycle of building hijackings continued to confound city officials, the inevitable process of slum-making appeared to spread into previously untouched areas, producing a downward spiral of neglect and deterioration of residential buildings. Property developers with considerable holdings in inner-city residential neighborhoods alleged that at least one building in almost every street in Yeoville, Berea, Hillbrow, Troyeville, Bertrams, Bezuidenhout Valley, Jeppestown, Rosettenville,

18. Another variant of the building hijacking scam is for syndicates to plant people inside the building as faux tenants who begin to systematically destroy the building. According to one property consultant, "they break pipes, smash windows, damage doors, and start inciting tenants, playing the race card. They tell tenants that the white owners are not interested in them and are exploiting them." In time the perpetrators form an erstwhile tenants' committee; on behalf of the committee these agents acquire signing powers on banks accounts and begin collecting rents. Initially the leaders do cosmetic repairs to give the impression of their good will. But thereafter, "they carry on collecting rentals without doing anything else, before disappearing [with the money]." In the end, the lawful owner is left with the costs of obtaining an eviction order, which ranges from R200,000 to R360,000 depending on the number of people who have to be removed. Quotation in text and information derived from Anna Cox, "Property Hijackers Coining Millions"; and Poloko Tau and Anna Cox, "Property Hijackers Threaten to Raze Building," *The Star*, April 5, 2005. Information for this and the following paragraph derived from interview with Geoff Mendelowitz; and interview with Lael Bethlehem, chief executive officer, Johannesburg Development Agency, City of Johannesburg, 30 May 2006. According to one journalistic account, residents of the Avril Malan building on the corner of Sauer and Commissioner streets in the heart of the provincial government precinct paid rent ranging from R400 to R1,000 per month. These rates are truly astronomical for a place of residence that was described as a cesspit and "the most disgusting building in Johannesburg." Ironically, the Avril Malan building, which was illegally converted from an office block into residential accommodation, is "flanked by the provincial departments of local government and housing—which shares its building with the provincial Department of Health." See Noor-Jehan Yoro Badat, "A Cesspool in the Middle of Joburg," *Saturday Star*, January 20, 2007.

19. *The Trafalgar Inner City* Report 2004. Information also derived from interview with Geoff Mendelowitz.

Turffontein, and Booysens had been hijacked. By 2007, the situation had reached such a low point that hijacking groups were turning their attention to already hijacked buildings. There is sufficient circumstantial evidence to suggest that international crime syndicates were using these buildings for drug-dealing and prostitution. Many city officials involved in investigating the syndicates and in arranging evictions resorted to permanently posting personal security guards at their homes because of death threats. One of the two main syndicates—the Isolabantu National Social Imbalances Movement—operates in the inner city and the eastern suburbs. The other focuses on residential neighborhoods, like Rosettenville and Turffontein, to the south of the central city. In looking into the modus operandi of these hijacking syndicates, it seemed clear that they were able to obtain fraudulent documents, like eviction orders, title deeds, official letterheads, and utilities bills, from their contacts in various municipal offices. Even though residents trapped in these hijacked buildings have repeatedly lodged complaints about their mistreatment, they have said that the police have provided little or no protection.[20]

The court proceedings initiated against two police inspectors assigned to the Hillbrow housing anti-hijacking task team provide an unusual glimpse into the shadowy world of building hijacking syndicates and how they operate. According to prosecution charges filed against Sean Twala and Tello Motu, these two men colluded with "gangster landlords" and "hitmen" to hijack dozens of buildings over a three-year period in such widely dispersed places as the central business district, Hillbrow, Turffontein, Yeoville, Kenilworth, and Bertrams. Part of their duties as members of the police anti-hijack task team was to prevent the illegal occupation of buildings and to track down building hijackers. But according to police investigators, the two men evicted illegal tenants from buildings, sometimes by falsifying eviction orders and enlisting the support of unsuspecting fellow officers to remove occupants. But instead of handing the buildings back to their legitimate owners, they moved in their own tenants and collected rents, which they pocketed for themselves.[21]

Responsible landlords—that is, those who have properly maintained and serviced their properties—have sought to distance themselves from the so-called

20. Quotation from Anna Cox, "Joburg Falls Victim to Building Hijackers," *The Star,* June 5, 2007. See also Anna Cox, "Owner Threatened in 'Bid to Hijack Building'," *The Star,* August 1, 2006; *The Star,* "Who Runs the Elusive Syndicate?" June 6, 2007; and *The Star,* "Modus Operandi: 1," June 6, 2007.

21. Quotations from Lee Rondganger, "Cops Allegedly Involved in Building-Hijacks," *Saturday Star,* September 23, 2006. See also Lee Rondganger, "Charges Pile Up against Alleged Corrupt Cop," *The Star,* July 31, 2007; and Phomello Molwedi, "Building-Hijack Probe Runs Deep, Says State." Information also derived from interview with Graeme Gotz.

slumlords. On the one side, they have welcomed the crackdown on the slum-lord economy and have praised municipal efforts to close down "bad build-ings," to clear out crime dens, and to evict illegal squatters. On the other hand, they have complained bitterly about bureaucratic sluggishness, about the reluctance of law enforcement officials to respond to problems with irre-sponsible tenants, and about housing regulations that favor the legal rights of tenants over their own as property owners.[22] Faced with the threat of building hijacking by occupants who stop paying rent, residential property owners who lease buildings to new occupants have resorted to the drastic tactic of demand-ing a substantial deposit and an initial payment to cover the first six months' rent. This practice has disproportionately hurt poor urban residents who typi-cally live from month to month.[23]

Ironically, the deterioration of the built environment has created numer-ous opportunities for illicit property scams. Amid great fanfare, municipal authorities have initiated a campaign (under the auspices of the Better Build-ings Programme) that, using forfeiture laws, is aimed at seizing dilapidated buildings whose lawful owners were desperately in arrears on municipal ser-vice payments. Once they have obtained the properties and removed the un-lawful occupants, city officials have placed the buildings on the auction block for resale to new owners with the stipulation that they make regular payments for municipal services, rehabilitate the buildings, and rent only to responsi-ble tenants. Much to their chagrin, housing authorities have discovered that this seemingly sensible rehabilitation strategy has sometimes inadvertently backfired. With only rudimentary background checks, valid identification documents, and a small 10 percent down payment, wily entrepreneurs have purchased run-down buildings at bargain-basement prices. With no intention of improving or repairing their properties, these slumlords quickly regain the initial outlay for the residential buildings and "never make another payment." When city officials step forward to collect the remainder of the promised pay-ment, they abandon the properties, triggering the renewal of a further cycle of property devaluation.[24]

22. *South African Press Association (SAPA)*, "Rental Act the 'Landlord's Best Friend,'" August 1, 2000. Information also derived from interview with Andrew Schaefer.

23. David Pincus, "Law Is Not on Landlords' Side"; Anna Cox, "Don't Look to SA to Invest, Warn Landlords," *The Star*, February 21, 2005; and Anna Cox, "Landlords to Ask for Bigger Deposits," *The Star*, October 8, 2004.

24. "[These slumlords] usually enlist people off the streets who are looking for work and who have little chance of being disturbed by bad credit. These people bid on the [dilapidated] houses, pay 10 percent, and the slumlord rents out the property" (Christina Gallagher, "Slumlords In-vade Johannesburg"). Information also derived from interview with Geoff Mendelowitz. See also Anna Cox, "'I Would Not Harm My Brothers,'" *The Star*, June 28, 2007; and Lynley Donnelly and Kwanele Sosibo, "Slumlords Cripple Inner City," *Mail & Guardian*, February 1–7, 2007.

Stemming the Tide of Inner-City Decay: The Opposing Dynamics of Inner-City Regeneration Strategies

> The first prescription for slum dwellers in the ghettos of
> the big cities is total, immediate, uncompromising surgical
> removal....When you operate in an over-built metropolis, you
> have to hack your way with a meat ax.
> ROBERT MOSES (1970, 468; CARO 1974, 849)

As a general rule, it is possible to distinguish between two analytically distinctive modes of thought—one creative and the other destructive—that have motivated opposing approaches to the housing question for low-income residents of the inner city (Page 1999, 70–71, 80). The creative impulse has constructed the housing problem within the framework of what Paul Boyer (1978, 123–133) has called "positive environmentalism": the starting point for dealing with the lack of decent, affordable residential accommodation for the worst-off urban residents begins with making improvements to the physical environment and with providing the kinds of amenities and social services required to sustain a satisfactory urban life. In contrast, the destructive impulse has viewed deteriorating inner-city housing through the demonizing lens of "negative environmentalism": the presumption that the protection and preservation of the orderly urban landscape requires the elimination of what is unhealthy in the city, just as a trained surgeon would remove a diseased part of a body in the interests of safeguarding the whole person (Page 1999, 70). At root, this ongoing tension between creative and destructive impulses reflects not only divergent institutional attitudes toward the urban poor and their rightful place in the city, but also opposing visions of the Johannesburg future city. These opposing modes of thought rely on different sets of images—and an accompanying vocabulary—to construct what cultural geographers call "shared mental maps" of the urban landscape. On the one side, the creative impulse relies on an image of the urban poor as hapless (and even helpless) victims of environmental circumstances beyond their control, and it takes the view that modifying the physical and social environment has the capability of transforming urban residents for the better. On the other side, the destructive impulse rests on the belief that inner-city slums have become breeding grounds for an agglomeration of urban evils, ranging from incivility, interpersonal violence, and substance abuse to disease, crime, and vice. Rather than locating the source of these problems with the environment that the slumlord economy has engendered, this mode of thought tends to place the blame for these deplorable conditions on the self-destructive and sometimes unlawful behavior of the inner-city residents themselves.[25]

---

25. As Page (1999, 78–79, 80–82) explains it, the destructive impulse rests on the presumption that it is just as important to eliminate unhealthy, crime-ridden places as it is to build better ones.

In theory and in principle, these conflicting modes of thought offer one-sided portraits of inner-city life and, as such, are ultimately irreconcilable. In practice, however, these two approaches sometimes overlap and reinforce each other, and their differences have been relatively easy to disguise and ignore. The institutional thinking that guides the implementation of housing policies for the inner-city poor has frequently moved back and forth between the two. The actual translation into action of the creative and destructive impulses has often turned out to be more a matter of emphasis than of substance. City officials have often used a dubious blend of the two positions to justify forced removals of low-income residents from dilapidated inner-city apartment buildings as an act of compassion because it has extricated vulnerable urban residents from the viselike grip of avaricious slumlords. The fact is that the logical incoherence contained in this way of thinking is relatively easy to overlook in the presence of a collective fantasy and myth. The faith that city officials have placed in forcibly evicting occupants from run-down buildings declared unfit for human habitation rests on the one-sided belief that slum-clearances would unleash the powerful impulses of inner-city regeneration whose benefits would eventually trickle down to the urban poor. Closing down "bad buildings" deprives slumlords of ill-gotten gain, but it also dumps impoverished people onto the streets with nowhere to go. Even though these policies have been couched in the pious idiom of progress and improvement, they effectively amount to an assault on the urban poor because they offer no realistic alternative for breaking the cycle of poverty epitomized by inadequate shelter and lack of formal employment.[26]

In the immediate aftermath of the transition to parliamentary democracy, the creative impulse dominated institutional ways of thinking about inner-city housing for the urban poor (Dirsuweit 1999). Flushed with the progressive zeal that came with the end of white minority rule and animated by the clarion call for rapid reconstruction and development, intellectuals, activists, and urban planners alike dreamed of new ways of making city life in the sprawling metropolis of Johannesburg a healthier, safer, more pleasant and inviting environment for all its residents, especially those who had been denied citizenship rights under white minority rule (see Page 1999, 70). Borrowing such contemporary urban planning motifs as the compact city, the sustainable city, and the integrated city, Johannesburg officials embarked on a far-reaching program of urban restructuring that aimed at not only reversing the structural imbalances of the apartheid city planning but also putting into motion new dynamics

---

26. Interview with Stuart Wilson, Centre for Applied Legal Studies, University of the Witwatersrand, June 7, 2006. For a detailed description of how these interwoven dynamics have played themselves out in practice, see du Plessis and Wilson (2005, 35–36).

that would close the income gap between the very rich and the very poor, rehabilitate and upgrade the marginal zones of the metropolitan landscape, and organically link parts of the urban landscape that had been artificially separated from one another as a consequence of racial segregation policies (Pieterse 2003, 2004; Robinson 1996). Brimming with confidence and optimism, early postapartheid inner-city housing authorities put in motion ambitious plans aimed at tackling the slumlord economy and ridding the inner city of indecent, insalubrious residential accommodation. City officials mounted various campaigns couched in the rhetoric of progressive reform and designed to promote a safe and healthy environment in inner-city residential areas (see Beall, Crankshaw, and Parnell 2002, 114–128).

Amid great fanfare, city officials launched their much-publicized social-housing initiatives in 1996. Hailed as the panacea to stem the tide of inner-city degeneration, social-housing schemes offered an alternative to outright private ownership or rental. But the rise and fall of the most celebrated of these programs—the Seven Buildings Project—provide a useful illustration of the difficulties of reconciling the goals of maintaining and upgrading inner-city housing stock with the cost-recovery principles that govern the capitalist marketplace.[27] Inaugurated in 1996 and greeted as the prototype for future co-operative housing developments, this R6-million initiative, designed to counteract the reluctance of large-scale commercial banks to finance low-income housing ownership in the inner-city, faltered almost from the start. Burdened with a complex management structure and occupied by low-income tenants who were unable to keep up their scheduled payments, five of the seven buildings had defaulted on their loans by 2002.[28]

The collapse of the Seven Buildings Project sealed the fate of social-housing programs modeled on cooperative ownership schemes for low-income residents. One by one, inner-city housing projects of this particular kind fell apart under the combined weight of nonpayment, mismanagement, inability to obtain loans, and simmering tensions between creditors and

27. See Anna Cox, "'Model' Housing Scheme Set to Crumble," *The Star,* March 7, 2000; and *The Star,* "Housing Plan Crumbling," May 30, 2001. The seven blocks of flats from which the Seven Buildings Project acquired its name are spread out among the Johannesburg inner-city neighborhoods of Hillbrow, Joubert Park, and Berea, and they make up approximately a third of all residential blocks in this precinct. In 1996 the Gauteng Provincial Housing Board agreed to allow the estimated two thousand tenants of these seven apartment buildings to become owners of the approximately 446 residential units in which they were living. This policy decision marked the successful completion of an almost six-year battle by the tenants for ownership of their homes and the beginning of cooperative housing programs in the Johannesburg inner city. See Cull (2001, 43–49); and SAPA, "2000 Johannesburg Families Face Eviction," *Financial Times,* May 28, 2001.

28. Vickie Robinson, "Policy Stumbles on Reality," *Mail & Guardian,* July 18–24, 2003.

borrowers.[29] Yet with such pent-up demand for moderate and low-income residential accommodation in the inner city, city officials turned to an alternative model in which social-housing units were owned or managed by institutional housing companies that offered security of tenure for relatively low monthly rental rates.[30] By adopting operational principles based on strict cost-recovery guidelines, the nonprofit Johannesburg Housing Company (JHC) filled the void for social housing. Jump-started with significant financing from the European Union in the mid-1990s, the JHC went on an extensive buying spree, purchasing existing blocks of flats and upgrading them, buying derelict hotels and converting them into housing units, and acquiring vacant land in the inner city and developing townhouse complexes there.[31]

The social-housing initiatives pioneered by the JHC exemplify the creative approach to meeting the needs for low-cost housing in the inner city. The JHC has adopted an approach toward residential accommodation for low-income city-dwellers that rests on three principles: by identifying where low-income residents want to live, social-housing schemes offer locational advantage; by carefully monitoring the premises, they ensure safe and secure environments; and through cross-subsidizing those households least able to pay, they provide good value for the money.[32] As an alternative to the powerful voices that call for the summary eviction of illegal squatters and demolition of "bad buildings," social-housing programs have substituted a philosophy that stresses the rehabilitation of decaying buildings as a means to both reshape the aesthetics of downtown and provide stable, safe, and decent residential accommodation at affordable prices for those trapped on the lower rungs of the housing ladder.[33]

In its ten-year existence, the JHC has succeeded in acquiring and refurbishing twenty-one separate buildings with an estimated 2,700 units accommodating

29. Out of the eight inner-city housing schemes that were introduced in the heady days immediately following the demise of apartheid, only one achieved the desired success. See Bongiwe Mlangeni, "Faltering Phoenixes," *Sunday Times*, January 12, 2003.

30. Vickie Robinson, "Policy Stumbles on Reality."

31. The JHC has functioned as an integral part of a complex public-private partnership involving such key players as the National Housing Finance Corporation, the Gauteng Department of Housing and Land Affairs, Anglo-American and Anglo Gold, ABSA, and ApexHi Properties. See Don Robertson, "Giving Downtown an Upbeat Outlook," *Sunday Times*, May 30, 2004.

32. Information for this and the following paragraphs derived from interview with Taffy Adler. The JHC is the only social-housing agency that has successfully garnered funding from private investors. In 2000, ABSA Bank and J. P. Morgan granted an R11 million loan with subsidized interest rates for a JHC residential development. This event marked the first time that a social-housing institution was able to obtain a loan since the large banks began redlining the inner city in the early 1990s. See Vickie Robinson, "Policy Stumbles on Reality"; see also Johannesburg Housing Company, *Landmarks and Learnings: 10 Years of the Johannesburg Housing Company* (Marshalltown: Johannesburg Housing Company, 2005).

33. Interview with Taffy Adler.

over eight thousand qualified buyers and low-income renters, thereby adding 8 percent to the residential stock of the inner city. The management and
maintenance of this substantial property portfolio has transformed the JHC
into one of the largest residential landlords in the inner city, overseeing a far-
flung geographical empire stretching from Troyeville and Jeppestown in the
east to Joubert Park and Hillbrow at the northeast corner and to Newtown
and Fordsburg in the west. While turnover is brisk, the occupancy rates have
remained high.[34]

Prices for inner-city properties have risen sharply over the past several years,
as private real estate developers, social-housing companies, and speculators
have joined in the fierce competition to acquire desirable buildings for conversion to residential accommodation.[35] Ironically, social-housing companies
like JHC have become the victims of their own success. Whereas in 1996–1997
three-quarters of residents of social-housing units fell below the subsidy band
(calculated at earning less than R3,500 per month), by 2006 only half the number of residents had monthly incomes that fell beneath this threshold. Faced
with rapidly rising property prices and the high cost of construction and maintenance, social-housing companies are no longer able to offer more than just
a room with a bed for the very poor. Social-housing programs have reached
an impasse: large-scale financial grants to fund construction of new housing have dwindled, the costs of building maintenance have climbed steadily,
and rental rates in the inner city have jumped 10 to 15 percent per year since
2001–2002. Although in 2006 the JHC was still able to offer rents at 20 to 30
percent below comparable private accommodation, social-housing programs
have increasingly served moderate-income groups whose earnings range from
R4,500 to R10,000 per month. The celebrated R210 million Brickfields Project
at the foot of the Nelson Mandela Bridge on the northern edge of the refurbished Newtown Cultural Precinct provides a telling example of the social-
housing dilemma. Built with the help of state subsidies and private financing,
the showpiece Brickfields housing development has set aside 30 percent of its
flats for low-income tenants who pay rents around 20 percent below market
rate. Yet rising property and construction costs, combined with the failure of
state subsidies to keep pace with the city's property boom, have meant that the
Brickfields development has been compelled by economic necessity to cater to
affluent clientele who can pay higher rents than early projects like Carr Gardens (Fordsburg) or Jeppe Circle (Jeppestown).[36]

34. Interview with Taffy Adler.
35. Interview with Geoff Mendelowitz.
36. Interview with Taffy Adler. The Brickfields project, incorporating Brickfields, Legae, and
Phumlani, was the inner city's first high-rise development in thirty years, and it is JHC's most
ambitious project so far. Comprising 742 units in a mix of low-rise and high-rise buildings, it is

Yet what has been often overlooked in this headlong rush to encourage a stable-income and middle-class presence in the inner city has been the underlying problem of displacement and relocation of the urban poor. Housing experts have shared the view that low-cost housing projects in the inner city can survive only through heavy doses of state subsidization.[37] Despite notable successes in providing affordable housing for low-income urban residents, social-housing initiatives have fallen short of goals and expectations, making only a modest impact on accommodating the poorest of the poor, the casually employed or jobless urban residents who are largely left to fend for themselves. In Johannesburg, individuals who do not have a stable and recurrent source of income of at least R3,500 per month are not likely to benefit from access to social-housing projects. This barrier to entry has excluded large numbers of urban residents who cannot qualify for subsidized housing. In 2006 the cheapest social-housing rents were R700 a month for spartan accommodation: a room and communal washing and kitchen facilities. The limited number of places available came nowhere close to satisfying the demand for low-cost housing in the inner city (du Plessis and Wilson 2005, 35–36; Huchzermeyer 2003a).[38]

City officials were faced with a perplexing dilemma partly of their own devising. On the one side, they were pledged to reversing the wrongs and inequities of a private real estate market that had failed to provide affordable housing for the poor. On the other side, they were obliged to work with property owners who have profited handsomely from horrendous slums, and, more broadly, they were bound to find a workable solution within the framework of profit-making investments in landed property and private ownership of housing stock. This dependence on the capitalist marketplace has limited their room for maneuvering. The housing market in the inner city, where there is little resistance to rising rents, has increasingly targeted moderate- and middle-income renters.[39] Despite populist rhetoric promising a better life for all, municipal

---

JHC's largest single investment and the first time that a consortium of financiers—including government, private banks, and private investors—have worked together in a social-housing project. See John Reed, "Brickfields Is Outpost of Progress in Inner City Blighted by Neglect," *Business Day*, August 14, 2006.

37. Richard Jansen van Vuuren, "City of Joburg Property Company on Building Refurbishment Campaign," *Housing in Southern Africa* (January 2006): 1–2.

38. Information derived from interview with Taffy Adler.

39. Beall, Crankshaw, and Parnell (2002, 116) capture the essence of this idea when they say: "What we can conclude…is that the role of the formal business community in the inner city has been indispensable to its reinvigoration. However, capital is invariably self-interested, and the investment of time, energy, and resources in improving residential accommodation is as much about keeping general property values up as about providing homes and shelter [for the urban poor]."

authorities have largely adopted a laissez-faire attitude toward urban development. Even as subsidized housing is desperately needed for low-income residents of the inner city, the municipality has given private developers a virtual free hand to convert former office blocks into luxury apartments.[40]

Despite mounting pressure, large-scale commercial banks have continued to resist what they regard as undue municipal interference with their prerogatives. In assessing the risk of loan defaults, these private lending institutions have remained extremely reluctant to offer mortgages to people wanting to buy in the low-income housing market.[41] Municipal authorities have faced an uphill battle in combating the cancerlike spread of the slumlord economy in the inner city, in containing the unlawful occupation of vacant buildings, and in forcing reluctant property owners and absentee landlords to bring their decaying buildings into conformity with existing standards for health and safety. These continuing frustrations have created fertile ground for the turn toward more unilateral and drastic action to rid the cityscape of unwanted ruin. In the context of this sense of impending crisis, the destructive impulse gained a foothold. As unauthorized shack settlements proliferated on the metropolitan fringe and the unlawful squatter occupation of decaying buildings in the inner city accelerated the downward spiral of the slum economy, city officials, urban planners, and law enforcement agencies began to turn toward drastic eradication strategies—not as a solution to an acute housing shortage but as a response to what was regarded as the growing threat of insalubrity, disorder, and crime.[42]

Identifying Sinkholes and Promoting Ripple-Pond Investments: Regulating the Market for Low-Income Housing

> Government must not confuse town planning with social
> engineering. We don't mind low-income housing, but we don't
> want socioeconomic issues dumped on us.
>
> PROPERTY DEVELOPER IN JOHANNESBURG

If the creative impulse has undergirded efforts of progressive urban planners to integrate low-income urban residents into the postapartheid urban fabric, then the destructive impulse has triggered attempts to implement a futurist

---

40. "The city doesn't have an urban design framework and it desperately needs one," said Neil Fraser, head of Urban Inc., a planning and development consultancy (quoted in John Reed, "Brickfields Is Outpost of Progress").

41. Interview with Paul Jackson, Trust for Urban Housing Finance (TUHF), very brief discussion, June 6, 2006; and interview with Kuben Govender.

42. Vickie Robinson, "Policy Stumbles on Reality."

vision of Johannesburg as a world-class city by eliminating whatever stands in the way.[43] This destructive impulse rests on the premise that spatial disorder undermines the moral and social boundaries on which respectable civic urbanism depends. In public pronouncements, personal interviews, and official documents, city officials have routinely painted the inner-city residential areas as crime-ridden slums characterized by severe overcrowding of existing residential units, illegal conversions, and unmanaged informal trading—all of which have resulted in a degraded built environment. For city boosters mesmerized by the intoxicating vision of postapartheid Johannesburg as a genuine world-class city, the inner-city landscape has come to resemble a sort of dystopian antimetropolis, a debilitating inversion of the ideals of civic virtue, refined urbanity, and cosmopolitanism befitting a globally desirable destination point for business, leisure, and tourism. By looking on dilapidated buildings as spawning grounds for disease, crime, and vice, they have turned to the forcible eviction of tenants and the wholesale demolition of these run-down structures as a viable solution to urban disorder. By labeling the status quo as intolerable, municipal authorities have been able to justify municipal intervention as both normal and logical and to legitimate the eviction of unwanted squatters, the expulsion of hawkers from the streets, the forcible removal of unlawful tenants, and the demolition of "bad buildings" as both beneficial and desirable (see Mele 2000, 632–633).

 This destructive impulse rests on the belief that inner-city rejuvenation requires the surgical removal of the "social evils" associated with "bad buildings" (Page 1999, 80). By placing the blame for inner-city decline on irresponsible tenants, profiteering slumlords, and unscrupulous building hijackers, city officials have tended to concentrate on surface appearances while ignoring the largely invisible structural underpinnings of the slumlord economy. The moralizing discourse of "bad buildings" and their illegal occupants not only glosses over how the private market in residential property has failed to deliver decent housing on a sufficient scale for the urban poor but also diverts attention away from the root cause of the slumlord economy, namely, the system of property exploitation that has sweated rental profits out of unimproved, dilapidated buildings unfit for human habitation. In short, municipal authorities have overlooked how slum-making is an integral feature of city building under the rule of real estate (Page 1999, 80–82, 88–89; Scobey 2002, 107–113).

By focusing almost exclusively on decaying residential dwellings and their unauthorized occupants, city officials have effectively anthropomorphized

---

43. The quote by a Johannesburg property developer is cited in Pauline Larsen, "Developers Voice their Support," *Financial Mail,* June 10, 2005.

"bad buildings," regarding them as incubators of irresponsible and illicit behavior rather than as available shelters of last resort for the urban poor (du Plessis and Wilson 2005). Framed in such a demonizing light, it not surprising that the advocacy of such one-sided, drastic measures has found a receptive ear. The ineffectiveness of code enforcement to regulate the landlord economy and to maintain uniform standards for proper housing, the absence of a self-regulating market in residential accommodation, the exponential growth in the demand for low-cost housing in the inner city, and the ability of unscrupulous slumlords to evade the law have spurred city officials to reconsider piecemeal strategies of consultation, negotiation, and cooperation. Instead, they adopted drastic measures to deal with crime, the decaying built environment, and insalubrious residential accommodation. The logic behind destroying dilapidated buildings in order to make way for new construction was deceptively simple. Since the private market in residential accommodation had failed to regulate itself, it therefore became incumbent on municipal authorities to intervene in order to reassert the power of market forces (Page 1999, 88).[44]

Seen from a wider angle, municipal authorities have not developed coherent policy guidelines or the requisite institutional capacity to deal adequately with the needs of the poor who inhabit inner-city slums. For the most part, urban planners, city officials, and law enforcement agencies have framed their collective approach to inner-city slums through the conventional discourses of urban renewal and regeneration. Viewed within this paradigmatic framework, slum properties are both the structural cause and the direct consequence of urban decay. To be successful, urban renewal or regeneration requires the eradication of these slum properties, either by rehabilitation or demolition. Urban management is left to the discretion of municipalities, where strategic initiatives largely focus on cleaning up the built environment in order to attract private investment. In Johannesburg, building codes, health and safety regulations, and municipal bylaws have provided the legal and administrative framework that has enabled city officials to deal with inner-city slums. In the discourse of urban renewal, decaying buildings are characterized as inner-city slums that require cleaning up, usually by means of property seizures and forcible evictions of residents (du Plessis and Wilson 2005, 35–36).[45]

As a way of combating the slumlord economy, municipal authorities established two programs: the Better Buildings Programme (BBP), designed to

---

44. Information for this and following paragraphs derived from interview with Neil Fraser; interview with Lael Bethlehem; and interview with Nazira Cachalia, program manager, City Safety Programme, City of Johannesburg, May 30, 2006. Interpretation is entirely mine.
45. Interview with Stuart Wilson.

refurbish buildings in the central city that had fallen into a state of disrepair but that remained structurally sound; and the Unsafe Buildings Programme, designed to demolish those buildings found to be structurally unsound and hence beyond rehabilitation. Since its inauguration in 1997 the BBP has become the cornerstone of the municipal goal of revitalizing the inner-city housing market.[46] As part of a wider strategy to rehabilitate decaying buildings and rid the inner-city of slumlords, the BBP has employed a two-sided approach: first, it has enticed property owners by offering debt forgiveness on outstanding municipal accounts (that more often than not outweigh the assessed value of buildings) in exchange for legally binding agreements by owners to revamp and maintain their buildings to compliant standards; and, second, it has used the powers of eminent domain to seize abandoned and derelict properties for auction to private developers who agreed to refurbish them as residential housing. As a way of encouraging private property developers to upgrade residential buildings, municipal authorities have offered various incentive packages, including reductions in property taxes and other subsidies. While tax rebates have cost the municipality in lost revenues, these incentives have encouraged private developers to rehabilitate buildings (Beall, Crankshaw, and Parnell 2002, 115–118).[47]

In documents prepared for the Inner-City Regeneration Strategy Business Plan 2004–2007, city officials identified close to 250 bad buildings in the inner city and estimated their occupation at somewhere between twenty-five thousand and eighty thousand residents. In addition to asserting that these bad buildings were unhealthy and unsafe, city officials have also characterized these decaying structures as veritable sinkholes: dead-end refuges for unlawful squatters, havens for criminals, and launching pads for illegal enterprises. Without any redeeming features, these "bad buildings" are obstacles to progress that stand in the way of urban regeneration. As part of a grand scheme to remake Johannesburg in the roseate image of a world-class city, urban planners have prescribed closing down these buildings—a neutral-sounding euphemism for using court-ordered eviction orders to force occupants out of the buildings and to seal them off. Some of the confiscated buildings are auctioned off to property developers at a fraction of their true value. Others are upgraded for the purposes of creating well-managed, low-cost housing for

46. Sabelo Ndlangisa, "Slum Busters," *Sunday Times,* August 18, 2002. Ideas and information derived from interviews with Neil Fraser; and interview with Yael Horowitz, Johannesburg Development Agency, June 20, 2003.

47. See *Sunday Independent,* "Jo'burg Targets City Buildings for Renewal," April 7, 2002; and Stephen Williams, "Can Jo'burg Regain Its 'Heart'?" *African Business* (May 2002): 13. Ideas and information derived from interviews with Neil Fraser; interview with Yael Horowitz; and interview with Geoff Mendelowitz.

moderate-income tenants under the BBP mandate. Still others are subjected to demolition at the hands of the wrecking ball.[48]

Extensive research conducted under the auspices of the Geneva-based Centre on Housing Rights and Evictions (COHRE) has suggested a far more complex and nuanced understanding of the "bad buildings" scenario than the one that municipal documents and city officials readily acknowledge.[49] Without a doubt, the inner city of Johannesburg has become a jumbled mixture of buildings, where many of them, poorly maintained and neglected and in violation of municipal bylaws, are mixed in with those that remain in compliance. While estimates of the numbers have varied considerably, researchers for COHRE suggested in 2005 that somewhere between 25,000 and 67,000 inner-city residents found shelter—sometimes unlawfully—in decaying buildings that are structurally unsafe, lacking in adequate sanitation facilities, often without running water and electricity, and with inadequate fire prevention and suppression systems (du Plessis and Wilson 2005, 41). These conditions have posed an immediate danger to life and health, so much so that some of these derelict buildings are not much more than collapsing shells, partially burned and stripped of everything of even modest value.[50] Inner-city deterioration has spread beyond the once-elegant residential neighborhoods of Hillbrow, Joubert Park, and Berea to include the edges of the historic downtown business core. For example, in 2004 city officials authorized the eviction of occupants of 16 percent of the 408 residential buildings in Bertrams for bylaw violations in the areas of health and safety, fire prevention, and overcrowding. In Malvern, at the southeastern edge of the inner city, there were eighty pending evictions at the start of 2005.[51]

48. Information derived from interview with Li Pernegger, program manager, Economic Area Regeneration, Department of Finance and Economic Development, City of Johannesburg, May 30, 2006; interview with Geoff Mendelowitz; and interview with Lael Bethlehem.

49. This report, called *Any Room for the Poor?*, was prepared by the Centre on Housing Rights and Evictions (COHRE), an international NGO (nongovernmental organization) with a secretariat in Geneva, Switzerland, and program offices in Brazil, Ghana, South Africa, Thailand, the United States, and Australia. Jean du Plessis coordinated the field research team in Johannesburg. Unfortunately, the Better Buildings Programme has typically provided residential accommodation in rehabilitated structures at rental rates that are beyond the means of the evicted occupants who have been ousted well before these renewal projects are completed (see du Plessis and Wilson 2005, 41–43).

50. Journalists have consistently reported that more than 67,000 poor people occupy derelict buildings in the inner city. See, for example, Beauregard Tromp, "JHB Council to Provide Housing for Evictees," *The Star*, November 2, 2007. See also interview with Graeme Gotz, specialist in policy and strategy, Corporate Planning Unit, Office of City Manager, City of Johannesburg, May 26, 2006; and interview with Kuben Govender. Information also derived from various on-site visits to the inner city. See also Tammy O'Reilly, "Evictions in the Inner City," JOBURG, City of Johannesburg Official Website, http://www.joburg.org.za/2003/nov/nov12_raid.stm, November 12, 2003.

51. The Inner City Task Force provided these figures. See Christina Gallagher, "Slumlords Invade Johannesburg."

For urban planners, derelict buildings that have fallen into disrepair not only pose an ongoing health and safety risk to their occupants, but they also have become breeding grounds for disease, criminality, and moral degradation.[52] In short, these insalubrious places were the physical embodiments of urban disorder. City officials have looked upon their strategies of forcibly removing unwanted tenants of "bad buildings" as a rational response to the problems of inhuman, degraded housing for the urban poor. They justified the hardships that evicted tenants faced as the unfortunate byproducts of well-meaning policies that serve the greater good. By 2006 the Inner City Task Force, which inspects buildings, enforces bylaws, and serves court-ordered eviction notices—has closed down an estimated 150 "bad buildings." The clampdown on unsafe buildings targeted a variety of bylaw violations, including the total collapse of sewerage infrastructure; illegal partitioning of rooms with combustible materials; inadequate fire-fighting equipment; pest and rodent infestation; overcrowding; open elevator shafts; illegal electrical connections; and unauthorized conversions from office to residential accommodation.[53]

According to the findings of the COHRE fact-finding mission in 2004 and testimonies of the unlawful squatters themselves, however, the municipal description of "bad buildings" as irredeemably crime-ridden sinkholes without any hope of redemption has overlooked the fact that these decaying buildings typically provide the only available residential accommodation for large numbers of ordinary people gainfully employed in low-paid formal-sector jobs and informal livelihood strategies that are anything but criminal. The fact that poor people have chosen to live under such appalling conditions is more a reflection of their desperation to obtain housing in the inner city than an indication of their criminal propensities. Poor people seeking to remain close to jobs and other income-generating activities, as well as schools, daycare centers, and health care clinics, have little choice but to rent the only residential accommodation they can afford in the inner city. Under the evolving circumstances of inner-city decay and neglect, some, but certainly not all, places designated as "bad buildings" have become magnets for illicit enterprises. Moreover, there is sufficient circumstantial evidence to suggest that ordinary occupants of decaying buildings "do their best to avoid and if possible to resist the activities of the criminals" (du Plessis and Wilson 2005, 41–42).[54]

52. Thomas Thale, "Jo'burg Moves In on Derelict Buildings," JOBURG, City of Johannesburg Official Website, http://www.joburg.org.za/april2002/bad_buildings.stm, April 2, 2002.

53. See David Jackson, "'Substantial Progress' in Revival of the CBD," *Business Day*, April 8, 2004; *Business Day*, "Jo'burg Team Tackles Unsafe City Buildings," June 28, 2005; Philippa Garson, "Better Buildings—New Push for Inner-City Revival," JOBURG, City of Johannesburg Official Website, http://www.joburg.org.za/2004/feb/feb13_better.stm, February 13, 2004. Information also derived from interview with Geoff Mendelowitz; and interview with Lael Bethlehem.

54. Information derived from interview with Shereza Sibanda, Inner City Resource Center, during on-site visit to inner-city buildings occupied by squatters, Johannesburg, May 29, 2006; and

In the official mind, closing down these despicable sinkholes was not the end point of municipal intervention but the start of a solution to inner-city decline. By accepting the calculus of eliminating the old in order to make way for the new, city officials embraced destruction as a creative act in itself. The logic behind this destructive impulse was deceptively simple: closing down "bad buildings" was a vital step in transforming the inner city from an agglomeration of moribund sinkholes into regenerated "ripple ponds," that is, targeted places where the injection of capital triggers investment in the surrounding areas. By linking one ripple pond with another, urban regeneration can spread in an ever-widening circle of confidence that in time meets the overall goal of "raising and sustaining private investment, leading to a steady rise in property values."[55] In the confident discourse of urban planning, ripple-pond projects consist largely of capital-intensive investments aimed at improving roads, traffic lights, drainage and utilities infrastructure, and the construction and restoration of sites of public, historic, or cultural interest. The purpose of this massive infusion of municipal funds is to lure private investment back to the inner city. The aim of such roseate language is not only to elicit much-needed public support for the difficult task of inner-city revitalization, but also to "promote integration and synergy" among the various government and private sector players required to bring these ambitious plans to fruition.[56]

But what typically appears as a relatively simple, straightforward process in the official manuals of urban planners has actually become extremely complicated in practice. For the most part, city officials have reduced the bewildering complexity surrounding the causes and consequences of dilapidated housing in the inner city, along with patterns and rhythms of unlawful squatting, to a single categorical refrain: "bad buildings" constitute a serious blight on the urban landscape, and those who occupy them need to be removed. Their attitude ignores the fact that poor tenants do not live in "bad buildings" out of choice but from necessity. The downward spiral of decline from good to "bad buildings" is a highly complex process that defies simple explanation. Yet this narrow approach to the problem of slum housing has come at the expense of the urban poor. Because many city officials have shown little regard for locating alternative accommodation for those evicted from condemned properties,

discussion with Nelson Khetani, alleged building hijacker, San José apartment complex, Olivia Street, Berea, May 29, 2006.

55. Neil Fraser, "Sinkholes and Ripple Ponds," JOBURG, City of Johannesburg Official Website, http://www.joburg.org.za/citichat/2003/mar10_citichat.stm, March 10, 2003.

56. See David Jackson, "'Substantial Progress' in Revival"; Nick Wilson, "Development Leaping Ahead in Johannesburg's CBD," *Business Day*, July 23, 2003; David Williams, "SA's Inner Cities Well on the Path to Rejuvenation," *Business Day*, September 29, 2003; and interview with Lael Bethlehem.

the urban poor have no alternative but to move into decaying housing elsewhere, thereby perpetuating the cycle of impermanence and virtually ensuring further rounds of evictions sometime in the future (du Plessis and Wilson 2005 43–48).[57]

Put in theoretical terms, urban planners worked with imaginary forms of spatial unity and historical continuity that served to suppress or deny the contested character of real estate capitalism. As they developed a deeply critical attitude toward profiteering slumlords, urban planners largely ignored how and why the private housing market has failed to provide decent accommodation for the urban poor and hence is the root cause of the slum problem. In the end, they tend to return to the "bad buildings" themselves as the literal personifications of urban decay. Because they have deteriorated beyond redemption, these derelict structures have to go before they bring down everything else within reach: closed down, sealed off, and put on the auction block. The stress on zealous destruction of "bad buildings," combined with weak or haphazard commitment to locating alternative shelter, has contributed to the reproduction of homelessness by scattering the urban poor to the four winds (du Plessis and Wilson 2005, 43–48).[58]

Despite concerted effort to stem the tide of decrepitude and to make redevelopment sustainable, the Johannesburg inner city has remained a bundle of contradictions. There are around 38,000 buildings (90 percent of which are multiunit housing properties) located in the residential neighborhoods of the inner city. The BBP listed 130 buildings under its mandate in 2006 and identified a thousand more as possible sites for renovation. Despite the notable achievements in rehabilitating "bad buildings," it has been estimated that housing authorities have refurbished a little more than 20 percent.[59]

57. Interview with Geoff Mendelowitz. See also Adri Kotze, producer, "People Are Living Here," *SABC Special Assignment,* February 23, 2003.
58. Interview with Stuart Wilson.
59. Vickie Robinson, "Policy Stumbles on Reality"; and interview with Geoff Mendelowitz.

6

The Struggle for Survival
in the Inner City

The more successful Government is in creating desirable living
conditions in areas that are close to jobs, the more likely it
is that low-income households will be driven out. This is
because when Government succeeds, the market replaces
Government programmes.

RICHARD TOMLINSON

In the Johannesburg central city large-scale property has remained primarily in the hands of the old white monopolies—prominent mining houses, banking establishments, insurance companies, pension and provident funds, and real estate holding companies.[1] In contrast, the streets, pavements, and public spaces of the cityscape are in the hands of ordinary people: sidewalk vendors, taxi drivers, the unemployed, and lower-income black consumers for whom the inner city has become the most convenient place to shop for foodstuffs and household items. Between these groups lies a great chasm, filled to a large extent by ignorance, misunderstanding, and fear. Rival perceptions of entitlement to the city invariably give rise to a volatile mixture of resentment and paranoia, competition and conflict. Seeing their fixed capital investments eroded by capital flight and demographic shifts, property owners have reacted strongly, blaming newcomers for all that has gone wrong with the city and casting aspersions on the new municipal authorities for their inability to deal effectively with crime or to manage the public environment (Bremner 2000, 2002).[2]

Although they are divided over their sources of wealth and power, the great constellations of private capital share a common vision: the restoration of the

1. Quote in epigraph is from Richard Tomlinson, "The Shape of Disadvantage," *Mail & Guardian*, September 15–21, 2001.
2. See Ferial Haffajee, "City Streets: Where South Africa's Economy Is Changing," *Mail & Guardian*, July 7–13, 1998.

downtown cityscape to something akin to its former glory. In their efforts to reverse the long-term decline of the central city, large-scale property owners have cobbled together an alliance of downtown stakeholders under the umbrella of the Central Johannesburg Partnership (CJP) with the aim of combating crime, restoring law and order, and encouraging investments (both public and private) in the built environment. Borrowing liberally from good governance strategies implemented (with varying degrees of success) in other cities throughout the world, this coalition of real estate capitalists and property developers have joined forces with leading city officials to launch number of urban revitalization projects, including the formation of the much-lauded city improvement districts (CIDs), the installation of closed-circuit surveillance cameras, the training of traffic officers in policing techniques, the establishment of licensed taxi ranks and the placement of informal marketplaces at authorized sites, the forcible removal of homeless squatters from vacant buildings, and clearing the sidewalks of unwanted curbside traders. The graduated implementation of these ambitious initiatives has signaled a concerted effort to protect and preserve the comforting image of middle-class prosperity in the face of increasing socioeconomic diversity in the central city, the steady deterioration of the built environment in certain areas, and the virtual absence of law and order in the interstitial spaces of the cityscape (Bremner 2004a).

Buoyed by the boosterist imagining of Johannesburg as an emergent world-class city, prominent civic leaders, top city officials, and large-scale property owners have put their faith in the synergistic ripple effects of private investments combined with public improvements as the driving force behind urban revitalization.[3] Yet despite these rhetorical appeals to an imagined future harmony, these new city-building efforts have contributed to the development of a partitioned urban landscape, in which the gap between the luxurious citadel office complexes in the central city, the affluent northern suburbs, and the enclosed leisure and entertainment sites for well-to-do urban residents, on the one hand, and the life-worlds of the inner-city slums, the prescribed formal townships, and the informal shack settlements on the metropolitan edge, on the other, have appreciably widened. All in all, according to recent figures, around 40 percent of the economically active population has remained without regular work in formal sector occupations over the past decade, and close to one-third of the urban residents of the greater Johannesburg metropolitan area were homeless, that is, without stable, affordable, and lawfully authorized

3. According to the Joburg 2030 revitalization plan introduced by the city council in 2002, "In 2030, the quality of life of a citizen in Johannesburg will have more in common with the quality of life of a citizen in San Francisco, London, or Tokyo than of a developing country's capital city" (Colin Hossack, "Next Generation Jo'burg—Africa's San Francisco?" JOBURG, City of Johannesburg Official Website, http://www.joburg.org.za/feb_2002/2030.stm, February 21, 2002).

shelter of their own. An estimated 120,000 households lived below the minimal standards set by the World Bank. An astounding 30 percent of Johannesburg households were eligible for special allowances available for registered
indigents—but these numbers did not include the hundreds of thousands of
undocumented migrants who refused to register with the proper authorities
for fear of deportation.[4] In Johannesburg after apartheid, the luxurious City
of Spectacle, consisting of those fancy playgrounds for the affluent that are
at once orderly, clean, enclosed, and fortified, stands in stark contrast to the
Other City—the one that contains those depleted, degraded, polluted, and
stagnant spaces of confinement inhabited by the urban poor, who are forced
to eke out daily existence under perilous and unstable conditions (Bremner
1999, 56–57; Lipman and Harris 1999, 731–733; Tomlinson 1999a).

Contradictory Impulses of Real Estate Capitalism: The Shifting Fortunes of Inner-City Johannesburg

Like other cities that originated on the margins of modernity, Johannesburg has always exhibited the contradictory impulses of cosmopolitan elitism
coupled with everyday marginalization of the poor and dispossessed, where
the intersection of global wealth and local poverty has fostered a peculiar
kind of urban instability, uncertainty, and unpredictability. Precisely at a time
when city boosters have hailed Johannesburg after apartheid as an upbeat, dynamic, world-class city on the verge of greatness, the metropolitan landscape
is marked by discomforting and debilitating disorders, or what can be called
the "frictions of space" (see Scobey 2002, 134–156). Always and everywhere,
real estate capitalism—and the city-building processes that accompany it—is
essentially contradictory and uneven, subject to periodic cycles of speculative expansion followed by stagnation and decline. In the greater Johannesburg metropolitan region the inevitable boom-and-bust cycles of real estate
capitalism have created a heteroscape of unstable dynamism and paralyzing
disorder. Once concentrated in the downtown urban core, large-scale corporate enterprises have moved out of the central business district and relocated
their headquarters office buildings in what once were homogeneous residential suburbs to the north. The resulting urbanization of suburbia has produced
a haphazard landscape that consists of a combination of booming edge cities
like Sandton, Fourways, and Midrand; cluster nodal points like Ilovo, Sunninghill, Melrose Arch, and Hyde Park; and a patchwork mosaic of high-rise

---

4. Interviews with Graeme Gotz, specialist in policy and strategy, Corporate Planning Unit,
Office of City Manager, City of Johannesburg, May 26 and June 3, 2006. See also Anna Cox,
"Joburg Faces Steep Rates and Service Fee Hike," *The Star*, May 29, 2003; and Richard Tomlinson,
"The Shape of Disadvantage."

office parks, overbuilt axial corridors, townhouse clusters, and look-alike strip malls scattered here and there. With the exception of the high-profile CIDs where large-scale property owners have created fortified enclaves in the central city, large stretches of the Johannesburg inner city, particularly along the frayed edges and the transitional spaces of shifting use, have fallen into disrepair. The massive capital flight that began in the 1980s and accelerated during the 1990s stripped the central business district of prestigious corporate owners and high-rent tenants, leaving boarded-up, vacant, and abandoned buildings—once the iconic symbols of the high modernist downtown building boom of the 1960s and 1970s—in its wake (Chipkin 1999; Czeglédy 2003; Robinson 1999).

The sluggishness of land development in the inner city, with its heavy initial investment in the built environment and slow income stream, encouraged two different but equally dysfunctional strategies. It promoted, first, the overuse or patchwork recycling of existing structures that eventually fall into ruin. Second, high entry costs and slow returns of investments in inner-city locations encouraged frenzied, horizontal building on the peri-urban fringe, where fly-by-night corporate builders constructed one cookie-cutter strip mall, townhouse cluster development, and look-alike office park after another (Bremner 1999, 56–57). While these responses to the real estate market appeared as unrelated and contradictory approaches to land use, they both amounted to alternative ways of "sweating the land." As the opposing faces of real estate capitalism, both disinvestment and speculative (rapid turnover) investment extracted value from real estate without significant improvements, and each has tended to retard, distort, or otherwise complicate city-building processes that have looked to rationality, efficiency, and coherence as the ideal (Page 1999; Scobey 2002, 143–146; Bremner 2000, 185–186).

Yet the most powerful impediment or disincentive to real estate improvement is the interdependence of the location market. Unlike most commodities, the exchange value of urban buildings is almost completely relational, their market prices fixed by the wider geography of adjacent networks and contiguous activities in which they are embedded. Thus, the rationality of the real estate market in buildings and property largely depends on its collective stability, "its capacity to generate zones of development within which real estate developers, corporate builders, and land speculators alike can calculate and secure the uses and prices of specific locations." Yet despite the efforts to create order and stability for the Johannesburg inner city, the real estate market has remained volatile, unpredictable, and uneven. The combination of capital flight by high-end property owners, environmental degradation, infrastructural decay, haphazard land use, and the tendency to extract immediate gain from property without enhancing its physical or locational value have contributed to the exposure of inner-city property to the constant threat of external devaluation (Scobey 2002, 134–146).

The Johannesburg inner city has become a vast, fluid zone of constant motion, fleeting interaction, and chance encounters. According to current figures, an estimated eight to nine hundred thousand commuters enter the Johannesburg central business district (CBD) on an ordinary weekday, whether to go to work, to shop, or simply to pass through on their way to somewhere else. Close to a half million long-distance migrant shoppers from surrounding countries venture into the CBD every year, purchasing items for resale elsewhere. The downtown cityscape consists largely of soaring skyscrapers, bulky office blocks, and low-rise commercial establishments (primarily on the eastern side). Yet the durability of the built environment—the fixity of real estate investments in buildings—contrasts sharply with the ephemerality of social interaction in the interstitial spaces of the city. What animates the streetscape are the volatile mixture and agglomerated concentration of pavement traders with their makeshift stalls, itinerant drifters, idle youth and loiterers, jobless work seekers, daily commuters, taxi drivers, and stationary security guards watching over someone else's property. While movement may seem aimless, it is always purposeful. The gravitational pull of the main transport hub—Park Station at the northern end of Eloff Street—lures passengers to the trains, buses, and taxis that operate there (Tomlinson 1999a).

Despite recent efforts to reclaim, recolonize, and refurbish the downtown streetscape, central Johannesburg has remained an incongruous mosaic of disconnected pockets of revitalization surrounded by marginal, indeterminate zones of uncertainty, instability, and possible danger. In the decade or so after the end of apartheid, city builders have reshaped the morphological form of the cityscape to conform to a new fortification aesthetic, adopting certain conventions in response to what is regarded as the ubiquitous threat of danger. The transparency of buildings that actually showcase their interior activities should not be confused with accessibility. Without exception, high-rise office buildings, lofty skyscrapers, and commercial shopping sites are defended by a multilayered grid of security checkpoints, bolted doors, barricaded entryways, surveillance cameras, and heavily armed security guards. The sequestered spaces of the private city—inhabited by bankers, financiers, and entrepreneurs along with their workforce of skilled professionals and unskilled wage earners—are duly fortified against the unruly others who are relegated to the public streetscape of the uncertain city. Property owners have boarded up vacant buildings, fenced off stairways, and walled off entrances in a sometimes unsuccessful effort to prevent their unwanted occupation by homeless squatters (Bremner 2002; Lipman and Harris 1999, 731–733).

As is the case with most aspirant world-class cities located at the margins of modernity, the Johannesburg central city has attracted more poor people than can be reasonably absorbed by the labor market or accommodated with affordable shelter that meets even the most minimal standards of health and safety. Spectacular displays of visible wealth provide a faulty impression of widespread socioeconomic buoyancy. The new affluence that has triggered upward mobility for some has not appreciably trickled down to the urban poor. In actuality the vast majority of urban residents are confined to the lower rungs of the labor market, where they move between low-paying wage work in the formal economy, casual labor on almost any terms, and various income-generating activities in the unregulated, informal, and shadow economies that have become the last refuge of the truly desperate. Under straitened circumstances where regular wage-paying work is often difficult to obtain and retain, various kinds of popular illegalities—unauthorized street trading, petty theft, prostitution, drug dealing, trafficking in stolen goods—have assumed exaggerated importance in the overall calculus of survival for the urban poor. The anxious rich who inhabit the urban landscape have sought to wrap their daily lives in one security envelope after another, furtively venturing from fortified residences to such sequestered destinations as enclosed shopping malls, cocooned places of work, and guarded leisure sites, traveling in high-speed automobiles with rolled-up windows, locked doors, and outfitted with the latest security paraphernalia (Bremner 1999, 56–57).[5]

In the immediate aftermath of apartheid, the explosive growth in the numbers of curbside hawkers, street vendors, and pavement entrepreneurs who flooded the sidewalks of the Johannesburg central city opened up new patterns of consumption for low-income urban residents. But by choking off pedestrian traffic and contributing significantly to the littered streetscape, these unregulated street traders have attracted the opprobrium of postapartheid urban planners who have sought to retain the semblance of an orderly city that conforms to the dictates of efficiency, rationality, and coherence. Likewise, the proliferation of unlicensed taxis created havoc on the roadways, as cutthroat competition between rival associations has sometimes erupted into senseless spasms of violence and mayhem on the streets.[6]

In the rough-and-tumble inner-city residential neighborhoods of Hillbrow, Berea, Joubert Park, Yeoville, Bertrams, and Doornfontein, lawfulness has become a middle-class affectation, a kind of romantic, utopian fantasy. Although the slow decline of the inner-city residential zone of Hillbrow, Berea, and Joubert Park can be traced to the 1970s, the bank redlining that began in

5. See interviews with Graeme Gotz.
6. See Stuart Graham, "Frustrated Taxi Drivers Take to the Streets," *The Star*, May 17, 2005.

the 1990s delivered the ultimate coup de grâce, condemning a once-elegant housing accommodation to overcrowding and neglect.[7] The steady deterioration of these former playgrounds for bohemian youth has only strengthened nostalgic remembrances of a time that no longer exists. The crowded streets and other public gathering places of the inner city come alive with networks of young people purposefully waiting for opportunities: selling stolen property and drugs, hawking goods, offering various services, targeting potential mugging victims, checking out the alarm systems of parked cars, begging, doing odd jobs. The once-vibrant commercial life of the street around such notorious "sleazy hotels" as the Safari, Heatherdenn, Monsneg, Mimosa, the Lloyd, Boulevard Guests, the Sands, the Chelsea, and Little Roseneath has vanished except for the eternal engine of the prostitution and the drug trade. Inner-city nightclubs that double as mass-market brothels generate enormous profits, fueling an underground, shadow economy that combines clandestine trafficking in women and underage girls with drugs and sex (Leggett 2001).[8]

The Spectral Geography of Homelessness: New Nomads in the Placeless City

> The homeless are forced into constant motion not because
> they are going somewhere, but because they have nowhere
> to go. Going nowhere is simultaneously being nowhere:
> homelessness is not only being without home, but more
> generally without place.
>
> SAMIRA KAWASH (1998, 327–328)

The vertiginous summit of the Carlton Centre offers a panoramic view from which to observe the urban landscape of Johannesburg in its totality. From this bird's-eye view on the observation deck fifty floors above the sprawling jumble of the cityscape below, the built environment of the central city looks like a vast, unpeopled orthogonal grid of street canyons (the "breezeways of modernity"), flanked by rows and rows of soaring office towers occasionally interspersed with low-rise buildings. This scenographic display of sheer monumentality provides ample testimony to high-modernist planning schemes gone awry. Historic city-building processes produced a harsh urban landscape

---

7. "Redlining takes place regardless of the borrower's credit worthiness or the condition of the house. It has harmed government's efforts to provide homes for the poor" (William Mervin Gumede, "The Banks Can and Must Do Better," *Financial Mail*, November 3, 2000). Information also derived from interview with Kuben Govender, Trust for Urban Housing Finance (TUHF), June 6, 2006.

8. Thomas Thale, "Jo'burg Moves In on Derelict Buildings," JOBURG, City of Johannesburg Official Website http://www.joburg.org.za/april2002/bad_buildings.stm, April 2, 2002.

devoid of greenbelt parklands and recognizable social gathering places defined by the qualities of openness and revelation. From the start, city builders forced the urban landscape to conform to the stark dictates of speed and motion, business and commerce, in contrast to the leisurely pace of pedestrian ambience. The original placement in the early twentieth century of the railway lines and vast switching yards brutally eviscerated the city center along a north-south axis. Unlike their counterparts in other aspirant world-class cities, urban planners—who were enamored with the restless urge to continuously reinvent Johannesburg in the image of heroic modernity—never allowed the city to "learn the art of growing old by playing on all its pasts." Following the lead of modernist urban planning protocols in vogue elsewhere, they encircled the tightly packed downtown business district with a tangled skein of high-speed freeways that propelled impatient motorists around the central city, rather than into it. As if ashamed by the city's rowdy, frontier past, city builders have readily torn down old buildings that seemed to stand in the way of progress, constructing ever-taller, -bigger, and more imposing structures that dwarfed the pedestrian streetscape and were defined primarily by their efficiency, functionality, and orderly appearance.[9]

Yet the panoptic picturing power of the Solar Eye produces only a deceptively simplified picture of the actual goings-on in the urban landscape—giving rise to what Michel de Certeau (1984, 91–93) has called the "fiction of knowledge." This view from above is associated with the planning perspective of elite city builders, privileging the demands of a generalized, orderly urbanism over the lives and needs of those who inhabit the margins, the gaps, and the edges of the city (Wigoder 2002). The Solar Eye view is the vantage point of city surveyors, town planners, or those whom Henri Lefebvre (1991, 38) called the "technocratic subdividers and social engineers." From this vantage point, it is easy to transform the variegated lives of city dwellers into quantities and numerical designations, to substitute grids for circuits and flows, and to imagine rational solutions for complex problems (Highmore 2005, 3–4).

These grand, visual representations provide a powerful mechanism for conveying a totalizing image of the city as a seamless and coherent whole. The "imaginary totalizations" (de Certeau 1984, 93) produced by the bird's-eye view, however, typically gloss over the breaks, the creases, and the discontinuities in the spatial continuum of the urban fabric. In contrast, mobile spatial practices—what de Certeau (1984, 91–93) has called "walking in the city"—open

9. The quotation comes from de Certeau (1984, 91–92). The Solar Eye presumes a socially undifferentiated and impersonal location of the point of observation, a disembodied vantage point, and the sole reference for the allocation of all objects in space.

up possibilities for multiple readings, or diverse understandings, of the urban landscape. Instead of seeking to construct an overwhelmingly coherent and logical view of the city, these movements through space conceive of the urban landscape as a series of relationships, where "the city is only experienced in time by a concrete, situated subject, as a passage from one 'unity of atmosphere' to another, not as the object of a totalized perception" (McDonough 1994, 65, 69). By disrupting the false continuity and the imaginary holism produced by cartographers, urban planners, and aerial photography in their cognitive mapping of the cityscape, mobile spatial practices stress the experiential dimension of city living, that is, the intersecting lifeworlds of the city, the variegated uses to which the built environment is put and the often conflicting meanings attached to place (de Certeau 1984, 91–93; McDonough 1994, 64, 65, 68–69).

Experienced on the ground, the physical deterioration of buildings in semi-industrial areas of the urban landscape that once catered to light manufacturing and large-scale commercial enterprises has created vast dead zones of under-utilized or unused properties, fenced, boarded up, and cordoned off. Central Johannesburg after dark resembles an eerie, high-rise ghost town, a virtually unpeopled place with little illumination except for the fortress office towers and an occasional fast-food outlet. The legions of homeless squatters who have cautiously and surreptitiously invaded the featureless zones of the central city have come in search of shelter, breaking into abandoned buildings, commandeering unused alleyways, and erecting makeshift hovels in empty lots. This new logic of homelessness triumphs every night in downtown Johannesburg, as hundreds of destitute people, whose bodies and meager possessions double as their homes, sleep in alleyways, sheltered doorways, in public parks and cemeteries, and under blankets on the cold pavements, transforming public space into private use (du Plessis and Wilson 2005).[10]

The sight-montage of such dystopian images as jobless drifters sleeping in public places, down-and-out beggars accosting insouciant passersby for handouts, and shoeless children roaming the crowded streets provide some of the most potent symbols of social exclusion in the postapartheid urban landscape. Homelessness in its most visible and graphic forms—abandoned street kids bedding down for the night on the sidewalks, idle youth perambulating the suburban streetscape, and destitute women with babies on their backs scavenging dumpsters for scraps of discarded food—has become a telling symptom of the failed promises of upliftment for the poorest of the poor after the end of apartheid. These dystopian images of urban distress contrast sharply

10. This information is derived from personal observation, as well as from interview with Stuart Wilson, Centre for Applied Legal Studies, University of the Witwatersrand, June 7, 2006.

with the portrayal of the homeless problem as it appears in the triumphalist language of neoliberal city boosterism. Rather than treating the existence of rootless people without stable residential accommodation as the inevitable outcome of stagnant economic growth, persistent poverty, and lifelong joblessness, the city boosterist construction of homelessness has framed it as an aberrant intrusion, a public nuisance, and an unsightly abnormality that poses a threat to urban order and stability. The conventional scripting of homelessness in the everyday discourse of the propertied classes typically conflates the homeless problem with adjacent symptoms of urban distress, decay, and disorder, thereby suggesting an elective affinity with such street criminalities as petty thieving, vagrancy, littering, public drunkenness, drug dealing, prostitution, loitering, and aggressive panhandling. Seen through the demonizing lens of triumphalist city boosterism, homelessness appears as an unwelcome disruption of normality that arrives from elsewhere and not as a visible sign of the failure of the labor market to absorb work seekers. In this way, homeless inhabitants of the city become complicit—through their own transgressive acts that violate the norms of middle-class propriety—in bringing about the ruination of the city and in creating problems that require decisive remedial action. What appears to trouble urban policy makers is not how to confront the root causes of homelessness and to provide long-term assistance, but, rather, how to regulate the cityscape through the effective spatial dispersal of homeless people and especially how to protect respectable middle-class urban residents from unwanted social interaction with them (Kawash 1998, 320–321; Mitchell 1997).

Persons who are homeless—that is, those without private domiciliary residences to call their own and therefore by definition inhabitants of the public spaces of the city—are precariously positioned in the ongoing battle over who rightfully belongs in the city, who has unhindered access to the different places of the urban landscape, and who has the right to decide what uses of public space fall within the public interest. The steady accretion of such luxurious post-public spaces of the city as upscale shopping malls, fortified office complexes, and sequestered leisure and entertainment sites has coincided with the introduction of new kinds of social exclusion designed to keep the poor, the unwanted, and the unacceptable on the outside looking in. The stringent application of the rules and regulations governing the use of such post-public sites of social congregation that constitute the City of Spectacle in the boosterist imagination corresponds to reconfigured conceptions of public security and new normative definitions of law enforcement that enable private security guards to operate with a great deal of impunity in harassing, intimidating, and even physically assaulting the urban poor on the pretense of maintaining public order (see Kawash 1998, 320–321).

To the extent that it collapses various life situations (such as joblessness, disability, extreme poverty, and lack of authorized shelter) under a single all-embracing rubric, the social category of homelessness disguises more than it reveals. Although most homeless people engage in all sorts of income-generating activities, they do not earn enough to afford shelter. The streets, sidewalks, and other places with public access become their primary venue for seeking work and acquiring money (Crawford 1995, 8). In the conventional construction of homelessness as a social problem, inhabitants of the city who lack secure shelter are seen as either passive victims of circumstances beyond their control, or menacing parasites who drain available resources and, hence, have become a burden on the city. In the first instance, the homeless require outside assistance in the form of a comprehensive social safety net, including elaborate support networks and social services, where the burden of caring can be shared. In the second instance, the presence of the homeless engenders demands for tighter surveillance, regulation, and control. Such simplified images of the homeless efface both the diversity of circumstances under which homelessness as a social condition is both produced and reproduced as part-and-parcel of city-building itself, and the various modes of social engagement and interpersonal activity in which homeless persons negotiate their everyday lives (Dear and Wolch 1987, 255–256; Kawash 1998, 321–322).

Whether considering the microgeographies of the urban homeless, the wider migrations of those in search of work or accommodation, the nomadic cycles of those moving around the circuits of informal trading, or the movement of those seeking simply to escape the straitened circumstances that precipitated the loss of home, it is clear that the conditionality of homelessness cannot be considered apart from the experience of movement. The homeless who move within, between, and through places where they are unwanted—sometimes by necessity, sometimes by choice—typically engender anxiety and hostility (May 2000, 737–738). As unsettled and restless people, these urban nomads are feared and despised "not because they are always on the move but because they might stay and 'contaminate' through their ambivalence and bring all manner of horrors upon the 'locals'" (Hetherington 1992, 91).

Until the relaxation of the influx control regulations that prohibited unauthorized black people from remaining in the urban areas in the early 1990s, city officials used the draconian policing powers at their disposal to cleanse the white cityscape of unwanted homeless squatters. With the collapse of apartheid, diverse groups of homeless people, including whole households, single mothers with children, work-seeking immigrants, abandoned children, and displaced farm workers from the nearby countryside, have ventured in expanding numbers into this once-forbidden urban wilderness, blending in in unexpected ways and metastasizing throughout the city. These new homeless groups—large numbers of whom were situationally without secure shelter rather than socially disaffiliated and cast adrift as isolated individuals—have brought with them an array of survival tactics, coping mechanisms, and innovative skills, including tenuous access to intermittent employment, ties to extended families, friends, and support networks, and an experiential knowledge of the urban landscape. Some homeless job seekers have established makeshift camps on vacant land, while others have commandeered unused multistory buildings that have been stripped of wires, pipes, and anything that could be converted to quick cash. Still others have fashioned transitory encampments under city bridges and freeway overpasses or constructed rudimentary shelter in alleyways, in partitioned cubicles in overcrowded apartment units, in abandoned cars, or in dense brush hidden from view.[11] These landscapes of despair consist of dwellings of necessity, and not residences of choice. With just a few tools and discarded building materials acquired through modern-day hunting and gathering, these are the outsider vernacular architects who continuously threaten to disrupt the hyped-up boosterist vision of the orderly city (Olufemi 1997, 2002; Rogerson 1996b; Groth and Corijn 2005).

It is impossible to estimate with any accuracy the absolute numbers of homeless people "sleeping rough" (i.e., on the sidewalks) in night shelters scattered around the central city, or in temporary accommodation in the countless numbers of interstitial, hidden spaces of the urban landscape. In 2005, city officials estimated that more than a hundred thousand people lived in squalid conditions in the Johannesburg inner city, primarily in the deteriorated residential zone of Hillbrow, Berea, Joubert Park; in clustered pockets scattered across the central business district; and along its frayed edges at places like Bertrams, Troyeville, Yeoville, and Doornfontein on the eastern rim. Large numbers of homeless people have squatted illegally in abandoned and derelict buildings, while others are severely exploited by heartless slumlords who charge exorbitant rents for minuscule spaces in partitioned rooms of houses or in high-rise apartment complexes (du Plessis and Wilson 2005, 1–20).[12] To be sure, these numbers provide no more than a rough approximation of numbers of people who live under deplorable conditions in the inner city, since they are largely guesses extrapolated from ethnographic field studies and journalistic accounts. Equally important, these estimates refer only to quantities. However accurate or reliable these figures may be, they fail to reveal any useful information about the circular movements of the urban poor in and out of homelessness, the diverse kinds of accommodation available in the spatial interstices of the inner city, or the evasive tactics

11. Ferial Haffajee, "Homeless Seize the High Ground," *Mail & Guardian*, June 5–11, 1998; and Ndivhuwo Khangale, "Blankets and Soup to Help Joburg's Homeless," *The Star*, July 24, 2003.

12. David Pincus, "Law Is Not on Landlords' Side"; and interview with Graeme Gotz. This information is also derived from on-site visits to places of temporary and irregular shelter.

that squatters employ to escape detection (Olufemi 1997, 1998; Nkomo and Olufemi 2001). Those who can afford it escape from the inner-city residential zone around Hillbrow as quickly as they can. In turn, new arrivals from the rest of South Africa have drifted in, joined by an estimated forty thousand (or more) immigrants from all over the African continent—most of them without official authorization. Amid the poverty and degradation, crime cartels have found a foothold, operating drug and prostitution rings, engaging in financial scams and other illicit activities, preying especially on the desperation of illegal immigrants and the most vulnerable. Overstretched local authorities have been unable to cope with the constant breakdown of the overtaxed infrastructure, like burst sewage and water pipes, electricity blackouts, and the mounting piles of rubbish that add to the general condition of urban decay. Into this cauldron of urban chaos sprout all sorts of small-scale entrepreneurial ventures—street vendors from Zimbabwe selling roasted chicken feet, Nigerian-owned pawn shops and Internet cafés, barbers and hairdressers from Democratic Republic of Congo, auto repair shops operated by Mozambican panel beaters, public telephone and fax kiosks run by Somali refugees—appearing wherever there is available space, serving the low end of a vast, buoyant market for rudimentary services (Landau 2005, 2006; Kihato 2007, 261–278; Simone 2000, 2001b, 2004a, 2004b).[13]

The morphological characteristics of the urban built environment have rendered homeless people more or less invisible. Certainly, homeless people routinely gather at indoor shelters, soup kitchens, church storefronts, and social service outlets. These facilities provide strategic landmarks on the "survival map" indicating where to obtain basic requirements such as food, health care, and information (Cloke, Milbourne, and Widdowfield 2000, 718–719). Yet for the most part, homeless squatters remain hidden in plain sight, surviving on the ruined edges and margins of the orderly cityscape in an opaque landscape of shadows. The broad contours of their circuitous movements are known, but the intimate details of how they eke out daily existence remain murky and cloaked under layers of ambiguity and deliberate subterfuge. Homeless people have established makeshift accommodation in discarded car wrecks in an old scrap yard at Lakeview near Booysens in the vacant mine belt south of the central city, in the cavernous spaces of Park Station, along the Braamfontein Spruit as it meanders through the affluent northern suburbs, in backyard storage buildings at a furniture-making workshop across from the German Old Age Home close to Vrededorp, and under freeway bridges in Braamfontein.[14]

13. United Nations Integrated Regional Information Networks, "Johannesburg—A City of Risk and Opportunity," *Africa News*, March 14, 2005.

14. *SAPA*, "A Warm Meal and a Blanket against the Cold," July 30, 2001; Roger Southall, "Taking a Walk on the Filthy Side," *Business Day*, October 16, 2003; Ndivhuwo Khangale, "Blankets and Soup"; and personal observation from on-site visits, June 3, 2006.

A woman named Sylvia Khumalo lived for several years in a bus stop in Alexander Street in Windsor West, a middle-class suburb west of Johannesburg central city. She survived by begging from passersby and on the meager pension she received.[15] Homeless and runaway mothers—typically just children themselves—anonymously deposit their unwanted infants at a specially designed hole in the outer wall of the Baptist Church in Berea.[16] In the early morning hours dozens of homeless men in Joubert Park can be seen stoically lying flat on their stomachs, a technique they claim relieves the pains of hunger.[17] At an abandoned house in Bertrams emergency workers had to crawl on all fours, one at a time, to rescue a critically ill woman who was living in a hole in the wall to take her to hospital. Before the police raided the premises and evicted the illegal squatters who occupied the place, twenty-three-year-old Pumzile Khuzwayo had squatted in a palatial old home in Jan Smuts Avenue in the heart of the posh northern suburbs. Stripped of windows, doors, and electrical fittings and its backyard used as a toilet, the property had deteriorated beyond repair. Khuzwayo was a recent arrival from KwaZulu-Natal, and since she was unable to find steady work, she sold beer in a nearby park. Welfare officials had taken her seven-year-old son from her. As she hastily stuffed her few belongings into a trolley cart and prepared to leave her squalid quarters, she had no idea where she was going.[18]

Beginning in the early 1990s makeshift shelters began to appear in vacant lots, in alleyways, and along sidewalks in central Johannesburg. After dark all across the city, homeless people, many just children, began to find refugee in the interstitial spaces of the cityscape, huddling under blankets and cardboard in available doorways, behind buildings, in stairwells, and parking garages. In the following years the few city parks in the central city have become the temporary home to entire families, where everyone sleeps in the open and children get dressed for school in the public toilets. In an obvious example, hundreds of homeless people have claimed Joubert Park as their own, building temporary encampments around the perimeter. On the northwestern edge of the central city, homeless people used the cover of nightfall to surreptitiously slip into Braamfontein cemetery where they cooked, slept, and washed among the grave sites. During the day the active presence of private security guards was a sufficient deterrent to keep the squatters away and out of sight. All that gave away the presence of the living were the telltale ashes of graveside cooking fires and discarded cardboard boxes.[19]

15. Chris Nthite, "A Bus Stop for a Home," *Sunday Times*, November 18, 2003.
16. Interview with Adale and staff members at The House, a refuge for homeless girls and young women at 60 Olivia Street, Berea, May 20, 2003.
17. Valentine Cascarino, "Raiders of the Lost Park," *Mail & Guardian*, January 6–12, 2000.
18. Anna Cox, "Police Force Squatters from Swanky Suburbs," *The Star*, June 16, 2004.
19. Ferial Haffajee, "Homeless Seize the High Ground."

From the start, these unauthorized land seizures and unlawful building occupations prompted an official backlash that combined indifference with quick action. Around the time of the historic liberation elections of April 1994, squatters moved into Jack Mincer Park, across the street from the ANC's former Shell House headquarters in the decaying eastern side of the city center. They laid out plots and erected rudimentary shacks. This urban land invasion reached a crisis point in May 1998. Property developers wanted to build a hotel nearby and city planners earmarked the park as a preferred site for an officially sanctioned taxi rank. In order to reclaim the land for these projects, the new municipal council sent tractors into "Jurassic Park"—as its residents christened the area—to demolish the makeshift shacks and forcibly remove the squatters to Weiler's Farm, a featureless dumping ground about 40 kilometers away to the south of Soweto.[20]

Around the country, many people who have received housing sites in far-away peri-urban settlement areas have sold the rights for under R1,000 in order to move back to the cities. In their view, city life provides an economic base that is just not available in many of the serviced sites or informal housing developments that have proliferated on the metropolitan fringe. With its emphasis on private home ownership, postapartheid housing policy has largely failed to take account of homeless squatters who cannot afford to purchase even a rudimentary structure and to outfit it with furniture and other amenities, or those who do not want to own a house, or who have not decided where they wish to settle. Beleaguered housing authorities have been unable to keep pace with the rising demand for decent and affordable shelter in the greater Johannesburg metropolitan region. While accurate figures are difficult if not impossible to obtain, it has been estimated that perhaps as many as one million people cannot find accommodation that is decent, affordable, and adequate. In addition to sprawling informal settlements on the urban peripheries and overcrowded residential apartment buildings in inner-city neighborhoods like Hillbrow, Berea, and Joubert Park, a new kind of impromptu exercise in self-provisioning has evolved in Johannesburg. Homeless squatters have seized vacant buildings—including empty factory shells, abandoned warehouses, unused office facilities, vacant garages—and construct indoor shacks using discarded materials in a similar manner to informal settlements. Access to water, sanitation, waste, and other basic environmental health services is severely limited, with the potential for serious health risks and poor quality of life among occupants (de Plessis and Wilson 2005, 41–74; Mathee and Swart 2001).[21]

20. Jonathan Ancer, "Homeless Man Felt Himself Freezing," *The Star*, August 22, 2003.
21. Information also derived from on-site visit to decaying neighborhoods on the inner-city periphery with Graeme Gotz, Corporate Planning Unit, Office of City Manager, City of Johannesburg, June 3, 2006.

In the absence of cheap rental units close to the central city, the owners of derelict warehouses have figured out ways to make extra money by sub-dividing these unused buildings into lucrative squats. Using plywood sheeting, makeshift doors, and a rudimentary lock, they have partitioned their vacant properties into small cubicles, which they rent for as much as R250 per month. Residents collect water from outside taps, light their rooms with candles, and cook over open fires. These wandering multitudes of homeless households do not include the totally destitute: disheveled beggars pleading with passersby for handouts; homeless children who roam the streets; the maimed and dis-figured; the mentally disturbed; abandoned women with small children; and the old and sick who survive in any way they can. These are the truly homeless, the classically dispossessed vagabonds who wander aimlessly around the city.[22]

In 2005 city officials reported that several homeless people a week died alone in abandoned houses, suffering in silence from dehydration, tuberculo-sis, HIV-AIDS, and cirrhosis of the liver brought on by drinking homemade beer, called *mbamba*, which contains battery acid and antifreeze.[23] In a par-ticularly egregious instance of the precarious circumstances surrounding the existential lifeworlds of the homeless, municipal authorities were horrified to discover around two hundred homeless squatters living in deplorable condi-tions described as "worse than animals" in ten abandoned buildings, known as the Pepperpot Houses, in the rapidly expanding slum lands of Bertrams. Once prized homes in a middle-class neighborhood on the east side of the central city, these buildings had declined to such a dilapidated state that thieves had stolen pipes and wiring, the ceilings had caved in, and the doors, windows, and floors were missing. Desperate squatters were squeezed into every available space—makeshift sleeping quarters under the floorboards, in backyard dog kennels, and even in filthy coal-storage holes about two meters square. Resi-dents crowded into darkened rooms subdivided into tiny cubicles, where card-board partitions provided the illusion of privacy. Without wage-paying work or regular sources of income, they survived on handouts from a nearby soup kitchen. The raw sewage that gathered in filthy pools, the piles of uncollected refuse, and leaking drainage pipes that emitted a revolting stench created a health hazard of crisis proportions. Some homeless families had lived on the premises without running water, electricity, or toilet facilities for as long as ten years, and many children were born there without proper medical attention.

22. Information derived from interview with Stuart Wilson.
23. "They'll get you drunk easily. And they'll prepare you for your grave sooner than you expected. They're called *mbamba*, *bitla le ahlame* and *mqomboli*, [they] are made from fer-mented maize or bread and are drunk mostly by the homeless, sometimes with a bowl of sugar.... Rumour has it they often contain chemicals from car batteries, brake fluid, dirty water, and rot-ten bread" (Valentine Cascarino, "A Potent Brew," *Mail & Guardian*, May 27–June 2, 2001).

As the glare of public scrutiny revealed one of the inner city's most "shameful secrets," municipal officials intervened, identifying three priority cases—Maria Nkabinda, Angelina Tobe, and Julia Paulus. These destitute, elderly, and malnourished women who had lived for three years in an abandoned dog kennel were provided with alternative accommodation at the Rhema Christian Service Foundation Home in Hillbrow.[24]

Despite the hardships of urban living and the constant harassment by municipal authorities, homeless squatters have found ways to scratch out a meager living on the city streets. Some earn money parking cars (up to R30 on a good day), picking pockets, washing taxis (between R5 and R10 a vehicle), collecting waste materials (like discarded cans, plastic bags, scrap metal, and newspapers) for recycling (R60 per load), and guarding goods for unlicensed hawkers—who pay them with overripe fruits and vegetables that they cannot sell. Others beg for handouts or resort to petty thievery. Still others wander the streets of affluent middle-class neighborhoods, offering to haul trash, mow lawns, clean yards, and dig ditches for money or food (Rogerson 1996b).[25]

Inner-City Wastelands: The Ravening Streetscape

> A homeless man broke into President Thabo Mbeki's Cape Town
> residence and lived there for days before being arrested on
> Tuesday. A presidential spokeswoman said the 27-year-old
> intruder had not gained entry to the private quarters of
> Mr. Mbeki, who was away when the man broke in last Friday.

City officials estimated that in 2005 at least 230,000 people lived in around thirty-seven thousand residential dwelling units located in the Johannesburg inner city.[26] In contrast to large-scale cities such as New York, London, and Paris, the residential accommodation that exists in the Johannesburg central business core is largely scattered in disconnected pockets away from the dense concentrations of high-rise commercial buildings, lofty skyscrapers,

24. Quotation taken from Anna Cox, "Jo'burg Homeless Go from a Hovel to Nothing," *The Star,* March 17, 2002; Anna Cox, "Joburgers Live and Die in Decay and Filth," *The Star,* September 6, 2001; and Anna Cox, "Jo'burg Destitute out of the Dog Box," *The Star,* October 29, 2001. According to the Registrar of Deeds, the Pepperpot Houses were owned by Ideal Insurance Brokers in Lynnwood, Pretoria, and Yu Keng Huang was listed as company director.

25. Vivian Warby, "Icy Chill Hits Homeless and Poor the Hardest," *The Star,* May 7, 2001; and Caiphus Kgosana, "Rubbish Collector's Savings Trashed," *The Star,* January 22, 2004.

26. Quotation under subhead is from "South Africa: Presidential Break-In," *New York Times,* November 17, 2000. See Trafalgar Properties, *The Trafalgar Inner City Report 2005* (unpublished pamphlet, pp. 4–5). The estimates for the residential population for the Johannesburg inner city have varied from a low of around two hundred thousand to a high of perhaps four hundred thousand people. The true figure would be nearly impossible to discern.

and mammoth office towers. For the most part, residential housing is situated along the outer edges of the central business district, in decaying areas like Doornfontein, New Doornfontein, and Bertrams, near the Ellis Park Stadium complex, on the east side; around Malvern, Jeppestown, and Belgravia at the southeastern corner; and Mayfair, Fordsburg, and Ferreirasdorp on the west. On balance, the central city has few amenities like eating establishments, cultural venues, or shopping outlets readily accessible to the ordinary public, especially on weekends and after dark. Most of the housing stock dispersed around the central city is substandard, as poor people have crowded into once-elegant apartment blocks that often lack the basic necessities of plumbing, water, and electricity (du Plessis and Wilson 2005, 41–42).[27] The high-density residential core of the inner city is located just northeast of the downtown business district in the contiguous neighborhoods of Hillbrow, Berea, and Joubert Park. This highly compact area consists in the main of cavernous streets flanked with a jumble of high-rise apartment blocs, short-stay hotels, and interspersed with ground-level retail shopping outlets.[28]

To truly grasp the significance of the insecurity in housing—spectral, ephemeral, and fleeting—requires moving beyond strictly empirical questions of socioeconomic inequality and material deprivation and into the intersecting and overlapping experiences of shortage, speculation, overcrowding, and improvisation in both public and private space. Impermanent shelter is inextricably linked with the everyday realities of collapsing infrastructure, unhygienic conditions, rodent infestations, absentee landlordism, rack-renting, gangsterism, crime, fleeting friendships, unstable households, sharing with strangers, and the almost total lack of privacy. The scarcity of affordable, decent, and stable housing goes hand in hand with the impermanence, transience, and provisionality of the everyday lives for the urban poor (Kihato and Landau 2005; Appadurai 2000, 635).

The scope of insecure, substandard housing is so varied and complex that it defies simple classification. The terrain of habitation ranges from dirty blankets or cardboard boxes of the truly destitute who sleep on the pavement, in alleyways, or in doorways to overcrowded flats in anonymous apartment blocks where revolving numbers of unrelated residents share a single room. At night, competition is fierce for pavement space. Hundreds of homeless people bed down on the corners of Rissik and Plein streets and Loveday and De Villiers streets in the heart of the central city. Sleeping in small groups on sidewalks in the open gives way to clusters of ramshackle

27. *Business Day,* "'Substantial Progress' in Revival of the CBD," May 20, 2004; and interviews with Graeme Gotz.
28. Neil Fraser, "Decade of Change Scorecard (2): How Are We Making Out in the Residential Sector?" *Citichat,* August 16, 2004.

Figure 7. City in Ruins. Photograph by Aubrey P. Graham

shacks hidden under bridges, along streams, and tucked away in little-used alleys. These, in turn, blend into semipermanent illegal structures along rail-road lines, erected in vacant lots, or secreted in dense vegetation, where residents have clandestinely tapped into electricity lines or even water pipes. Still other poor residents have invaded abandoned buildings, vacant warehouses, or any unused properties, where they have divided the interior spaces into makeshift dwellings. Anywhere from five hundred to eight hundred homeless people, including large numbers of politically stranded refugees from Zimbabwe, find nightly refuge in the halls of the Central Methodist Church in the central city.[29] Those with reliable and steady sources of income have found accommodation in substandard rental units, particularly in over-crowded flats in decaying apartment blocks concentrated in the inner-city high-rise neighborhoods of Hillbrow, Berea, and Joubert Park, spilling over into nearby Yeoville and Orange Grove. All along the vast southern side of the city—from Jeppestown on the southeast to Marshalltown in the center and Fordsburg in the southwest—homeless squatters have squeezed into abandoned buildings, seized unused office blocks, and invaded vacant ware-houses. The urban poor have also surreptitiously moved into decaying residential neighborhoods that virtually encircle the central city in an elongated, gentle arc that extends from Pageview and Mayfair on the western edge, Brixton on the northwest, Belgravia on the east, and Highlands and Bellevue on the northeastern side.[30]

In 2005 municipal authorities reacted with growing alarm to what they regarded as the almost unstoppable advance of a decaying slum belt that had spread not only to the high-rise zones of the inner city but was also quickly extending to once-stable residential areas on the periphery, including Bertrams, Troyeville, Doornfontein, Lorentzville, and Malvern. Health officials, town planning experts, and law enforcement agencies complained bitterly about wily slumlords who have "conquered large chunks of Johannesburg, 'hijacking' houses and blocks of flats from their legitimate owners" and diverting rental payments from tenants into their own pockets and absconding on debt. As vast areas of the residential landscape are turned into decaying slums occupied by tens of thousands of poor people living in appalling conditions, the City of Johannesburg has been unable to evict illegal tenants and recoup unpaid water, electricity, and rates bills. As a multibillion rand business that has deprived the municipality of much-needed revenue, slumlording has become, in the words of Allan Wheeler, the manager of the Department of Planning,

29. See Tamlyn Stewart, "Crowded House of Hope," *Business Day,* June 17, 2006; and Reesha Chibba, "It's a Hard Life on the Streets of Johannesburg," *Mail & Guardian,* June 9–15, 2006.

30. Christina Gallagher, "Slumlords Invade Johannesburg"; David Pincus, "Law Is Not on Landlords' Side"; and Anna Cox, "Jo'burgers Live and Die."

Transportation, and Environment, "the biggest scourge of the city and almost impossible to control."[31]

Cartographic maps of the urban streetscape produce a discourse about the city that is predicated on the appearance of optical coherence, or what Henri Lefebvre (1991, 355–356) called the reduction of the urban landscape to "the undifferentiated state of the visible-readable realm." This kind of spatial representation homogenizes differences and hence conceals gaps or fissures in the urban fabric, where the seemingly unallowable and the unwanted are sometimes able to creep in (McDonough 1994, 65, 69). Despite the illusion of clarity that comes with identifying areas on a city map with degrees of socioeconomic status, the various sorts of insecure housing arrangements for the poor cannot be neatly segregated and distinguished by area, neighborhood, or sometimes even street. The reason for this ontological difficulty is simple: although insecure housing is concentrated in particular zones of the inner city, the poor have carved out accommodation for themselves—albeit unevenly— across the length and breadth of the urban landscape. When expressed as cartographic representations on maps, the boundaries separating different parts of the city appear geographically fixed. In the mundane conduct of daily life, however, there is a constant flow of people across these putative boundaries, since affluent suburban residents have come to rely on a large number of underpaid serving people, occupying a wide range of occupations, to support their opulent and leisurely lifestyles. Law enforcement agencies have reported numerous cases of squatters who illegally occupied grand, stately homes that were temporarily left vacant by their affluent owners in such upscale residential neighborhoods as Houghton, Parkwood, and Saxonwold (where properties have routinely sold for anywhere from R3 million to R7 million).[32] Almost without exception, access to insecure housing, including pavement spots, backyard shacks behind middle-class homes in suburbia, and rental units in tenement buildings, is subject to much negotiation and bargaining. Because of the vast opportunities for self-enrichment, powerful figures often try to use their control over access to shelter to extort rent, protection money, and favors from powerless tenants.[33]

31. Quoted in Christina Gallagher, "Slumlords Invade Johannesburg." Information and ideas derived from interview with Nazira Cachalia, program manager, City Safety Programme, City of Johannesburg, May 30, 2006; interview with Lael Bethlehem, chief executive officer, Johannesburg Development Agency, City of Johannesburg, May 30, 2006; and interview with Graeme Gotz.

32. For example, squatters illegally occupied a once-beautiful home belonging to Orlando Pirates chairperson Irvin Khoza in Saxonwold. Squatters vandalized the house, removing windows, doors, and electrical fittings. Neighbors complained of drug dealing and prostitution on the premises (Anna Cox, "Police Force Squatters").

33. Anna Cox, "My Building Has Been Hijacked," The Star, September 29, 2004.

In the upper-middle-class neighborhoods of the affluent northern suburbs, the live-in poor—typically, those working as domestic helpers, gardeners, or child-minders—have fashioned tenuous rights to backyard shacks, converted garages, or disconnected servants' quarters. They have engaged in an endless variety of tactical maneuvers to accommodate friends and dependents in their living quarters. For their part, property owners, large and small, have waged a protracted and relentless war against this colonization of space from below. Yet the urban poor can never be completely excluded and driven away from the affluent middle-class areas of the city. Merchants, shop owners, and affluent homeowners are dependent on the labor of the poor for the odd jobs they choose not to do for themselves, whether as domestic servants, child-minders, gardeners, drivers, handymen, carpenters, or private security guards. The trade-off for continued and reliable access to low-cost labor for menial tasks is often the provision of some sort of makeshift housing accommodation (du Plessis and Wilson 2005, 12–25).[34]

The fragmented, tangled, and harrowing stories of a few of the desperately poor who have found temporary refuge in the inner-city neighborhoods of Johannesburg can help to illuminate the circumstances surrounding homelessness. Liumwani Ramaliuhana, a refugee from Zimbabwe, found temporary refuge for herself and her four children in a cramped cubicle in a high-rise Hillbrow apartment building. For as little as R200 per month, women like Liumwani share accommodation in a single room with as many as seven others. With bed sheets dangling from strings to protect their privacy, they share practically everything else, from bathroom facilities to kitchen space. Oftentimes, immigrants—from Kenya, the Democratic Republic of Congo, Nigeria, Senegal, Mozambique, Zimbabwe, Angola, or Cameroon—prefer to occupy one whole flat with others from their home country. With a staggering fifty-nine thousand crimes committed in Hillbrow between 1999 and 2001 (the last year detailed statistics were released), including 640 murders, 988 rapes, 7,521 assaults, 6,775 armed robberies, and 3,523 stolen vehicles, the area is especially dangerous, particularly for immigrants (whether documented or undocumented) who cannot afford to move to the less insecure, but still hostile, neighborhoods of Yeoville and Berea, and who are frequently preyed upon by thieves, corrupt police, and criminal gangs.[35]

Sixteen-year-old Ahmed Ebrahim Ali fled war-ravaged Somalia in December 2001 and eventually reached Johannesburg. Suffering with severe gastric ulcers, he is afraid to leave his tiny, one-room living quarters in Fordsburg,

34. For the source of these ideas, see Appadurai 2000, 627–651, esp. 635–637.
35. "South Africa: The Hell Where Illegal Immigrants Seek Refuge," *The East African Standard* (Nairobi), May 2, 2004.

except to cross the road to work at a local restaurant, where he waits tables in exchange for food and a place to stay. As an unaccompanied minor without a parent or legal guardian, Ahmed is ineligible to apply for asylum. The teenager does not hang round street corners and talk with others his own age, for if he is arrested, he faces immediate deportation. Faced with similar circumstances, Kabongo Ngoy, a twenty-four-year-old refugee from Zaire, cares for eight children, all family relatives, ranging in age from three to twelve years old. Out of money and out of work, the children's parents abandoned them almost two years ago. After their mother stopped sending money, the children were expelled from their school in Yeoville. The children spend their days in the house, bored and hungry, playing on a pile of worn, urine-soaked mattresses. Water and electricity have been disconnected because of failure to pay the bills. Over time, the interior of the house was emptied of its contents because Ngoy sold most of their meager belongings, one by one, to pay for food.[36]

The homeless poor survive in the shadow of urban ruins. The overlapping and intersecting stories of the homeless poor take place among the fading glories of decaying buildings and the deteriorating built environment. In his autobiography, *Long Walk to Freedom*, Nelson Mandela (1994, 130) reminisced about the law practice he and his partner, Oliver Tambo, established in 1952 at Chancellor House, "a small building just across the street from the marble statues of Justice standing in front of the Magistrate's Court in central Johannesburg." The fate of Chancellor House, a nondescript building that has fallen into an advanced state of disrepair, illustrates the overall pattern of heritage triage that has befallen many iconic structures in the central city. In the late 1990s homeless squatters seized the vacant building, located in Fox Street in a decaying part of the downtown landscape, partitioning its interior into makeshift rooms. Suffering from years of neglect, and with more than three hundred squatters crammed into every available interior space, the two-story building has deteriorated so badly that it was "rotting into oblivion." Lacking water and electricity and with all the windows broken, the building has become a crime den, where prostitution and drug dealing are rife. While historical preservation advocates proclaimed that the site "serves as a reminder of the suffering and sacrifice that led to democracy in our country," the South African Heritage Resources Agency (SAHRA), a state-sponsored agency established to look at the development of nationally significant locations, said that Chancellor House was actually never on their priority list of recommended preservation sites.[37]

36. Khadija Magardie, "AAGM: The Plight of Africa's Refugee Children," *Mail & Guardian*, February 2–8, 2002.
37. "Madiba's [Mandela's] Old Offices a Crime Den," *Mail & Guardian*, February 6–12, 2004.

Killer Cold

[Solly Mdluli], 33, who had slept in sub-zero temperatures at
Park Station, said: "I'm scared of going to sleep tonight because
I don't know if I will wake up in the morning.... I had made
a blanket out of sacks and plastic bags, but it was useless. It
became so cold that I couldn't feel my body."

In the bitter cold of winter the plight of the urban poor always turns from
bad to worse.[38] When temperatures have dipped below freezing, countless numbers of homeless people over the years have died of exposure, and many more
have suffered from hypothermia and frostbite. As the icy winter weather en-
gulfs the high veldt, the homeless routinely flood emergency shelters, churches,
and soup kitchens to seek relief from the bitter cold. The Salvation Army dis-
tributes thousands of blankets and food packets at donation points around
the central city; it also sends out these much-needed items in mobile soup
kitchens that make regular nightly stops at dozens of out-of-the-way places
where small numbers of homeless squatters huddle against the cold. In times
of severe weather crisis, emergency crews take to the streets, scouring the by-
ways, alleyways, and parks, seeking to rescue the unfortunate ones who face the
immediate threat of freezing to death. With limited resources, Salvation Army
workers are often engaged in a kind of impromptu triage, providing hot meals,
blankets, and warm clothing to women and children before adult males.[39]

In mid-July 2000 a severe cold front brought icy temperatures to the greater
Johannesburg metropolitan region. At least one person—discovered in an
alley in Norwood—died from exposure to the freezing conditions that gripped
the city over the weekend. While hundreds of homeless sought refuge at soup
kitchens, churches, or the homeless shelters, emergency crews from the Salvation Army and local churches rescued dozens from almost certain death,
including sixteen homeless people who were found in very critical condition
in Joubert Park. According to Captain Timothy Mabaso, mission development
officer of the Salvation Army, some of the victims could not walk or speak
properly when they were found. The victims had tried unsuccessfully to use
flimsy cardboard boxes to shield themselves from the bitter cold, and some had
made fires with discarded refuse in order to provide a modicum of warmth.
All across the greater Johannesburg metropolitan region, charitable organizations were stretched to the limit to provide assistance for the homeless. Salvation Army volunteers staffed soup kitchens at places like New Doornfontein

---

38. Quote found in Jonathan Ancer, "Homeless Man."
39. *SAPA*, "A Warm Meal and a Blanket against the Cold," July 30, 2001; *SAPA*, "Salvation
Army Hands Out Food, Blankets to Homeless," July 21, 2001; and Ndivhuwo Khangale, "Blankets
and Soup."

and at their downtown storefront in Simmonds Street, as men, women, and children sought protection from the freezing temperatures. Salvation Army sanctuaries throughout the inner city and beyond were filled to capacity, with more than double the number of people usually seeking shelter. Emergency crews reported a sharp rise in the numbers of sick children needing assistance. With hundreds of people trying to warm themselves with burning wood, trash, and other debris in open-pits, firefighters responded to more than fifty incidents of out-of-control fires over the weekend.[40]

Single events like this one typify the ongoing struggle of homeless people, who are forced to find rudimentary shelter on the unforgiving streets of Johannesburg. Like those living in informal settlements, homeless squatters rely on fires for warmth—sometimes with disastrous consequences. Those who live in inadequate housing are disproportionately affected by such cold-related emergencies as devastating shack fires, electrocutions, and inhalation of poisonous gases and smoke from brazier-type fires. In addition, high-tension failures resulting from the overuse of electrical appliances to escape the cold cause frequent power outages.[41]

Squatting in the Central City: The Fire Next Time

> For here, right in the heart of one of the continent's cleaner cities, is without doubt the filthiest place in the world. The dirtiest places that Lagos could have offered—large areas of Mushin, Ajegunle, and Osholdi—pale in comparison to the Drill Hall homeless place, which bestrides Twist and Plein streets. A military barracks until 1994, 8 Plein Street is an example of a society gone awry.
>
> OSITA NWAJAH

Just as firestorms have routinely swept through informal squatter settlements on the outlying metropolitan fringe, raging infernos have seriously damaged or destroyed once-majestic buildings scattered around the central city.[42] Catastrophic fires typically break out in derelict buildings that are more often than not occupied by homeless squatters, desperate people who prefer the wretched conditions of interior hovels to the unpredictable vagaries of life

---

40. Chimaimba Banda, Melanie-Ann Feris, and SAPA, "Icy Weather Gnaws at Jo'burg Rescue Services," *The Star*, July 16, 2000; *Mail & Guardian*, "Cold Snap a Killer," July 17, 2000; and Nandi Ngcobo, "Fire and Ice Have SA in Killer Grip," *The Star*, July 19, 2000.

41. Jonathan Ancer, "Homeless Man"; and Isaac Mahlangu, "I Feel It in My Bones," *Sunday Times*, July 13, 2003.

42. The quote is from Osita Nwajah, "The Filthiest Place in the World," *Mail & Guardian*, October 7–13, 2000.

on the street. In the Johannesburg inner city, the persistent demand for affordable housing, coupled with the departure of middle-class property owners and apartment tenants, has accompanied the steady deterioration of the built environment. The vicious cycle of "inadequate regulation and negligent enforcement" has given rise to a burgeoning slumlord economy, where absentee ownership, deliberate overcrowding, rack-renting, and building hijacking have expanded alongside deteriorating service delivery, inattention to maintenance and repair, and declining standards of code enforcement and building safety (quotation from Davis 1998, 114, 119–120).[43]

The intense fire that swept through the historic Drill Hall in April 2002 signified not only a catastrophic event of tragedy and death but also the end point of complex historical processes of ongoing spatial restructuring culminating in urban ruination. This fiery conflagration, which resulted in the deaths of five people—one a disabled man with artificial legs who was unable to outrun the flames—came less than a year after a similar blaze completely gutted the front of the building and caused the deaths of five squatters.[44]

Yet to adequately narrate this linkage between events and processes requires multiple stories—told from sometimes intersecting, overlapping, or conflicting points of view. As Erin Manning (2000), Michel-Rolph Trouillot (1995), and other scholars have suggested, stories cannot be "expected to unfold sequentially as ever-accumulating histories marching straight forward in plot and dénouement—too much is happening against the grain of time, traversing the story-line laterally" (Manning 2000, 77). Stories are encapsulated in space. Contested meanings and changing uses attached to place complicate and interrupt the temporal flow of a single, all-encompassing story line.

City ruins signal the destructive power of history, as the past remains in the present as visual, physical reminders of destruction, decay, and trauma. As fragments of the past, ruins disrupt and unsettle the present. Just as the field of psychoanalysis is dedicated to uncovering the power of the past as it acts on the lives in the present, the investigation of urban culture must look to history to understand the power of the past to haunt the city of the present. As material objects, city places are located in historical time and hence are subject to the seemingly inexorable temporal forces of decay, breakdown, and ruination that threaten oblivion (Edensor 2005a, 2005b; Highmore 2005, 4–5).

43. See Christina Gallagher, "Slumlords Invade Johannesburg"; Anna Cox, "'My Building Has Been Hijacked'"; David Pincus, "Law Is Not on Landlords' Side"; and Anna Cox, "Landlords to Ask for Bigger Deposits," *The Star*, October 8, 2004.

44. Vivian Warby, "Historic Jo'burg Hall Burns Down, Killing Two," *The Star*, April 8, 2002; *SAPA*, "Rescuers Search for Missing in Hall Fire," April 8, 2002; *SAPA*, "Five Bodies Pulled from Drill Hall Ruins," April 8, 2002; *SAPA*, "Five Die after Woman Sets Husband Ablaze," April 8, 2002; and *SAPA*, "Five Die in Jo'burg Drill Hall Blaze," *The Star*, June 16, 2001.

The Drill Hall, located on the corner of Plein and Twist streets in the heart of the city and facing Joubert Park, is one such place where the past has continued to impinge on the present. Over the course of its almost century-long existence, this sprawling building served all sorts of different uses, with different and conflicting meanings attached to it. In the end, it came to an ignominious demise in a raging fire that reduced the place to a pile of smoldering debris in a matter of minutes.[45]

There is no urban space without folds and creases, gaps and silences, light and shadow, and memory and loss (Doel 1996, 422–437). As artifacts of another time and place, decaying buildings become stark reminders of the outdatedness of visions that have lost their luster. Built in 1904 immediately after the end of the Anglo-Boer War, the Drill Hall originated as the home to the victorious British military forces, and as such it functioned as an iconic symbol of the geographic extension of the British Empire on African soil. For decades it served as the headquarters of the Witwatersrand Military Command and as the only military installation in the middle of the city. In the 1950s the huge, hulking building achieved a different kind of notoriety when it doubled as the courtroom site for the Treason Trial, which began in 1957 and dragged on until 1961, in which 156 activists were charged with conspiring to overthrow the apartheid government. In his autobiography, Nelson Mandela (1994, 176)—one of the accused in the trial—described the structure as "a great barn of a building with a corrugated iron roof, and considered the only public building large enough to support a trial of so many accused." In 1962, in a symbolic gesture of defiance, the late Joe Slovo—a well-known Communist Party stalwart and ANC activist—failed to burn the building down with an incendiary device. When the military left the premises in the early 1990s as a result of downsizing, the building stood empty and deserted, prompting homeless squatters—led by the Johannesburg Tenants Association—to invade the vacant building in 1994 and reconfigure its interior for their own purposes.[46]

For the urban poor, squatting has always involved collective action and mobilization. Many of the original squatters who occupied the vacant Drill Hall were jobless work seekers who had been living nearby, in shacks and on pavements around Park Station and Joubert Park. With the squatter invasion, the Drill Hall no longer accomplished the grand visual spectacle that the military had designated for it. The homeless occupation of the building signaled the beginning of an accelerated process of irreversible decline.[47]

---

45. Thomas Thale, "Shackland in the Halls of Darkness," *The Star*, March 28, 2002.
46. *SAPA*, "Five Bodies Pulled"; Gudrun Hecki, "Apartheid Relic Bulldozed," *The Star*, April 11, 2002; and Thomas Thale, "Shackland in the Halls of Darkness."
47. Gudrun Hecki, "Apartheid Relic Bulldozed."

Before it was completely destroyed by fire, the Drill Hall—when viewed from a distance—still managed to retain the look of imposing, baroque grandeur despite obvious signs of neglect etched on its faded and crumbling facade. The streetscape surrounding the building was crowded with the mobile poor, shuttling from place to place in search of opportunities to make ends meet. Indifference, negligence, and outright abuse slowly consumed the cavernous structure, transforming what had been a well-maintained building into a derelict shell without electricity, running water, or heat. Squatters erected shacks in the deep shadows of the interior, living in virtual darkness even on the brightest days. Ruins were evident everywhere: in the stench of uncollected piles of discarded garbage, in the open sewers, in the emaciated bodies of the aimless poor surviving on homemade beer and cannabis. By the time of its demise the Drill Hall had deteriorated into a hulking, decaying relic of another time and place in world history that had become a fugitive place for discarded urban outcasts, the last refuge for truly desperate squatters imprisoned in the futureless world of joblessness, hunger, and despair. Daily living under overcrowded conditions led invariably to filthy surroundings. Piles of uncollected rubbish and exposed toilet facilities created an unbearable stench. Some of the hundreds of poor people who squatted in the rat-infested building lived in makeshift shacks erected around the perimeter. Others carved its vast, cavernous interior spaces into a warren of tiny cubicles divided by cardboard partitions. An entire squatter community of close to three hundred fifty families lived in randomly scattered rows of corrugated iron shacks erected in the main hall, each the size of an average room and shrouded in shadows. The more fortunate residents occupied about a dozen rooms that used to be army offices in the double-story building adjacent to the main hall. Gideon Mvelase, the recognized chairperson of the Drill Hall squatters committee, lived in one of these rooms, partitioned with a curtain, with his wife and two other men. The building was without electricity, running water, or toilet facilities, yet residents did not complain, since they were used to relying on candles for light and paraffin for cooking.[48]

The squatter occupation of the building set in motion a very different use of the interior space and its objects. Because of their straitened circumstances, the inhabitants of the squalid place looked on such accoutrements as doorways, windows, appliances, electrical fixtures, wiring, and plumbing not for their symbolic or aesthetic value, but as items for trade, barter, or sale. The social interactions that took place inside the building represented a microcosm of the wider social world of homelessness and survivalism in the central city.

---

48. Osita Nwajah, "The Filthiest Place in the World"; and Thomas Thale, "Shackland in the Halls of Darkness."

Enterprising entrepreneurs had erected a *spaza* shop next to the entrance, and stocked it with small quantities of the prosaic necessities of daily living, along with other odds and ends, like soap, toilet rolls, cooking oil, cigarettes, biscuits, chewing gum, and matches.[49]

For years, city officials complained that the dilapidated Drill Hall had become a health and fire hazard, accusing the homeless squatters who had commandeered the premises of reducing the building to a city slum. Even though the building was designated as a historic heritage site that fell under the stewardship of SAHRA, little progress had been made in finding alternative housing for the homeless who lived there and in marshalling the funding required to restore the derelict building. In the end, years of neglect and the two devastating fires took their toll. Declared structurally unsafe by the City of Johannesburg in April 2002, city officials authorized wrecking crews to bulldoze significant portions of the sprawling building.[50]

For the homeless poor, the driving force behind illegal squatting in the inner city is the unmet demand for rental accommodation that is affordable and that conforms to at least minimal health and safety standards. For city officials, however, unauthorized squatting—in all its variegated modalities—signifies the breakdown in the boundaries separating the orderly city from the disorderly city. In the official mind, policing these boundaries requires ever more-vigilant monitoring and surveillance of decay and neglect, the stringent enforcement of city bylaws, and the forcible eviction of tenants inhabiting bad buildings. Municipal authorities looked upon squalid sites like the Drill Hall as disreputable places, cesspools of disease and human degradation, dens of all sorts of iniquity, and safe havens for illegal aliens. In their view, these places have become terra incognita, sites outside the official gaze of authority that have slipped beyond the grasp of law and order. In the months preceding the devastating fire that finally destroyed the building, city officials unveiled plans to evict the squatters by force if necessary and relocate them either to Vlakfontein, south of Soweto, or to a temporary transit camp outside the city pending a final decision.[51]

For urban planners, control of the everyday uses of urban space was an indispensable part of the establishment of municipal sovereignty. With the end of apartheid, urban planners introduced new rules and regulations designed

49. Osita Nwajah, "The Filthiest Place in the World."
50. Buhle Khumalo, "Joburg Mayor Promises a Clean Sweep of the City," *The Star*, February 18, 2001; Gudrun Hecki, "Apartheid Relic Bulldozed." One small section of the original building was preserved and restored in late 2003 (Gudrun Hecki, "About Turn," *Sunday Times*, December 14, 2003).
51. Moipone Malefane, "Woman Arrested after Drill Hall Fire Kills 5," *SAPA*, April 8, 2002.

to produce an orderly cityscape and govern the everyday uses of urban space. In short, sovereignty over the municipal landscape meant that measures had to be taken to make the poor relate to the urban environment according to the rules of elite imagination, not their own. In order to ensure conformity to this social arrangement, city officials have found it necessary to obtain the obedience of the poor to the normative ideal of the city as orderly, hygienic, and predictable. As one city councilor, Sizakele Nkosi, pointedly put it, "these people [i.e., illegal squatters] are not used to paying for services and we must first teach them to develop a sense of ownership and responsibility."[52]

City officials have sought to distance themselves from normative notions of public obligation and responsibility, suggesting instead that the burden of survival rested with the ability of the poor to earn a living for themselves. Rather than viewing the cesspool at the Drill Hall as a vivid symbol of the failure of the city to adequately deal with the homeless problem, city officials seemed content to focus on the self-destructive behavior of desperately poor people and the disreputable actions of criminals who preyed on the residents there. In the wake of the disaster, executive mayor Amos Masondo promised that "our zero-tolerance stance on illegal squatting and bad buildings in the inner city will go ahead with more vigour and speed." The mayor proclaimed that there were a number of low-rent options available to transient-type communities who needed shelter. When questioned about how the homeless and unemployed were expected to find money to pay rent, Masondo responded by saying that the city "will not tolerate 'transients' who did not pay their dues.... You cannot use human rights to promote anarchy," he declared.[53] City councilor Sol Cowen echoed these hard-line sentiments, proclaiming that the municipality was under no legal obligation to find housing for people who occupied buildings illegally. In the meantime, city officials managed to transport some of the burned-out residents of the building to a temporary transit camp at Eikenhof to await their eventual relocation to Vlakfontein near Orange Farm. Nevertheless, less fortunate victims of the devastating fire were "back on the streets with nowhere to go."[54]

Three months later, in an incident eerily reminiscent of the gutting of Drill Hall, a huge fire virtually destroyed the old Marshall Street Barracks, a three-story edifice that had been built in 1913. The building originally served as police headquarters for central Johannesburg before it became home to the Transvaal

---

52. See Thomas Thale, "Shackland in the Halls of Darkness."

53. The first quotation from Amos Masondo comes from Gudren Hecki, "Apartheid Relic Bulldozed." The second comes from *SAPA*, "Four Derelict JHB Buildings to Be Demolished," April 24, 2002.

54. Moipone Malefane, "Woman Arrested"; and Gudrun Hecki, "Apartheid Relic Bulldozed." Quotation from Vivian Warby, "Historic Jo'burg Hall."

Light Horse Regiment and, later, the Irish Regiment. When the South African military downsized and moved most of its operations out of Johannesburg, the Marshall Street Barracks was left empty and virtually abandoned until homeless squatters began to occupy the premises. At the time of the outbreak of the fire, close to one thousand people lived inside the rambling structure, which was owned by the provincial public works department. Sidewalk hawkers used the large inner courtyard area as a storage facility for their wares—ranging from shoes and clothing to electronic goods and foodstuffs. Once firefighters arrived to extinguish the blazing inferno, most of the inhabitants—largely undocumented immigrants—fled the scene. Fearing arrest or harassment, those who remained behind were largely hostile and uncooperative with municipal authorities.[55]

The deplorable housing situation in the inner city has unleashed a tripartite struggle among desperate inner-city residents seeking inexpensive accommodation, irresponsible landlords aiming to squeeze profits out of neglected buildings, and harried city officials trying in vain to maintain proper health and safety standards in decaying residential neighborhoods. Whether as legitimate rent-paying tenants or as unauthorized squatters, the urban poor who have crowded into blighted buildings in the inner city face a host of inconveniences, hardships, and dangers, ranging from lack of electricity and water to exposure to toxins and other contaminants. But it is the sudden outbreak of fire that poses perhaps the greatest threat to bodily harm. Just days before Christmas 2005 four people, including three children, were burned to death in a blaze that destroyed a double garage in Kimberly Road, Judith Park, in the central city. In August 2006 another eight people were killed and one was critically injured when two dilapidated Johannesburg inner-city buildings that had been illegally converted for residential use caught fire. While they often go unreported in conventional media outlets, incidents like these take place with frightening regularity in the inner-city neighborhoods where dilapidated residential accommodation is the norm.[56]

Under circumstances where the slumlord economy has thrived and where health and safety precautions are largely ignored, fires in dilapidated buildings have become inevitable occurrences, often with tragic consequences.[57] The

55. *SAPA*, "Fire Partially Destroys Historic Building," *The Star*, October 23, 2002; and *SAPA*, "Arson Investigated in Historic Jo'burg Blaze," October 23, 2002. The African Council of Hawkers and Informal Businesses reported that around two thousand informal traders lost goods to the value of R10-million [$1.3 million] in the fire. See *SAPA*, "Police Probe Arson Claims at Historic Jo'burg Building."

56. Jillian Green, "Fire Kills Four in Johannesburg City Centre," *The Star*, December 23, 2005; and *SAPA*, "Eight Killed in Joburg Fires," August 27, 2006.

57. City officials placed the blame for a blaze in April 2001 on an illegal electrical connection; the fire tore through a block of flats at the corner of Nugget and Bree streets and resulted in the

raging inferno that swept through the derelict Johnny's Woodcraft building at the corner of Commissioner and Nugget streets in the heart of the central city in the early morning hours of March 27, 2006, represents in microcosm the precariousness of everyday living in the inner city. With eight men and four women dead, nine more people in critical condition, and nineteen others seriously injured, this horrific episode was one of the worst fire-related tragedies in Johannesburg's history. The fire began shortly after 1:00 A.M. on the top floor of the unused two-story workshop when a stove used as a heater overloaded the electrical fuse and burst into flames. The blaze spread quickly and soon engulfed the entire building in swirling black smoke and intense heat. In their unsuccessful effort to save some of their belongings, many residents had piled TVs, bicycles, blankets, radios, and clothes into the hallways, inadvertently trapping themselves and others inside the burning building. As panic-stricken people rushed to escape the raging fire, they discovered to their horror that the single entrance was locked and the key was missing. A passing tow-truck operator saw the flames and stopped his vehicle, tying a steel cable to the locked steel gate and ripping it off its hinges. If this driver had not come to the rescue, many more people would have undoubtedly perished in the fire.[58]

Only weeks earlier, at least a hundred fifty homeless squatters—mainly undocumented immigrants from Malawi and Zimbabwe—had quietly invaded the abandoned building, converting the disused carpentry workshop into makeshift dormitories, where anywhere from two to six people crowded into each room. The abandoned building was totally unsuitable for human habitation, with only two toilets and one entrance—which was locked every night at 10:00 P.M. to protect residents from unwanted intruders—and an emergency exit, which was blocked by debris. This tragedy was just another horrific episode in an uninterrupted (but largely invisible) pattern of similar tragedies that highlight the everyday dangers faced by desperate residents of the hundreds of dilapidated inner-city buildings, who live without electricity or sanitation and are forced to prepare meals and warm themselves on primus stoves

---

deaths of five people. Fire inspectors speculated that a locked security gate restricting access to the upstairs rooms prevented trapped victims from escaping the inferno. Like other slum dwellings in the central city, this six-bedroom, double-story apartment complex was severely overcrowded: about forty people were crammed into the building, someone had constructed a makeshift shack in the kitchen, and at least one person was living under the stairwell. In seeking to arrange alternative accommodation for those displaced by the devastating fire, municipal authorities tried in vain to identify and locate the owner of the building (Simon Nare, "Two Children Killed in Johannesburg Fire," *SAPA*, April 3, 2001).

58. Lee Rondganger, "'I Walked on People to Escape the Flames,'" *The Star*, March 30, 2006; Benita Enoch, "Council 'Must Provide for Poor Residents,'" *SAPA*, March 29, 2006; and *SAPA*, "Shelters Set Up for Joburg Fire Survivors," March 29, 2006.

and open fires.[59] City officials used this calamity to once again reiterate the need for the Inner-City Task Force to accelerate its efforts to enforce health and safety standards in derelict buildings and to defend their policy of condemning "bad buildings" and evicting their illegal occupants. In contrast, critics suggested that such horrible fires like this one symbolized in microcosm the lack of secure, affordable shelter in the inner city, arguing further that such senseless deaths and serious injuries demonstrated the "dismal failure" of the municipality "to deal productively with unsafe living conditions," as indicated by their refusal to provide "viable, decent, safe alternatives" for poor people.[60]

The fire also drew attention to the plight of immigrant work seekers who have typically found insecure residential accommodation with fellow nationals in the inner city. "We came here for a better life and to make money," Jeffrey Malama, an undocumented immigrant from Malawi who lost everything in the fire, explained. "If we go back home, we will be seen as failures."[61] In the meantime, while determined work seekers like Jeffrey Malama sought to put their lives back in order and to once again blend into the anonymity of the inner city, the unexpected outbreak of fires in residential buildings continued to subject the poorest of the poor to grave danger. At a dilapidated residential high-rise called Lorna Court at the corner of Twist and Wolmarans streets in Hillbrow, Michael Ndlovo made a miraculous, life-saving catch of a eight-month-old baby named Likhona Mviko after her desperate mother threw her from the top floor of a burning five-story building into the waiting arms of rescuers gathered below. Other residents of the block of flats were not so lucky: one person was burned to death, and the baby's mother, Thandiwe, and her cousin, Andisiwe Njwezana, were rushed to the hospital in critical condition after plunging to the ground when trying to escape the fire.[62] Several weeks later, a man and woman died after jumping out of the window of a burning building at the corner of Bree and Nugget streets. Once an upscale office block, the abandoned Frank and Hirsch building had been taken over

59. *SAPA,* "Inferno Workshop 'Should Have Been Condemned,'" March 29, 2006; Lee Rondganger, "'I Walked on People'"; *SAPA,* "Shelters Set Up"; Kwanele Sosibo and Lynley Donnelly, "Caught between Eviction and Dereliction," *Mail & Guardian,* March 30–April 5, 2006; *SAPA,* "Johannesburg Blaze Claims 12 Lives," March 29, 2006; and Lee Rondganger, "Immigrants Battle to Survive after Inferno," *The Star,* March 31, 2006.

60. The quotations are from Stuart Wilson, Centre for Applied Legal Studies (CALS), and are provided in Benita Enoch, "Council 'Must Provide for Poor Residents.'" See also "Inner City Fire Shows the Need for Adequate Housing, not Evictions," Media Statement, Centre for Applied Legal Studies (CALS) and Centre on Housing Rights and Evictions (COHRE), March 30, 2006.

61. *SAPA,* "Malawi Requests Details of Blaze Victims," March 31, 2006. Jeffrey Malama quoted in Lee Rondganger, "Immigrants Battle to Survive."

62. Poloko Tau and Linda Mbongwa, "Life-Saving Catch Made amid the Flames," *Pretoria News,* May 4, 2006; *SAPA,* "Domestic Quarrel Sparks Blaze in Joburg Flat," May 3, 2006; and Poloko Tau, "Mother in Coma after Baby Escapes from Fire," *The Star,* May 5, 2006.

by homeless squatters. In a three-month period ending in May 2006, at least fourteen deaths and scores of serious injuries were attributed to residential fires in the inner city.[63]

Seen from a wider angle of vision, these chronic fire tragedies are visible expressions of the deeply entrenched socioeconomic inequalities that have crystallized in the dual city. Desperate work seekers are inexorably drawn to the Johannesburg inner city because of its concentration of economic opportunities unavailable on the metropolitan periphery. Policy makers generally agree that, despite some notable achievements in the field of social-housing delivery, the supply of safe, secure residential accommodation for low-income residents has failed to keep up with the accelerating demand. While municipal authorities have pushed ahead with strategic initiatives designed to accelerate inner-city regeneration via a kind of middle-class gentrification, they have not implemented programs directed at meeting the conventional standards of inclusionary housing—where urban residents, no matter the income level of their households, have access to decent, affordable shelter.[64]

To a certain extent, policy makers have allowed the essential kernel of inner-city impoverishment—desperately poor people exploited by unscrupulous slumlords because they are unable to afford available, privately owned, moderately private rental housing—to be camouflaged by a normative discourse of "bad buildings," illegal squatting, and unsafe living conditions. While property owners, landlords, managing agents, and slumlords have largely escaped responsibility for the deplorable state of inner-city housing, the poor who have occupied these decaying buildings with crumbling infrastructure have borne the brunt of the social consequences, including evictions, disruption of their livelihoods, and displacement.[65]

Without access to low-cost, safe housing in the inner city, the urban poor have gambled with their lives, crowding into derelict buildings that have been allowed to fall into ruin. With a near monopoly on low-end shelter, slumlords and their managing agents have mercilessly exploited the desperately poor by charging exorbitant rents by the month, the week, and even the day. Dilapidated buildings with unworkable elevators, broken-down fire escapes, and blocked

63. *SAPA*, "One Dead after Fire at Joburg Building," May 21, 2006; *Independent Online*, "Street Kid Burns to Death in Basement," May 4, 2006; and Alex Eliseev, "Lensman Captures Drama of Plunge from Flames," *The Star*, May 23, 2006.

64. Kevin Allan and Karen Hesse, "The Dilemmas of a Growing Metropolis," *Business Day*, March 30, 2006; and Neil Fraser, "Breaking New Ground in the Inner City," *CitiChat*, March 6, 2006.

65. "My gripe has been that evictions do not solve the housing problem in the inner city, they exacerbate it" (Neil Fraser, "City Must Explore Ways to House the Poor," *CitiChat*, December 5, 2005). For the issue of nonprosecution of slumlords, see Neil Fraser, "Fire Raises Issue of Housing Needs—Again," *CitiChat*, April 3, 2006.

exits constitute the centerpiece of the hazardscape that the urban poor have to negotiate in the conduct of their everyday lives. Lacking alternative accommodation in the inner city, the desperate urban poor who have squeezed into these firetraps expose themselves to grave danger. With even privately owned low-income housing beyond their financial reach, the poorest of the poor are the most vulnerable to the ongoing social catastrophe.[66]

66. Information derived from on-site visit to decaying neighborhoods on the periphery of the inner city, June 3, 2006. See Neil Fraser, "Evictions—Between a Rock and a Hard Place," *CitiChat,* March 13, 2006; and "Inner City Fire Shows the Need," Media Statement, CALS and COHRE.

7

Revitalization and Displacement in the Inner City

> At the end of the day, inner cities [like Johannesburg] will become too expensive for the [poor] people that presently inhabit them.
>
> NEVILLE SCHAEFER, chief executive officer, Trafalgar Properties

S ometimes seemingly prosaic and unremarkable events, when looked at retrospectively, can be seen to signal a turning point in public perceptions and attitudes.[1] One such pivotal moment may have occurred on a particularly balmy June evening in 2004, as dozens of Jo'burg's new elite—representatives of the first generation of affluent urbanites who have come of age after the end of apartheid—gathered together for a gala social occasion on the thirteenth floor of the old Ernst and Young Building at the corner of Diagonal and Pritchard streets. As the young, trendy, and unmistakably well-to-do sipped white wine and colorful cocktails, tasted chocolate truffles, and gazed at the magnificent view of the surrounding skyline, young entrepreneurs Alfonso Botha and his partner Duan Coetzee, who together operate a property company called Urban Ocean, used the festive event to showcase their latest upscale residential development project. Rechristened as The Franklin, this completely renovated residential complex—with eighty individual units— bears only a superficial resemblance to its former life as the headquarters for a prestigious accounting and professional services company located in the historic financial district, situated opposite the old Johannesburg Stock Exchange building and overlooking the newly refurbished Newtown Cultural Precinct. The developers assured investors that The Franklin was fully equipped with 24-hour security, a central reception area, exclusive office and conference facilities, undercover parking, a gymnasium and wellness center,

---

1. Neville Schaefer quoted in *Business Day,* "Downtown Jo'burg Leads Urban Renewal," November 4, 2004.

an indoor swimming pool and spa, and exclusive street cafés and restaurants nearby. As demand for residential units at The Franklin increased, prices inched steadily upward, ranging from about R400,000 for a sixty-one square meter unadorned shell to R4 million for a top-floor penthouse, complete with an open-air garden, swimming pool, and large entertainment area with a stunning view of the cityscape.[2]

Urban Ocean is one of a handful of well-financed property development companies that have begun to buy under-utilized high-rise office buildings in blighted areas in downtown Johannesburg and to retrofit them into luxury residences for upwardly mobile young professionals and wealthy foreigner buyers.[3] Property developers catering to an upscale clientele envision the revival of downtown Johannesburg in terms of grand apartment complexes and luxurious condominiums with spectacular vistas, cozy street cafés, designer boutique hotels, and trendy nightspots.[4] While skeptics have remained unconvinced that these rejuvenation efforts have expanded beyond a comparatively narrow preoccupation of a few urban pioneers, ever-exuberant city boosters have pointed to stabilized rents for office space in the central city (albeit at levels far lower than during the heyday fifteen to twenty years earlier), declining vacancy rates, and rising business confidence as clear indications that inner-city decline had reached its nadir and that the central city was poised for an imminent recovery.[5]

---

2. Former quarterback for the Philadelphia Eagles Randall Cunningham purchased one of the first luxury penthouse apartments at The Franklin (Chantelle Benjamin, "Gridiron Star Buys Inner-City Penthouse," *Sunday Times*, September 26, 2004).

3. Urban Ocean acquired Corner House, one of the most ornate and historic office blocks located on the corner of Commissioner and Simmonds streets, converting its spacious interiors into expensive loft apartments with spectacular views of the city skyline. Apparently flushed with huge cash reserves, the company's two owner-entrepreneurs also purchased the former Stuttafords department store on the corner of Pritchard and Rissik streets, a once elegant art deco building in Loveday Street, the National Bank Building (80–84 Market Street), and Penmore Towers at the southern end of Rissik Street (renamed No. 1 Rissik Street). They planned to outfit all these refurbished luxury apartment buildings with swimming pools, spas, gymnasiums, rooftop gardens, on-site delis and cocktail lounges, limousine shuttle service for residents, and 24-hour doormen posted outside the buildings. Some penthouse apartments at No. 1 Rissik Street boast of their own private helicopter landing pads and clearance rights. For the information here and some of the following paragraphs, see Ian Fife, "Johannesburg CBD: The City Comes to Life," *Financial Mail*, September 19, 2003; Shanthini Naidoo, "Highlife in the Inner City," *Business Day*, June 28, 2004; and *Sunday Times*, "Sexing Up the City," September 21, 2003. The Urban Ocean foray into the property market of the old financial district was sponsored by a consortium of investors, including Athaenor Investments (with significant holdings in London), Alon Apteker (Internet Solutions), and Chris Convery, founder of Gray Security Services (now Securicor).

4. Ian Fife, "The City Comes to Life," *Financial Mail*, September 23, 2003.

5. See Marianne Pretorius, "The Relics We Relish," *Sunday Times*, August 15, 2004; and Nick Wilson, "Finest in City Living Back in Town," *Business Day*, January 28, 2004.

The Choreography of Urban Revitalization: Reinventing Inner-City Johannesburg Once Again

Since around 2001, prices for residential real estate in the inner city have climbed steadily upward, prompting city boosters to speak in upbeat terms of a "second gold rush" for downtown Johannesburg.[6] "Once a beleaguered and desolate place with little or no nightlife and a reputation for endemic crime and grime," the decidedly upbeat Trafalgar Inner City Report for 2005 declared, "the inner city is gentrifying with a vengeance."[7] The uplifting discourse accompanying urban regeneration efforts has laid particular stress on the return to the city as an expression of an emancipatory, liberatory, and trendy urbanism, an upscale social practice at work in other aspirant world-class cities around the globe. Property developers wanting to jump on the gentrification bandwagon have looked longingly on the downtown cityscape as a densely packed treasure trove of under-utilized historic buildings, efficient transport hubs, and an ample streetscape of broad pavements, "waiting to be transformed into the blends of commercial, residential, and retail development sweeping the cities of the world."[8] The "staggering demand" for inner-city real estate produced a groundswell of optimistic forecasts about the pace and scale of urban revitalization. City officials, municipal authorities, and real estate developers alike have joined their voices in proclaiming the coming Manhattanization of downtown Johannesburg, by which they mean a steady influx of affluent professionals seeking the chic cosmopolitanism of New York- and London-style loft living amid the high-rise office complexes.[9] Throwing caution to the wind, real estate developers and property speculators have poured huge amounts of investment capital into inner-city redevelopment on the belief that the gentrifying impulse has reached the tipping point of a Rostowian takeoff.[10]

Yet not unlike other cities on the margins of modernity, city-building efforts in Johannesburg have long suffered from a kind of self-interested, profit-driven presentism that has blinded property developers from the longer view. Despite the early signs of socioeconomic recovery, skeptics like property consultant François Viruly have suggested that unless commercial banks and

6. Anna Cox and Nalisha Kalideen, "'Second Gold Rush' for Joburg," *The Star,* August 17, 2004.

7. Trafalgar Properties, *The Trafalgar Inner City Report 2005* (unpublished pamphlet, p. 4).

8. Pauline Larsen, "Call of the Pied Pipers," *Financial Mail,* April 18, 2005; Janice Healing, "Inner-City Blues Starting to Lift," *Business Times,* April 4, 2005; and Danielle de Jager, "Finesse in the District," *Business Day,* August 20, 2004.

9. Trafalgar Properties, *The Trafalgar Inner City Report 2004* (unpublished pamphlet, pp. 1–13). (Quotation from p. 5.)

10. Lucille Davie, "Investments Revive Inner City," JOBURG, City of Johannesburg Official Website, http://www.joburg.org.za/2005/april/april21_inner.stm, April 21, 2005.

other lending institutions provide their full support for underwriting inner-city property markets, these new pristine pockets of redevelopment will most likely be marooned in a "sea of urban degeneration," with the result that real estate developers will only succeed in creating "a second-rate American city in Johannesburg."[11] Critics have argued that, despite the well-known boom-and-bust cycles in property markets and the anarchy of capitalist investment, municipal authorities have deliberately subordinated their urban redevelopment to the logic of capital and profit. Yet it was this same economic logic that led large property developers to relocate their real estate investments to suburban malls and alternative office block developments during the 1980s and 1990s. With limited financial and institutional resources at their disposal, city officials have placed their faith in a revitalization strategy that uses subsidies, tax abatements, and other incentives to lure private real estate developers back to the inner city. While city boosters have declared that inner-city vacancy rates have stabilized, they largely gloss over the fact that about a quarter of A- and B-grade (that is, prime and close-to-prime) office space remains empty. Rentals in the central business district have increased, but from a very low base. In addition, they remain well below those of the northern business nodes. A large number of the tenants who rent office space in the central business district are small- and medium-scale business enterprises. The high failure rate of these businesses in their first year of operation and the high turnover underscore the precariousness of the alleged stabilization. What also adds to the stress on inner-city recovery is the fact that the office-building stock is aging fast and, with prime A- and B-grade rentals at subeconomic levels, the chances that property owners are prepared to maintain or upgrade their buildings are slim.[12] In their haste to jump-start inner-city regeneration, city officials have failed to adequately address problems associated with urban poverty, particularly the availability of affordable housing for low-income residents, the lack of decent-paying jobs, and the availability of proper social services.[13]

Beyond the conflicting rhetorical depictions of the Johannesburg inner city as either on the verge of a spectacular Phoenix-like rebirth or trapped once again in yet another round of overly optimistic forecasting and self-delusion,

11. François Viruly quoted in Nick Wilson, "City Living—Glamorous," *Business Day,* September 1, 2005; and Nick Wilson, "Regeneration Will Take More than Tax Breaks," *Business Day,* October 27, 2004.

12. "Rentals at subeconomic levels" refers to returns on investment at declining or below market value. See Inner City Forum, "Johannesburg's Better Buildings Programme: A Response," *Development Update* 5, no. 1 (2004): 187–194. See *Rode Property News,* "Is the Johannesburg CBD Stabilizing?" July 31, 2003; and Rode Property News, "Johannesburg CBD 'Stabilizing,'" September 8, 2003.

13. See Neil Fraser, "Evictions—Between a Rock and a Hard Place," *CitiChat,* March 13, 2006; and *Sunday Independent,* "City Living," November 12, 2005.

it is possible to detect actual movements on the ground that indicate where the complex processes of urban restructuring are heading and why. Exploring these concrete mechanisms by which power relations are embedded in the spatial form of the city enables us to identify the winners and losers in the process of revalorizing landed property in the Johannesburg inner city. Despite the dire warnings of numerous doomsayers who have long forecast the virtual disappearance of the central business district as a viable economic entity, downtown Johannesburg has held out against the forces of total annihilation and ruin. Although the diminishing demand for prestigious high-grade corporate office space has caused the central business district to shrink to a fraction of its former size, a vibrant core footprint has remained intact, concentrated primarily around the historic financial and mining district at the southwest corner but also including a galaxy of fortress-like clusters scattered across the urban landscape (Beavon 2004).[14]

Efforts aimed at the regeneration of the Johannesburg inner city have not conformed to a single, all-encompassing master logic but instead are governed by the complex interaction of overlapping and intersecting processes. Far from eliminating metropolitan blight and decay, the piecemeal uplifting of parts of the inner city has largely displaced it, pushing the urban poor out of newly gentrified enclaves and into blighted places not appreciably different from where they were before. Urban revitalization has proceeded more or less in tandem with spatial deterioration elsewhere. Unlike cities where the extension of the gentrification frontier has taken place along a wide front, revitalization of inner-city Johannesburg has produced a number of notable fortified enclaves that abut zones of blight and decay.[15]

Yet the boosterist association of the anticipated rebirth of the Johannesburg inner city with the extension of the gentrification frontier in other aspirant world-class cities conceals a much more mundane and brutal reality. For the physical location of this imagined future city is also the place where municipal authorities, in a class-based alliance with property owners and real estate developers, have opened up a new front in a war of position against an impoverished and increasingly vulnerable population who live a precarious existence in the Johannesburg inner city. The immediate aim of urban revitalization is to dislodge largely redundant, supernumerary multitudes of underemployed urban residents by wresting control over inner-city buildings and housing stock and turning it over to real estate developers for upgrading (Deutsche and Ryan 1984, 93). At its core, the gentrifying impulse that has gripped

14. Nick Wilson, "Jo'burg's Inner-City Office Market Still in Decline," *Business Day*, September 1, 2004.
15. Nick Wilson, "City Living—Glamorous."

downtown Johannesburg is about the revalorization of real estate values for higher-income newcomers rather than the revitalization of urban communities and neighborhoods for current moderate- and low-income residents (see Rutheiser 1999, 317–318; Smith 2002).

The Business of Gentrification: The Exalted Place of Private Enterprise

> We have seen insatiable demand for upmarket rentals in the city [central city Johannesburg]. We are targeting young up-and-coming professionals as living in the city becomes an increasingly attractive option.
>
> RICHARD RUBIN, Aengus Lifestyle Properties

Urban redevelopment of the Johannesburg inner city cannot be traced to a single source (Bremner 2000).[16] What can be said is that a diverse array of city builders (real estate entrepreneurs, property developers, corporate builders, commercial business interests, architecture and design experts, heritage advocates, journalists, city officials, and well-meaning reformers) have devoted a great deal of attention to reshaping and reconfiguring the urban landscape in the spatial imaginary of a world-class city. As a temporal process, revitalization has taken place in fits and starts. Although the huge influx of start-up capital in state-sponsored projects like Constitution Hill (Braamfontein) and the Newtown Cultural Precinct—along with generous tax incentives that have leavened the turnaround—inner-city revival has been largely driven by private enterprise. Borrowing heavily from international best practices that have generated success stories in other aspirant world-class cities, private developers, urban planners, and municipal authorities have devised all sorts of public-private partnerships as a means of energizing revitalization efforts. City builders have also taken their cue from the stylistics popularized under the rubric of the New Urbanism and imagined the wholesale reinvention of the Johannesburg inner city as a collage of semiautonomous "urban villages," each consisting of mixed residential, commercial, and office space. Unlike high-modernist planning principles that emphasized efficient and functional linkages across a hierarchically demarcated urban grid, the practice of urban redevelopment in postapartheid Johannesburg has structured the cityscape as a patchwork assemblage of almost semiautonomous and disconnected localities—rechristened as the jewelry, legal, retail, cultural, fashion, constitution, government, media, corporate, mining, and health precincts as a way of stressing distinctiveness.[17]

---

16. Rubin's quote is from Aengus Lifestyle Properties, "Aengus Lifestyle Properties Redefines City Living," *EPROP Commercial Property Marketplace*, August 15, 2006.
17. Interview with Neil Fraser, Urban Inc., Urban Consultants, May 29, 2006.

These city-building efforts to rejuvenate the Johannesburg central business district have taken place in stages. One of the first projects was the rehabilitation of the derelict bus terminus, called Van der Bijl Square, between Eloff and Rissik streets. With an estimated 250,000 bus passengers passing through the area each day, this transport hub is one of the busiest in downtown Johannesburg. Armed with a municipally approved forty-five-year lease on the precinct renamed Gandhi Square, a major property development company called Olitzki Property Holdings (OPH) purchased about half the properties in the area, introducing cafés and restaurants, "genteel retail" shops, and a 24-hour security service. City boosters hailed these commercial upgrades catering to an upmarket clientele as an incipient "retail revolution" in the southern section of the central business district.[18]

In 2006 city builders initiated a number of joint ventures between property owners and municipal agencies to revamp the built environment along Main Street, connecting Gandhi Square in the center of the city to the Anglo American headquarters at the southwestern edge. In a similar vein, ApexHi Properties, the largest property holding company in the central city, installed a special pedestrian-friendly precinct around the High Court buildings near Pritchard and Von Brandis streets. As part of its private urban management program, the Central Johannesburg Partnership (CJP) has overseen the conversion of parts of Fox and Main streets into pedestrian thoroughfares and has completed a R30 million upgrade of the Braamfontein business corridor that included road repairs and new landscaping. Provincial and municipal agencies have pumped a great deal of money into a number of key development projects with the aim of stimulating private business investments in real estate development. In this urban entrepreneurial model the role of the municipality is to improve the investment climate through the provision of infrastructure, urban management, and crime prevention. In trying to lure private investments to places where private investors have feared to tread, municipal agencies such as the Johannesburg Development Agency (JDA), Blue IQ initiative, and the CJP spearheaded the completion of a number of infrastructural projects, including the Nelson Mandela Bridge as the soaring gateway to the Newtown Cultural Precinct, the historic Constitution Hill complex, the vendor and taxi rank projects in Jeppe Street, and the establishment of a distinct fashion district that spans a twenty-block area from Pritchard Street to End Street on the eastern edge of downtown.[19]

18. Dan Robertson, "Giving Downtown an Upbeat Outlook," *Sunday Times,* May 30, 2004; quotations from Nick Wilson, "Social, Shopping Vibe Back in Downtown Jozi," *Business Day,* November 23, 2006; David Pincus, "Johannesburg's Heart Beats to a New Rhythm," *The Star,* November 11, 2006.

19. Ian Fife, "Johannesburg CBD"; Pauline Larsen, "Call of the Pied Pipers," *Financial Mail,* April 18, 2005; and interview with Lael Bethlehem, chief executive officer, Johannesburg Development Agency, City of Johannesburg, May 30, 2006.

At first glance, it might appear that urban regeneration is a straightforward, linear process of replacing the old, the decrepit, and the outmoded with the new, the efficient, and the functionally useful. Upon closer inspection, however, it becomes clear that landed property is a different kind of commodity where its marketability and profitability are inextricably linked to location and "highest and best use." Urban regeneration is a complex, multilayered, and contradictory process played out on the shifting terrain of real estate capitalism (see Blomley 2004, 29–74).

The economic geography of capitalist reinvestment in the Johannesburg inner city is not a random process. Property developers do not just plunge into derelict parts of the city without serious reflection. They tend to follow an incremental strategy of colonizing the cityscape piece by piece.[20] The feral energy of the gentrifying impulse has triggered its share of wildly speculative investments in ill-considered undertakings. Yet while city boosters like to talk of rugged entrepreneurialism and the pioneering spirit of risk takers, fixed investments in landed property are typically tempered by financial caution (Smith 1996, 23).

Sketched in bold strokes, urban revitalization in downtown Johannesburg must be understood as the complex interaction of such supply factors as availability of land, the marketing strategies of real estate entrepreneurs and firms, and intervention of municipal authorities, operating in tandem with such demand factors as perceptions of economic opportunity, shifting consumer tastes, and evolving land uses. The municipality has provided ample institutional support promoting market-led revitalization of the Johannesburg inner city, yet the driving force behind these efforts has originated with private entrepreneurs. The resurgent interest in downtown real estate has been fueled in part by low property prices and in part by the efforts of the city administration to provide a host of incentives, including tax write-offs for risk-taking real estate entrepreneurs. With buildings selling at a fraction of their replacement costs, land speculators and property developers have looked on the built environment of downtown Johannesburg as an untapped source of value that languished in neglect for too long. As corporate giants with substantial property portfolios (e.g., Sanlam, Old Mutual, and Liberty Life) have sought to diversify their investment holdings into more liquid assets by off-loading their fixed properties in the central business district, small- and medium-scale investors have been quick to seize what they have regarded as an opportunity to acquire under-utilized buildings at low prices.[21]

20. Interview with Geoff Mendelowitz, program manager, Better Buildings, City of Johannesburg Property Company, June 2, 2006; and interview with Lael Bethlehem.

21. *Business Day,* "Small Investors Strive to Rescue CBD," February 27, 2003; and Chantelle Benjamin, "Joburg CBD Revamp Appears to Be Paying Off," *Business Day,* November 14, 2006.

Inner-city revitalization has linked together changing property values, land uses, and ownership patterns. Rising demand for residential accommodation close to the central city, coupled with the availability of a large inventory of inexpensive and unused office properties, has triggered a boom in the downtown property market. All sorts of property investors, ranging from large-scale companies specializing in conversions of unused office space into residential accommodation to small-scale speculators (lawyers, real estate agents, and other professionals seeking to take advantage of quick profits) have joined the fray. A great deal of this entrepreneurial activity has been project-based, small-scale, and noninstitutional, thereby making it very difficult to accurately calculate the scale of invested capital, to track investor habits, and to identify overall patterns.[22]

Private investments in real estate involve complex relationships among property developers, corporate lenders, and equity investors on the production side and among purchasers, borrowers, and tenants on the consumption side. The business of real estate revolves around money and location. The reluctance over the past two decades of commercial banks, mortgage lenders, and other financial institutions to provide financing for inner-city property transactions and home mortgage loans in the Johannesburg inner city brought the real estate market to a virtual standstill.[23] As a counterweight to these redlining practices, the Trust for Urban Housing Finance (TUHF) has taken a leading role in providing financing for residential property purchases and upgrading in the inner city. The purpose of these short- and medium-term loans has been to stimulate new real estate investment, underwriting property rehabilitation and promoting socioeconomic revitalization in the inner city.[24] Borrowing from a well-tested model of inner-city revitalization pioneered by Shore Bank of Chicago, TUHF has specialized in providing risky financing for property purchases and upgrading within decaying urban neighborhoods where established financial institutions have steadfastly refused to lend money. While TUHF was created as a not-for-profit company, it has adopted stringent business principles in its lending policies. Although its financial managers insist on a down payment of 20 percent of the purchase price as the collateral requirement for obtaining a loan, TUHF is willing to authorize funds to cover the entire cost for building refurbishments. Its primary clients are established

22. Interview with Andrew Schaefer, managing director, Trafalgar Property Management, June 5, 2006; and Nick Wilson, "How Degeneration Became Regeneration," *Business Day,* November 24, 2006.

23. Nick Wilson, "Regeneration Will Take More than Tax Breaks," *Business Day,* October 27, 2004.

24. Trust for Urban Housing Finance (TUHF), *Annual Report 2005* (Braamfontein: TUHF, 2006); and interview with Kuben Govender, Trust for Urban Housing Finance (TUHF), 6 June 2006.

property companies with substantial portfolios of inner-city buildings. For the most part, these investors are seeking to purchase blocks of flats and under-utilized office buildings in the inner city and to refurbish them for middle-income tenants.[25]

In breaking out of the conventional mold of a development finance corporation, TUHF has taken the unusual step of working with two other kinds of housing entrepreneurs and aspiring landlords in the inner city. The first group is composed of expatriates from Zimbabwe, Malawi, Mozambique, and even the Democratic Republic of Congo who are interested in purchasing inner-city properties. The second (and more surprising) group of property owners consists of middle-aged black women who have slowly but surely accumulated portfolios of sectional title units in the inner city. Typically working as nurses or social workers, these small-scale entrepreneurs "are creating their own, well-managed property empires." Generally speaking, these women own and rent units in the apartment complexes where they themselves live, thereby ensuring hands-on management and a firm commitment to the long-term well-being of the neighborhood.[26]

As the real estate market has picked up steam, a number of large-scale companies with substantial property holdings in the inner city have shifted their business focus away from conventional rent-seeking investments in commercial office buildings and toward joint-venture partnerships as equity capital providers in residential development projects of varying quality, price, and market niche. For example, two of the largest corporate property-holding companies in the inner city—Old Mutual and ApexHi Properties—have joined forces with medium-scale property developers to enter into the profitable residential housing market. In several undertakings, Old Mutual has provided the buildings and the financing, while companies like the Affordable Housing Company (AFHCO) and the Pretoria-based City Properties took charge of the actual conversions of under-utilized commercial office blocks into residential units. Not to be outflanked in the rush to cash in on the anticipated residential property bonanza, ApexHi Properties has followed a similar investment strategy. With an ever-expanding portfolio of close to fifty buildings in the Johannesburg central city and Braamfontein, this large-scale property holding company has specialized in the acquisition of B-grade and even

25. Although TUHF has restricted its lending practices to decaying residential areas, the trust does not price for risk. Financing is approved at a nonnegotiable interest rate of prime plus one percentage point, and investments are expected to provide an initial yield of no less than 20 percent (interview with Kuben Govender).

26. Pauline Larsen, "Inner-City Investment: TUHF for Tough Times," *Financial Mail*, February 13, 2004.

C-grade (i.e., mid-level) properties in secondary locations.[27] In 2006 ApexHi Properties transferred ownership of the closed-down office components of five of its central Johannesburg properties (Castle Mansions, Biccard House, 66 Smal Street, African City, Kelhof) to make way for their conversion into residential apartments and condominiums. ApexHi Properties has retained an equity stake in the properties, along with ownership of the retail component of the refurbished buildings.[28]

Generally, small- and medium-sized property developers have surged to the forefront of residential property development. For example, at the end of 2005 the Johannesburg Property Company, a semiautonomous agency operating under the auspicious of the City of Johannesburg, estimated that there were more than two hundred private investors and property developers seeking to establish a stake in the rehabilitation of inner-city buildings.[29] By specializing in the conversion of mothballed commercial office buildings into places of residence in underperforming nodes in the inner city, Aengus Property Holdings (APH) has taken advantage of a niche opportunity in the housing market for moderate- and low-income residential accommodation. By 2005 APH gathered together 350 residential units in at least a dozen buildings in the inner city under its ownership and management. The company, whose core business is residential property refurbishment, provides what the real estate business calls "turnkey development," in which real estate development projects are taken from an initial idea through the construction phase, culminating in either leasehold or ownership and ongoing management.[30]

The real estate industry is primarily a service business, making different types of physical space available to a variety of property owners, investors, developers, managers, and users. Property developers have created complex ownership arrangements that involve mobilizing resources in new and creative ways.[31] For example, as part of a long-term strategy to take advantage

27. ApexHi was formed in 2001 out of the merger of the old Apex Property Trust and the property arm of Anglo-American Corporation (known as AMPROS). Under the leadership of its chief executive Gerald Leissner, the property giant has built a portfolio consisting of at least 235 office, residential, and commercial buildings spread over the country but primarily located in Johannesburg, Pretoria, and Durban. See *The Star*, "ApexHi Sees Opportunity in the CBD," August 20, 2003; and Lindsay Williams and Gerald Leissner, "Success in the City," *Business Day*, August 16, 2004. Some information also derived from interview with Taffy Adler, chief executive officer, Johannesburg Housing Company, City of Johannesburg, May 31, 2006.

28. Monica Meyer, "Feeding the Inner City's Hungry Housing Needs," *EPROP Commercial Property Marketplace*, September 7, 2006.

29. Chantelle Benjamin, "Inner-City Demand Intensifies," *Business Day*, December 30, 2005.

30. Nick Wilson, "Braamfontein Finds Its Home in Residential Market," *Business Day*, November 15, 2006.

31. Xolile Bhengu, "Developers Sold on City of Gold," *Financial Mail*, November 22, 2005.

of market opportunities for inner-city residential property, APH has joined forces with ApexHi Properties, Standard Bank, and Trafalgar Properties. These triangular partnerships reflect a new kind of synergistic approach to urban revitalization led by private, profit-making property companies. Standard Bank Properties, a division of Standard Bank South Africa, has provided mortgage financing on several APH developments. Besides making available for sale buildings from its property portfolio, ApexHi Properties has become a minority equity stakeholder in three of APH's inner-city projects and has invested heavily within the nodes where APH has developed its residential properties. Trafalgar Properties, the leading residential property management company in Johannesburg and South Africa, has assumed management responsibilities for all of APH's buildings.[32]

At the high end of the real estate market, companies like Urban Ocean have specialized in the retrofitting of stately office buildings into luxury apartments and expensive condominiums. Despite claims of success, skeptics have expressed reservations about the economic viability of such upmarket residential developments in the central city. Only large property developers with deep financial pockets are able to undertake such high-priced projects that require huge outlays of initial capital and that have relatively long turnover time and narrow market appeal. With few social amenities such as upscale restaurants, retail outlets, and leisure and entertainment sites in the central city, most property developers have been hesitant to sink too much capital into development projects that cater exclusively to affluent clients.[33]

The rising demand for moderate and low-income rental units in the inner city has triggered a buying spree in which property developers and speculators have eagerly gobbled up available properties at an accelerating pace. Small- and medium-scale property development companies have been at the forefront of

32. APH converted Biccard House (renamed Braamfontein Lofts) at Juta and Biccard streets into upgraded retail space and fifty-four luxury apartments, consisting of studios and one-bedroom flats. Similarly, APH refurbished 66 Smal Street, a fifteen-floor building in the central city between President and Pritchard streets (rechristened as Lofts@66), into 150 themed apartments designed around motifs borrowed from various cities around the world, including New York, Paris, Tokyo, and Johannesburg, which the real estate developers have imagineered as "Jozi." The two penthouse suites on the top floor have virtually unencumbered views of the cityscape. Finally, APH has rebuilt a commercial building called African City that had been abandoned for close to ten years; it now contains 145 bachelor and one-bedroom apartments with raw and industrial finishes and is called Tribeca ("Property Firm Snaps Up Commercial Stock for Residential Conversions," *Housing in Southern Africa* (January 2006): 11–12).

33. By 2006 Urban Ocean had acquired twenty-one buildings clustered around the historical financial district of the central city. These include Shakespeare Place, a former office block facing City Hall (Wilson Johwa, "Making Joburg's Downtown Upmarket," *SAPA*, March 29, 2006).

these efforts. Companies such as Atterbury Properties, City Properties, Connawright Properties, APH, Jungle Holdings, the architectural firm Urban Solutions, Jozi Housing Company, and the Johannesburg Land Company have specialized in the conversion of under-utilized office buildings into residential accommodation catering largely to middle-income renters and buyers. Other property developers and management companies, such as Trafalgar Properties, Ithembu Properties, and AFHCO, have sought to take advantage of the unfulfilled demand for moderate- and low-income residential housing close to the central city.[34]

With so many rental units coming onto the market so quickly, the management of residential properties in the Johannesburg inner city has become a profitable business. Pioneering property management companies, such as Trafalgar Properties, City Properties, and a host of others, have surged to the forefront in extending the residential frontier into derelict inner-city neighborhoods. In addition to its residential property holdings, insurance business, and other entrepreneurial ventures, Trafalgar Properties has aggressively pursued the property management side of the real estate business. In 2006 Trafalgar managed fifty-two residential buildings with twenty-five hundred separate units, in addition to eight hundred individual units in other buildings. These residential buildings are concentrated primarily in the inner city (Hillbrow, Berea, Joubert Park), but some are located in Yeoville, Newtown, and Troyeville.[35] In order to counteract the problems associated with residential rentals, companies such as Trafalgar Properties have instituted strict debt-control measures, backed by "strong, day-to-day operational management." Building supervisors oversee the collection of monthly rents, strictly control access to the premises, and do not hesitate to initiate legal proceedings to evict defaulting tenants. The social profile of the typical inner-city tenant is a testimony to the changing circumstances of the new South Africa: young, black, male, single, and a recent arrival to the inner city with the ultimate aspiration of moving into rental property in upscale Sandton.[36]

34. By 2006 property development and management company City Property had accumulated a portfolio of forty-three buildings, mostly located in the central city. Similarly, the Affordable Housing Company owned thirty-three buildings in the central city, Braamfontein, and New Doornfontein. Most of these were residential buildings, with twenty-five hundred units for rent (Lucille Davie, "More Residential Blocks Planned for Inner City," *EPROP Commercial Property Marketplace,* March 30, 2006).

35. In 2006 Trafalgar owned eight residential buildings, which it also managed. Interviews with Jaco Ferreira, portfolio manager, and Andrew Schaefer, managing director, Trafalgar Property Management, June 5, 2006. See also Trafalgar Properties, *The Trafalgar Inner City Report 2005* (unpublished pamphlet, pp. 1–19); and Trafalgar Properties, *The Trafalgar Inner City Report 2006* (unpublished pamphlet, pp. 1–26).

36. Quotation from *The Trafalgar Inner City Report 2004,* p. 4.

Disciplining Urban Space: Producing the New Residential Landscape in the Inner City

We have to bring discipline back to [inner-city] residents.

DALLAS DELPORT, deputy director of court liaison,
Johannesburg

While some property owners have expressed guarded optimism about the municipal progress toward inner-city regeneration, others have lodged serious complaints that the existing planning and legal regimes have failed to adequately protect the rights of property owners against irresponsible tenants, unlawful squatters, and building hijackers.[37] Landlords and managing agents have also objected to what they regard as cumbersome, time-consuming, and expensive procedures required to carry out legal evictions sanctioned by city courts. Despite assurances from city officials that they were fully committed to establishing and maintaining a favorable business climate in the inner city, corporate developers have expressed hesitation about investing in commercial or residential property in the inner city because of what they regarded as the blatant disregard for city bylaws, inadequate law enforcement, and poor service delivery in such areas as timely refuse removal and street cleaning.[38]

Property developers have enlisted the assistance of municipal authorities to carry out the more prosaic, mundane tasks of enforcing bylaws, evicting illegal squatters, and preventing crime. Under the umbrella of its "bad buildings" program, city officials have provided clear signals that they are willing to seize properties for nonpayment of taxes and to sell off the foreclosed buildings to the highest bidder. In 2004 the metro police conducted weekly raids in the inner city, confiscating goods from an average of six hundred unlicensed traders each week. Police public relations officials claimed that fines for putting up unauthorized posters in the inner city alone amounted to about R50,000 per week, and that those caught littering were handed a R100 "spot fine."[39]

Despite the rhetoric of capitalist competition as the driving force behind economic growth, real estate entrepreneurs generally operate best when they do not work alone. The Property Owners and Managers Association (POMA), a lobbying organization representing thirty property owners and managers with an estimated one thousand residential buildings in the inner city, has

37. Delport cited in Pauline Larsen, "Inner City: By the Way, Zip Up," *Financial Mail,* October 8, 2004.

38. *The Star,* "Rental Act the 'Landlord's Best Friend,'" August 1, 2000; *Business Day,* "Contented Tenants the Best Defense against Building Invasion," July 4, 2005; and Anna Cox, "Property Hijackers Coining Millions in Joburg," *The Star,* April 5, 2005.

39. Lucille Davie, "Joburg's Inner City Property Boom," City of Johannesburg Official Website, November 22, 2004.

become the principal vehicle promoting private entrepreneurial efforts to re-energize the inner-city property market. As the collective voice representing the interests of inner-city landlords and managing agents, POMA has spearheaded the drive to pressure the municipality to tighten enforcement of city bylaws and to accelerate infrastructural improvements and service delivery.[40] From its inception, POMA has argued quite vociferously that the competitive disadvantage of residential property ownership in the inner city is the persistence of blighted buildings and derelict neighborhoods that have become fertile breeding grounds for building hijackers and illegal squatting. At the start of the revitalization effort, municipal authorities took a piecemeal approach, targeting the most egregiously dilapidated buildings wherever they were located, forcibly removing illegal squatters, and boarding up these collapsing structures in anticipation of resale and refurbishment at a future date. In light of the failure of this shotgun approach to quickly jump-start the private real estate market, POMA has taken a leading role in promoting a precinct plan for inner-city revitalization. This strategy for taking back the cityscape rests on the premise that successful urban renewal can take place only incrementally, that is, building by building, street by street, and precinct by precinct.[41]

In implementing what it termed a "holistic approach," POMA has sought to forge alliances between the main property owners and managing agents of residential buildings in blighted hot spots in the inner city. This strategy involves bringing together the main stakeholders—landlords and tenants, the city council, municipal utility departments, Johannesburg metropolitan police, and the South African Police Service—to identify and address common concerns, ranging from safety and security, street maintenance, infrastructural upgrading, code enforcement, and municipal service provision in inner-city residential zones where "crime and grime" have discouraged investments.[42]

Urban planning and design practices typically involve intersecting and overlapping processes, creating specific kinds of spatial products in particular institutional environments. Hoping to trade on the success of the business-sponsored city improvement district blueprint for urban regeneration, POMA (along with its member affiliates) has unveiled comprehensive plans for the eventual establishment of five residential improvement districts in inner-city

40. POMA was created in 2002 with sixteen original founder-members (Anna Cox, "Joburg Building Managers Gunned Down in CBD," *The Star*, August 1, 2005; and Anna Cox, "Cops Seek 3 in Building Manager Murder Case," *The Star*, August 23, 2005).

41. According to a company portfolio manager for Trafalgar Property Management, "Owners are doing their own thing" (interview with Jaco Ferreira).

42. *Business Day*, "POMA Targets Hot Spots in Inner-City Jo'burg," June 23, 2005; and interview with Andrew Schaefer.

neighborhoods, including Hillbrow, Berea, and Braamfontein.[43] Borrowing from spatial strategies implemented around key business nodes in the city, property owners have banded together to install closed circuit television (CCTV) monitoring systems linked to private security companies and the metropolitan police, to establish private security checkpoints and patrols to control access, and to hire cleaning and maintenance crews.[44] As part of its wider planning for urban revitalization, the municipality has introduced tax incentive schemes designed to encourage property development companies to invest in the refurbishment of buildings in the inner city, particularly commercial redevelopments and the office-to-residence conversions. POMA has worked closely with its members to take full advantage of these municipal giveaways.[45]

The celebratory talk that has accompanied the planned implementation of these residential improvement districts provides a somewhat one-sided view of their sociohistorical significance. As alien spatial products deliberately inserted into the urban social fabric, these island-like enclosures bring together the essential features of privatized urbanism, where municipal authorities cede sovereignty over specific locations to private property owners who, in turn, use these sites to generate profitable returns on initial investments. To the extent that they operate as efficient engines for the production of rental income, residential improvement districts are exemplary expressions of the idealized entrepreneurial city. But, as lubricating agents facilitating the market for rental housing, these pioneering business enterprises are neither innocent nor neutral interventions into the urban landscape: they are political statements that reinforce the view that residential accommodation is a commodity for sale and not a human right. Just like detention camps, prisons, and military bases, residential improvement districts are spatial formations that establish their own rules of conduct governing behavior distinct from the normative order that prevails outside their boundaries. As distinct from ordinary residential neighborhoods, these privatized locations substitute strict enforcement of entry and exit and careful supervision of circulation and movement for conventional considerations of convenient location, affordable price, and aesthetics. Like gated residential communities or refugee camps, these spatial enclosures seek legal immunity as an exceptional condition, operating as deterritorialized

43. *Business Day,* "POMA Targets Hot Spots."

44. Lucille Davie, "Joburg's Inner City Property Boom."

45. See *BuaNews,* "Tax Relief for Inner-City Development," October 15, 2004; and *Business Day,* "Developers Welcome Inner-City Tax Breaks," October 20, 2004. Information also derived from interview with Li Pernegger, program manager, Economic Area Regeneration, Department of Finance and Economic Development, City of Johannesburg, May 30, 2006; and interview with Andrew Schaefer.

enclaves entitled to special sovereignty and exemption from law. By excluding those who cannot afford the price of admission, these spatial products aspire to become manageable utopias, singular domains, and microworlds seeking to coerce compliance and compatibility from that which does not fit with their operative principles (Easterling 2005, 1–5, 48–49).

Large-scale property owners have looked upon residential improvement districts as quarantined outposts of order and tranquility, urban beachheads that can serve as launching pads for further incursions across the gentrification frontier. Designed to counter the perceived danger of decaying inner-city neighborhoods, the success of these spatial strategies depends on creating a self-interested alliance of invested stakeholders who agree to work in concert to achieve common ends of safe and secure residential properties that generate competitive rates of return. This precinct approach has formed the bedrock of urban revitalization strategy in decaying inner-city residential neighborhoods. Two such places are in operation or an advanced state of preparation: Saratoga Precinct (centered on Ponte City) and the Legae La Rona Precinct (with the Helderburg apartment complex in Joel Street, Berea, at the core).[46]

The revamped Ponte City represents a prototype for the planned reconquest of inner-city residential neighborhoods. It offers an ideal setting for the critical appraisal of residential improvement districts. With its distinctive cylindrical shape wrapped around a hollowed-out core, this soaring high-rise apartment complex consists of fifty-four floors of residential units sitting incongruously on seven levels of parking bays. The exterior of the building is finished with a rough, gray concrete patina, called "hacked concrete," a style commonly referred to as new brutalism. For a building once voted one of the ten ugliest in Johannesburg, Ponte City has certainly never experienced any difficulty in drawing considerable attention to itself. Perched on a prominent ridge in Berea in an unfashionable part of the city, this dizzyingly high apartment complex is an unmistakable civic beacon that dominates the vertical skyline. The pinnacle of the building offers spectacular panoramic views of the city and an ideal setting to cultivate an aesthetic detachment from the bustling streets below.[47]

46. On-site visit of Trafalgar Properties in Hillbrow and Berea with Jaco Ferreira, portfolio manager, Trafalgar Property Management, June 5, 2006.

47. Rounded structures are infinite, and Ponte City's peculiar tubular shape is what makes it so visually hypnotic. Without a fixed relationship to east-west and north-south polarities, visitors are easily disoriented. Not only does its sheer size and unique cylindrical shape make it one of Johannesburg's most distinct spatial landmarks, but since 1996 this gigantic high-rise tower has been crowned, first, by a distinctive, five-story-high Coca-Cola logo emblazoned on one side and, more recently, by a brightly illuminated, neon Vodacom cell-phone advertisement (Lucille Davie, "Ponte: Rent the Best View in Town," JOBURG, City of Johannesburg Official Website, http://www.joburg.org.za/2003/dec/dec24_ponte.stm, December 24, 2003). Information for this and the following paragraphs is derived from on-site visit to Ponte City, June 5, 2006.

Figure 8. Ponte City. Photograph by Aubrey P. Graham

At its completion in 1975, Ponte City achieved instant fame as the tallest residential complex on the African continent. Designed by the architectural firm Manfred Hermer and Rodney Grosskopff in the romantic, sleek, and modernist image of the Radiant City of Le Corbusier, this "strangely beautiful" building represented the pinnacle of upmarket success for the affluent white professionals yearning for sophisticated urban living close to the central city. But the glory years faded quickly. As neglect and decay gripped the surrounding residential neighborhoods during the 1980s and 1990s, this toroidal building suffered a similar fate: garbage piled three-stories high at the base of the hollow cylinder, the six lifts stopped working, and residents lived in fear. The low point for Ponte City came in 1998 when U.S. prison architect Paul Silver toured the premises at the invitation of the Ministry of Correction Services with a view to converting the building into a maximum security prison. "It's a lousy apartment building, but a perfect prison," Silver remarked.[48]

In 2000 Vincemus Investments (the owners of Ponte City) launched a new management strategy designed to restore order by removing undesirable tenants and introducing a strict supervisory regime over the premises. By removing weapons from private security guards and by replacing the bulletproof safety glass from the reception area, the management has created a less ominous atmosphere for the 2,200 residents who occupy the 470 apartments. The spatial redesign of the exterior limits street-access routes to the premises from three to one—off Lily Avenue. The new techniques for securing these kinds of residential enclaves involve the fusion of up-to-date technologies with conventional private policing. The installation of floor-to-ceiling turnstiles, coupled with a sophisticated biometric fingerprint scanning system, provides a secure method of identity verification, thereby eliminating any unauthorized access to the building. Private security officers patrol the building and its perimeter 24 hours a day. The names, identity numbers, and fingerprints of all registered tenants are stored in the central computerized data system. In screening prospective tenants, the management team accesses the Tenant Profile Network, a database that provides, along with other information, the criminal records of those who submit written application forms. With such high demand for apartment units, management has no trouble keeping the vacancy rates close to zero.[49]

As the largest residential management company in South Africa, Trafalgar Properties has worked with Ithemba Properties to develop its own pilot

48. Quotation and comment from Paul Silver found in Richard Jansen van Vuuren, "Ponte City Sets Example for Hillbrow Turnaround," *Housing in Southern Africa* (August 2005), pp. 1–3.
49. On-site visit to Ponte City, June 5, 2006.

precinct project. While still in the planning stages, the Legae La Rona ("Our Place" in southern Sotho) neighborhood consists of six or seven contiguous residential blocks (with close to seventy multiunit apartment buildings and close to sixty property owners) in the heart of Berea.[50] At its completion this sequestered enclosure promises to provide military-like security by around-the-clock armed patrols, biometric fingerprint identification systems for access to every building, three (or more) sentry towers strategically placed to provide unimpeded views of the streetscape, and a tight grid of CCTV surveillance cameras connected to an on-site police control center.[51]

The pivotal piece in the Legae La Rona Precinct is the Helderburg bloc of flats in Joel Street in Berea. With its twenty-two stories, 269 apartments, and thirty staff rooms, the Helderburg building presents a formidable challenge to innovative management techniques. The management team enforces strict access control through a biometric fingerprint identification system. Firearms are strictly forbidden on the premises. In a practice borrowed from prisons, security personnel are routinely rotated in order to prevent too much familiarity or fraternization between guardians and residents. Management has maintained a strict policy of zero tolerance for tenants and maintenance staff alike: any member of security or cleaning crews caught stealing from residents or breaking rules are summarily fired, and tenants who fail to pay rent or other bills are evicted immediately.[52]

Just as military bases, prisons, and other sequestered spaces express the outlook of their principle designers, so residential improvement districts reflect the power and beliefs of those who construct them. In seeking to ensure profitable returns on their investments, property developers have subjected ordinary residential buildings to the logic of the capitalist marketplace. On the one hand, their spatial design conforms to the modernist principles of efficiency and rationality. Retrofitted to maximize occupancy and minimize costs, these residential buildings resemble, to use Le Corbusier's phrase, "machines for living in": spartan, dormitory-like accommodation where individual rooms are outfitted with prepaid meters for electricity and water in order to individualize costs and where their limited access points enable management to maintain strict supervision of who enters the premises and to monitor their activities once inside. On the other hand, the function of these residential properties

50. The Legae La Rona neighborhood pilot project is bordered by Beatrice Lane on the west, Park Lane on the north, Lily Avenue on the east, and Olivia Road on the south, with Joel Road at its center. Trafalgar Properties and Ithemba Properties have sought to establish Legae La Rona as a formal city improvement district and approached private investors for funding for security towers, CCTV monitoring systems, and infrastructural upgrading of the area.

51. For this and the following paragraph, see interview with Jaco Ferreira.

52. On-site visit to Trafalgar Properties in Hillbrow and Berea, June 5, 2006.

is linked to the need to generate profitable returns for their owners. Some critical observers have suggested that these sequestered enclosures, which resemble military-style barracks, amount to little more than prison-like "rent factories" specializing in the extraction of profitable returns from low-income residents.[53]

The Discourse of Inner-City Regeneration: Imagining World-Class Johannesburg

> One must incredulously ask whether electoral democracy as now observed in the city of Johannesburg has horribly resulted in an official culture of denial of the human and constitutional rights of the city's extremely poor.
>
> RON AMATO

The discourse of urban regeneration cannot be separated from sociospatial practices of urban restructuring.[54] As a general rule, city builders promote and market urban revitalization through the judicious use of moralizing narratives of past harmony, present decline, and future regeneration. For the most part, these spatial stories employ a combination of images, symbolic representations, flowery language, analogies, and other convenient fictions in order to sway public opinion and to influence municipal planning policy choices (see Mele 2000).

Just as earlier generations of urban planners exaggerated threats to health and public safety to legitimate the forced removal of the urban poor from where they were not wanted, city boosters in Johannesburg after apartheid have come to rely on a heady mixture of nostalgia for a lost golden age, indignation at the slide into ruin, and fantasy-projection about the promised radiant future in order to justify efforts to clean up the city and remake the inner-city landscape in ways that conform to the image of a world-class city. Narratives of decline and regeneration are always entangled with wider aesthetic and cultural understandings of the orderly city of the middle-class imagination. By forming a kind of mental landscape or imaginary map of the urban uncanny (or the spaces of the city that are unseen and unknown and hence beyond the scope of control), these storied constructions readily become powerful tools in the hands of city boosters, lending legitimacy to drastic actions that

53. Interview with Shereza Sibanda, Inner City Resource Center, Johannesburg, May 29, 2006; and interview with Stuart Wilson, Centre for Applied Legal Studies, University of the Witwatersrand, June 7, 2006.

54. Ron Amato, "Masando 'Lacks the Will' to Manage Urban Poverty," *Sunday Independent*, April 2, 2006.

might appear at face value to be unduly cruel and harsh.[55] In order to produce these seamless narratives, it is necessary to ignore or discard as irrelevant inconvenient facts, divergent opinions, and nuanced understandings. To the extent that they have caricatured blighted inner-city areas as incoherent spaces devoid of meaning and identity, city boosters have largely glossed over the complexities of daily life for the urban poor in order to clear the way for capital reinvestment and residential displacement (Whitzman and Slater 2006). In their proleptic projection of the Radiant City, they imagine—in the present—a future metropolis without disorder or disruption (Vidler 1992, 182).

The preoccupation of city officials with cleaning up the inner city—specifically, the focus on eliminating unlawful squatting, illegal immigrants, idle youth, street kids, criminality, and unauthorized trading—has provided an opening for speaking about (or on behalf of) existing residents. Contemporary practices of urban revitalization frequently employ the language, if not the outright methods, of military conquest and colonial settlement (Smith 1992, 61–92; Virilio 1983). Municipal officials, urban planners, and law enforcement authorities have typically characterized the inner-city neighborhoods of Hillbrow, Berea, and Joubert Park as bastions of lawlessness, places teeming with drug-dealing rackets, illegal aliens, street gangs, unhealthy prostitutes, and runaway children. In their sometimes self-appointed role as moral guardians of the orderly city, they have routinely portrayed inner-city residents in the most demeaning and dismissive terms, as unsavory characters who impede progress and who are adversaries in the ongoing battle for good governance. These one-sided characterizations have laid the groundwork for efforts to legitimate such coercive interventions as harassment of street traders, forcible evictions of unlawful squatters, and the arrest and deportation of undocumented immigrants. Taken together, these actions have resulted in the displacement of respectable rent-paying tenants, particularly women and children, who have been pushed onto the streets with nowhere to go, and they have sometimes led to the arrests, detention, and threatened deportation of innocent victims of overzealous police.[56]

55. In his discussion of "the uncanny" in modern urbanism, Anthony Vidler identifies the unknown and the unseen as the source of unease and anxiety. The urban uncanny originates in the contrast between the planned city of the modernist imagination and the uncertainties and ambiguities of modern city living. The "alien presence" of the unknown and unseen Other constitutes a menace because it threatens to disrupt the normal spaces of the orderly city. In order to counter what Vidler calls this "fearful invasion of an alien presence," city builders seek to erase disorderly spaces and eliminate chaos, filling in the voids and empty spaces with tangible objects (Vidler 1992, xiii, 3 [source of quotation], 13, 167–168).

56. See *The Star,* "Hillbrow Inner City Regeneration Strategy Aims to Build a Safer and Better Place," July 19, 2004.

Because they are freighted with symbolism, metaphors are never neutral figures of speech. Put more precisely, while they assist in describing the social world, they also function as tools for arguments about and in the social world. In the ongoing war of words, city boosters have appropriated the dubious metaphorical imagery of the urban jungle as a way of encoding the inner city as a battlefront, pitting the civilizing impulses of disciplined property management against the barbarity of ravening beasts preying on innocent victims.[57] Overlaid with the mythical idealization of a Hobbesian war of all against all, the urban jungle is a way of life as much as a place. This unflattering portrait of everyday life in the inner city is neither innocent nor purely decorative, and it carries considerable ideological weight. The urban jungle imagery enables city builders to downplay the root causes of social conflict in impoverished inner-city neighborhoods by externalizing the social complexities of urban lifeworlds to the realm of a mythologized uncivil nature. By naturalizing the lifeworlds of the inner-city poor, this figural image reaffirms class-specific social norms of civility, discipline, and respectability. While chronic stress and persistent danger are indeed real features of the inner city, the urban jungle metaphor flattens out the complexities of the survivalist calculations that characterize the everyday lives of the urban poor. As such, it provides a ready-made vocabulary to lend legitimacy to the pacification and reconquest of what is deemed a threatening, disorderly, and unruly urban frontier and to rationalize residential displacement and social exclusion as a natural and otherwise inevitable outcome of urban revitalization (Smith 1996, 23).

City officials are able to render urban development more acceptable and persuasive when the promises they make, such as upgraded neighborhood appearance (or beautification) and enhanced public safety, are endowed with a universal appeal that cuts across social and class boundaries. Yet hidden within progressive conceptions of city improvement and regeneration sometimes lie the ideological trappings of cruel indifference to the plight of the urban poor. In implementing their vision of a world-class city, municipal officials have used the uplifting discourses of urban revitalization to validate coercive action and to legitimate the forcible removal of the urban poor. They engage in a complicated moral calculus that equates derelict buildings with urban pathology and that naturalizes displacement as the unfortunate but necessary byproduct of remedial action. In the rhetoric of inner-city revitalization, the narrow self-interests of real estate developers are often subsumed under the "noble abstraction of community betterment." City officials have thus disguised—intentionally or otherwise—the desired outcome of capital

---

57. *EPROP,* "The Property Asset: Urban Jungles with a Range of Beasts," April 26, 2005; and *The Trafalgar Inner City Report 2004.*

mobility and reinvestment in the real estate market under the coded sign of an improved quality of life for all without specifying the deleterious impact on those uprooted and displaced (see Mele 2000, 632–633).

Extending the Gentrification Frontier: Urban Revitalization and the Vanishing Poor

> The blind spot in this increasing formalization of the inner city, and the increasing management of the social and financial terrain, is to threaten the presence of the poor. The eviction of people in dilapidated buildings without alternative accommodation deprives not only gangster landlords of a captive income but also decent, honest people of the cheapest accommodation available.... This blind spot, caused by the necessary processes of development, undermines the very development in whose name it is being done.
>
> MURPHY MOROBE, chairperson, Johannesburg Housing Company

In the early morning hours of November 20, 2002, when most city residents were still asleep, the metro police, backed by six hundred private security guards from Wozani Security Company (nicknamed the Red Ants because of their distinctive "red boiler" suits), descended on Armadale Place, a seventeen-story converted office block in Bree Street in the central city to carry out the forcible removal of an estimated two thousand tenants living there.[58] Armed with a court-sanctioned eviction order giving them permission to clear the building of illegal squatters, police and private security guards bounded into the building, raced up the stairs, and banged on doors before smashing them open with crowbars and axes. Sheriff's deputies gave sleeping residents less than five minutes to get themselves and their children dressed and out of their flats. As frightened residents tried to protest, the metro police brandished their weapons, threatening those who did not move quickly enough with bodily harm. Some residents fought back, refusing to vacate the premises and blocking the entrances with debris. In the ensuing melee, a private security guard was shot in the shoulder and another had his nose broken, while scores of residents were physically assaulted and severely beaten. While metro police cordoned off Bree and Jeppe streets between Delvers and Troye streets and closed off traffic for six hours, the dreaded Red Ants entered the building to finish the dirty work of physically removing the remaining occupants who had

---

58. Morobe is quoted in Philippa Garson, "Speakers Urge Solution for Inner-City Poor," JOBURG, City of Johannesburg Official Website, http://www.joburg.org.za/2004/aug/aug24_inner1.stm, August 24, 2004.

barricaded themselves in their flats and nonchalantly dumping their personal belongings in piles on the sidewalks.[59]

City authorities justified the evictions on the grounds that the dilapidated structure contravened fire, health, town planning, and building control by-laws. But these reasons provided little comfort or solace to the evictees thrown onto the streets. A weeping Mimi Skosana, a young mother sitting disconsolately on her discarded mattress along with her five-month-old baby in the scorching sun, told reporters that the tenants had been made scapegoats of the landlord who had obtained a court order against them, alleging that their rent was R2 million in arrears. "How can we be responsible for such a huge debt when we pay our rentals through the bank every month?" she asked. "The truth is the landlord has accumulated this debt long before we moved in here; now we are made to shoulder his problem." Like most of the Armadale Place tenants, Skosana was not formally employed, and she eked out a living by selling vegetables from a curbside stand. While some women and children managed to secure temporary housing at a nearby Hillbrow church hall, other residents were forced to sleep on the sidewalk for five nights until they found refuge at the B. G. Alexander shelter in Hillbrow. In order to prevent squatters from surreptitiously reentering the building, city officials posted round-the-clock security guards at the premises. A tense standoff ensued, as a large contingent of evicted men remained at the boarded-up building, trying to guard household possessions piled on pavements just around the corner. A common lament among distraught evictees was that private security guards had carted away valued belongings that they were forced to leave inside the building because there was no room on the streets. Despite lodging numerous formal complaints with the police, only three private security guards and another man were arrested for looting goods while forcibly removing tenants from the building. Police officials refused to assist the evicted residents with caring for or moving their belongings, proclaiming that those thrown out on the streets had been given plenty of warning of what was going to happen.[60]

The forcible removal of unlawful tenants at Armadale Place provides a particularly graphic illustration of the callous indifference associated with legally sanctioned and municipally sponsored evictions of the urban poor living in the inner city. Yet this episode offers only a partial glimpse of the broader patterns of spatial restructuring of the inner-city urban landscape. What began in the immediate aftermath of the 1994 transition to parliamentary democracy as largely haphazard, piecemeal interventions to extricate unauthorized

59. *SAPA*, "One Shot as 1,000 Evicted in Johannesburg," November 20, 2002.
60. *SAPA*, "Evicted Tenants Facing Future in the Veld," November 20, 2002; *SAPA*, Homeless Armadale Tenants Vow to Continue Fight against Eviction," November 26, 2002; and *SAPA*, "City Centre Calm after Mass Evictions," November 21, 2002.

squatters from abandoned buildings, to expel homeless families from public parks, and to drive pavement vendors off congested sidewalks quickly metamorphosed into a comprehensive campaign to rejuvenate the inner city. By systematically targeting violations of city bylaws, health and safety codes, and land-use regulations, municipal authorities have effectively criminalized the survival tactics of the urban poor.[61]

While apologists typically portray the gentrifying impulse as an art form resulting in the desired beautification of the cityscape, the actual process of bringing gentrification into being often requires the blunt instrument of brute force. City officials have embraced this revitalization strategy in the name of improvement, progress, and betterment. The driving force behind these military-like campaigns to uproot and dislodge homeless squatters from the insecure niches they carved for themselves—sometimes illegally—in the interstitial spaces of the inner city is to restore the glitter to the City of Gold by "bleaching away" the urban poor. The long-term goal of these deliberate efforts designed to clean up the inner city is to implement the corporate vision of Johannesburg as a world-class city.[62]

Residential property owners, low-income tenants, and city officials have become locked in a bitter struggle over access to affordable housing in the inner city, where the battle lines are fluid, porous, and mutable. Administrative fragmentation of underfunded enforcement agencies has prevented city planning officials from mounting a coordinated approach to monitoring badly managed, insecure, and improperly maintained buildings.[63] City officials have assembled a vast administrative machinery for carrying out the arduous work of inner-city regeneration. To get the process under way, building inspectors canvass derelict neighborhoods, categorizing and classifying buildings. Municipal courts provide eviction orders for "bad buildings," thereby authorizing the forcible removal of unlawful occupants. In the typical case, law enforcement agencies carry out lightning raids conducted with military-like precision, on targeted buildings where scores of municipal police officers and private security guards swoop down without warning on unsuspecting residents in the early morning hours. Municipal authorities have relied on private security companies (particularly the Wozani Security Company and its notorious Red Ants),

61. Demain van der Reijden, "Red Ants Evict City Squatters," *The Star*, May 10, 2006; and Nalisha Kalideen and Kevin Scott, "Dawn Evictions Put Hundreds out in the Cold," *The Star*, November 7, 2001.

62. This phrase is borrowed from a press release entitled "Johannesburg Inner City Anti-Eviction Campaign March Saturday 14 December" and issued by the Anti-Privatisation Forum, December 12, 2002.

63. Interview with Nazira Cachalia, program manager, City Safety Programme, City of Johannesburg, May 30, 2006; and interview with Geoff Mendelowitz. Interpretation is mine.

as the primary instrument for carrying out the dirty work of forcible evictions. With the means to mobilize a sizable force of six thousand shock troops at a time, Wozani Security has the functional capacity of a small army.[64]

As authorized agents empowered to act on behalf of the municipality, the Red Ants form an integral part of the privatized shadow state. They are perpetrators of officially sanctioned force and violence. The logistics of carrying out forced removals are permeated with such enormous metaphorical force that they effectively dehumanize their victims.[65] In conducting their military-like operations, the Red Ants move systematically through the buildings, floor by floor, ordering frightened residents to immediately vacate the premises, breaking down locked doors, and cavalierly throwing their personal effects into piles on the street. The use of these mundane technologies of social terror constitutes a key component of the municipal strategy of clamping down on popular illegalities. Because of their callous disregard for homeless people and their meager possessions, the Red Ants gained a reputation as cruel and indifferent enforcers acting at the behest of municipal authorities. In numerous incidents those evicted from "bad buildings" have complained bitterly that these hired thugs have stolen money and personal belongings, ruined household items, and started fires to drive them into the streets.[66]

Municipal authorities have demonstrated their willingness to go to extremes to remove unwanted squatters from unlawfully occupied buildings. Armed with a demolition order for the several residential properties in Bertrams, city officials removed the roofs of several buildings, known as the Pepperpot Houses, to force the two hundred or so occupants to leave. Without water, electricity, or toilet facilities, squatters were living in miserable conditions. Leaking drainage pipes emitted a revolting stench and huge piles of refuse were scattered everywhere. Some people carved out makeshift quarters under the floorboards, others occupied abandoned dog kennels, and several slept in old coal bins. Some squatter families lived for up to ten years—with many children having been born there—in darkened rooms partitioned off

64. Demain van der Reijden, "Red Ants Evict City Squatters." In February 2005 the Johannesburg Metropolitan Council quietly terminated its multimillion-rand contract with Wozani Security after charges of corruption, bribery, and fraudulently misrepresenting itself in terms of "black economic empowerment." This move proved to be temporary (*Mail & Guardian*, "Johannesburg Fires Hated Red Ants," February 5–11, 2005).

65. See, for example, Alex Eliseev, "Red Ants Evicted Us like Animals, Says Family," *The Star*, October 27, 2006.

66. See Tammy O'Reilly, "Evictions in the Inner City," JOBURG, City of Johannesburg Official Website, http://www.joburg.org.za/2003/nov/nov12_raid.stm, November 12, 2003; Lee Rondganger, "Commotion as Red Ants Evict Squatters," *The Star*, May 31, 2006; SAPA, "East Rand Relocation Turns Violent," May 30, 2006; and Cornelia du Plooy, "Red Ants Leave Squatters Facing Bleak Xmas," *Pretoria News*, December 13, 2005.

with cardboard boxes for privacy. While some mothers with newborn babies were moved into another abandoned building across the road, the rest were left to fend for themselves. The councilor for the area, Nomaswazi Mohlala, welcomed the move of the city authorities to demolish the houses. "Unfortunately people will have to find other accommodation," she said, "as the council cannot do it for them."[67]

Circuits of Power and Powerlessness: Living in the City of Nightmares

The celebrated launch of the Inner City Regeneration Strategy in 2001 marked a key turning point in the municipal campaign to clean up derelict parts of the city by closing down bad buildings and eradicating sinkholes. Armed with a new repertoire of administrative tools designed to streamline the regeneration effort, city officials accelerated the scale and scope of evictions of unauthorized occupants squatting in dilapidated buildings that were classified as unsafe, dangerous, and otherwise unfit for human habitation. While scores of forced removals of unlawful squatters were carried out without much fanfare or adverse publicity, several episodes came under intense media scrutiny, largely because of the tragic circumstances surrounding them. In July 2005 the Red Ants surrounded a sixteen-story building called Bree Chambers and began to systematically remove the terrified residents from their rooms and unceremoniously toss their possessions in a common dumping site on the sidewalk. Like dozens of other downtown office blocks that slumlords had illegally converted into residential use in order to rack-rent tenants, Bree Chambers had fallen into an advanced state of disrepair.[68] In declaring that the dilapidated building was a death trap, city officials provided a long litany of reasons: the sewer infrastructure had collapsed, toilets and bathing facilities were insufficient for residential use, the building lacked proper ventilation and was severely invested with rodents and other vermin, illegal electrical connections created a dangerous fire hazard, existing fire exits were blocked and locked, and the tiny rooms were subdivided using highly combustible materials. But for the hundreds of low-income occupants of the building, this awful place was their only home. Irate residents proclaimed vehemently that while they paid an initial deposit of around R1,000 to occupy the premises and a regular monthly rent of R600 the property owners did nothing to improve the condition of the place. In observing the tragic events unfold, one legal expert

67. Mohlala quoted in Anna Cox, "Jo'burg Homeless Go from a Hovel to Nothing," *The Star,* March 17, 2002.

68. Poloko Tau, "Foul Hellhole Is What Hundreds Call Home," *The Star,* September 21, 2005.

at the scene referred to this mass eviction as "utterly barbaric," due in large measure to the excessive use of physical force and the lack of preparation for interim emergency shelter for those evicted. Although city officials disagreed, housing rights advocates insisted that residents were not properly informed of the eviction order and hence did not have a reasonable opportunity to legally oppose the court order. While steps were taken to relocate the elderly and infirm, a spokesperson for the City of Johannesburg declared that "Everyone else must find other accommodation on their own."[69]

In 2005 municipal authorities extended the reach of the eviction dragnet beyond Joubert Park, Berea, and Hillbrow to include the outer fringe of Doornfontein, Troyeville, Bertrams, and Jeppestown. In July 2005 widespread rioting erupted in Doornfontein, just to the east of the central city, after private security guards swooped down on several buildings, forcibly removing scores of unlawful occupants and throwing their belongings into the street. Police fired rubber bullets to disperse the crowd of angry tenants who had gathered to protest the action, forcing innocent bystanders to flee the area in utter panic. When pressed, the sheriff for Johannesburg East declared that these evictions, which were carried out at the behest of private property owners, were illegal. Yet the damage had already been done. These Doornfontein properties are close to Ellis Park Stadium, an area earmarked for significant upgrading in anticipation of the 2010 World Cup matches.[70]

The accelerated pace of evictions has triggered widespread protests. In order to counter the violent tactics of the Red Ants, unlawful occupants of "bad buildings" have turned to barricading entryways, tossing petrol bombs from roofs, and fighting back with makeshift weapons. On occasion, gunfire has erupted.[71] In August 2005 large crowds of protestors in Marlboro (at the outer edge of Alexandra) barricaded roads with burning tires and other debris in response to rumors that the Red Ants were preparing to evict them from the sixteen abandoned factories that they had illegally occupied since the mid-1990s. These derelict buildings were without water, sanitation, electricity, and emergency fire exits. When the crowd that had swelled to close to nine hundred protesters failed to disperse, police fired rubber bullets and stun grenades to clear the streets.[72]

---

69. For this and next paragraph, see Jillian Green, "Red Ants Swarm on Inner City 'Death Trap,'" *The Star*, July 15, 2005 [Source of quotation]; and Caroline Hooper-Box and SAPA-AFP, "Egoli Evictions Slammed by Rights Groups," *Sunday Independent*, July 31, 2005.

70. Henriëtte Geldenhuys, "Red Ants March On, Says Their Boss," *Sunday Times*, August 14, 2005; and Jermaine Craig, "New Deal to Boost Ellis Park Precinct," *The Star*, July 19, 2006.

71. Alex Eliseev, "'Barbaric' Eviction Leaves Hundreds Homeless," *SAPA*, July 14, 2005; and *SAPA*, "Return of the Red Ants," July 14, 2005.

72. *SAPA*, "Squatters Clash with Police in Marlboro," August 3, 2005; and *SAPA*, "Rubber Bullets Used to Disperse Rioters," August 3, 2005.

Human rights groups have accused municipal authorities in Johannesburg of copying Zimbabwean President Robert Mugabe's controversial urban clearance program, in which hundreds of thousands of homes were demolished by city officials. While recognizing that these derelict buildings were indeed structurally unsafe and unhealthy and that they sometimes served as gathering places for criminals, housing rights advocates have stressed that the great majority of unlawful occupants of "bad buildings" were ordinary poor people trying to earn a daily living on the streets of Johannesburg and were largely the victims rather than perpetrators of crime.[73]

According to joint research released in 2005 by the Geneva-based Centre on Housing Rights and Evictions (COHRE) and the Centre for Applied Legal Studies, tens of thousands of poor urban residents live in dilapidated buildings because they cannot afford decent accommodation in the private residential market and because they fail to meet the income requirements for any of the chronically oversubscribed social-housing units available in the inner city. Researchers estimated that the backlog of decent, low-cost housing in the inner city stood at eighteen thousand households, or somewhere between seventy thousand and eighty-two thousand people (du Plessis and Wilson 2005, 35–47). The overwhelming majority of these poor urban residents have no choice but to live in what are deemed "bad buildings." Many of these buildings were originally intended as office sites, but have been illegally converted by slumlords into residential accommodation to crowd as many people in as possible in order to maximize rental income.[74] Those who live here have chosen to do so because they want to be close to income-generating activities and to have access to social services. Many inner-city residents eke out a daily existence in the informal economy as curbside hawkers, car guards, and scrap collectors. Others perform the most poorly paid jobs in the formal labor market: factory workers, security guards, cleaners, and gas station attendants.[75]

The thinking behind the Inner City Regeneration Strategy unveiled in 2001 was the belief that the elimination of sinkholes would trigger an increase in property values, spark private investment in refurbished residential buildings, and help to transform Johannesburg into an African world-class city. But according to critics, these forced removals of unlawful occupants were actually "arbitrary, inhumane, and in violation of human rights law and the South African

73. Henriëtte Geldenhuys, "Red Ants March On"; and *SAPA*, "'Joburg Centre Will End Up like Zimbabwe,'" July 24, 2005.

74. Caroline Hooper-Box, "Residents of 60 Jo-burg Buildings Face Eviction," *Sunday Independent*, November 12, 2005.

75. Stuart Wilson and Jean du Plessis, "Housing and Evictions in Johannesburg's Inner City: Forced Evictions Are Not a Legitimate Tool of Development," Statement to the Cities and Slums Workshop, World Housing Congress, September 25, 2005.

constitution." Research figures released in the 2005 COHRE report found that at least twenty-five thousand poor people living in the Johannesburg inner city were at grave and immediate risk of "losing the roof over their heads" if city officials continued to push ahead with their urban renewal plans (du Plessis and Wilson 2005, 1–55). Human rights advocates also noted the irony that city officials were carrying out forced removals from "bad buildings" by using apartheid-era legislation—the National Building Regulations and Building Standards Act—to secure eviction orders.[76]

In a ground-breaking ruling on March 3, 2006, the High Court of South Africa ordered the City of Johannesburg to cease and desist from carrying out evictions of inner-city residents as a violation of their constitutional rights, until such time as municipal authorities were able to provide adequate alternative accommodation. The legal dispute centered on the efforts of municipal authorities to evict unauthorized tenants from three properties in the inner-city: a multistory apartment complex known as the San José apartment complex in Olivia Street, Berea; four condemned row houses in Joel Street, Berea; and an abandoned auto repair workshop at 197 Main Street in the central city.[77] In reaching this decision, Judge Mahomed Jajbhay argued that city-sponsored evictions were unconstitutional, as they violated the rights of the urban poor to adequate housing close to places of work.[78]

The High Court judgment turned on the question of whether city officials were entitled to exercise their administrative powers to remove unauthorized squatters from unsafe buildings without taking into consideration the ability of these desperate people to find alternative accommodation, and without having to devise and implement a coherent plan to rehouse evicted people who were too poor to do so for themselves. The High Court ruling revealed the failure of the city administration to provide adequate low-cost housing for the estimated seventy to eighty-two thousand poor residents living in unsafe conditions. Municipal authorities have sponsored a number of social-housing initiatives, yet the poorest of the poor are unable to qualify for these subsidized programs because their monthly incomes fall below the required R3,500 monthly earnings threshold.[79] At the same time, rising rental rates have placed

76. Caroline Hooper-Box and SAPA-AFP, "Egoli Evictions Slammed."

77. Chantelle Benjamin, "Squatters Take Jo-burg to Court over Evictions," *Business Day*, February 7, 2006.

78. Rob Amato, "Judge, Counsel in the Bowels of Jozi," *Sunday Independent*, February 12, 2006. See "Evictions from 'Bad Buildings' in Johannesburg Unconstitutional Rules High Court," COHRE/CALS Joint Media Release, March 3, 2006.

79. Because of steadily rising prices and increasing property values, social-housing schemes were increasingly unable to accommodate the demand for shelter coming from the tens of thousands stuck at the lower rungs of the socioeconomic ladder. The urban poor are unable to pay a deposit of R4,000 and monthly rent of around R1,500 for the least expensive private rental

the availability of low-cost housing in the private housing market well out of reach for the overwhelming majority of urban residents living in decaying buildings without running water or electricity. At the time of the High Court decision, city officials had identified 235 properties on its list of "bad buildings" (i.e., properties where absent owners have accumulated rate debts in excess of the current market values), and they were sitting on a backlog of sixty court orders to carry out evictions.[80]

City officials have stressed that they were both obligated and empowered by municipal regulations to evict people from decaying buildings structurally unsound, unhealthy, and otherwise unsuited for human habitation. They have argued that simply because they were unable immediately to accommodate or provide for the rights of occupiers to a basic roof over their heads did not mean they should be prevented by the courts from fulfilling their legal and governmental obligations in maintaining health and safety standards. Property developers also joined the chorus of opposing voices, proclaiming that the landmark court ruing would undoubtedly "scare investors away."[81]

In contrast, while readily acknowledging that conditions in many inner-city buildings were deplorable, critics have argued that wholesale evictions have accomplished little toward providing a realistic, equitable, or lasting solution to the housing crisis of the inner-city poor and the problem of unsafe living conditions. In their haste to restore order to the city, municipal authorities have aggressively removed unlawful occupants of decaying buildings, yet often with little thought as to the overall consequences or what options are available for affordable alternative housing accommodation. Housing rights advocates have charged that city officials have often obtained urgent interdicts under circumstances of questionable legality in order to carry out eviction orders against inner-city residents.[82] Without the availability of well-managed, secure, and affordable alternative accommodation, large numbers of evicted occupants of "bad buildings"—usually after extended periods of homelessness on the streets or in temporary accommodation—eventually gravitate to

---

accommodation in the inner city (Stuart Wilson, "Bottom Line Is Rights, Not a Quick Profit," *Business Day,* March 24, 2006). See also interview with Stuart Wilson.

80. Jackie Dugard, "Any Room for the Poor?" *Mail & Guardian,* February 21–27, 2006; Chantelle Benjamin, "Illegal to Evict Joburg Squatters—Judge," *Business Day,* March 24, 200; and Ron Amato, "Masando 'Lacks the Will' to Manage Urban Poverty," *Sunday Independent,* April 2, 2006.

81. Isaac Mahlangu, "Brakes Put on City Spruce-Up," *Sunday Times,* July 24, 2005.

82. Many of those forcibly removed from inner-city buildings complained that they regularly paid rents and received no prior notice warning them of pending eviction. See Bafana Nzimande, "City Clears Out Unsafe Building," JOBURG, City of Johannesburg Official Website, http://www.joburg.org.za/2004/oct/oct27_reg.stm, October 27, 2004.

equally deteriorated 'slum housing' elsewhere because they have no choice. Those evicted with nowhere to go are exposed to far worse dangers on the streets, thereby "rendering them even more vulnerable than they were while living in the 'bad building'" (du Plessis and Wilson 2005, 43–44).[83]

The four-year legal dispute pitting the City of Johannesburg against housing rights advocates gradually worked its way through the judicial system before ending in an negotiated compromise brokered by the Constitutional Court. But before this settlement was reached, city officials steadfastly resisted efforts to force them to address the housing needs of those evicted from buildings that posed health and safety hazards. In March 2007, the Supreme Count of Appeal (SCA) upheld the appeal of the City of Johannesburg against the previous year's High Court ruling that had temporarily halted evictions in the inner city.[84] This landmark SCA decision declared that attempts of municipal authorities to evict three hundred residents from six derelict buildings in the inner city were neither unconstitutional nor unlawful, maintaining that "even if the effect of complying with the [eviction] order will be that they [i.e., the evictees] are left without access to adequate housing."[85] For their part, city officials were quick to hail the SCA judgment as vindication that they acted within their rights to evict unlawful occupants of unsafe and unhealthy buildings in the inner city.[86] Yet the SCA ruling acknowledged that the eviction of desperately poor people "triggers a constitutional obligation upon the city to provide at least minimum [emergency] shelter to those occupants who have no access to alternative housing."[87]

Although housing rights advocates considered the SCA decision at least a partial victory for the inner-city poor, the overall thrust of the judgment was not particularly sympathetic to the plight of low-income earners who wanted to remain in the inner city. Literally within days of the SCA ruling, municipal authorities called on the dreaded Red Ants to forcibly evict more than one hundred refugees and asylum seekers from the Coronia Gardens, a thirteen-story apartment block in the city center, where they had lived for many years.

83. Anna Cox, "Squatters Illegally Evicted, Says Councilor," *The Star,* September 7, 2006; Rob Amato, "Judge, Counsel"; and *SAPA,* "The Red Ants Are Coming," November 9, 2005. Information also derived from interview with Stuart Wilson.

84. *SAPA,* "Court Gives Residents a Month to Move," March 26, 2007; Chantelle Benjamin, "World Cup Cities Await Ruling on Fate of Jo'burg Squatters," *Business Day,* February 13, 2007; and Beauregard Tromp, "Joburg Evictions to Continue," *Pretoria News,* March 27, 2007.

85. This passage from the SCA decision is quoted in UN Integrated Regional Information Networks, "South Africa: Poor Squatters Make Way for the 2010 World Cup," *Africa News,* April 13, 2007.

86. City officials quoted in Chantelle Benjamin, "Appeal Ruling Lets Jo'burg Clear Derelict Buildings," *Business Day,* March 27, 2007.

87. Stuart Wilson, "Before Jo'burg Starts Toasting a 'Victory'," *Business Day,* April 10, 2007.

While city officials justified their actions on the grounds that the building had become a sordid gathering place for prostitutes and drug dealers, the evictees spent more than a week on the pavement, "braving the approaching winter in makeshift shelters assembled from sagging mattresses and whatever they could salvage from their apartments and off the streets."[88]

In August 2007 the four-year dispute finally reached the Constitutional Court, the terminal point of the judicial system. Although city officials were soundly criticized for carrying out mass evictions without a plan in place to accommodate those who were rendered homeless, the Constitutional Court reserved judgment in the matter, urging instead that the two parties resolve the issue through negotiation. By taking this course, the Court effectively let stand the earlier SCA ruling that permitted city officials to evict residents of "bad buildings" without consultation and without guarantees of alternative housing in the inner city.[89] In terms of the negotiated settlement, city officials agreed to put in place interim measures to improve living conditions at two of the affected buildings, including providing basic services and a general clean-up of the properties, and to provide temporary shelter until suitable alternative housing could be found.[90]

Yet there are broader structural dynamics at work here. By focusing so much attention on the legal wrangling over the city's eviction policies, it is easy to overlook how the shifting fortunes of real estate capitalism have fundamentally altered the playing field on which property developers and the urban poor compete in the marketplace as buyers and sellers of commodities. Between 2002 and 2007, rising prices for inner-city buildings and skyrocketing rents have ensured that the force of economic circumstances was inexorably driving the poor out of inner-city neighborhoods where private developers were gobbling up properties at a rapid pace.[91] Despite restrictions on their legal right to use private security firms to conduct mass evictions, private owners were under no obligation to find alternative housing for tenants evicted from their buildings.[92] This revival of the inner city has resulted in an escalation of property values, thereby making it virtually impossible for city agencies and non-profit organizations to provide much-needed social housing for low-income

88. Quotation from *SAPA*, "Joburg Evictions Leave Refugees Stranded," April 12, 2007. See UN Integrated Regional Information Networks, "South Africa: Poor Squatters Make Way for the 2010 World Cup."

89. *SAPA*, "Judgment Reserved on Joburg Evictions," August 28, 2007.

90. *Business Day*, "Jo'burg May Not Evict Residents of Derelict Buildings," October 25, 2007.

91. See Chantelle Benjamin, "Jo'burg's Poor Reject Offer of Makeshift Accommodation," *Business Day*, March 12, 2007.

92. See Anna Cox, "'Squatters Can't Be Evicted in One Go'," *The Star*, April 15, 2007. For descriptions of evictions, see Solly Maphumulo, "Mother and Child Wrenched Apart in Dawn Chaos," *The Star*, March 20, 2007; *SAPA*, "More Inner-city Joburg Evictions," March 19, 2007.

earners. Faced with a buoyant real estate market, particularly ahead of the Soccer World Cup in 2010, private property developers found it more difficult to offer residential accommodation at affordable prices for those at the lowest rungs of the income ladder.[93]

Clearing the Buildings and Sweeping the Streets: Driving the Urban Poor Out of the Inner City

> Will the entire inner city be turned into a vibrant mixed-income society like other first-world cities around the globe or will we have a few pristine areas like Newtown and the Johannesburg financial district (southwestern inner-city areas that house mainly banks and mining companies) surrounded by a sea of decay in the form of Hillbrow, Berea, Yeoville, and Bertams?
>
> NICK WILSON

The moralizing discourse that has accompanied the projected revitalization of the Johannesburg inner city mobilizes a distinct spatial mise-en-scène organized around the contrast between degenerate sinkholes and uplifting ripple-pond investments.[94] By putting so much stress on the ill effects of "bad buildings," the official discourse of inner-city revitalization has tended to overlook the straitened circumstances that have led ordinary people to seek shelter in these run-down, unhealthy places in the first place. Despite its objective language, the inner-city regeneration strategy is, by virtue of its selective focus, its boundaries, and its exclusions, also an ideological statement that has set boundaries for defining the problems associated with urban blight and for posing solutions that will bring about projected redevelopment. This focus on "bad buildings" rather than their desperately poor occupants obscures the role of power and choice in decision-making processes of city officials, thereby rendering the politics of place seem strangely apolitical. Neglecting to consider alternative accommodation for those evicted corresponds with a general indifference to the plight of the urban poor more generally (Deutsche 1996, 6–7, 11–21, 45–48).[95]

---

93. Chantelle Benjamin, "Property Prices in Jo'burg City Centre out of Reach for the Poor," *Business Day,* January 4, 2007; and Beauregard Tromp, "Joburg Evictions to Continue." It was reported, for example, that the waiting list for access to low-income housing at Diepsloot to the north of the central city was already 300,000 families long. See *SAPA,* "Joburg Evictions in 'Breach of Law'," August 28, 2007.

94. Nick Wilson, "City Living—Glamorous."

95. "I have voiced the opinion previously that the City [of Johannesburg] does not have a coherent policy in its approach to the urban poor. This concern is exacerbated when it comes to residential accommodation. I think it is time to take a step back and look critically at where we are and where we are going. I think it is time to develop a new model that breaks with apartheid

The Inner-City Regeneration Strategy may offer an elegant story of a successful path toward urban regeneration for real estate developers who stand to benefit. But for the poorest of the poor who stand in the way, its implementation represents a disgraceful example of urban tyranny. The High Court ruling provided a glimpse into the tensions, contradictions, and ambiguities that have accompanied inner-city revitalization in Johannesburg after apartheid. Although entrepreneurial investments and market forces drive the process of inner-city revitalization, municipal authorities have taken an active role in facilitating this impulse toward gentrification. The High Court ruling interfered with this seamless narrative that identified the problem as degenerate sinkholes and the solution as closing down "bad buildings" and evicting their occupants as a way of clearing the path for regenerative ripple-pond investments. By focusing on the constitutional rights of evicted occupants to alternative accommodation, the legal decision restored the connections that official discourses of inner-city regeneration severed, ignored, or sanitized: without the availability of alternative housing, large-scale evictions of the urban poor do not eliminate the slumlord economy and its deleterious effects but only displace these problems to another location.[96]

Unlawful occupation of abandoned buildings not only reveals the contradiction between the post–liberation promise of improvement and the actual realities of urban deprivation. Forced removals have continued to take place after the end of apartheid, but paradoxically there is a kind of collective amnesia about the continuity between the past and the present. Particular events generate attention for a brief moment, only to become part of a cycle of forgetting where they disappear from memory. Evictions remain largely hidden from view and generally undocumented. The anonymity of displaced people makes them vulnerable to misunderstanding and incomprehension because their lives are so easily stereotyped (Beningfield and Gaule 2006, 24–26).

---

planning because I really don't think we have achieved that. In fact I see little evidence of revolutionary thinking when it comes to housing policy at any level of government. I must sadly concur with Stephen Greenberg,…who says 'In the face of a coldly rational model of planning, the horror of forced removals has not been consigned to history along with apartheid, but remains alive in postapartheid South Africa'" (Neil Fraser, "Decade of Change Scorecard (2): How Are We Making Out in the Residential Sector?" *CitiChat*, August 16, 2004).

96. Kwanele Sosibo and Lynley Donnelly, "Caught between Eviction and Dereliction," *Mail & Guardian*, March 31–April 6, 2006.

8

The Banality of
Indifferent Urbanism

We are left to die.

TABISO, a homeless man

On September 21, 2004, Simon Magaliso Radebe, a fifty-seven-year-old homeless man, collapsed on President Street in downtown Johannesburg.[1] The security guards who discovered him lying in the gutter realized that he required immediate medical attention, and they quickly radioed Johannesburg Emergency Management Services (EMS) for urgent assistance. The two EMS paramedics who arrived on the scene looked at the prostrate man—who was covered in grime, fleas, and ticks—and complained that he was too filthy to put in the ambulance. Instead, they put on surgical gloves, lifted Radebe out of the street and propped him against a nearby wall, telling the security guards who had gathered there that the barely conscious man was not really sick, but "just dirty" and was "stinking." Within five minutes, and without even a cursory medical examination, they quickly sped away, leaving the helpless man to suffer, abandoned and alone. Less than sixteen hours later, Radebe was found dead, unmoved from the spot where he had been unceremoniously dumped.[2]

The ignominious death of Simon Radebe undoubtedly would have gone unnoticed, and his body interred in a pauper's grave without even a headstone to mark his passing, if this merciless chain of events had not been captured on video footage by CCTV monitors. An attentive operator at Cueincident, a private security company with CCTV cameras dotted all over the central city, first noticed the man lying on the pavement, and he alerted security guards who then called the parametics.[3] As the story of what happened came to light,

1. Tabiso is quoted in Jonathan Ancer, "Nobody Sees Us as People, Say the Homeless," *The Star,* September 28, 2004.
2. Jonathan Ancer, "Medics Who Left Dying Vagrant Get the Axe," *The Star,* November 19, 2004.
3. *SAPA,* "Dead Homeless Man: Paramedics Face Tribunal," October 15, 2004.

city officials, human rights activists, and homeless advocates reacted with outrage at the shocking manner in which this incapacitated person was left to perish without assistance on the streets of Johannesburg. In seeking to learn the name of the unidentified man, investigators discovered that Radebe had been "sleeping rough" on the streets, in the vicinity of the Newton Cultural Precinct for about four months. Along with a group of around fifty others, he spent his days begging for food and money at Mary Fitzgerald Square in front of MuseumAfrica.[4]

City officials were quick to condemn this deliberate act of wanton cruelty directed at a helpless vagrant who was unable to care for himself. The two EMS paramedics, Jacobus Craukamp and Johan Erasmus, were brought before a disciplinary tribunal, where they were found guilty of negligence and dismissed from their jobs. Yet focusing too much attention on this single episode and treating it as an isolated, aberrant deviation from standard practice has the effect of overlooking and ignoring broader patterns of silent violence aimed at the poor and dispossessed of the city. When asked about the incident, the homeless people who knew the hapless victim expressed little surprise that paramedics had acted with such callous disregard for human life. Over the past decade scores of other homeless people have perished, alone and abandoned, on the streets of Johannesburg, and their deaths have gone largely unnoticed. According to city officials in Johannesburg, the number of pauper's burials—unidentified bodies unclaimed by family or friends—had increased from an estimated seven hundred between 2000 and 2001 to a staggering twelve hundred between 2005 and 2006. Johannesburg City Parks, the department responsible for managing burial sites, disposed of these bodies three or four to a grave without a headstone.[5]

The Seamy Underside of Urban Revitalization: Displacement, Exclusion, and Marginality

> When we have returned to normalcy, we won't have to crack down anymore.
>
> OSWALD REDDY, Johannesburg police commissioner

The presence of homeless people living in makeshift cardboard shelters on sidewalks, sleeping in dirty cubicles in abandoned buildings, or squeezing into already overcrowded flats in residential apartment complexes in the inner city

---

4. Jonathan Ancer and Solly Maphumulo, "News of Vagrant's Death Greeted with Horror," *The Star*, September 24, 2004; and Jonathan Ancer, "Nobody Sees Us as People."

5. Caiphus Kgosana, "'Too-Dirty' Hobo: Medics Guilty of Negligence," *The Star*, October 4, 2004; and Phomello Molwedi, "1,200 Pauper's Burials in Joburg this Year," *The Star*, July 21, 2006.

is emblematic of a larger crisis of jobless economic growth where the promises of prosperity after the end of apartheid have mostly failed to trickle down to the poorest of the poor.[6] For affluent urban residents, the fear, anxiety, and annoyance caused by the visible presence of homeless vagrants, beggars, and drifters has contributed to a visceral impulse to segregate, exclude, and sometimes even to confine and repress them in the name of public order and personal safety. Taken together, the accumulation of single acts—like the refusal to transport Simon Radebe to the hospital—have formed the incremental building blocks of a broader pattern of structural violence—intentional or otherwise, it matters little—directed at the urban poor. The serial accretion of seemingly isolated events has amounted to a kind of invisible yet all-out war against the poor, the disenfranchised, and the dispossessed. When police officers issue huge spot fines to unlicensed street traders and confiscate their wares, they effectively take away the livelihood of the most marginalized hawkers who occupy the lowest rungs of the informal economy. When city officials impound aging and unsafe vehicles as part of an overall municipal campaign to promote safety on the roads and to upgrade the city's taxi fleet, they deprive independent operators of their only source of income.[7] When municipal authorities carry out the forcible eviction of residents from condemned residential buildings in the name of eradicating crime dens or because of violations of health and safety codes, they throw responsible tenants who have paid their rents and maintained their flats into the streets with no provision for alternative accommodation. When law enforcement agencies conduct massive crime blitzes in the inner city, they invariably sweep up innocent victims into their dragnet. Taken together, these seemingly disparate actions aimed at implementing a vision of a stable, orderly city have contributed to a broader juggernaut directed at the most marginalized and vulnerable urban residents where the battle lines are drawn between the anxious rich who want to take back the city and the victimized poor who have nowhere else to go (du Plessis and Wilson 2005, 1–10, 35–42, 85–87; Olufemi 1998).

Official discourse about urban well-being has moved from calls for redistributive justice to an endorsement of the virtues of personal responsibility. The ideological roots for this profound shift in thinking can be traced to a reinvigorated belief in the enabling powers of the hidden hand of the market to bring about the trickling down of wealth. The triumph of liberalism—with its emphasis on individual choice, entrepreneurial initiative, and private ownership—has marked a decisive "sociocultural and ideological 'turn'

6. Oswald Reddy, quoted in Peter Honey, "The Man Who Is Trying to Bring Down an Elephant," *Financial Mail,* October 10, 2003.
7. Stuart Graham, "Frustrated Taxi Drivers Take to the Streets," *SAPA,* May 17, 2005.

which [has] relegated considerations of social justice to the back burner of urban politics" (Swyngedouw 2005, 127). In Johannesburg and elsewhere, municipal authorities have jumped on the bandwagon of market-driven urban development, embracing an entrepreneurial approach to city building in which municipal officials, urban planners, real estate developers, architects, and designers have joined forces to fashion urban growth machines that endorse grand projects and programs designed to enhance their attractiveness in the competition to achieve world-class status. Framed within the context of diminishing attention to matters of social welfare and the collective consumption of scarce resources, this kind of market-led development has triggered powerful centripetal forces of social polarization, spatial exclusion, and marginalization (Bremner 2005, 32–47; Degan 2003; Swyngedouw 2005, 125).

In an ominous sign of a (possible) turn toward a "Brazilianization" of the Johannesburg urban landscape, law enforcement officers—operating outside legally sanctioned mandates—have contributed to the institutionalized violence directed at the homeless poor.[8] Social workers, church staffers, and homeless advocates have raised a chorus of complaints about the ill treatment of the shelterless poor at the hands of the municipal police. Places like Nugget Park, a small, litter-strewn square at the corner of Nugget and Saratoga streets in the central city, have become battlegrounds in the unofficial war against the homeless. Homeless people tell harrowing stories of "men in street clothes" who regularly confiscate their simple possessions, including identity documents. Others complained that the police regularly beat them, doused them with water cannons, and sprayed them with tear gas to drive them out of city parks and other public places of the city. "We cannot sit back and watch the place going to the dogs," Arthur Adendorff, city manager for the Eastern Metropolitan Council, proclaimed with pride. "Our job is to keep the parks clean and safe. We cannot allow people to sleep and do business in our parks." Homeless people who have been rounded up in periodic street sweeps were routinely relocated to Weiler's Farm—nicknamed "Tula, Ntwana" ("Quiet, my children"), as a reference to the shame and pain that homeless people experience at being relocated there.[9] In response to complaints from motorists and pedestrians, municipal authorities have mounted numerous campaigns to rid the city of beggars, claiming that these truly

8. "Brazilianization" refers to the extra-legal violence directed at street children and aimed at cleansing public places of those who are regarded as an annoying nuisance. It is a term borrowed from the experience of cities in Brazil, like Rio de Janeiro and São Paulo.

9. Quotations from homeless people and Arthur Adendorff are taken from Aaron Nicodemus, "A Precarious Existence in Nugget Park," *Mail & Guardian*, March 20–26, 1999.

destitute people created a public nuisance at street intersections and near entrances to upscale shopping malls. In the name of public health and safety, the metro police and social service personnel worked together to place children detained in police sweeps in homeless shelters and to transfer those without proper identity documents to the Department of Home Affairs for deportation to their country of origin.[10] The approximately four hundred fifty to five hundred blind people from Zimbabwe who survived in Johannesburg by begging were particularly vulnerable. After joining the mass exodus fleeing the socioeconomic collapse north of the Limpopo river, these disabled people crowded into inner-city slums—sometimes more than thirty people in a single-room flat. The visible presence of blind beggars led around by child handlers at street corners made them easy targets for police dragnets.[11] Salvation Army employees have reported that the police, in trying to drive homeless people off the streets, particularly those sleeping rough on the sidewalks, under bridges, and under the M1 and M2 highway overpasses, have regularly smashed their flimsy shelters, impounding their belongings and setting them alight in huge bonfires.[12] Advocates for the homeless have long charged that the Johannesburg Metropolitan Council has all too often resorted to force and the threat of violence to remove unwanted young people from the city pavements with the aim of cleaning up the streets and promoting tourism. This revanchist approach toward street kids has taken many forms, including petty harassment by police, arbitrary arrests, physical assaults, and confinement in detention centers for runaway youth. According to homeless advocates like the Reverend Les Sanabria of the Gauteng Alliance for Street Children (GASC), both the Johannesburg Metro Police and the Red Ants have routinely resorted to confiscating blankets donated to homeless street children and either discarding them or burning them under the flimsy pretext that they were littering.[13]

In early 2007, rumors circulated that street children had been "'cleaned off' the streets and spirited away to secret institutions or camps, in a mock dress

10. United Nations Integrated Regional Information Networks, "Johannesburg—A City of Risk and Opportunity," *Africa News*, March 14, 2005; Phomello Molwedi and Solly Maphumulo, "'We Don't Like Begging, But We Have To,'" *The Star*, February 4, 2005; and Melanie-Ann Feris, "Super Blitz to Clean Up Jo'burg's Streets," *The Star*, February 4, 2005.

11. Melanie-Ann Feris and Anna Cox, "Egoli Police Launch 'Blitz on Beggars,'" *The Star*, February 4, 2005; Basildon Peta, "Blind Zimbabweans Coining It in Joburg," *The Star*, February 4, 2005; and Solidarity Peace Trust, "Hillbrow Horror: 31 Blind People Live in One Room," *Sunday Independent*, November 21, 2004.

12. SAPA, "Salvation Army Blankets 'Go Up in Flames,'" July 6, 2003.

13. Thembisile Makgalemele, "Cops Are Burning Street Kids' Blankets," *Saturday Star*, July 11, 2003; and Ndivhuwo Khangale, "Cops Beat Me to Teach Me a Lesson—Teen," *The Star*, May 19, 2003.

rehearsal for the expected influx of visitors for the 2010 soccer World Cup." These unconfirmed speculations proved untrue when it was learned that the street children had merely shifted from their usual haunts to be closer to shelters in Hillbrow, Berea, and End Street, where mid-day meals were available. Advocates for homeless children pointed with alarm to three disturbing developments in recent years that have changed the social composition of parentless young people living on the streets. First, the average age of homeless youths has risen so sharply that young adults outnumber those under eighteen. Second, the numbers of homeless girls and young women has increased dramatically. Third, the proportion of immigrants from other parts of Africa has increased steadily. Although city officials denied it, street children claimed that the Metro police regularly burned their blankets in order to drive them off the streets and into shelters.[14]

Human rights advocates have also pointed with alarm to an upsurge of vengeful attacks on the urban poor organized by shadowy gangs of ostensibly law-abiding citizens operating on their own accord and in secret. In 2002 a group of seven men carried out a vigilante-like assault on a squatter settlement in Muldersdrift on the West Rand, burning numerous shacks and leaving at least fifty shack dwellers homeless. In charging the men with arson, malicious damage to property, and assault, law enforcement officials suspected that these attacks and others like them were racially motivated.[15]

Ironically, it is the combination of unrelenting constancy, the ordinariness, and the anonymity that has rendered the everyday insecurity of the urban poor so frightening. Formal citizenship, including access to civil society, respect for human rights, and the sanctity of the person—in a word, the inalienable rights to proprietorship over one's own body—have seemed to disappear in the face of persistent harassment, intimidation, and callous disregard. The routinization of everyday violence, the cavalier indifference, and the callous neglect of their straitened circumstances have fostered a "climate of anxious, ontological insecurity" that has trapped the urban poor in its grip, a stranglehold that the most marginalized and vulnerable urban residents have found nearly impossible to escape (Scheper-Hughes 1992, 219–220). The relentless efforts to exclude the poor through walls and barriers, to evict the homeless from the only shelter they can find in the inner city, and to deny the most impoverished ways to make a living add up to, as Michael Taussig (1989, 3–20) has put it in another context, "terror as usual."

---

14. Quotation and information derived from Jeremy Gordin, "Wave of Homeless Youths Overwhelming Joburg," *Sunday Independent*, June 17, 2007.

15. *SAPA*, "Case against Four Alleged Arsonists Postponed," February 4, 2002.

Policing the Carceral City: The Clampdown on Popular Illegalities

[The police] have decided the only way to stop the mayhem is to tackle the criminals head-on with military-style raids on crime-ridden buildings. It's neither pretty nor easy, and it sparks mayhem of its own. Often innocent people's rights get trampled, or they are trapped in crossfire when criminals fight back.

PETER HONEY

Despite the rhetorical commitment to upliftment and improved quality of life for the urban poor, Johannesburg city officials have remained fixated on the roseate image of Johannesburg as a "world-class, globally competitive city."[16] By establishing rigorous standards to regulate land uses and spatial aesthetics, urban planners have sought to shape the provision of residential housing through far-reaching efforts to regulate the capitalist market in urban space. Municipal authorities have sought to promote and sustain economic growth in the central city by embracing the privatization of bulk service delivery (electricity, water, sewerage, and road maintenance), by fostering the creation of public-private partnerships as a means of spurring much-needed investment in the built environment, and by providing financial and institutional support to small- and medium-scale enterprises. Simultaneously, they have actively courted big business, both nationally and internationally, in a concerted effort to hold investment grade financial ratings and maintain Johannesburg's place as the dominant economic hub of southern Africa.[17] Although the Greater Johannesburg Metropolitan Council (GJMC) endorsed the creation of safety nets and targeting mechanisms, in addition to infrastructure and tariff subsidies, to benefit the most impoverished urban residents, urban policy makers have largely ignored the formulation of a coherent and comprehensive poverty reduction strategy for the city (Beall, Crankshaw, and Parnell 2000, 110–111; 2002, 109–128).[18]

In seeking to achieve their goal of encouraging private entrepreneurs to invest in the upgrading of residential and commercial properties in the inner

16. Peter Honey, "The Man Who Is Trying"; Rapule Tabane, "Expertise, Cash Boost for Igoli 2002," *The Star,* October 13, 1999; and Prince Hamnca, "Jo'burg Boss Moloi Aims for World-Class City," *The Star,* April 3, 2001.

17. Ideas and information derived from interview with Yael Horowitz, Johannesburg Development Agency, June 20, 2003; interview with Li Pernegger, program manager, Economic Area Regeneration, Department of Finance and Economic Development, City of Johannesburg, May 30, 2006; and interview with Lael Bethlehem, chief executive officer, Johannesburg Development Agency, City of Johannesburg, May 30, 2006. Interpretation is mine.

18. Ideas and information derived from interviews with Neil Fraser, chief executive officer, Central Johannesburg Partnership, June 12 and July 3, 2003.

city, municipal authorities have mobilized an entire repertoire of new policing technologies in order to clean up the city and clamp down on popular illegalities.[19] In late 2004 the City of Johannesburg established a new municipal court with the primary objective of enforcing city bylaws, particularly infractions regarding unlawful squatting in abandoned buildings, unregistered businesses, and unauthorized street trading. As part of a wider strategy to create an orderly streetscape, law enforcement agencies have targeted unlicensed taxi drivers and telephone kiosk operators, illegal shebeens, street prostitution, drug dealing, and panhandling.[20] By also promising to crack down on such seemingly innocuous and irritating public nuisances as littering, loitering, hanging washing on apartment balconies, sleeping on the sidewalks, and urinating in public places, municipal authorities have introduced a get-tough policy that bears a striking resemblance to the zero-tolerance approach to city policing adopted in New York City under the guidance of Mayor Rudolph Giuliani and Chief of Police William Bratton. By focusing on minor infractions, city officials have hoped to reverse the crime and grime syndrome that has plagued the image of the inner city for decades. "If we start small," one city official stated, "we believe we can clean up the inner city."[21] The underlying premise of this anticrime strategy is that police should not just enforce the law but impose a rigorous set of values on those who wished to use urban space: saturating the streets with uniformed police officers and expelling potential troublemakers reduces the risk of crime.[22] While advocates of this zero-tolerance approach to recolonizing disorderly space have praised its track record in reducing crime in the areas where it is put into practice, civil libertarians have suggested that this strategy often boils down to police harassment of the poor and the unwanted (Smith 1998).[23]

Municipal police have targeted sidewalk hawkers, using the stringent enforcement of city bylaws to effectively criminalize their small-scale enterprises. By confiscating their goods and issuing exorbitant fines to those least able to pay, municipal authorities have subjected the poorest and most marginal street traders (namely, the bottom 10–20 percent who cannot secure places for themselves in the authorized informal marketplaces scattered around the

---

19. Interview with Nazira Cachalia, program manager, City Safety Programme, City of Johannesburg, May 30, 2006. The views expressed here are mine alone.

20. Despite declining crime rates in the central city, Johannesburg has remained South Africa's most dangerous city. A recent victim study has suggested that in 2003 nearly one-third of inner-city residents were robbed at gunpoint or knifepoint (Peter Honey, "The Man Who Is Trying").

21. Pauline Larsen, "Inner City: By the Way, Zip Up," *Financial Mail*, October 8, 2004.

22. Jonny Steinberg, "Zero-Tolerance Rhetoric May Have Worked in New York, but Johannesburg Is a Different Kettle of Fish," *Business Day*, February 8, 2000.

23. Peter Honey, "The Man Who Is Trying."

cityscape) to the severest hardships.[24] Police officials have defended their aggressive street patrols and periodic road blocks as a requisite step to apprehend criminals and reduce the crime rate, but these actions have also disguised a strong xenophobic current. Undocumented migrants and asylum seekers have frequently borne the brunt of police violence. Nativist discourses that blame foreigners for a host of social ills have lent legitimacy to the circumvention and even suspension of existing legal procedures, thereby creating what are in effect urban zones of exception where the rule of law no longer applies. According to the South African Human Rights Commission, "people of foreign appearance"—including dark-complexioned South African citizens—have been routinely subjected to arbitrary arrest and unlawful detention, harassment, extortion, and assault at the hands of overzealous police and private security officials (Landau 2005).[25]

Despite the stated commitment to universal human rights and the introduction of new training programs, old policing habits die hard. There is plenty of evidence to suggest that the police have not completely "left behind the culture of torture and abuse that characterized their modus operandi under apartheid." In their concerted effort to combat crime and clean up the city, law enforcement agencies and private security operatives have often resorted to harsh and brutal methods that have claimed innocent victims.[26]

Blurring the Boundaries between Urban Renaissance and Revanchism: Urban Outcasts and the Heartless City

> The [squatter] camp is thus the structure in which the state of exception...is realized *normally*.
>
> GIORGIO AGAMBEN (1998, 170)

The efforts of city builders to stimulate the urban renaissance of the historic urban core of Johannesburg have become to be a double-edged sword. On the

24. The implementation of the Informal Trading Development Programme has meant the restriction of street trading to twenty-seven areas in the city. The effect of channeling traders into eight newly constructed market areas has been to deprive hawkers of access to passing pedestrians and to intensify competition (Harrison 2006, 330).

25. Interview with Nathi Radebe, former street trader and inner-city building manager, Johannesburg, May 25, 2006. Some of these ideas are derived from "Johannesburg Inner City Anti-Eviction Campaign March Saturday 14 December," press release issued by the Anti-Privatisation Forum, December 12, 2002. Some ideas are derived from personal observation. See also Lee Rondganger, "Masondo at Loggerheads with Joburg Hawkers," *The Star*, October 14, 2004.

26. Quotation from Khadija Magardie and Glenda Daniels, "Torture and Abuse by Cops," *Mail & Guardian*, November 10–16, 2000. See Khadija Magardie, "Migrants and Refugees among Top Targets," *Mail & Guardian*, November 10–16, 2000.

one hand, in fashioning the new Johannesburg in the cosmopolitan image of a vibrant world-class city, municipal authorities and planning professionals have tried to construct a sustainable and orderly urban realm, founded upon the principles of social mixing, connectivity, high densities, walkability, efficient services, and aesthetically pleasing streetscapes. On the other hand, in allowing the principles of market rationality to drive the process of urban revitalization, the boundaries between urban renaissance and revanchism are often blurred. For city officials and planning professionals alike, the continued existence of disorderly and unregulated places represents all the outward symptoms of an unwanted "space pathology," where the readily available default option is elimination. As a general rule, urban regulatory regimes combine design-led solutions to unwanted unruliness through the embedding of defensive architectural features into the urban fabric with the strict enforcement of codes and bylaws intended to displace and disperse dangers, risks, and threats to the stability of the orderly city (Coaffee, 2005, 448). Broadly speaking, the creation of sequestered zones that design out "crime and grime" privileges those with a stable foothold in the urban social fabric, that is, propertied and affluent residents, at the expense of the unstable urban poor.

In seeking to bring Johannesburg into conformity with the standards of a world-class city, city builders have adopted new forms of urban management that seek to produce secure landscapes, which minimize personal risk by excluding unwanted persons, rather than to focus on the apprehension of lawbreakers. These new strategies of spatial governmentality rely on sequestering places through architectural design and security devices, removing incivilities, and excluding offensive behavior (Merry 2001, 16–18). The solution to the problem of urban disorder, whether it takes the form of criminality, unauthorized occupation of buildings, unsanctioned use of public space, homelessness, panhandling, or illegal immigration, is to rid the cityscape of the people who embody it, that is, in order to deal with unauthorized use of urban space, it is necessary to eliminate potential lawbreakers (Bouillon 2002, 96).

Revanchist urbanism consists of more than a dual city bisected by extremes of wealth and poverty, or a divided-city partitioned into citadels and ghettos. What distinguishes revanchist urbanism from the benign neglect of either the dual-city or the divided-city paradigms is the striking image of the city at war with itself, where urban stakeholders are actively engaged in a seemingly zero-sum competition over access to scarce resources, and where the victorious haves are willing to go to great lengths to defend their privilege, such as it is, and have become increasingly vicious in keeping the have-nots at bay. The conventional liberal paradigm of social control, characterized by the effort to balance repression with reform, has been superceded by a vindictive rhetoric of incipient social warfare that calculates the interests of the middle classes and the urban poor as a zero-sum game where there are either winners or losers (Flusty 2001, 659; Jewson and MacGregor 1997; Lees 1998; Mitchell 1997; Smith 1996, 1998).

The language of liberation, collective improvement, and redistribution that accompanied the post-1994 transition to parliamentary democracy in the new South Africa has gradually faded, and a new rhetoric of entitlement has filled the void. The active defense of privilege has assumed the form of criminalizing the poor, effectively blaming the hapless victims of a stagnant labor market that cannot provide jobs for all (Davis 1990, 223–226; Smith 1996, 227). A punitive, revanchist vernacular has become an integral part of a middle-class political response intended "to discipline the deleterious social consequences and the escalating sociospatial contradictions that continue to be generated by a neoliberalising political economic agenda" (MacLeod 2002, 603). In the emergent revanchist city, the assembled forces of private property and the municipal administration are blended together in a new disciplinary ensemble that seeks to impose sociospatial order on the disorderly cityscape by driving the urban poor away. The geographical contours of this emergent urban form are increasingly choreographed through the control over and purification of urban space. By pushing the disadvantaged out, municipal authorities have made it "clear that, as broken windows rather than people, [the poor] simply have *no* right to the city" (Mitchell 2001, 71).

The slide toward revanchist urbanism reflects a changing conception of connection, entitlement, and belonging to the city as such. Contrary to the hard-won extension of formal citizenship rights that accompanied the collapse of white minority rule, revanchism has sought to reassert various kinds of social exclusion and to justify these as somehow just and good. When in competition with the middle-class desire for order, comfort, and relaxation, the rights of jobless and homeless urban dwellers to a legitimate place in the city have come under attack. Under circumstances where marketplace bargaining power determines access to the post-public spaces of the city, those without work, without shelter, and without steady income "are not really citizens in the sense of free agents with sovereignty over their own actions." The exclusionary practices that keep the unwanted out of the new post-public privatopias that characterize the urban glamour zone have helped to institutionalize this conviction by restricting the movements of the urban poor to the depleted zones of the city, with their overcrowded streets, nonexistent social services, broken-down infrastructure, and blighted built environment. In seeking to regulate the use of urban space, a host of measures, ranging from city bylaws covering loitering, sleeping, littering, trading, and begging to municipal codes governing the use of streets, sidewalks, and parks effectively annihilate the public spaces of the city, thereby ensuring that there is literally no room for the urban poor (Mitchell 1997, 320–321). In exploiting the compassion fatigue of affluent urban residents who have grown weary of the presence of the poor in their midst, municipal authorities have accelerated efforts to root the homeless out of their temporary redoubts under bridges, in abandoned buildings, in alleyways, and other interstices of the urban streetscape. Law enforcement agencies have evicted unlawful squatters without providing alternative accommodation, have targeted idle youth for petty harassment and arbitrary arrest, and have placed the blame for urban crime on the shoulders of illegal immigrants.[27]

Just as the right to the city is not an ontological entitlement that spans time and space, so, too, does formal citizenship not translate into equal access to all that the city has to offer. At the end of the day, the right to the city can be boiled down to the opening up of (or making available) opportunities to use the cityscape in order to realize one's individual or collective aspirations. But different ways of using the city as a platform for translating ambitions into concrete realities do not take place in a void (Simone 2004c, 3–4). The social fabric of the cityscape itself—that is, its movements toward growth and decline, its juxtaposition of planning and improvisation, its balance between private luxury and public amenities, and the availability of shared spaces and the resources of collective consumption—sets the limits and possibilities for the realization of a decent urban life.

27. See, for example, Michael Wines, "As the Police Get Smarter, the Highwaymen Get Meaner," *New York Times*, September 23, 2005.

References

Periodical Publications

African Business
Architecture SA
Engineering News
Financial Mail
Housing in Southern Africa

Newspapers

Africa News
Agence France-Presse
Baltimore Sun
BuaNews
Business Day
Cape Argus
City Press
Daily Telegraph (London)
East African Standard (Nairobi)
Financial Times
Mail & Guardian
New York Times
Pretoria News
Reuters
Saturday Star
South African Press Association (SAPA)
The Financial Gazette
The Star

The Star Business Report
Sunday Independent
Sunday Times

Periodicals and Other Sources Online

BBC News [http://www.iol.co.za]
CitiChat [http://www.joburg.org.za/citichat]
Facing Reality [http://www.journalism.berkeley.com]
EPROP Commercial Property Marketplace [http://www.eprop.co.za]
Independent Online [http://www.iol.co.za]
JOBURG, City of Johannesburg Official Website [http://www.joburg.org.za]
Johannesburg News Agency [http://www.joburg.org.za]
Rode Property News [www.rode.co.za/news/]

Primary Materials

INTERVIEWS WITH AUTHOR

Adler, Taffy. 2006. Chief executive officer, Johannesburg Housing Company, City of Johannesburg, May 31.

Beavon, Keith. 2003. Professor, Department of Geography, University of Pretoria, June 20.

Bethlehem, Lael. 2006. Chief executive officer, Johannesburg Development Agency, City of Johannesburg, May 30.

Bremner, Lindsay. 2003. Head of architecture, School of Architecture and Planning, University of the Witwatersrand, June 12.

Cachalia, Nazira. 2006. Program manager, City Safety Programme, City of Johannesburg, May 30.

Charlton, Sarah. 2006. Professor, School of Architecture and Urban Planning, University of the Witwatersrand, June 1.

Ferreira, Jaco. 2006. Portfolio manager, Trafalgar Property Management, June 5.

Fraser, Neil. 2003. Chief executive officer, Central Johannesburg Partnership, June 12.

——. 2003. Chief executive officer, Central Johannesburg Partnership, July 3.

——. 2006. Partner, Urban Inc., Urban Consultants, 29 May 2006.

Gotz, Graeme. 2006. Specialist in policy and strategy, Corporate Planning Unit, Office of City Manager, City of Johannesburg, May 26.

——. 2006. Specialist in policy and strategy, Corporate Planning Unit, Office of City Manager, City of Johannesburg, June 3.

Govender, Kuben. 2006. Programme Officer, Trust for Urban Housing Finance (TUHF), June 6.

Horowitz, Yael. 2003. Project manager, Johannesburg Development Agency, June 20.

Jackson, Paul. 2006. Director, Trust for Urban Housing Finance (TUHF), very brief discussion, June 6.

Jones, Bronwen. 2006. Director, Children of Fire Trust, May 27.

Mendelowitz, Geoff. 2006. Program manager, Better Buildings, City of Johannesburg Property Company, June 2.

Penberthy, John. 2003. Executive director, Business against Crime (BAC) Surveillance Technology, June 19.

Pernegger, Li. 2006. Program manager, Economic Area Regeneration, Department of Finance and Economic Development, City of Johannesburg, May 30.
Radebe, Nathi. 2006. Former street trader and inner-city building manager, Johannesburg, May 25.
Rust, Kecia. 2006. Consultant in housing finance and development policy, June 1.
Schaefer, Andrew. 2006. Managing director, Trafalgar Property Management, June 5.
Sibanda, Shereza. 2006. Inner City Resource Center, Johannesburg, May 29.
Staff members. 2003. The House, a refuge for homeless girls and young women at 60 Olivia Street, Berea, May 20.
Tomlinson, Richard. 2001. Consultant in urban economic development and project management, Johannesburg, June 4.
Wilson, Stuart. 2006. Researcher, Centre for Applied Legal Studies, University of the Witwatersrand, June 7.

ON-SITE OBSERVATIONS BY AUTHOR

Alexandra Township. 1999. With David Letsia, Lulu Mothapo, Johnny Mpho, and Sam Maredi of RHREDI, an NGO specializing in health and environment issues, May 21.
Alexandra Township. 2001. With Lulu Mothapo, Johnny Mpho, and Sam Maredi of RHREDI, an NGO specializing in health and environment issues, May 19.
Alexandra Township. 2003. With Mzwanele Mayekiso, May 22.
Better Buildings projects in Johannesburg inner city. 2006. With Geoff Mendelowitz, Better Buildings Programme, City of Johannesburg Property Company, June 2.
Dainfern, Cosmo City, and Diepsloot. 2006. With Sarah Charlton, School of Architecture and Planning, University of the Witwatersrand, June 4.
Decaying neighborhoods on the inner-city periphery. 2006. With Graeme Gotz, Corporate Planning Unit, Office of City Manager, City of Johannesburg, June 3.
Elias Motsoaledi informal settlement, Soweto. 2006. With long-time resident and self-declared anarchist Phillip Nyalungu, June 8.
The House, a refuge for homeless girls and young women at 60 Olivia Street, Berea. 2003. With staff members, May 20.
Informal settlements of Chicken Farm, Mandelaville, Elias Motsoaledi, and Thembelihle near Soweto. 2006. With Trevor Ngwane, community activist and resident of Pimville, Soweto, June 8.
Inner-city buildings. 2006. With George Chauke, Better Buildings Programme, City of Johannesburg Property Company, June 7.
Inner-city buildings occupied by squatters. 2006. With Shereza Sibanda, Inner City Resource Center, Johannesburg, May 29.
Inner-city housing projects in Yeoville, Hillbrow, and the central city. 2006. With Kuben Govender, Trust for Urban Housing Finance (TUHF), June 6.
Inner-city neighborhoods. 2001. With Josephine Malala and Mashadi Dumelakgosi, Hillbrow social workers, May 31.
Joe Slovo informal settlement near Coronationville. 2006. With volunteers from Children of Fire, May 28.
Johannesburg inner city. 2003. With Professor Keith Beavon, University of Pretoria, June 18.

Johannesburg inner city. 2003. With Neil Fraser, Central Johannesburg Partnership, July 3.

Orange Farm and Weiler's Farm informal settlements. 2003. With Adrian Meyer, June 14.

Ponte City. 2006. With Danie Celliers and Elna Celliers, manager of Ponte City, Vincemus Investments, June 5.

San Jose apartment complex, Olivia Street, Berea. 2006. With Nelson Khetani, alleged building hijacker, May 29.

Trafalgar Properties in Hillbrow and Berea. 2006. With Jaco Ferreira, portfolio manager, Trafalgar Property Management (Pty), June 5.

Media Statements

"Johannesburg Inner-City Anti-Eviction Campaign March Saturday 14 December." 2002. Press release issued by the Anti-Privatisation Forum, December 12.

"Inner-City Fire Shows the Need for Adequate Housing, Not Evictions." 2006. Media statement, Centre for Applied Legal Studies (CALS) and Centre on Housing Rights and Evictions (COHRE), March 30.

"Evictions from 'Bad' Buildings in Johannesburg Unconstitutional, Rules High Court." 2006. Joint media release, Centre on Housing Rights and Evictions (COHRE) and Centre for Applied Legal Studies (CALS), March 3.

Wilson, Stuart, and Jean du Plessis. 2005. "Housing and Evictions in Johannesburg's Inner City: Forced Evictions Are Not a Legitimate Tool of Development." Statement to the Cities and Slums Workshop, World Housing Congress, September 25.

TELEVISION DOCUMENTARY PROGRAMMING

Kotze, Adri, Producer. 2003. "People Are Living Here." *SABC Special Assignment,* February 23.

Mancunga, Zukile, and Anneliese Burgess, Directors. 2000. "Slums." *SABC Special Assignment,* June 20.

Secondary Materials

Abbas, Ackbar. 1994. "Building on Disappearance: Hong Kong Architecture and the City." *Public Culture* 6 (3): 441–459.

Agamben, Giorgio. 1998. *Homo Sacer: Sovereign Power and Bare Life.* Translated by Daniel Heller-Roazen. Stanford: Stanford University Press.

——. 2005. *State of Exception.* Translated by Kevin Attell. Chicago: University of Chicago Press.

Appadurai, Arjun. 2000. "Spectral Housing and Urban Cleansing: Notes on Millennial Mumbai." *Public Culture* 12 (3): 627–651.

——. 2002. "Deep Democracy: Urban Governmentality and the Horizon of Politics." *Public Culture* 14 (1): 6–37.

Augé, Marc. 1992. *Non-places: Introduction to an Anthropology of Supermodernity.* Translated by John Howe. New York: Verso.

Baeten, Guy. 2002. "Hypochondriac Geographies of the City and the New Urban Dystopia." *City* 6 (1): 103–116.

Bales, Kevin. 2004. *Disposable People: New Slavery in the Global Economy.* Berkeley: University of California Press.

Ballard, Richard, Adam Habib, Imraan Valodia, and Elke Zuern. 2005. "Globalization, Marginalization, and Contemporary Social Movements in South Africa." *African Affairs* 104: 615–634.

Bauman, Zygmunt. 1998. *Globalization: The Human Consequences.* Cambridge, UK: Polity Press.

———. 2003. *Wasted Lives: Modernity and Its Outcasts.* Cambridge, UK: Polity Press.

Baviskar, Amita. 2003. "Between Violence and Desire: Space, Power, and Identity in the Making of Metropolitan Delhi." *International Social Science Journal* 175: 89–98.

Bayat, Asef. 1997a. "Un-Civil Society: The Politics of the 'Informal People.'" *Third World Quarterly* 18 (1): 53–72.

———. 1997b. *Street Politics: Poor People's Movements in Iran, 1977–1990.* New York: Columbia University Press.

Beall, Jo, Owen Crankshaw, and Susan Parnell. 2000. "Local Government, Poverty Reduction, and Inequality in Johannesburg." *Environment and Urbanization* 12 (1): 107–122.

———. 2002. *Uniting a Divided City: Governance and Social Exclusion in Johannesburg.* London: Earthscan.

Beauregard, Robert. 1989. "Between Modernity and Postmodernity: The Ambiguous Position of U.S. Planning." *Environment and Planning D* 7 (4): 381–396.

———. 1993. "Constituting Economic Development: A Theoretical Perspective." In *Theories of Local Economic Development,* edited by Richard Bingham and Robert Mier, 267–283. Newbury Park, CA: Sage.

———. 2005. "The Textures of Property Markets: Downtown Housing and Office Conversions in New York City." *Urban Studies* 42 (13): 2431–2445.

Beavon, Keith. 1992. "The Post-Apartheid City: Hopes, Possibilities, and Harsh Realities." In *The Apartheid City and Beyond: Urbanisation and Social Change in South Africa,* edited by David Smith, 292–302. London: Routledge.

———. 1997. "Johannesburg: A City and Metropolitan Area in Transformation." In *The Urban Challenge in Africa,* edited by Cathy Rakodi, 150–191. Tokyo: United Nations University Press.

———. 2004. *Johannesburg: The Making and Shaping of the City.* Pretoria: University of South Africa Press.

Beerends, Sjoerd. 2000. "In Formality, Westgate Station, Johannesburg." *Planning* 169: 58–59.

Beningfield, Susan, and Sally Gaule. 2006. "Circuits of Power and Powerlessness: Newtown." *Leading Architecture and Design* (January–February): 24–26.

Bénit, Claire, and Philippe Gervais-Lambony. 2005. "The Poor and the Shop Window: Globalisation, a Local Political Instrument in the South African City?" *Transformation* 57: 1–23.

Benjamin, Walter. 1978. *Reflections.* Translated by Edmund Jephcott. New York: Harcourt Brace Jovanovich.

———. 1999. *The Arcades Project.* Translated by Howard Eiland and Kevin McLaughlin. Cambridge, MA: Belknap Press of Harvard University Press.

Blomley, Nicholas. 2003. "From 'What?' to 'So What?': Law and Geography in Retrospect." In *Law and Geography,* edited by Jane Holder and Carolyn Harrison, 17–34. Oxford: Oxford University Press.

———. 2004. *Unsettling the City: Urban Land and the Politics of Property.* New York: Routledge.

Body-Gendrot, Sophie, and Robert Beauregard. 1999. "Imagined Cities, Engaged Citizens." In *The Urban Moment: Cosmopolitan Essays on the Late-20th-Century City,* edited by Sophie Body-Gendrot and Robert Beauregard, 3–21. Thousand Oaks, CA: Sage.

Bond, Patrick. 2000. *Elite Transition: From Apartheid to Neo-Liberalism in South Africa.* Durban, South Africa: University of Natal Press.

Borden, Iain, Joe Kerr, and Jane Rendell. 2001. "Things, Flows, Filters, Tactics." In *The Unknown City: Contesting Architecture and Social Space,* edited by Iain Borden, Joe Kerr, and Jane Rendell (with Alice Pivaro), 2–27. Cambridge, MA: The MIT Press.

Bouillon, Antoine. 2002. "Between Euphemism and Informalism: Inventing the City." In *Under Siege: Four African Cities—Freetown, Johannesburg, Kinshasa, Lagos,* edited by Okwui Enwezor et al., 81–98. *Documenta 11_Platform 4.* Ostiledern-Ruit, Germany: Hatje Cantz.

Boyer, M. Christine. 1983. *Dreaming the Rational City: The Myth of American City Planning.* Cambridge, MA: The MIT Press.

———. 1992. "Cities for Sale: Merchandising History at South Street Seaport." In *Variations on a Theme Park: The New American City and the End of Public Space,* edited by Michael Sorkin, 181–204. New York: Hill and Wang.

———. 1994a. *The City of Collective Memory: Its Historical Imagery and Architectural Entertainments.* Cambridge, MA: The MIT Press.

———. 1994b. "The City of Illusion: New York's Public Places." In *The Restless Urban Landscape,* edited by Paul Knox, 111–126. Englewood Cliffs, NJ: Prentice Hall.

———. 1995. "The Great Frame-Up: Fantastic Appearances in Contemporary Spatial Politics." In *Spatial Practices,* edited by Helen Liggett and David Perry, 81–109. Thousand Oaks, CA: Sage.

———. 2001. "Twice-Told Stories: The Double Erasure of Times Square." In *The Unknown City: Contesting Architecture and Social Space,* edited by Iain Borden, Joe Kerr, and Jane Rendell (with Alice Pivaro), 30–53. Cambridge, MA: The MIT Press.

Boyer, Paul. 1978. *Urban Masses and Moral Order in America, 1820–1920.* Cambridge: Harvard University Press.

Brechin, Gray. 1999. *Imperial San Francisco: Urban Power, Earthly Ruin.* Berkeley: University of California Press.

Bremner, Lindsay. 1999. "Crime and the Emerging Landscape of Post-Apartheid Johannesburg." In *Blank___: Architecture, Apartheid, and After,* edited by Hilton Judin and Ivan Vladislavić, 49–63. Rotterdam: NAi.

———. 2000. "Reinventing the Johannesburg Inner City." *Cities* 7 (13): 185–193.

———. 2002. "Closure, Simulation, and 'Making Do' in the Contemporary Johannesburg Landscape." In *Under Siege: Four African Cities—Freetown, Johannesburg, Kinshasa, Lagos,* edited by Okwui Enwezor et al., 153–172. *Documenta 11_Platform 4.* Ostiledern-Ruit, Germany: Hatje Cantz.

——. 2004a. "Bounded Spaces: Demographic Anxieties in Post-Apartheid Johannesburg." *Social Identities* 10 (4): 455–468.

——. 2004b. *Johannesburg: One City, Colliding Worlds.* Parktown (Johannesburg): STE.

——. 2005. "Remaking Johannesburg." In *Future City,* edited by Stephen Read, Jürgen Rosemann, and Job van Eldijk, 32–47. New York: Spon.

Brodie, Janine. "Imagining Democratic Urban Citizenship." In *Democracy, Citizenship, and the Global City,* edited by Engin Isin, 110–128. London: Routledge.

Buck-Morss, Susan. 1995. "The City as Dreamworld and Catastrophe." *October* 73: 3–26.

Caldeira, Teresa. 1996a. "Building Up Walls: The New Pattern of Spatial Segregation in São Paulo." *International Social Science Journal* 48 (147): 55–66.

——. 1996b. "Fortified Enclaves: The New Urban Segregation." *Public Culture* 8: 303–328.

Caldeira, Teresa, and James Holston. 1999. "Democracy and Violence in Brazil." *Comparative Studies in Society and History* 41 (4): 691–729.

Castel, Robert. 2000. "The Roads to Disaffiliation: Insecure Work and Vulnerable Relationships." *International Journal of Urban and Regional Research* 24 (3): 519–535.

Castells, Manuel. 1996. *The Rise of the Network Society.* Oxford: Blackwell.

Calvino, Italo. 1974. *Invisible Cities.* Translated by William Weaver. New York: Harcourt Brace Jovanovich.

Caro, Robert. 1974. *The Power Broker: Robert Moses and the Fall of New York.* New York: Alfred Knopf.

Castells, Manuel. 1996. *The Rise of the Network Society.* Oxford: Blackwell.

Chipkin, Clive. 1993. *Johannesburg Style: Architecture and Society, 1880s–1960.* Cape Town: David Philip.

——. 1999. "The Great Apartheid Building Boom: The Transformation of Johannesburg in the 1960s." In *Blank____: Architecture, Apartheid, and After,* edited by Hilton Judin and Ivan Vladislavić, 248–267. Rotterdam: NAi.

Choay, Françoise. 1980. *La regle et le modele: Sur le theorie de l'architecture et de l'urbanisme.* Paris: Seuil.

Christopherson, Susan. 1994. "The Fortress City: Privatized Spaces, Consumer Citizenship." In *Post-Fordism: A Reader,* edited by Ash Amin, 409–427. Oxford: Blackwell.

Cloke, P., P. Milbourne, and R. Widdowfield. 2000. "Homelessness and Rurality: 'Out-of-Place' in Purified Space?" *Environment and Planning D* 18: 715–735.

Coaffee, Jon. 2005. "Urban Renaissance in the Age of Terrorism: Revanchism, Automated Social Control, or the End of Reflection?" *International Journal of Urban and Regional Research* 29 (2): 447–454.

Crankshaw, Owen, and Christine White. 1995. "Racial Segregation and Inner-City Decay in Johannesburg." *International Journal of Urban and Regional Research* 19 (3): 622–638.

Crawford, Margaret. 1995. "Contesting the Public Realm: Struggle over Public Space in Los Angeles." *Journal of Architectural Education* 49 (1): 4–9.

Cronon, William. 1991. *Nature's Metropolis: Chicago and the Great West.* New York: W. W. Norton.

Crush, Jonathan. 1993. "Darkness Falls: Imagining the South African City." *Social Dynamics* 19: 128–148.

Crush, Jonathan. 1994. "Gazing on Apartheid: Post-Colonial Travel Narratives of the Golden City." In *Writing the City: Eden, Babylon, and the New Jerusalem,* edited by Peter Preston and Paul Simpson-Housley, 257–284. London: Routledge.

Cuff, Dana. 2000. *The Provisional City: Los Angeles Stories of Architecture and Urbanism.* Cambridge, MA: The MIT Press.

Cull, Tracy. 2001. "The Seven Buildings Project." *Africa Insight* (March): 43–49.

Curtis, Barry. 2001. "That Place Where: Some Thoughts on Memory and the City." In *The Unknown City: Contesting Architecture and Social Space,* edited by Iain Borden, Joe Kerr, Jane Rendell (with Alice Pivaro), 54–67. Cambridge, MA: The MIT Press.

Czeglédy, André. 2003. "Villas of the Highveld: A Cultural Perspective on Johannesburg and Its Northern Suburbs." In *Emerging Johannesburg: Perspectives on the Postapartheid City,* edited by Richard Tomlinson, Robert Beauregard, Lindsay Bremner, and Xolela Mangcu, 21–42. New York: Routledge.

———. 2004. "Getting around Town: Transportation and the Built Environment in Post-apartheid South Africa." *City and Society* 16 (2): 63–92.

Davis, Mike. 1985. "Urban Renaissance and the Spirit of Postmodernism." *New Left Review* 151: 106–114.

———. 1990. *City of Quartz: Excavating the Future of Los Angeles.* London: Verso.

———. 1991. "Fortress Los Angeles: The Militarization of Urban Space." In *Variations on a Theme Park,* edited by Michael Sorkin, 154–180. New York: Hill and Wang.

———. 1998. *Ecology of Fear: Los Angeles and the Imagination of Disaster.* New York: Vintage.

———. 2002. *Dead Cities and Other Tales.* New York: New Press.

———. 2006. *Planet of Slums.* New York: Verso.

Dawson, Ashley. 2005. "Geography of Fear: Crime and the Transformation of Public Space in Postapartheid South Africa." In *The Politics of Public Space,* edited by Setha Low and Neil Smith, 123–142. New York: Routledge.

Dear, Michael. 1989. "Privatization and the Rhetoric of Planning Practice." *Environment and Planning D* 7 (4): 449–462.

Dear, Michael, and Jennifer Wolch. 1987. *Landscapes of Despair: From Deinstitutionalism to Homelessness.* Princeton: Princeton University Press.

De Boeck, Filip. 2002. "Kinshasa: Tales of the 'Invisible City' and the Second World." In *Under Siege: Four African Cities—Freetown, Johannesburg, Kinshasa, Lagos,* edited by Okwui Enwezor et al., 243–286. Ostfildern-Ruit, Germany: Hatje Cantz.

De Boeck, Filip, and Marie-Françoise Plissart. 2004. *Kinshasa: Tales of the Invisible City.* Ghent/Tervuren: Ludion/Royal Museum for Central Africa.

De Cauter, Lieven. 2002. "The Capsular City." In *The Hieroglyphics of Space: Reading and Experiencing the Modern Metropolis,* edited by Neil Leach, 271–280. London: Routledge.

———. 2004. *The Capsular Civilization: On the City in the Age of Fear.* Rotterdam: NAi Publishers.

De Certeau, Michel. 1984. *The Practice of Everyday Life.* Translated by Steven Rendall. Berkeley: University of California Press.

———. 1988. *The Writing of History.* Translated by Tom Conley. New York: Columbia University Press.

Degan, Monica. 2003. "Fighting for the Global Catwalk: Formalizing Public Life in Castlefield (Manchester) and Diluting Public Life in el Raval (Barcelona)." *International Journal of Urban and Regional Research* 27 (4): 867–880.

Delaney, David. 2004. "Tracing Displacements; or, Evictions in the Nomosphere." *Environment and Planning D* 22: 847–860.

Desai, Ashwin, and Peter van Heusden. 2002. "'Is This Mandela's Park?' Community Struggles and State Response in Post-Apartheid South Africa." Occasional Paper Series. Centre for Civil Society, University of KwaZulu-Natal, Durban.

Deutsche, Rosalyn. 1996. *Evictions: Art and Spatial Politics.* Cambridge, MA: The MIT Press.

Deutsche, Rosalyn, and Cara Gendel Ryan. 1984. "The Fine Art of Gentrification." *October* 31: 91–111.

Dewar, David. 1999. "Settlements, Change, and Planning in South Africa since 1994." In *Blank____: Architecture, Apartheid, and After*, edited by Hilton Judin and Ivan Vladislavić, 368–375. Rotterdam: NAi.

Dirsuweit, Teresa. 1999. "From Fortress City to Creative City." *Urban Forum* 10 (2): 183–213.

Dirsuweit, Teresa, and Florian Schattauer. 2004. "Fortresses of Desire: Melrose Arch and the Emergence of Urban Tourist Spectacles." *GeoJournal* 60: 239–247.

Doel, Michael. 1996. "A Hundred Thousand Lines of Flight: A Machinic Introduction to the Nomad Thought of Gilles Deleuze and Felix Guattari." *Environment and Planning D* 14: 422–437.

Doron, Gil. 2000. "The Dead Zone and the Architecture of Transgression." *City* 4 (2): 247–262.

Dovey, Kim. 1999. *Framing Places: Mediating Power in Built Form.* New York: Routledge.

du Plessis, Jean, and Stuart Wilson. 2005. *Any Room for the Poor? Forced Evictions in Johannesburg South Africa.* Geneva: Centre on Housing Rights and Evictions.

Easterling, Keller. 2005. *Enduring Innocence: Global Architecture and Its Political Masquerades.* Cambridge, MA: The MIT Press.

Edensor, Tim. 2005a. "Waste Matter—The Debris of Industrial Ruins and the Disordering of the Material World." *Journal of Material Culture* 10 (3): 311–332.

———. 2005b. "The Ghosts of Industrial Ruins: Ordering and Disordering Memory in Excessive Space," *Environment and Planning D* 23: 829–849.

Emdon, Erica. 2003. "The Limits of Law: Social Rights and Urban Development." In *Emerging Johannesburg: Perspectives on the Postapartheid City,* edited by Richard Tomlinson, Robert Beauregard, Lindsay Bremner, and Xolela Mangcu, 215–230. New York: Routledge.

Engels, Friedrich. 1970. *The Housing Question.* Moscow: Progress Publishers.

Fainstein, Susan. 1994. *The City Builders: Property, Politics, and Planning in London and New York.* Oxford: Blackwell.

———. 2000. "New Directions in Planning Theory." *Urban Affairs Review* 35 (4): 451–478.

Fainstein, Susan, and Dennis Judd. 1999. "Global Forces, Local Strategies, and Urban Tourism." In *The Tourist City,* edited by Susan Fainstein and Dennis Judd, 1–17. New Haven: Yale University Press.

Faulkner, Simon. 2004. "'Asylum Seekers,' Imagined Geography, and Visual Culture." *Visual Culture in Britain* 5 (1): 93–114.

Fitzsimmons, Diana. 1995. "Planning and Promotion: City Reimaging in the 1980s and 1990s." In *Reimaging the Pariah City: Urban Development in Belfast and Detroit,* edited by William J. V. Neil, Diana Fitzsimmons, and Brendan Murtagh, 1–49. Aldershot, UK: Avebury.

Flusty, Steven. 1994. *Building Paranoia: The Proliferation of Interdictory Space and the Erosion of Spatial Justice.* Los Angeles: Los Angeles Forum for Architecture and Urban Design.

———. 1997. "Building Paranoia." In *Architecture of Fear,* edited by Nan Ellin, 47–59. New York: Princeton Architectural Press.

———. 2001. "The Banality of Interdiction: Surveillance, Control, and the Displacement of Diversity." *International Journal of Urban and Regional Research* 25 (3): 658–664.

Foucault, Michel. 1977. *Discipline and Punish: The Birth of the Prison.* New York: Vintage.

———. 1980. *Power/Knowledge: Selected Interviews and Other Writings, 1972–1977.* Translated by Colin Gordon. New York: Pantheon.

Gandy, Matthew. 2000. "Urban Visions." *Journal of Urban History* 26 (3): 368–379.

———. 2005a. "Learning from Lagos." *New Left Review* 33: 36–52.

———. 2005b. "Cyborg Urbanization: Complexity and Monstrosity in the Contemporary City." *International Journal of Urban and Regional Research* 29 (1): 26–49.

Ghirado, Diane. 1996. *Architecture after Modernism.* London: Thames and Hudson.

Goga, Soraya. 2003. "Property Investors and Decentralization: A Case of False Competition?" In *Emerging Johannesburg: Perspectives on the Postapartheid City,* edited by Richard Tomlinson, Robert Beauregard, Lindsay Bremner, and Xolela Mangcu, 71–82. New York: Routledge.

Goldberger, Paul. 1996. "The Rise of the Private City." In *Breaking Away: The Future of Cities,* edited by Julia Vitullo-Martin, 135–147. New York: Twentieth Century Fund Press.

Govender, Prem, and James Aiello. 1999. "Johannesburg's Strategic Plan for Municipal Service Partnerships." *Development in Southern Africa* 16 (4): 649–667.

Greenberg, Stephen. 2004a. "The Landless People's Movement and the Failure of Post-Apartheid Land Reform." Research Report, Centre for Civil Society and School of Development Studies, University of KwaZulu-Natal, Durban.

———. 2004b. "Post-Apartheid Development, Landlessness, and the Reproduction of Exclusion in South Africa." Research Report No. 17. Centre for Civil Society and School of Development Studies, University of KwaZulu-Natal, Durban.

Groth, Jacqueline, and Eric Corijn. 2005. "Reclaiming Urbanity: Indeterminate Spaces, Informal Actors, and Urban Agenda Setting." *Urban Studies* 42 (3): 503–526

Guillaume, Philippe, and Myriam Houssay-Holzschuch. 2002. "Territorial Strategies of South African Informal Dwellers." *Urban Forum* 13 (2): 86–101.

Hall, Tim, and Phil Hubbard. 1996. "The Entrepreneurial City: New Urban Politics, New Urban Geographies?" *Progress in Human Geography* 20 (2): 153–174.

Hajer, M. J. 1999. "Zero-Friction Society." *Urban Design Quarterly* 71: 29–34.

Hannigan, John. 1998. *Fantasy City: Pleasure and Profit in the Postmodern Metropolis.* London: Routledge.

Harrison, Philip. 2006. "On the Edge of Reason: Planning and Urban Futures in Africa." *Urban Studies* 43 (2): 319–335.

Harvey, David. 1982. *The Limits to Capital.* Chicago: University of Chicago Press.

——. 1989a. *The Condition of Postmodernity: An Enquiry into the Origins of Cultural Change.* New York: Basil Blackwell.

——. 1989b. "From Managerialism to Entrepreneurialism: The Transformation in Urban Governance in Late Capitalism." *Geografiska Annaler B* 79: 3–17.

——. 1997. "The New Urbanism and the Communitarian Trap." *Harvard Design Magazine* (Winter/Spring): 68–70.

——. 2003. *Paris, Capital of Modernity.* New York: Routledge.

Herwitz, Daniel. 1999. "Modernism at the Margins." In *Blank____: Architecture, Apartheid, and After,* edited by Hilton Judin and Ivan Vladislavić, 404–421. Rotterdam: NAi.

Hetherington, Kevin. 1992. "Stonehenge and Its Festival: Spaces of Consumption." In *Lifestyle Shopping: The Subject of Consumption,* edited by Rob Shields, 83–98. London: Routledge.

Highmore, Ben. 2002. "*Street Life in London:* Toward a Rhythmanalysis of London in the Late Nineteenth Century." *new formations* 47:171–193.

——. 2005. *Cityscapes: Cultural Readings in the Material and Symbolic City.* New York: Palgrave Macmillan.

Hillis, Helen, and Paul Tyler. 2002. "The Fetishized Past: Post-Industrial Manchester and Interstitial Spaces." *Visual Culture in Britain* 3 (2): 103–117.

Holcomb, Briavel. 1999. "Marketing Cities for Tourism." In *The Tourist City,* edited by Dennis Judd and Susan Fainstein, 54–70. New Haven: Yale University Press.

Holston, James. 1989. *The Modernist City: An Anthropological Critique of Brasília.* Chicago: University of Chicago Press.

——. 1999. "Spaces of Insurgent Citizenship." In *Cities and Citizenship,* edited by James Holston and Arjun Appadurai, 155–173. Durham: Duke University Press.

Holston, James, and Arjun Appadurai. 1999. Introduction to *Cities and Citizenship,* edited by James Holston and Arjun Appadurai, 1–20. Durham: Duke University Press.

Hommels, Anique. 2005. *Unbuilding Cities: Obduracy in Urban Sociotechnical Construction.* Cambridge, MA: The MIT Press.

Huchzermeyer, Marie. 2003a. "A Legacy of Control? The Capital Subsidy for Housing and Informal Settlement Intervention in South Africa." *International Journal of Urban and Regional Research* 27 (3): 591–612.

——. 2003b. "Housing Rights in South Africa: Invasions, Evictions, the Media, and the Courts in the Cases of Grootbloom, Alexandra, and Bredell." *Urban Forum* 14 (1): 80–107.

——. 2004. *Unlawful Occupation: Informal Settlements and Urban Policy in South Africa and Brazil.* Trenton, NJ: Africa World Press.

Huyssen, Andreas. 1997. "The Voids of Berlin." *Critical Inquiry* 24: 57–81.

Inner City Forum. 2004. "Johannesburg's Better Buildings Programme: A Response." *Development Update* 5 (1): 187–194.

Jacobs, Jane. 1961. *The Death and Life of Great American Cities.* New York: Random House.

Jameson, Fredric, and Michael Speaks. 1990. "Envelopes and Enclaves: The Space of Post-Civil Society—An Architectural Conversation." *Assemblage* 17: 32–37.

Jaguaribe, Beatriz. 1999. "Modernist Ruins: National Narratives and Architectural Forms." *Public Culture* 11 (1): 294–312.

Jewson, Nick, and Suzanne MacGregor. 1997. Introduction to *Transforming Cities: Contested Governance and New Spatial Divisions,* edited by Nick Jewson and Suzanne MacGregor, 1–17. London: Routledge.

Johannesburg Housing Company. 2005. *Landmarks and Learnings: 10 Years of the Johannesburg Housing Company.* Marshalltown: Johannesburg Housing Company.

Jurgens, Ulrich, and Martin Gnad. 2002. "Gated Communities in South Africa—Experiences from Johannesburg." *Environment and Planning B: Planning and Design* 29 (4): 337–353.

Kaika, Maria. 2005. *City of Flows: Modernity, Nature, and the City.* New York: Routledge.

Kaika, Maria, and Erik Swyngedouw. 2000. "Fetishizing the Modern City: The Phantasmagoria of Urban Technological Networks." *International Journal of Urban and Regional Research* 24 (1): 120–138.

Kaviraj, Sudipta. 1997. "Filth in the Public Sphere: Concepts and Practices about Urban Space in Calcutta." *Public Culture* 10 (1): 83–113.

Kawash, Samira. 1998. "The Homeless Body." *Public Culture* 10 (2): 319–339.

Kesper, Anna. 2003. "Making a Living in the City: The Case of Clothing Manufacturers." In *Emerging Johannesburg: Perspectives on the Postapartheid City,* edited by Richard Tomlinson, Robert Beauregard, Lindsay Bremner, and Xolela Mangcu, 85–100. New York: Routledge.

Keyder, Caglar. 2005. "Globalization and Social Exclusion in Istanbul." *International Journal of Urban and Regional Research* 29 (1): 124–134.

Khan, Firoz. 2003. "Continuities, Ambiguities, and Contradictions: The Past, Present, and (Possible) Future of Housing Policy and Practice in South Africa." In *Housing Policy and Practice in Post-Apartheid South Africa,* edited by Firoz Khan and Petal Thring, 1–76. Sandown, South Africa: Heinemann.

Khan, Firoz, and Cecile Ambert. 2003. Introduction to *Housing Policy and Practice in Post-Apartheid South Africa,* edited by Firoz Khan and Petal Thring, i–xxv. Sandown, South Africa: Heinemann.

Kihato, Caroline. 1999. "A Site for Sore Eyes: Johannesburg's Decay and Prospects for Renewal." Centre for Policy Studies, Policy Brief 10, April. Pretoria: Centre for Policy Studies.

Kihato, Caroline, and Loren Landau. 2005. "The Uncaptured Urbanite: Migration and State Power in Johannesburg." Forced Migration Working Paper Series No. 25. Forced Migration Studies Programme, University of the Witwatersrand, Johannesburg.

———. 2007. "Governing the City? South Africa's Struggle to Deal with Urban Immigrants after Apartheid." *African Identities* 5 (2): 261–278.

King, Anthony. 1996. "Worlds in a City: Manhattan Transfer and the Ascendance of Spectacular Space." *Planning Perspectives* 11: 97–114.

———. 1997. "The Politics of Vision." In *Understanding Ordinary Landscapes,* edited by Paul Groth and Todd Bressi, 134–144. New Haven: Yale University Press.

Klein, Norman. 2002. "Mapping the Unfindable: Neighborhoods West of Downtown L.A. as a Magic Realist Computer Game." In *Unmasking L.A.: Third Worlds and the City,* edited by Deepak Narang Sawhney, 77–96. New York: Palgrave Macmillan.

Kolson, Kenneth. 2001. *Big Plans: The Allure and Folly of Urban Design.* Baltimore: Johns Hopkins University Press.

Koolhaas, Rem. 1994. *Delirious New York: A Retroactive Manifesto for Manhattan.* New York: Monacelli Press.

Landau, Loren. 2005. "Urbanization, Nativism, and the Rule of Law in South Africa's 'Forbidden Cities.'" *Third World Quarterly* 26 (7): 1115–1134.

———. 2006. "Transplants and Transients: Idioms of Belonging and Dislocation in Inner-City Johannesburg." *African Studies Review* 49 (2): 125–145.

Lees, Loretta. 1998. "Urban Renaissance and the Street: Spaces of Control and Contestation." In *Images of the Street: Planning, Identity, and Control in Public Space,* edited by Nicholas Fyfe, 236–253. London: Routledge.

———. 2000. "A Reappraisal of Gentrification: Toward a 'Geography of Gentrification.'" *Progress in Human Geography* 24 (2): 389–408.

———. 2004. "The 'Emancipatory City': Urban (Re)Visions." In *The Emancipatory City? Paradoxes and Possibilities,* edited by Loretta Lees, 3–20. Thousand Oaks, CA: Sage.

Lefebvre, Henri. 1991. *The Production of Space.* Translated by Donald Nicholson-Smith. New York: Blackwell.

———. 1996. *Writings on Cities.* Translated by E. Kofman and E. Labas. Oxford: Blackwell.

Leggett, Ted. 2001. *Rainbow Vice: The Drugs and Sex Industries in the New South Africa.* Cape Town: David Philip.

Leontidou, Lila, Hastings Donnan, and Alex Afouxenidis. 2005. "Exclusion and Difference along the EU Border: Social and Cultural Markers, Spatialities, and Mappings." *International Journal of Urban and Regional Research* 29 (2): 389–407.

Lester, Alan, Etienne Nel, and Tony Binns. 2000. "South Africa's Current Transition in Temporal and Spatial Context." *Antipode* 32 (2): 135–151.

Lim, William S. W. 2002. "Spaces of Indeterminacy." In *Bridge the Gap,* edited by Miyake Akiko and Hans Ulich Obrist, 377–397. Kitakyushu, Japan: Center for Contemporary Art.

Lipietz, Barbara. 2004. "'Muddling-Through': Urban Regeneration in Johannesburg's Inner City." Unpublished paper presented at N-Aerus annual conference, September 16–17, Barcelona, Spain.

Lipman, Alan. 1998. "Cash and Carry History Store." *South African Architect* (June): 21–22.

———. 2006. "Beyond Our Urban Mishaps." In *From Jo'burg to Jozi: Stories about Africa's Infamous City,* edited by Heidi Holland and Adam Roberts, 133–136. Johannesburg: Penguin.

Lipman, Alan, and Howard Harris. 1999. "Fortress Johannesburg." *Environment and Planning B* 26 (5): 731–733.

Logan, John, and Harvey Molotch. 1987. *Urban Fortunes: The Political Economy of Place.* Berkeley: University of California Press.

Loukaitou-Sideris, Anastasia. 1993. "Privatization of Open Public Space." *Town Planning Review* 64 (2): 139–168.

Loukaitou-Sideris, Anastasia, and Tridib Banerjee. 1998. *Urban Design Downtown: Poetics and Politics of Form.* Berkeley: University of California Press.

Lukose, Ritty. 2005. "Empty Citizenship: Protesting Politics in the Era of Globalization." *Cultural Anthropology* 20 (4): 506–533.

Mabin, Alan. 1990. "On the Problems and Prospects of Overcoming Segregation and Fragmentation in Southern Africa's Cities in the Postmodern Era." In *Postmodern Cities and Spaces,* edited by Sophie Watson and Keith Gibson, 187–198. Oxford: Blackwell.

Mabin, Alan. 1999. "Reconstruction and the Making of Urban Planning in 20th-Century South Africa." In *Blank____: Architecture, Apartheid, and After,* edited by Hilton Judin and Ivan Vladislavić, 269–277. Rotterdam: NAi.

MacLeod, Gordon. 2002. "From Urban Entrepreneurialism to a 'Revanchist City'? On the Spatial Injustices of Glasgow's Renaissance." *Antipode* 34 (3): 602–623.

Macpherson, C. B. 1987. *The Rise and Fall of Economic Justice and Other Essays.* Oxford: Oxford University Press.

Madanipur, Ali. 2003. *Public and Private Spaces of the City.* London: Routledge.

Mandela, Nelson. 1994. *Long Walk to Freedom.* Boston: Little, Brown.

Mangcu, Xolela. 2003. "Johannesburg in Flight from Itself: Political Culture Shapes Urban Discourse." In *Emerging Johannesburg: Perspectives on the Postapartheid City,* edited by Richard Tomlinson, Robert A. Beauregard, Lindsay Bremner, and Xolela Mangcu, 281–291. New York: Routledge.

Manning, Erin. 2000. "Compromising Encounters: Reading History through Geography in Anne Michaels's *Fugitive Pieces.*" *Space and Culture* 6: 77–89.

Mathee, Angela, and Andre Swart. 2001. "A Description of Living Conditions and Health Status in Informal Settlements in Johannesburg." *Medical Research Council of South Africa: Urban Health and Development Bulletin* 4, 1 (March).

May, Jon. 2000. "Of Nomads and Vagrants: Single Homelessness and Narratives of Home and Place." *Environment and Planning D* 18: 737–759.

Mayer, Margit. 1995. "Urban Governance in the Post-Fordist City." In *Managing Cities: The New Urban Context,* edited by Patsy Healey, Stuart Cameron, Simin Davoudi, Stephen Graham, and Ali Mandani-Pour, 231–250. New York: John Wiley and Sons.

Mbembe, Achille. 1992. "The Banality of Power and the Aesthetics of Vulgarity in the Postcolony." *Public Culture* 4 (2): 1–30.

———. 2004. "The Aesthetics of Superfluity." *Public Culture* 16 (3): 373–405.

McClung, William Alexander. 2000. *Landscapes of Desire: Anglo Mythologies of Los Angeles.* Berkeley: University of California Press.

McDonald, David. 1998. "Hear No Housing, See No Housing: Immigration and Homelessness in the New South Africa." *Cities* 15 (6): 449–462.

McDonough, Thomas. 1994. "Situationist Space." *October* 67: 59–77.

Mele, Christopher. 2000. "The Materiality of Urban Discourse: Rational Planning in the Restructuring of the Early Twentieth-Century Ghetto." *Urban Affairs Review* 35 (5): 628–648.

Melvin, Jeremy. 2000. "Letter from Johannesburg." *Architectural Review* 208 (1243): 36–37.

Merrifield, Andy. 2000. "The Dialectics of Dystopia: Disorder and Zero Tolerance in the City." *International Journal of Urban and Regional Research* 24 (2): 473–489.

Merry, Sally Engle. 2001. "Spatial Governmentality and the New Urban Social Order: Controlling Gender Violence through Law." *American Anthropologist* 103 (1): 16–29.

Mitchell, Don. 1997. "The Annihilation of Space by Law: The Roots and Implications of Anti-Homeless Laws in the United States." *Antipode* 29 (3): 303–335.

———. 2001. "Postmodern Geographical Praxis? Postmodern Impulse and the War against Homeless People in the 'Post-Justice' City." In *Postmodern Geography: Theory and Praxis,* edited by Claudio Minca, 57–92. Oxford: Blackwell.

——. 2003. "Cultural Landscapes: The Dialectical Landscape—Recent Landscape Research in Human Geography." *Progress in Human Geography* 26 (3): 381–389.

Moses, Robert. 1970. *Public Works: A Dangerous Trade.* New York: McGraw-Hill.

Muwanga, Christina. 1998. *South Africa: A Guide to Recent Architecture.* London: Ellipsis.

Nkomo, Mokubung, and Olusola Olufemi. 2001. "Educating Street and Homeless Children in South Africa: The Challenge of Policy Implementation." *International Journal of Education Policy, Research, and Practice* 2 (4): 337–356.

Olufemi, Olusola A. 1997. "The Homeless Problem: Planning, Phenomenology, and Gender Perspectives." Ph.D. thesis, School of Architecture, University of the Witwatersrand.

——. 1998. "Street Homelessness in the Johannesburg Inner-city: A Preliminary Survey." *Environment and Urbanization* 10 (2): 223–234.

——. 2002. "Barriers That Disconnect Homeless People and Make Homelessness Difficult to Interpret." *Development Southern Africa* 19 (4, 1): 455–466.

Ong, Aihwa. 1999. *Flexible Citizenship: The Cultural Logics of Transnationality.* Durham: Duke University Press.

Otter, Chris. 2002. "Making Liberalism Durable: Vision and Civility in the Late Victorian City." *Social History* 21 (1): 1–13.

Page, Max. 1999. *The Creative Destruction of Manhattan, 1900–1940.* Chicago: University of Chicago Press.

Pakenham, Thomas. 1979. *The Boer War.* New York: Random House.

Palestrant, Ellen. 1986. *Johannesburg One Hundred: A Pictorial History.* Johannesburg: Ad Donker.

Park, Robert. 1925. "The City: Suggestions for Investigation of Human Behavior in the Urban Environment." Reprinted in *The City: Suggestions for Investigation of Human Behavior in the Urban Environment,* edited by Robert Park, Everett Burgess, R. D. McKenzie, and Louis Wirth, 1–46. Chicago: University of Chicago Press, 1984.

Parker, David, and Paul Long. 2004. "'The Mistakes of the Past'? Visual Narratives of Urban Decline and Regeneration." *Visual Culture in Britain* 5 (1): 37–58.

Parker, Simon. 2004. *Urban Theory and the Urban Experience: Encountering the City.* New York: Routledge.

Parnell, Susan. 1997. "South African Cities: Perspectives from the Ivory Tower of Urban Studies." *Urban Studies* 34 (5–6): 891–906.

Patke, Raveev. 2000. "Benjamin's *Arcades Project* and the Postcolonial City." *Diacritics* 30 (4): 3–14.

Pieterse, Edgar. 2003. "Unraveling the Different Meanings of Integration: The Case of the *Urban Development Framework* of the South African Government." In *Confronting Fragmentation: Housing and Urban Development in a Democratising Society,* edited by Philip Harrison, Marie Huchzermeyer, and Mzwanele Mayekiso, 122–139. Cape Town: University of Cape Town Press.

——. 2004. "Untangling 'Integration' in Urban Development Policy Debates." *Urban Forum* 15 (1): 1–35.

Pile, Steve. 1997. "Introduction: Opposition, Political Identities, and Spaces of Resistance." In *Geographies of Resistance,* edited by Steve Pile and Michael Keith, 1–32. London: Routledge.

Pile, Steve. 2001. "The Un(Known) City…or, an Urban Geography of What Lies Buried Below the Surface." In *The Unknown City: Contesting Architecture and Social Space*, edited by Iain Borden, Joe Kerr, and Jane Rendell (with Alice Pivaro), 262–279. Cambridge, MA: MIT University Press.

Pinder, David. 1996. "Subverting Cartography: The Situationists and Maps of the City." *Environment and Planning A* 28: 405–427.

Porteous, David, and Keith Naicker. 2003. "South African Housing Finance: The Old Is Dead—Is the New Ready to be Born?" In *Housing Policy and Practice in Post-Apartheid South Africa*, edited by Firoz Khan and Petal Thring, 192–227. Sandown, South Africa: Heinemann.

Ramutsindela, Maano. 2002. "'Second Time Around': Squatter Removals in Democratic South Africa." *GeoJournal* 57 (1–2): 53–60.

Read, Stephen. 2005. "The Form of the Future." In *Future City*, edited by Stephen Read, Jürgen Rosemann, and Job van Eldijk, 3–17. New York: Spon.

Relph, Edward. 1987. *The Modern Urban Landscape*. Baltimore: Johns Hopkins University Press.

Robbins, David. 1997. *Wasteland*. Johannesburg: Lowry.

Roberts, Adam. 2002. "From Jo'burg to Jozi." In *From Jo'burg to Jozi: Stories about Africa's Infamous City*, edited by Heidi Holland and Adam Roberts, 1–14. London: Penguin.

Robins, Kevin. 1993. "Prisoners of the City: Whatever Could a Post-Modern City Be?" In *Space and Place: Theories of Identity and Location*, edited by Erica Carter, James Donald, and Judith Squires, 303–330. London: Lawrence and Wishart.

Robins, Steven. 2002. "At the Limits of Spatial Governmentality: A Message from the Tip of Africa." *Third World Quarterly* 23 (4): 665–689.

Robinson, Jennifer. 1992. "Power, Space, and the City: Historical Reflections on Apartheid and Post-Apartheid Urban Orders." In *The Apartheid City and Beyond: Urbanisation and Social Change in South Africa*, edited by David Smith, 292–302. London: Routledge.

——. 1995. *The Power of Apartheid: State, Power, and Space in South African Cities*. London: Heinemann.

——. 1996. "Transforming Spaces: Spatiality and the Transformation of Local Government in South Africa." In *Contemporary City Structuring: International Geographical Insights*, edited by R. J. Davies, 333–354. Cape Town: International Geographical Union Commission on Urban Development and Urban Life.

——. 1997. "The Geopolitics of South African Cities: States, Citizens, Territories." *Political Geography* 16 (5): 365–386.

——. 1998. "Spaces of Democracy: Remapping the Apartheid City." *Environment and Planning D* 16 (5): 533–548.

——. 1999. "(Im)Mobilising Space—Dreaming of Change." In *Blank____: Architecture, Apartheid, and After*, edited by Hilton Judin and Ivan Vladislavić, 163–171. Rotterdam: NAi.

——. 2002. "Global and World Cities: A View from Off the Map." *International Journal of Urban and Regional Research* 26 (3): 531–554.

——. 2003. "Johannesburg's Futures: Beyond Developmentalism and Global Success." In *Emerging Johannesburg: Perspectives on the Postapartheid City*, edited by Richard

Tomlinson, Robert A. Beauregard, Lindsay Bremner, and Xolela Mangcu, 259–280. New York: Routledge.

——. 2005. *Ordinary Cities: Between Modernity and Development.* New York: Routledge.

Rogerson, Christian. 1996a. "Image Enhancement and Local Economic Development in Johannesburg." *Urban Forum* 7 (2): 139–158.

——. 1996b. "Urban Poverty and the Informal Economy in South Africa's Economic Heartland." *Environment and Urbanization* 8 (1): 167–179.

Rose, Gillian. 1993. *Feminism in Geography: The Limits of Geographical Knowledge.* Cambridge, MA: Polity Press.

Rose, Nikolas. 2000. "Governing Cities, Governing Citizenship." In *Democracy, Citizenship, and the Global City,* edited by Engin Isin, 95–109. London: Routledge.

Rossi, Aldo. 1992. *The Architecture of the City.* Cambridge, MA: The MIT Press.

Royston, Lauren. 2003. "On the Outskirts: Access to Well-Located Land and Integration in Post-Apartheid Human Settlement Development." In *Housing Policy and Practice in Post-Apartheid South Africa,* edited by Firoz Khan and Petal Thring, 234–255. Sandown, South Africa: Heinemann.

Rust, Kecia, Andreas Bertoli, and David Gardner. 2005. "Review of Johannesburg's City Strategy. Opinion Piece 1: Housing Pressures, Residential Opportunities, and Asset Investment Choices." Report prepared for City of Johannesburg Corporate Planning Unit, June 23.

Rutheiser, Charles. 1986. *Imagineering Atlanta: The Politics of Place in the City of Dreams.* London: Verso.

——. 1999. "Making Place in the Nonplace Urban Realm: Notes on the Revitalization of Downtown Atlanta." In *Theorizing the City: The New Urban Anthropology Reader,* edited by Setha Low, 317–341. New Brunswick, NJ: Rutgers University Press.

Sanchez, Lisa. 1997. "Boundaries of Legitimacy: Sex, Violence, Citizenship, and Community." *Law and Social Inquiry* 22 (3): 543–580.

——. 2001. "Enclosure Acts and Exclusionary Practices: Neighborhood Associations, Community Police, and the Expulsion of the Sexual Outlaw." In *Between Law and Culture: Locating Sociolegal Studies,* edited by David Theo Goldberg, Michael Musheno, and Lisa C. Bower, 122–140. Minneapolis: University of Minnesota Press.

——. 2004. "The Global E-rotic Subject, the Ban, and the Prostitute-Free Zone: Sex Work and the Theory of Differential Exclusion." *Environment and Planning D* 22: 861–883.

Sandercock, Leonie. 1998a. "Introduction: Framing Insurgent Historiographies for Planning." In *Making the Invisible Visible: A Multicultural Planning History,* edited by Leonie Sandercock, 1–36. Berkeley: University of California Press.

——. 1998b. *Towards Cosmopolis: Planning for Multicultural Societies.* Chichester: Wiley.

Sassen, Saskia. 2000. "New Frontiers Facing Urban Sociology at the Millennium." *British Journal of Sociology* 5 (1): 143–159.

Sawhney, Deepak Narang. 2002. "Journey beyond the Stars: Los Angeles and Third Words." In *Unmasking L.A.: Third Worlds and the City,* edited by Deepak Narang Sawhney, 1–20. New York: Palgrave.

Scheper-Hughes, Nancy. 1992. *Death without Weeping: The Violence of Everyday Life in Brazil.* Berkeley: University of California Press.

Scobey, David. 2002. *Empire City: The Making and Meaning of the New York City Landscape.* Philadelphia: Temple University Press.

Scott, James. 1985. *Weapons of the Weak: Everyday Forms of Peasant Resistance.* New Haven: Yale University Press.

———. 1990. *Domination and the Arts of Resistance: Hidden Transcripts.* New Haven: Yale University Press, 1990.

———. 1998. *Seeing Like a State: How Certain Schemes to Improve the Human Condition Have Failed.* New Haven, CT: Yale University Press.

Shields, Rob. 1989. "Social Spatialization and the Built Environment: The West Edmonton Mall." *Environment and Planning D* 7: 147–164.

———. 1991. *Places on the Margin: Alternative Geographies of Modernity.* New York: Routledge.

Sihlongonyane, Mfaniseni Fana. 2005. "The Rhetoric of Africanism in Johannesburg as a World African City." *Africa Insight* 34 (4): 22–30.

Simmel, Georg. 1911. "The Ruin." Reprinted in *Georg Simmel, 1858–1911,* edited by Kurt Wolff, 259–266. Columbus: Ohio State University Press, 1959.

Simone, AbdouMaliq. 1999. "Globalization and the Identity of African Urban Practices." In *Blank____: Architecture, Apartheid, and After,* edited by Hilton Judin and Ivan Vladislavić, 173–187. Rotterdam: NAi.

———. 2000. "Going South: African Immigrants in Johannesburg." In *Senses of Culture: South African Cultural Studies,* edited by Sarah Nuttall and Cheryl-Ann Michael, 426–442. Cape Town: Oxford University Press.

———. 2001a. "Between Ghetto and Globe: Remaking Urban Life in Africa." In *Associational Life in African Cities: Popular Responses to the Urban Crisis,* edited by Arne Tostensen, Inge Tvedten, and Mariken Vaa, 46–63. Stockholm: Nordiska Afrikainstitutet.

———. 2001b. "Straddling the Divides: Remaking Associational Life in the Informal City." *International Journal of Urban and Regional Research* 25 (1): 102–117.

———. 2002. "The Visible and Invisible: Remaking Cities in Africa." In *Under Siege: Four African Cities—Freetown, Johannesburg, Kinshasa, Lagos,* edited by Okwui Enwezor et al., 23–43. *Documenta 11_Platform 4.* Ostiledern-Ruit, Germany: Hatje Cantz.

———. 2003. "Resource of Intersection: Remaking Social Collaboration in Urban Africa." *Canadian Journal of African Studies* 37 (2–3): 513–537.

———. 2004a. "People as Infrastructure: Intersecting Fragments in Johannesburg." *Public Culture* 16 (3): 407–429.

———. 2004b. *For the City Yet to Come: Changing African Life in Four Cities.* Durham, NC: Duke University Press.

———. 2004c. "South African Urbanism: Between the Modern and the Refugee Camp." Dark Roast Occasional Paper Series, No. 17. Islandla Institute, Cape Town.

Simone, AbdouMaliq, and Graeme Gotz. 2003. "On Belonging and Becoming in African Cities." In *Emerging Johannesburg: Perspectives on the Postapartheid City,* edited by Richard Tomlinson, Robert Beauregard, Lindsay Bremner, and Xolela Mangcu, 123–147. New York: Routledge.

Smith, Neil. 1992. "The Lower East Side as Wild, Wild West." In *Variations on a Theme Park: The New American City and the Death of Public Space*, edited by Michael Sorkin, 61–99. New York: Hill and Wang.

———. 1996. *The New Urban Frontier: Gentrification and the Revanchist City.* London: Routledge.

———. 1998. "Giuliani Time: The Revanchist 1990s." *Social Text* 57: 1–10.

———. 2002. "New Globalism, New Urbanism: Gentrification as Global Urban Strategy." *Antipode* 34 (3): 427–450.

Solnit, Rebecca, and Susan Schwartzenberg. 2000. *Hollow City: The Siege of San Francisco and the Crisis of American Urbanism.* New York: Verso.

Sorkin, Michael. 1992. "Introduction: Variations on a Theme Park." In *Variations on a Theme Park: The New American City and the End of Public Space*, edited by Michael Sorkin, xi–xv. New York: Hill and Wang.

Staub, Alexandra. 2005. "St. Petersburg's Double Life: The Planners' vs. the People's City." *Journal of Urban History* 31 (3): 334–354.

Swilling, Mark. 1999. "Rival Futures: Struggle Visions, Post-Apartheid Choices." In *Blank____: Architecture, Apartheid, and After*, edited by Hilton Judin and Ivan Vladislavić, 285–299. Rotterdam: NAi.

Swyngedouw, Eric. 2005. "Exit 'Post'—The Making of 'Global' Urban Modernities." In *Future City*, edited by Stephen Read, Jürgen Rosemann, and Job van Eldijk, 125–144. New York: Spon.

Taussig, Michael. 1989. "Terror as Usual: Walter Benjamin's Theory of History as a State of Siege." *Social Text* 23: 3–20.

Tomlinson, Richard. 1992. "Competing Urban Agendas in South Africa." *Urban Forum* 3: 92–105.

———. 1999a. "From Exclusion to Inclusion: Rethinking Johannesburg's Central City." *Environment and Planning A* 3 (9): 1665–1678.

———. 1999b. "Ten Years in the Making: A History of Metropolitan Government in Johannesburg." *Urban Forum* 10 (1): 1–39.

———. 2002. "International Best Practice, Enabling Frameworks, and the Policy Process: A South African Case Study." *International Journal of Urban and Regional Research* 26 (2): 377–388.

Tomlinson, Richard, Robert A. Beauregard, Lindsay Bremner, and Xolela Mangcu. 2003. "The Postapartheid Struggle for an Integrated Johannesburg." In *Emerging Johannesburg: Perspectives on the Postapartheid City*, edited by Richard Tomlinson, Robert A. Beauregard, Lindsay Bremner, and Xolela Mangcu, 3–20. New York: Routledge.

Tomlinson, Richard, and Pauline Larsen. 2003. "The Race, Class, and Space of Shopping." In *Emerging Johannesburg: Perspectives on the Postapartheid City*, edited by Richard Tomlinson, Robert Beauregard, Lindsay Bremner, and Xolela Mangcu, 43–55. New York: Routledge.

Trafalgar Properties. 2004. *The Trafalgar Inner City Report 2004.* Unpublished pamphlet.

———. 2005. *The Trafalgar Inner City Report 2005.* Unpublished pamphlet.

———. 2006. *The Trafalgar Inner City Report 2006.* Unpublished pamphlet.

Trouillot, Michel-Rolph. 1995. *Silencing the Past: Power and the Production of History.* Boston: Beacon Press.

Trust for Urban Housing Finance (TUHF). 2006. *Annual Report 2005*. Braamfontein: TUHF.

Van Niekerk, Marlene. 1999. "Take Your Body Where It Has Never Been Before." In *Blank____: Architecture, Apartheid, and After*, edited by Hilton Judin and Ivan Vladislavić, 321–329. Rotterdam: NAi.

Van Onselen, Charles. 1981a. *Studies in the Social and Economic History of the Witwatersrand, 1886–1914*. Vol. 1: *New Babylon*. London: Longman.

——. 1981b. *Studies in the Social and Economic History of the Witwatersrand, 1886–1914*. Vol. 2: *New Ninevah*. London: Longman.

Virilio, Paul. 1983. *Pure War*. New York: Semiotext(e).

Weber, Rachel. 2002. "Extracting Value from the City: Neoliberalism and Urban Redevelopment." *Antipode* 34 (3): 519–540.

Whitzman, Carolyn, and Tom Slater. 2006. "Village Ghetto Land: Myth, Social Conditions, and Housing Policy in Parkdale, Toronto, 1879–2000," *Urban Affairs Review* 41 (5): 673–696.

Wigoder, Meir. 2002. "The 'Solar Eye' of Vision: Emergence of the Skyscraper-Viewer in the Discourse of Heights in New York City, 1890–1920." *Journal of the Society of Architectural Historians* 61 (2): 152–169.

Winkler, Tanya. 2006. "Reimagining Inner-City Regeneration in Hillbrow, Johannesburg: Identifying a Role for Faith-based Community Development." *Planning Theory & Practice* 7 (1): 80–92.

Zukin, Sharon. 1995. *The Culture of Cities*. Cambridge, Mass.: Blackwell.

Index